Pharmacy Law in Alabama

Marilyn N. Bulloch • Scott Penzak
Lena McDowell

Pharmacy Law in Alabama

A Comprehensive Review Guide for the MPJE

Springer

Marilyn N. Bulloch
Harrison College of Pharmacy
Auburn University
Auburn, AL, USA

Scott Penzak
Harrison College of Pharmacy
Auburn University
Auburn, AL, USA

Lena McDowell
Harrison College of Pharmacy
Auburn University
Auburn, AL, USA

Editorial Contact: Jessica Chio

ISBN 978-3-031-84770-7 ISBN 978-3-031-84771-4 (eBook)
https://doi.org/10.1007/978-3-031-84771-4

This Springer imprint is published by the registered company Springer Nature Switzerland AG
The registered company address is: Gewerbestrasse 11, 6330 Cham, Switzerland

Preface

The Multistate Jurisprudence Examination (MPJE) is an examination that all pharmacists must pass before they can legally practice pharmacy in the state of Alabama. Given the high-stakes nature of this examination, preparation can be wrought with anxiety, at the core of which is the question, "Am I studying everything I need to be studying in order to pass this exam?" One of the reasons that this is a common question among Alabama MPJE candidates is that there is not a single, comprehensive source that contains "everything one needs to know" to pass the Alabama MPJE. While it is possible, if not likely, that this book will unintentionally omit a topic that will be covered on the Alabama MPJE, it is our sincere hope that any such oversights will be minimal. At the opposite end of the spectrum, the reader will notice that a number of topics in this book are addressed in multiple chapters. This is intentional and is meant to reinforce areas of importance. Lastly, since the MPJE is the focus of this book, it does not contain lengthy background material on law history, nor does it provide legal cases with detailed discussions of pharmacist liability. There are already excellent sources available that provide this information.

This book was written by a team of Alabama pharmacists who both practice pharmacy in the state and actively educate pharmacy trainees. Federal and state laws and regulations relevant to the profession are scattered throughout various administrative websites which can be at times burdensome to locate, much less understand. This book was designed to be a comprehensive resource for the learner while at the same time providing context to the information presented. While the book is intended to be a study tool for pharmacy law, it is important that the learner be able to gain a solid understanding of the laws, rules, regulations, and policies that govern our profession on the Federal level and within the state of Alabama. Years after the test taker completes and passes the Alabama MPJE, they are still expected to know, understand, and comply with these legal requirements. It is a certainty that some laws, rules, or regulations will change with time, new ones will be introduced, and others repealed. In that regard, the Alabama Board of Pharmacy (ALBOP) provides updates to statutory and regulatory changes on their website by calendar year. The information presented in this book is accurate as of the time of publication, but learners are advised to visit the ALBOP website to note any changes that may have occurred since the time of publication.

The book purposefully does not include "practice questions." These can be found in other resources, including a practice exam provided directly from the same organization that oversees the MPJE. It does, however, provide tips and advice for learning, studying, and understanding the content to help the learner feel prepared to answer questions about the content.

Auburn, AL, USA

Marilyn N. Bulloch
Scott Penzak
Lena McDowell

Contents

Abbreviations

3PL	Third-Party Logistics Provider
AACP	American Association of Colleges of Pharmacy
ACIP	Advisory Committee on Immunization Practices
ACPE	Accreditation Council for Pharmacy Education
ADHD	Attention Deficit Hyperactivity Disorder
ADPH	Alabama Department of Public Health
ADU	Automated Dispensing Units
AE	Adverse Event
ALBME	Alabama Board of Medical Examiners
ALBOP	Alabama Board of Pharmacy
ANDA	Abbreviated New Drug Application
APA	Alabama Pharmacy Association
ARCOS	Automation of Reports and Consolidated Orders System
ATT	Authorization to Test
BTC	Behind the Counter
CDTM	Collaborative Drug Therapy Management
CE	Continuing Education
CFR	Code of Federal Regulations
CMEA	Combat Methamphetamine Epidemic Act
CNM	Certified Nurse Midwife
CNS	Central Nervous System
CPA	Collaborative practice agreement
CPR	Cardiopulmonary Resuscitation
CPSC	Consumer Product Safety Commission
CRNP	Certified Registered Nurse Practitioner
CSA	Controlled Substances Act
CSAT	Center for Substance Abuse Treatment
CSOS	Controlled Substances Ordering System
CSRPA	Controlled Substance Registration Protection Act
DEA	Drug Enforcement Administration
DESI	Drug Efficacy Study Implementation
DOT	Department of Transportation
DQSA	Drug Quality and Security Act
DSHEA	Dietary Supplemental Health and Education Act

DUR	Drug Utilization Review
eLTP	Electronic License Transfer Program
EMR	Electronic Medical Record
FAERS	FDA Adverse Event Reporting System
FATA	Federal Anti-Tampering Act
FDA	Food and Drug Administration
FDAAA	Food and Drug Administration Amendment Act
FDCA	Food, Drug, and Cosmetic Act of 1938
GMP	Good Manufacturing Practice
HIPAA	Health Insurance Portability and Accountability Act
HIV	Human Immunodeficiency Virus
ID	Identification
IND	Investigational New Drug
IRS	Internal Revenue Service
IV	Intravenous
LPSP	Limited Purpose Schedule II Permit
LTC	Long Term Care
MD	Doctor of Medicine
MDA	Medical Device Amendments
Mg	Milligrams
MLP	Mid-Level Practitioners
MPJE	Multistate Jurisprudence Examination
NABP	National Association of Boards of Pharmacy (NABP)
NAPLEX	North American Pharmacist Licensure Examination
NDA	New Drug Application
NDC	National Drug Code
NF	National Formulary
NTP	Narcotic Treatment Program
OBRA-90	Omnibus Budget Reconciliation Act of 1990
OD	Doctor of Optometry
OTC	Over-the-Counter
PA	Physician Assistant
PAIA	Alabama Pharmacy Audit Integrity Act
PBM	Pharmacy Benefit Manager
PDMA	Prescription Drug Marketing Act
PDMP	Prescription Drug Monitoring Program
PDUFA	Prescription Drug User Fee Act
PEEHIP	Public Education Employees' Health Insurance Plan
PET	Positron Emission Tomography
PHI	Protected Health Information
PHS	Public Health Service
PPA	Phenylpropanolamine
PPPA	Poison Prevention Packaging Act
PRN	As Needed
QACSC	Qualified Alabama Controlled Substance Certificate

REMS	Risk Evaluation and Mitigation Strategy
RN	Registered Nurse
SAMHSA	Substance Abuse and Mental Health Services Administration
SLCP	Scheduled Listed Chemical Products
SNDA	Supplemental New Drug Application
TB	Tuberculosis
TPP	Third-Party Program
TV	Television
U.S.	United States
USAN	United States Adopted Names
USP	United States Pharmacopeia
VAERS	Vaccine Adverse Event Reporting System

List of Figures

List of Tables

Introduction to the Alabama Multistate Jurisprudence Examination (MPJE)

1

Believe you can and you're half way there.

—Theodore Roosevelt

1 Purpose of the MPJE

The objective of the Multistate Pharmacy Jurisprudence Examination® (MPJE®) is to assess the knowledge and application of laws and regulations pertaining to the practice of pharmacy in a particular state or jurisdiction (i.e., Alabama) [2]. Before a pharmacist can obtain a license to practice in one of these states or jurisdictions, they must succesfully pass the MPJE. This includes recent graduates from an accredited pharmacy school, or individuals licensed to practice pharmacy in another state who wish to reciprocate (i.e., transfer) their license to Alabama.

Key Concept
This book is designed to assist those studying for the Alabama MPJE; however, if the test taker requires clarity or desires a better understanding of a concept or topic, they are strongly encouraged to access the source documents referenced throughout this book.

2 About the MPJE

The Multistate Pharmacy Jurisprudence Examination® (MPJE®) is a national exam overseen by the National Association of Boards of Pharmacy (NABP) and individualized for each state (that participates) [1]. The 2.5-h test contains 120 test questions that are administered via a computer using adaptive technology. "Adaptive" simply means that as you answer successive questions correctly, the harder questions become. The goal of this approach is to match the knowledge of the test taker with

M. N. Bulloch et al., *Pharmacy Law in Alabama*,
https://doi.org/10.1007/978-3-031-84771-4_1

the difficulty level of the question. To illustrate, if a student selects an incorrect answer, the next question provided by the computer will be easier than the previous question that the student got wrong. Conversely, if the test taker selects the correct answer, the next question will be more challenging. It is important to not stress too much about whether a question seems "easy" or "hard" during the test. It is entirely possible that the reason you feel a question is "easy" is because you know the information well, and not because you are answering previous questions incorrectly. The system determines the measure of "easy" versus "hard" using testing statistics from previous exam takers; questions themselves are not intentionally written to be easier or harder than others. Of the 120 questions, only 100 count toward the test taker's score; 20 questions are "trial questions," which may be included on future MPJEs depending on how well candidates answer them. In order for the exam to be scored, the test taker must complete at least 107 out of the 120 questions. It is difficult to imagine that anyone would not answer all 120 questions, but be that as it may, that is the rule. Test takers have 2.5 hours to complete the MPJE. This translates to 1 min and 15 s per question, which is plenty of time for most individuals. It is important to note that once a question is answered, it cannot be revisited. Similarly, questions cannot be skipped and answered later on.

The questions on the exam are written by volunteers in pharmacy practice and faculty from colleges and schools of pharmacy from across the United States. The questions, which may be referred to as exam items, or simply items, are then extensively reviewed by a review committee to determine their appropriateness and validity. They may be formatted as traditional multiple choice, select all that apply, or K-type questions, all of which are discussed later in this chapter. The question format should not be used as a clue for whether the system considers the question to be "easy" or "hard." It may simply be that the item writer thought it was the best format for the particular question. The review committee vets each question for relevance and clarity. Questions are sent to the individual state boards of pharmacy to ensure that only questions that are applicable to that state's laws and regulations are represented. To be able to receive a score, at least 107 of the 120 exam items must completed. If the candidate answers 107 or more questions, but not all 120, a penalty is applied to the exam score. Ideally, the candidate will pass on their first attempt. Results are generally available within 14 business days. However, candidates have a total of five attempts to pass the Alabama MPJE.

3 Registering and Scheduling the Exam

Recent graduates are in the challenging position of having to schedule both their NAPLEX and MPJE examinations. It is up to each person which exam they prefer to take first; this is an individual decision that may vary based on multiple factors. An important piece of advice is to try and focus on one exam at a time, and allow plenty of time to study.

The timeline from applying to actually taking the MPJE can be lengthy, and you should begin the process as early as possible. The first step in registering to take the

Alabama MPJE is to visit the ALBOP's website and make sure that all of the criteria for pharmacist licensure have been met. While the NABP confirms eligibility for testing for some states, in Alabama, this process is still completed by the ALBOP. Therefore, you will need to apply to both the ALBOP and the NABP to be able to take the MPJE. Application through the ALBOP is found on the board's website. Separately, you will apply for the Alabama MPJE in the "Exam Services" section of the NABP e-Profile. If you have never taken the MPJE before in any state, an official transcript from your college/school of pharmacy (sent directly from the registrar and not the candidate) must be sent to the NABP. It will take up to 10 days for the transcript to be processed, so be patient and plan for that time course. Once the ALBOP confirms your eligibility with the NABP and the NABP receives your transcript, a link to purchase the Alabama MPJE will appear in your NABP e-Profile. All testing accommodations must be made using the "Request for Testing Accommodations form" on the NAPB website. After purchasing the exam, an authorization to test (ATT) will be emailed to you. You must have this ATT to schedule your exam with Pearson VUE. Pearson VUE is a company that administers a large variety of high-stakes computer-based tests and licensure exams for multiple industries. The company has a limited number of testing centers in each state, and many candidates will need to integrate this travel time to the center into their exam day preparations. You will receive test-day instructions via email (which can also be found on the NABP website) and it is essential that they follow those instructions, or they risk not being able to take the test at their scheduled day and time.

Alabama is one of several states who offer and recognize a waived fee for testing for active military and veterans and a discounted fee for military spouses. If you qualify for this discount, you should request the discount before applying for the exam. Documentation necessary to obtain the discount can be uploaded to your e-Profile.

4 Associated Costs

There are a number of costs associated with the MPJE. There is an online registration fee, which includes an application fee. Specific fees are not included here, as they are subject to change. The reader is referred to the NABP website for up-to-date costs related to the MPJE.

5 Test-Taking Considerations

While a detailed treatise on how best to prepare for a major exam such as the MPJE is beyond the scope of this chapter, there are some general recommendations we would like to highlight. First, we acknowledge that this is a "high-stakes" examination, in that an individual cannot practice pharmacy (and in many cases, begin a residency) in the state of Alabama without achieving a passing score on the Alabama MPJE. Hence, there is often significant social, psychological, and financial pressure upon those preparing to take the MPJE exam. To this end, it is strongly suggested that all MPJE test takers adopt a healthy respect for the importance and difficulty level of this examination.

In 2023, 82.5% of all first-time test takers passed the Alabama MPJE [2]. The percentage of test takers who passed was 85.4% among in-state test takers and 77.1% among out-of-state test takers, suggesting that pharmacists reciprocating their license to Alabama have a more difficult time with the MPJE. Of note, these pass rates were considerably higher compared to national rates, which were 72.2% for all MPJE test takers (74.4% for in-state, and 67.6% for out-of-state test takers) [2]. In other words, not everyone passes the MPJE on their first try. You should do everything in your power in terms of preparation to give yourself the best chance of passing this exam. This means—if at all possible—preparing over a period of months, as opposed to weeks. It is extremely difficult to learn everything you need to know to pass the MPJE in a few short weeks. Hence, set aside dedicated periods of time each day or week to prepare for the MPJE. Writing questions for self-study is extremely helpful in preparing for the MPJE. This can be achieved using note cards or via electronic means. Pneumonic devices are useful when memorizing cumbersome lists. Some of these will be shared in various chapters throughout this book. Lastly, some people find group studying to be an effective means of preparation. It is best to first study on your own, before getting together with others to discuss items that may not be clear. Soliciting the viewpoint of others in these situations can often be quite helpful.

▶ **Study Pro Tip** It is not advised to schedule the NAPLEX and the MPJE too close in time together. Most test takers allow sufficient time between the two tests. How much time you separate the tests by depends on how much time was dedicated to studying prior to the test dates. Test takers should NOT wait until they have taken the NAPLEX to begin studying for the MPJE unless they are planning to separate the two test dates by several months.

Specific approaches to the different types of question formats will be discussed below. Each type of format may have its own, unique considerations, but there are some test-taking strategies that can be applied regardless of the type of question. Pay attention to seemingly "small" words in the question stem so that you are entirely clear on what the question is asking. Words such as "may," "shall," "must," "not," "except," and "include" can provide context to what correct response the item writer is seeking. The word "Alabama" may or may not appear in the question stem; if a question was meant to be adaptable for multiple states, a phrase such as "in your jurisdiction" may be used to ask about state specific content. If the question uses a word such as "federal," or "federally," it will be asking about federal content specifically. Not all questions will make a distinction between federal and state laws/regulations in the question stem; it will assume that the test taker knows both. Sometimes, the federal and state requirements are the same, which makes answering the question easier. When there is a discrepancy, the test taker should always use the stricter law/regulation to answer the question.

5.1 General Preparation Considerations

MPJE candidates are encouraged to review the MPJE competency statements published by the NABP. Candidates should also review sample items to become familiar with question formatting. Individuals may also choose to access the Pre-MPJE practice exam, which is available through the NABP website for a fee [1]. The purpose of the Pre-MPJE is to provide students with a realistic test-taking experience that helps them prepare for the actual MPJE. The Pre-MPJE consists of 40 past-MPJE questions that the test taker has 50 minutes to answer. Upon completion, the examinee is provided with a scaled score. Key documents to study in preparation for the Alabama MPJE are listed in the Recommended Reading section at the end of this chapter.

Pay close attention to the MPJE competency statements and outline. The exam is broken down into four content areas (Fig. 1.1). Area 1 will be state specific, but Areas 2, 3, and 4 could include both federal and state content. You must study, *in detail*, the state specific Pharmacy Practice Act for any state's MPJE that you take. It is also important to study the state specific Controlled Substance Act and to be able to compare and contrast it with the federal Controlled Substances Act. Because laws often simply authorize agencies to write rules, you must also study, *in detail*, the Alabama Board of Pharmacy Administrative Code. Do not neglect studying federal laws and regulations. This is particularly notable if you have taken the MPJE for another state. The amount of federally tested content varies from state to state.

It is helpful to be aware that exam items may refer to medications using brand or generic names, particularly controlled substances. When you are studying, you should prepare yourself to be able to recognize a medication by either name.

Fig. 1.1 MPJE makeup by area [1]

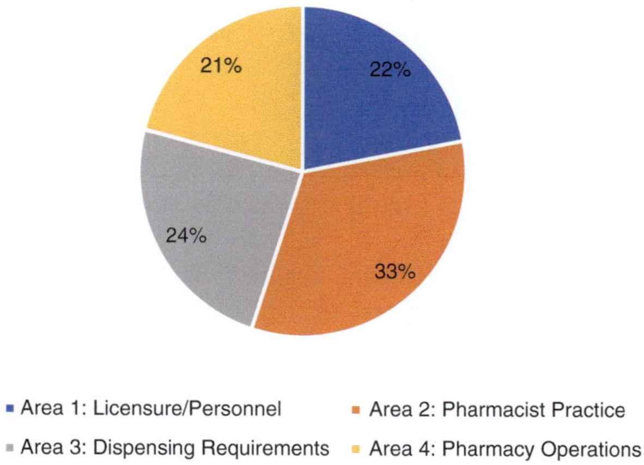

5.2 Approach to Multiple-choice Questions

There are several free online resources that provide general advice to individuals taking multiple choice examinations [3]. Most people are familiar with the general guidance provided, which includes advice to read each question carefully, consider each possible answer before making a choice, and to choose an initial selection if attempting to decide between two answers. It is important to note that most of these resources recommend skipping difficult questions and coming back to them; however, as noted above, the MPJE does not allow for this strategy, as all questions must be answered sequentially. This recommendation notwithstanding, most institutions of higher education offer excellent online strategies to keep in mind when taking multiple-choice exams. One key piece of advice is to try and break down/simplify each question by asking, "What is this question asking?" For example, consider the following question:

It is permissible for a patient to be given a 72-h supply of which medication(s) if they are out of refills and the pharmacist is unable to reach their provider? (Select ALL that apply)

A. Hydrocodone/acetaminophen.
B. Gabapentin.
C. Oxandrolone.
D. Alprazolam.

Approach this question by asking, "What is this question asking?" After preparing for the Alabama MPJE, you will know that a pharmacist may provide a 72-h emergency supply of medication that the patient requires for chronic treatment except medications that are in Schedule 2. So then, the question is actually asking you to "Select those medications that are unscheduled or Schedule 3, 4, or 5 (i.e., omitting Schedule 2 medications). Assessing choices A-D, you determine that these medications are in the following Schedules:

A. Hydrocodone/acetaminophen: Schedule 2.
B. Gabapentin: Schedule 5 (in Alabama).
C. Oxandrolone: Schedule 3.
D. Alprazolam: Schedule 4.

The correct answers then are (B), (C), and (D). The question becomes notably easier once you determine what it is attempting to ask. Let us look at another example:

A pharmacy technician obtained their initial Alabama registration in December 2023. Upon first renewal of their registration, how many live hours of continuing education (CE) are required?

A. 6 h
B. 3 h

C. 2 h
D. 1 h

Again, ask yourself, "What is this question asking?" When you do that, you find that all this question is asking is, "How many live CE hours must a registered pharmacy technician obtain per every renewal period?" The date in the question (December 2023) only serves to let you know that this is the beginning of a new registration period for technicians, who must renew their registration biennially on odd years [4]. Therefore, since pharmacy technicians must obtain SIX (6) hours of CE every registration period, TWO (2) hours of which must be live, the answer is 2 h (Answer C). Often times, questions will contain information that is not necessary to answer the question. By zeroing in on what a question is asking, you can often identify extraneous information and set it aside so that it does not interfere with your ability to correctly answer the question.

5.3 Approach to a Multiple-choice, K-Type Question

A "K-type question" is a type of multiple-choice question where the answers a single response or be combined. Generally, there are three options listed as Roman numerals "I," "II," and "III." The actual answers (e.g., "A," "B," "C," and "D") may list one or more of the Roman numerals as correct. The test taker must determine which of the three, or if appropriate, which combination, is the correct response. For example, consider the following question:

True statements regarding eligibility for pharmacist licensure in Alabama include which of the following?

I. Candidates must be at least 21 years of age.
II. Candidates must have completed at least 400 h of practical pharmacy training in a traditional pharmacy setting.
III. All candidates must consent and be subject to a criminal background check.

A. I only.
B. III only.
C. I and II only.
D. II and III only.
E. I, II, and III only.

It may be easy to get overwhelmed when one of these questions comes up in the exam. Education literature indicates that K-type questions are not an optimal way to test learner knowledge and take significantly longer to answer compared to other test item formats. Many schools and colleges have stopped using this format on examinations given in the classroom. However, the question format has not been eliminated from the MPJE. As a result, it is entirely possible that your first encounter with the K-type question is on the MPJE. In many ways, a K-type question is similar to a "select all that apply"-type multiple question. Start by looking at the three individual options and determining if it is true or not. In the case of the answer above, you know that Alabama law only requires a candidate to be 19 years of age, but that 400 h of training in a traditional pharmacy setting and a background check are both required for licensure. Therefore, the correct answer to this question is D," indicating that both choices II and III are correct, but choice I is incorrect. With this type of question, determining the accuracy of item II may also help approach the question. If item II is incorrect, then only A or B are potential answers. If item II is correct, then only C, D, or E are options. This may elevate some angst in knowing that if item II is correct, either or both I and III must be correct. At times, the stem may help narrow down the choices. For example, a question may request the "most appropriate" item(s). If the item writer used appropriate grammar, the use of the word "a" versus the word "are" *may* help indicate if a single or multiple items are correct. Unfortunately, there is no way to guarantee this assumption.

5.4 Recognize when Generalizations Can and Cannot Be Made

Upon initial examination, it may seem daunting when faced with the challenge of knowing the Schedule of each benzodiazepine as assigned by the Controlled Substance Act [5]. However, once you realize that all benzodiazepines are Schedule 4 (CIV) medications, you simply have to be able to recognize the names (brand and generic) of the various benzodiazepines [4]. Most of these medications end in "pam" or "lam," so even if you haven't heard of a particular benzodiazepine, if a drug ends in "pam" or "lam," there is a good chance it will be a CIV medication. But take your studying a step further and ask yourself, "Are there any benzodiazepines that don't end in "pam" or "lam? If so, what are their generic and brand names?" Two examples would be clorazepate (Tranxene®) and chlordiazepoxide (Librium®). It is important to always consider exceptions to any general patterns you notice. Taking this a step further, you might ask, "What schedule is the combination medication chlordiazepoxide 5 mg plus clidinium 2.5 mg (Librax®)?" The answer is that Librax® isn't a controlled substance at all!

An example where a "class effect" does not apply when it comes to DEA scheduling are appetite suppressants [4]. Phendimetrazine and benzphetamine are Schedule III medications, while phentermine is a schedule IV drug. Other medications for weight loss, such as liraglutide, orlistat, semaglutide, setmelanotide, and bupropion/naloxone, are not controlled substances. It is important to examine drugs from different classes and be able to identify differences.

► **Study Pro Tip** Make an honest, unbiased assessment of your knowledge base and focus heavily on any deficiencies you identify. However, in so doing, take care not to overlook (i.e., take for granted) subjects with which you feel most comfortable. Study everything albeit to varying degrees based on your strengths and weaknesses.

6 Results and Licensure

MPJE exam results are revealed within 14 business days after the exam is taken. Examinees access their results via their NABP e-Profile. Exam results consist of a Pass or Fail notification. Although candidates are required to achieve a scaled score of at least 75 (minimum score of zero and a maximum score of 100), actual scores are no longer reported as of January 18, 2021. If a candidate receives a failing result, they are provided with a performance report, which contains details from the different competency areas. This will hopefully allow the examinee to see what topics they need to study further to achieve a passing score. If an individual fails the MPJE, they must wait at least 30 days prior to retaking the exam. Note that this differs from the NAPLEX in that a person who fails the NAPLEX must wait 45 days before sitting for the exam again. It is important to note that after an individual receives notice that they passed their MPJE exam, they are not automatically licensed to practice pharmacy in the state of Alabama at that time. After receiving a passing notification, the ALBOP will contact the individual and work with them to schedule their attendance at an upcoming Alabama Board of Pharmacy meeting (i.e., board meeting). Once they appear before the board, typically along with others who recently passed the Alabama MPJE, the person will then be eligible to practice pharmacy in Alabama.

Recommended Reading

1. Code of Alabama: Available at: https://alison.legislature.state.al.us/code-of-alabama
   (a) Alabama Practice of Pharmacy Act 205—Title 34 Chap. 23.
   (b) Controlled Substances Act—Title 20.
   (c) Drug Offenses—Title 13A Chap. 12 Article 5.
2. Alabama Administrative Code 680: Available at: https://albop.com/statutes-rules/
   (a) Administration- 680-x-1.
   (b) Practice of Pharmacy—680-x-2.
   (c) Alabama Uniform Controlled Substances—680-x-3.
3. The Pharmacist's Manual: an informational Outline of the Controlled Substances Act: Available at: https://www.deadiversion.usdoj.gov/GDP/(DEA-DC-046R1)(EO-DEA154R1)_Pharmacist%27s_Manual_DEA.pdf

References

1. National Association of Boards of Pharmacy. Multistate Pharmacy Jurisprudence Examination (MPJE) | NABP. National Association of Boards of Pharmacy. Accessed July 11, 2024. https://nabp.pharmacy/programs/examinations/mpje/
2. MPJE data. National Association of Boards of Pharmacy. Data on File. 2024.
3. How to ace multiple choice questions: tips and tricks. Multiple choice advice https://studyright.net/blog/multiple-choice-questions-tips/ (accessed January 10, 2024)
4. Alabama Administrative Code r. 680-X-2.14
5. United States. Drug Enforcement Administration. Office of Compliance and Regulatory Affairs. (1980). Pharmacist's manual: an informational outline of the Controlled Substances Act of 1970. Washington, D.C.:U.S. Dept. of Justice, Drug Enforcement Administration. 2022 Edition. chrome-xtension://efaidnbmnnnibpcajpcglclefindmkaj. https://www.deadiversion.usdoj.gov/GDP/(DEA-DC-046R1)(EO-DEA154R1)_Pharmacist's_Manual_DEA.pdf

Understanding Laws, Statutes, Rules, and Regulations

2

Poisons and medicines are often the same substance given with different intents.

–Peter Latham, 1865 (nineteenth-century English Physician and Educator).

1 Fundamentals of the U.S. Government Structure

The U.S. Federal Government is made up of three branches of equal power (Table 2.1). Laws are written and passed by the legislative branch, and then implemented by the executive branch. The judicial branch determines if a law is in alignment with the U.S. Constitution and oversees cases involving criminal of civil violations of law or regulatory requirements.

Table 2.1 Branches of the U.S. Government

Branch	Members	Roles and responsibilities
Executive	President Federal Agencies (e.g., Department of Health and Human Services)	Implement laws
Legislative	House of representative Senate	Write and pass laws
Judicial	Courts	Determine constitutionality of laws

M. N. Bulloch et al., *Pharmacy Law in Alabama*,
https://doi.org/10.1007/978-3-031-84771-4_2

2 What Is a Law?

Laws are passed by both branches of the U.S. Congress at the federal level and by both branches of the Alabama State Legislature at the state level. They can outline allowances, requirements, or prohibitions. Laws identify crimes and prohibit civil (i.e., noncriminal) behavior. Passing, removing, or changing a law can be difficult because of the requirement that it pass both components of the legislative branch and be signed by the President or Governor (depending on if it is a Federal or State process) [1]. Laws passed by the U.S. Congress are incorporated into the U.S. Code, which is divided by subject into titles. The titles focus on a specific area of the law, and can be further subdivided into chapters, subchapters, parts, sections, paragraphs, and clauses [2].

3 Understanding Regulations, Rules, Statutes, and Guidance

Laws include references to designated U.S. Departments and/or Federal Agencies that are tasked with implementing the law. Not all laws require agency involvement or regulation, though the majority of laws involving drugs and pharmacy practice do direct a department and/or agency to act. The federal agencies publish regulations to clarify their interpretation of the law as well as how the law will be implemented [2, 3]. Similar to laws, regulations may include requirements or prohibitions. All regulations must be consistent with the law. While regulations are easier to modify because they do not require legislative action, they still go through a structured process that is outlined in a law, the Administrative Procedure Act, unless otherwise directed by the individual law providing the agency with the authority to act [4]. Once an agency writes a proposed regulation, it is published in the Federal Register [2]. Anyone, including the public, can provide comments, request clarification, or propose modifications to the proposed regulation for a designated period of time. After the comment period concludes, the agency evaluates and considers the feedback received, and may amend the regulation based on that feedback. The final version of the regulation is once again published in the Federal Register. This final version holds the force and effect of law, and can be enforced with similar criminal or civil consequences [2, 4]. Each year, the most recent version of regulations are codified in the Code of Federal Regulations (CFR). Just as laws are inserted into the U.S. Code with a specific organization, the CFR is categorized by titles, which are based on subject area. Titles are divided into chapters, that typically contain the name of the agency issuing the regulation(s). Chapters are divided into parts to address specific regulatory topics and into numerical sections. When referencing a regulation, only the title and the section are used [5] (Fig. 2.1).

Depending on the situation, agencies may pass guidance or policy statements to provide further explanation on how the agency understands and implements current laws and regulations [2, 6]. While these outline suggested or recommended actions,

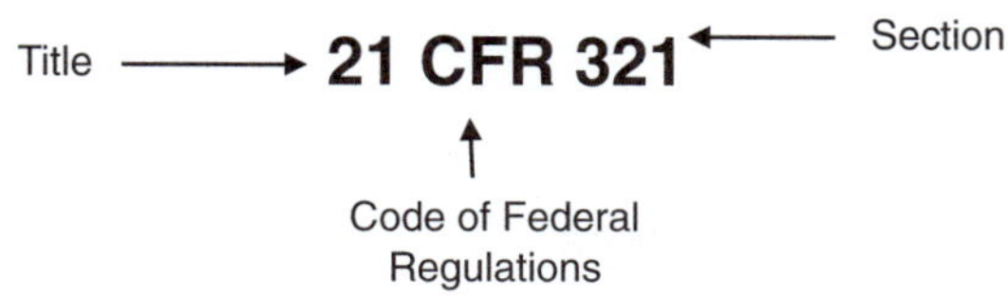

Fig. 2.1 Referencing a federal regulation

they are not commonly mandatory, unless they are integrated into a regulation or are included within the terms of an agency-overseen agreement or contract (e.g., funding agreement).

4 Key Regulatory Bodies Impacting Pharmacy

There are multiple key federal agencies whose oversight impacts pharmacy. The most recognizable of these is the Food and Drug Administration (FDA). The origins of the modern FDA date to the 1906 Pure Food and Drug Act [7]. The FDA is responsible for protecting public safety. Part of its mission includes ensuring that drugs, biological products, and medical devices (among other products) are safe for use in humans (and as applicable, animals). The FDA does not have a direct impact on the practice of pharmacy per se, but its enforcement of the Food, Drug, and Cosmetic Act means that the FDA determines what medications and devices are available for use in the United States, how medications and devices are produced and packaged, how research on these products must be conducted, quality and purity of any drug or device that enters interstate commerce, and what information is required to be included in the package labeling. The agency also determines what drugs require a prescription and which ones may be sold over the counter. The Drug Enforcement Administration (DEA) is tasked with enforcing the Controlled Substances Act. It has a narrower focus than the FDA in that it only focuses on drugs that may cause physical or psychological dependence. However, the average pharmacist is often impacted to a greater degree by DEA regulations in the daily aspect of their work. The DEA determines how controlled substances may be ordered, stored, inventoried, prescribed, dispensed, and disposed of. The agency sets federal requirements about what must be on a prescription for a controlled substance, and determines what missing information a pharmacist may, or may not, add. DEA agents have the authority to enter a pharmacy and inspect operations and records, and if necessary, to take punitive action for any violation it identifies. To a smaller extent, the Environmental Protection Agency has some regulatory authority over drug disposal from an environmental perspective and the Department of Transportation issues certain regulations regarding the literal transportation of medication through interstate commerce. At the state level, the Alabama Board of Pharmacy (ALBOP) is the primary agency directed with overseeing the practice of pharmacy through enforcement of the Alabama Practice of Pharmacy Act. Pharmacists must adhere both to specific laws within the Practice Act as well as regulations released by the ALBOP in applying the law. The ALBOP employs investigators who may inspect medications made, packaged, or sold in the state of Alabama, search medication and pharmacy-related records, and may enter a pharmacy or other facility where drugs are kept during business hours. These inspectors have the same authority as other law enforcement officials and can search, seize, issue citations, and initiate criminal proceedings for violations [8].

5 Legislative and Regulatory Considerations Within Alabama

Most aspects of pharmacy practice in Alabama are controlled by the profession itself. Every member of the ALBOP must be a practicing pharmacist who is nominated by their peers. Two of the three are directly voted on by licensed pharmacists within the state. The Alabama Practice of Pharmacy Act is specifically found in 34 Alabama Code 23. Similar to the way laws are organized at the federal level, laws in the state of Alabama are incorporated into the Code of Alabama. The Code of Alabama is organized into titles by subject area which are then divided into chapters by a more specific chapter area. For example, the Practice of Pharmacy Act is found in Chapter 23 of Title 34 of the Code of Alabama. Chapters are organized into articles and articles are subdivided into divisions that are further broken down into sections. This act has a few explicit items within it. For example, the act directly states that a person must be at least 19 years of age to receive a pharmacist license and it sets the minimum size of a pharmacy dispensing area [8]. However, for most aspects of the pharmacy profession, the act authorizes the ALBOP to issue specific rules, regulations, and guidelines which can be located in the Alabama Administrative Code 680. When the ALBOP adopts a new rule or requirement, it must be sent electronically to every registrant (i.e. anyone with a license issued by the board) at least *10 days* prior to when the rule or regulation is to become effective.

▶ **Study Pro Tip** You are unlikely to be asked the specific numerical title, chapter, section, or other reference point of a law or regulation. However, it is helpful for your ability to locate these references throughout your practice as a pharmacist to recognize where they are located.

References

1. Sullivan JV. How Our Laws Are Made – Congress.gov Resources. House Document 110-49. Congressional Session 110-1. Published online July 24, 2007. Accessed January 17, 2024. https://www.congress.gov/help/learn-about-the-legislative-process/how-our-laws-are-made
2. United States Department of Health and Human Service. Introduction to U.S. Law & Policy. Published February 15, 2018. Accessed January 17, 2024. https://www.phe.gov/s3/law/Pages/default.aspx

3. U.S Department of Health ahnd Human Services. S3: Science, Safety, Security. Published February 15, 2018. Accessed February 7, 2024. https://www.phe.gov/s3/law/Pages/Regulations.aspx
4. Administrative Procedure Act | National Archives. National Archives. Published August 15, 2016. Accessed January 18, 2024. https://www.archives.gov/federal-register/laws/administrative-procedure/552.html
5. U.S. Archives and Records Administration. About the Code of Federal Regulations. National Archives. Published August 15, 2016. Accessed February 7, 2024. https://www.archives.gov/federal-register/cfr/about.html
6. U.S. Department of Health and Human Services. Guidance & Guidelines. S3: Science, Safety, Security. Published February 15, 2018. Accessed February 7, 2024. https://www.phe.gov/s3/law/Pages/Guidance.aspx
7. Office of the Commissioner. FDA History. FDA. Published March 29, 2021. Accessed February 7, 2024. https://www.fda.gov/about-fda/fda-history
8. Alabama Legislature. Pharmacists and Pharmacies (Chapter 23). Code of Alabama Title 34. Code of Alabama. Published February 7, 2024. Accessed February 7, 2024. https://alison.legislature.state.al.us/code-of-alabama

3 Federal Laws That Impact Pharmacy Practice

The safety of the people shall be the highest law.

–Marcus Tullius Cicero, Roman philosopher (b. 106 B.C.)

1 The Food and Drug Act of 1906 and Other Early Laws

The first major law regulating pharmacy at the federal level was The Food and Drug Act of 1906. The law was passed after the publication of a shocking (for the time) book detailing the workings of the meat packing industry. The Food and Drug Act of 1906 prohibited the shipment in interstate commerce food or drugs that were misbranded or adulterated. [1] The Bureau of Chemistry—later to become the Food and Drug Administration (FDA), was given limited authority to regulate and enforce the act [2]. Given the stimulus for the law's origin, the agency gave more attention to food oversight. For drugs, the it primarily focused on substandard synthetics and adulterated crude drugs and essential oils [2]. The Food and Drug Act of 1906 was amended seven times between 1906 and 1935, most of them unrelated to drugs [1]. The Sherley Amendment of 1912 codified that a drug was considered misbranded if the label had any "false and fraudulent" information regarding the drug's therapeutic effect. Unfortunately, this regulation was difficult to enforce because legally, intent to deceive must be shown to prove fraud [1]. The first time a requirement for a prescription before dispensing any type of drug appeared in federal legislation occurred almost a decade later. In 1914, the passage of the Harrison Narcotic Act required pharmacies who wanted to dispense narcotics to register with the Internal Revenue Service (IRS) and pay a fee [2]. The act stipulated that the pharmacist could only dispense a narcotic pursuant to a valid written prescription from an authorized physician or dentist. However, in general, the Food and Drug Act of 1906 had minimal authority over new drugs as long as they were not misbranded or adulterated.

M. N. Bulloch et al., *Pharmacy Law in Alabama*,
https://doi.org/10.1007/978-3-031-84771-4_3

2 Food, Drug, and Cosmetic Act of 1938

2.1 Background of the Food, Drug, and Cosmetic Act

The Food and Drugs Act of 1906 was considered obsolete by the 1930s, but there were strong disagreements about what it should be replaced with [3]. In 1937, a tragedy that claimed the lives of over 100 people. The "sulfanilamide tragedy" impacted patients in 15 states and involved a liquid version of sulfanilamide, an antibiotic that had been available in tablet and powder formulations. In 1937, a salesman for the company that produced the drug reported demand for a liquid form and in response, the manufacturer's chief chemist (and pharmacist) found a way to dissolve sulfanilamide in diethylene glycol. The product was tested for flavor, appearance, and fragrance, but because tests for safety and efficacy were not required, it was made available without animal or human testing. Unfortunately, diethylene glycol can be toxic, particularly to children. Though federal officials worked tirelessly to track down the product, it lacked the authority to seize the product except through a technicality [1]. The only consequence that could be applied was to charge the company for misbranding the product as an "elixir" instead of a solution." In less than a year, the Food, Drug, and Cosmetic Act (FDCA) of 1938 was passed. This law remains in please to this day and is the basis for the FDA's regulation of medications. It is important for those involved with the pharmacy profession be familiar with the contents of the FDCA; violation of the law can result in severe civil and criminal penalties. It is worth recognizing the FDCA is a lengthy law. As of 2023, the law contains approximately 925 pages and only a portion of them is relevant to pharmacy.

2.2 General Overview of the Food, Drug, and Cosmetic Act

The FDCA provides the FDA the authority to regulate the production, sale, and distribution of food, drugs, medical devices, and cosmetics in order to protect U.S. patients and consumers from misleading and unsafe products through enforcement of the FDCA and subsequent FDA regulations [4, 5]. Specifically, the FDCA prohibits the introduction into interstate commerce any drug or device (or food, cosmetic, or tobacco product) which is adulterated or misbranded. It also bans the act of adulteration or misbranding, including the receipt into interstate commerce of any product that is adulterated or misbranded. In order to allow the FDA, appraise adulteration, the original FDCA authorized factory inspections. Additionally, the act required the *safety* of drugs to be shown *before* marketing. This was extended by later amendments to more explicit proof of both safety and efficacy. Where the term "drug" was vaguely defined in the Food and Drug Act of 1906, the FDCA defined the term more broadly to the inclusion of articles used in the *diagnosis or treatment of disease and those intended to affect the structure or function of the body* [1, 4]. The original 1938 law implemented new expectations for drug labels (which have been expanded upon are amended since). For example, a product produced from ≥2 ingredients must have a label disclosing those ingredients. Labels were also required to state net weight and any differences in composition from an official standard (e.g., listed in an official compendium) and narcotics and hypnotics had to be listed as habit forming. The law eliminated the requirement to prove intent in the regulation of misbranding.

Key Concept
In 1938, the FDCA was focused primarily on *safety*, particularly regarding adulteration and misbranding of products. Because it is a federal law, it directs much of its application to those products intended for or introduced into interstate commerce.

The FDCA has multiple key prohibitions. These include:

- Banning the production, sale, disposal, possession, control, or concealing of anything that could be used to counterfeit a drug, drug container, or label.
- Counterfeiting drugs or devices.
- Prohibiting the alteration, mutilation, destruction, obliteration, or removal of the whole or any part of the labeling of or the doing of any other act with respect t o a drug or device (or food, cosmetic, or tobacco product) if the act is done while the product is held for sale after shipment into interstate commerce and results in the product being adulterated or misbranded.
- The failure of the manufacturer, packer, or distributor of a prescription drug to maintain for transmittal or to transmit, upon written request, to any licensed practitioner (by a State) information related to such a drug that is *true and correct* copies of printed matter which is required to be included in any package in which the drug is distributed or sold.
- The introduction of or delivery for introduction into interstate commerce any dietary supplement that is unsafe.
- The resale of a compounded drug that is labeled "not for resale."
- Failure of a registered entity to report adverse events.
- Failure to retain records required by the FDCA.
- Failure to comply with any portion of the FDCA.

2.3 Key Definitions Important to Pharmacy Practice

The law contains key definitions that provide the legal framework for pharmacy practice, legislations, and regulation [4]. Because the FDCA applies to more than just pharmaceuticals, not all of the definitions are relevant to pharmacy. However, there are many key terms that those within the pharmacy profession should be very familiar with (Tables 3.1 and 3.2) [4, 6]. Whenever these terms appear in the FDCA, other legislation, or within regulations, it is these definitions that are referenced,

Table 3.1 Key pharmacy terms defined in Federal Pharmacy Law and Regulations [4, 6]

Term	Definition	Notes
Drug	Articles recognized in the official U.S. Pharmacopeia, official Homeopathic Pharmacopeia of the U.S. , or official National Formulary, or any supplement to any of them Articles intended for use in the diagnosis, cure, mitigation, treatment, or prevention of disease in man or other animals Articles (which are not food) indented to affect the structure or function of the body of man or animals Articles intended for use as a component of any other part of this definition.	Does not include other substances (e.g., food, dietary supplements) who do not meet these criteria regardless of any label or labeling claims
Adulterated	A drug or device that consists in whole or in part of any filthy, putrid, or decomposed substance or If a drug or device has been prepared, packed, or held under insanitary conditions where it may have been contaminated with filth or rendered injurious to health or A drug where the methods used in the facilities or controls used for its manufacture, processing, packing, or holding do not conform to or are not operated or administered in conformity with current good manufacturing practices to assure that such a drug meets the requirements of the FDCA as to safety, has the identity and strength, and meets the quality and purity characteristics which it purports or is represented to possess Other definitions described in Table 3.2	
Counterfeit drug	A drug, or its container or labeling, without authorization, bears the trademark, trade name, or other identifying mark, imprint, or device, or any likeness thereof, of a drug manufacturer, processor, packer, or distributor other than the person(s) who in fact manufactured, processed, packed, or distributed the drug	
New drug	Any drug whose composition is not generally recognized among experts qualified by scientific training and experience to evaluate the safety and effectiveness of drugs, as safe and effective for use under the conditions prescribed, recommended, or suggested in the labeling Any drug whose composition is a result of investigations to determine its safety and effectiveness for use under such conditions has become so recognized, but which has not, except for in such investigations, been used to a material extent or time under such conditions	Does not apply to any drug subject to the Food and Drugs Act of 1906 whose labeling contained the same representation. Does not apply to new animal drug or animal feed containing a new animal drug

(continued)

Table 3.1 (continued)

Term	Definition	Notes
New animal drug	A drug intended for use in animals other than man, including any drug for use in animal feed and whose composition is not generally recognized among experts qualified by scientific and experience to evaluate the safety and effectiveness of animal drugs, as safe and effective for use under the conditions prescribed, recommended, or suggested in the labeling Whose composition is a result of investigations to determine its safety and effectiveness for use under such conditions has become so recognized, but which has not, except for in such investigations, been used to a material extent or time under such conditions	Does not apply to animal feed without a drug Does not apply to any drug subject to the Food and Drugs Act of 1906 whose labeling contained the same representation
Device	An instrument, apparatus, implement, machine, contrivance, implant, in vitro reagent, or other similar or related article which is: Recognized in the U.S. Pharmacopeia, National Formulary, or any supplement of them Intended for use in the diagnosis of disease, or other conditions, or in the cure, mitigation, treatment, or prevention of disease in man or other animals Intended to affect the structure or function of the body of man or other animals Does not achieve its primary purpose through chemical action within or on the body of man or other animals and is not dependent upon being metabolized to achieve its primary purpose	Does not include software functions
Official compendium	Official U.S. Pharmacopeia Official Homeopathic Pharmacopeia of the United States Official National Formulary Any supplement to the above	
Label	A display of written, printed, or graphic matter upon the immediate container AND outside container or wrapper (if applicable) of any article	"Immediate container" does not apply to package liners
Labeling	All labels and other written, printed, or graphic matter upon any article or any of its connection or wrappers, or accompanying any article	
Ingredient	Any substance in the drug, whether added to the formulation as a single substance or in admixture with other ingredients	

(continued)

Table 3.1 (continued)

Term	Definition	Notes
Color additive	Dye, pigment, or other substances made by a process of synthesis or similar artifice or extracted, isolated, or otherwise derived with or without intermediate or final change of identity from a vegetable, animal, mineral, or other source When added or applied to a food, drug, or cosmetic, or to the human body or any part thereof, is capable (alone or in reaction with other substance(s)) of imparting color thereto	Does not apply to any substance whose intended purpose is not coloring Color includes black, white, and intermediate grays among its options
Knowingly or knew	The person with respect to the information has actual knowledge of the information or acts in deliberate ignorance or reckless disregard of the truth or falsity of the information	
Dietary supplement	A product intended to supplement the diet and bears or contains ≥1 of the following: vitamin, mineral, herb, botanical, amino acid, dietary substance for use by man to supplement the diet by increasing total dietary intake, or a concentrate, metabolite, constituent, extract, or combination of any of these Is intended for ingestion Is not represented for use as a conventional food or as a sole item of a meal or the diet Is labeled as a dietary supplement Is not approved as a drug or certified antibiotic, licensed as a biologic, or an article authorized for investigation as a new drug, antibiotic, or biologic for which substantial clinical investigations have been instituted and for which the existence of such investigations has been made public	Excludes tobacco
Antibiotic or antibiotic drug	Any drug composed wholly or partly of any kind of penicillin, streptomycin, chlortetracycline, chloramphenicol, bacitracin, or any other drug intended for human use containing any quantity of any chemical substance which is produced by a microorganism, and which has the capacity to inhibit or destroy micro-organisms in dilute solution (including chemically synthesized equivalent) or any derivative thereof	

(continued)

Table 3.1 (continued)

Term	Definition	Notes
Compounded positron emission tomography drug	A drug that exhibits spontaneous disintegration of unstable nuclei by the emission of positron Is used for the purpose of providing dual photon positron emission tomographic diagnostic images Has been compounded by or on the order of a practitioner who is licensed by a State to compound or order compounding for a drug in accordance with State law Includes any nonradioactive reagent, reagent kit, ingredient, nuclide generator, accelerator, target material, electronic synthesizer, or other apparatus, or computer program to be used in the preparation of such a drug	
Single-use device	A device that is intended for one use or on a single patient during a single procedure	
Current good manufacturing practice	The implementation of oversight and controls over manufacture of drugs to ensure quality, including managing the risk of and establishing the safety of raw materials, materials used in the manufacturing of drugs, and finished drug products	
Established name	Applicable official drug name (i.e., generic name) or official device name If there is no official name and such drug or ingredient is an article recognized in an official compendium, then the official title listed in that compendium If none of the above, the common or usual name	
Wholesale distribution	Distribution or receipt of a drug to a person other than a consumer or patient	
Intended use(s)	The objective intent of the persons legally responsible for labeling. Intent may be shown by person's expressions, labeling claims, advertising material, oral or written statements, article design or composition, or by circumstances surrounding the distribution of the article	

FDCA Food, Drug, & Cosmetic Act, *US* United States

Table 3.2 Understanding adulteration and misbranding according to the FDCA [4, 6]

Adulterate, adulterated, or adulteration	Misbrand, misbranded, or misbranding
A drug or device that consists in whole or in part of any filthy, putrid, or decomposed substance or If a drug or device has been prepared, packed, or held under insanitary conditions where it may have been contaminated with filth or rendered injurious to health A drug where the methods used in the facilities or controls used for its manufacture, processing, packing, or holding do not conform to or are not operated or administered in conformity with current good manufacturing practices to assure that such a drug meets the requirements of the FDCA as to safety, has the identity and strength, and meets the quality and purity characteristics which it purports or is represented to possess A drug that purports to be or is represented as a drug recognized in an official compendium, but whose strength differs from or whose quality or purity falls below the standards set forth in the compendium Any drug that has been mixed or packed so as to reduce its quality or strength (wholly or in part) A device that fails to conform with the standard for devices A banned device A device and the methods used in or the facilities or controls used for its manufacture, packing, storage, or installation do not conform with applicable requirements of the FDCA A drug or device which has been manufactured, processed, packed, or held in any factory, warehouse, or establishment where the owner, operator, or agent delays, denies, or limits an inspection or refuses to permit entry or inspection	Labeling for a drug or device is false or misleading in any way A drug or device in package form without a label containing the following information: (1) name and address of the manufacturer, packer, or distributor, (2) an accurate statement of quantity in terms of weigh, measure, or numerical count (reasonable variations and exceptions to small packages allowed) If any word, statement, or other information required by or under the authority of (e.g., required by the FDA) to appear on the label or labeling is not prominently placed with conspicuousness and in such terms as to render it likely to be read and understood by the ordinary individual under customary conditions of purchase and use A drug without a label bearing any of the information required by the FDCA A product that purports to be a drug recognized in an official compendium but is not packaged and labeled as prescribed in the compendium A drug that is liable to deterioration which is not packaged in such a form and manner and without a label stating such precautions necessary for the protection of public health A drug container made, formed, or filled to be misleading or is an imitation of another drug, or offered for sale under the name of another drug A drug that is dangerous to health when used in the dosage or manner or with the frequency or duration prescribed, recommended, or suggested in the labeling If there is color additive whose intended use is for the purpose of coloring only unless the packaging and labeling conform to the requirements applicable for a color additive Failure of the manufacturer, packer or distributor to include in all advertisements and other descriptive printed matter issued or caused to be issued with respect to that drug information required by the FDCA A drug or device not manufactured, prepared, propagated, compounded, or processed in an establishment not duly registered as required by the FDCA A drug imported or offered for import by a commercial importer of drugs not registered as required by the FDCA A device that does not bear symbols from the uniform system for identification of devices as required by the FDCA A drug and its packaging or labeling that violates the Poison Prevention Packaging Act A drug or device whose advertising is false or misleading in any way A reprocessed single-use device that fails to prominently and conspicuously bear the name of the manufacturer of the reprocessed device (or a generally recognized name abbreviation or symbol identifying the manufacturer) A reprocessed single-use device that fails to prominently and conspicuously bear the statement "reprocessed device for single use. Reprocessed by__________" with the statement including the manufacturer of the reprocessed device An original device or attachment that fails to prominently and conspicuously bear the name of the manufacturer (or a generally recognized name abbreviation of symbol identifying the manufacturer) A new animal drug whose label does not conform to the FDAC or for whom the labeling fails to include the application number as "Approved by the FDA under (A)NADA # xxx-xxx" An OTC drug whose label fails to list a domestic (i.e., U.S.) address or phone number through which a responsible person may receive a report of a serious adverse event with the drug Drugs subject to an approved REMS where the responsible person fails to comply with a requirement of the strategy Drugs that violate FDCA requirements related to labeling for post marketing (e.g., Phase IV) studies and clinical trials Drugs or active pharmaceutical ingredients manufactured, propagated, compounded, or processed in a facility for which fees have not been paid as required by the FDCA Advertising or promotion of a compounded drug that is false or misleading in any way A drug that fails to bear the product identifier required by the FDCA An antimicrobial or OTC drug whose label does not conform to specific requirements for those types of drugs under the FDCA An investigational drug or device without a clear statement identifying it as such

FDA Food and Drug Administration, *FDCA* Food, Drug, And Cosmetic Act, *OTC* over-the-counter, *REMS* risk evaluation and mitigation strategy, *US* United States unless otherwise stated. Please note that the law uses the legal default of "man" to indicate a human, regardless of gender. The FDCA's definition of drug is essential to the context of many other pieces of pharmacy legislation and regulation. Both inclusion and omission involving these definitions are used to shape pharmacy expectations. For example, if a product is alleged to be misbranded due to misleading labeling or advertising, not only are the representations made or suggested by the labeling or advertising considered, but the failure to reveal factual information could qualify a product as meeting the definition of misbranding.

> **Study Pro Tip** Preparing flash cards or using another method of repeated method of applying or connecting a term with the definition should be part of your studying process. Most people find it difficult to fully learn and understand the definitions by reading it once. After you create your initial flash cards (or other method), it can be helpful to review the term(s) each time you encounter it in pharmacy laws or regulations (including others besides the FDCA) until you are fully confident in your knowledge of the definition(s).

Much of the FDCA focuses on ensuring that a drug is not adulterated or misbranded. These terms have extensive definitions under the FDCA. For certain products, the definition of either adulteration or misbranding can be item specific. For example, a compounded positron emission tomography (PET) drug can qualify as adulterated under the same criteria as another drug except that instead of failing to meet good manufacturing practices (GMP) , an adulterated PET drug would not be in conformity with the PET standards and the official monographs of the U.S. Pharmacopeia (USP) [4]. A PET drug is also considered adulterated if its container is composed (wholly or in part) of any poisonous or deleterious substance, if it contains a unsafe color additive, or if it is an unsafe new animal drug. In some situations, criteria qualify under both adulteration and misbranding. According to the FDCA, a drug is both adulterated and misbranded if it does not meet the standards listed in the official compendium. However, the law has a caveat that it is not adulteration if the difference in strength, quality, and purity from the compendium standards are plainly stated on the label. Should there be a drug listed in both the USP and the Homeopathic Pharmacopeia of the United States, the USP standards take precedence *unless* the product is specifically labeled and offered for sale as a homeopathic drug (in which case the Homeopathic Pharmacopeia of the United States is the standard). Some exemptions are also made. A few criteria defining adulteration or misbranding read as though it should fall under the opposite term, and it is important to be knowledgeable of these distinctions. Some exceptions are explicitly listed throughout the law. As an example, while the FDCA is very clear that labeling cannot be false or misleading, it does not consider health care economic information provided to a payor, formulary committee, or similar entity to be subject to the definition misbranding in regard to labeling.

2.4 Labels and Labeling

The FDCA and subsequent FDA regulations are pretty specific regarding what information is required on the label of a drug or device. If any of this information is missing or false, the product is considered misbranded [4, 6]. Required information on the *label* includes:

1. The established (i.e., generic) drug name and quantity, or proportion of each active ingredient (including quantity, kind, and proportion of any alcohol).
   (a) For prescription drugs, the established name of the drug or (if applicable) ingredient on the label must be printed prominently and in a font size at least half as large as the font size of the proprietary (i.e., brand) name or designation for such ingredient.
   (b) For over-the-counter (OTC) drugs, the net quantity of the package contents must also be listed.
2. If applicable, whether active or not, the established name and quantity (or if applicable, proportion) of any bromides, ether, chloroform, acetanilide, acetophenetidin, amidopyrine, antipyrine, atropine, hyoscine, hyoscyamine, arsenic, digitalis, digitalis glucosides, mercury, ouabain, strophanthin, strychnine, thyroid, or any derivative or preparation of these substances (unless not intended for human use).
3. The established name of each inactive ingredient is listed.
   (a) For OTC drugs, this list must be in alphabetical order on the outside container of the retail package and on the immediate container.
4. Adequate directions for use—directions which the average person can use to take a drug safely for the intended purpose(s).
5. Adequate warnings against use in those pathological conditions or by children where its use may be dangerous to health.
   (a) For OTC drugs, warnings related to use in pregnancy or lactation is required (unless intended for exclusive use in pediatrics), including a specific warning for aspirin or aspirin-containing products.
   (b) For oral OTC drugs with sodium from active and/or inactive ingredients, the amount of sodium content per dosage unit as milligrams per dosage unit must be listed. (Usually under "Other information") If the labeled maximum daily dose includes ≥140 mg sodium, a warning label must also appear.
      (i). The term "sodium free" may be used to indicate that there is ≤5 mg sodium in the maximum daily dose and "Very low sodium" may indicate when that amount is ≤35 mg.
      (ii). Rectal products must list sodium content if the amount per dose is ≥5 mg.
   (c) For OTC drugs—warnings regarding Reye's syndrome, allergic reactions, asthma alerts, sore throats, contraindications, patient age (particularly pediatrics).

6. Adequate warnings against unsafe dosage or methods of duration or administration or application.
   (a) For OTC drugs non intended for ingestion, the statement "For external use" (in bold font) is required for topical products. The phrase "For rectal use only" or "For vaginal use only" must appear on appropriate labels in bold font.
   (b) For OTC drugs—warnings on flammability, chocking, and signs of toxicity are required.

Study Pro Tip There are many more requirements for OTC drug labels that are not listed in this chapter. The information not listed is more important for a manufacturer or packer and is less likely to appear on the MPJE.

Labeling for drugs is much more extensive, serves as a summary of the essential scientific information necessary (whenever possible derived from human experience) to use the drug safely and effectively and should be informative and accurate and not promotional or misleading [6]. The list of contents will likely be familiar to anyone who has seen a drug's package insert. In general, labeling follows a particular template preceded by a table of contents. If an item is omitted, an asterisk (*) should be used by its designation on the table of contents with a statement at the end of such contents that the item(s) are not listed. Items included in labeling include:

1. Highlights of prescribing information—a summary of more extensive information.
   (a) Product names.
   (b) Boxed warning(s).
   (c) Recent major changes (if applicable).
   (d) Indications and usage.
   (e) Dosage forms and strengths.
   (f) Contraindications.
   (g) Warnings and precautions.
   (h) Adverse reactions.
   (i) Drug interactions.
   (j) Use in specific populations (e.g., age, organ function, disease state).
2. Full prescribing information.
   (a) Boxed warning(s).
   (b) Indication and usage.
   (c) Dosage forms and strengths.
   (d) Contraindications.
   (e) Warnings and precautions.
   (f) Adverse reactions.
   (g) Drug interactions.
   (h) Use in specific populations (to include pregnancy, lactation, people of reproductive potential, pediatric use, and geriatric use).

(i) Drug abuse and dependence (to included controlled substance, abuse, and dependence information as necessary).
(j) Overdosage information.
(k) Description of the product.
(l) Clinical pharmacology (to include mechanism of action, pharmacodynamics, and pharmacokinetics).
(m) Nonclinical toxicology (to included carcinogenesis, mutagenesis, fertility impairment, and animal toxicology and/or pharmacology).
(n) Clinical studies.
(o) References.
(p) How the product is suppled and how it should be stored and handled.
(q) Patient counseling information.

The presence of *adequate* directions for use is a frequently referenced label and labeling requirements of the FDCA. It is important to remember that if they are not present, the drug is considered misbranded. Directions are considered inadequate if they omit (wholly or in part) or incorrectly specify intended purpose(s) or use(s). All purposes or uses of the prescription or OTC drug must be stated except for prescription drugs that are only advertised to licensed prescribers [6]. Other reasons for directions for use being considered inadequate include omission or incorrect specification of the dose quantity (including usual quantities AND doses for patients of different ages or physical conditions), frequency of administration/application, duration of administration/application, timing of administration or application (specifically in regards to food, onset of symptoms, or other relevant time factors), route or method of administration or application, or preparation for use (specifically, shaking, dilution, temperature adjustment, or other manipulation or process [6]. When certain criteria do not differ, it is prudent to list in the labeling as such rather than omitting that information. For example, if dosing for patients ≥65 years is the same as younger adults, a statement is commonly included to indicate that (e.g., no dosage adjustment in geriatric patients is required). If a drug has "commonly known directions," they do not have to be stated on the label *as long* as they are known to the *ordinary* individual.

There are other label and labeling requirements found in FDA regulations rather than within the FDCA itself, but are nonetheless still important to know and the absence of which can also render a product misbranded [6]. When required, the drug's expiration date should appear on the immediate container and the outer package, unless the outer package is designed so the date on the immediate container is visible or for single-use containers, the date may appear on the individual carton. The label should include a lot number that can be used to identify the product's complete manufacturing history. Systemic antimicrobials require specific statements regarding the risk of drug-resistant bacteria. Insulin labels have dedicated requirements on statement of identify, net quantity of contents, and dosage.

For drugs with ≥2 ingredients, referring to the drug by a name that suggests only one of the ingredients is considered misleading and therefore rendered misbranded [6]. The label should not be misleading by listing ingredients in an order so as to give misleading prominence, failing to state the proportion or amount of each included ingredient, engaging a "fanciful" proprietary (e.g., brand) name to imply that the drug or ingredient has a unique effectiveness or composition when that drug or ingredient is a common substance, or featuring names of inert or inactive ingredients so as to imply they have more value than their true functional role in the product. The law requires that the label and labeling always include the established (e.g., generic) drug name, and that it be listed in a font size that is no less than 50% of the font used to state a proprietary name.

> **Study Pro Tip** Unless otherwise specified, the use of the word "label" in the FDCA refers to the label on a drug package supplied by a manufacturer, repackager, or other similar source. Labels applied by a pharmacist to a prescription vial, bottle, or other package for a drug dispensed by the pharmacy have their own requirements for what must be included, according to federal and Alabama law. When studying, it is helpful to be able to compare and contrast these requirements.

The law also takes a detailed approach to information presented by manufacturers, packers, or distributors of prescription drugs or devices in advertisements or other descriptive print matter. These must include a true statement of:

1. The established name printed prominently and in font size at least *half* as large as any trade or brand name.
2. For drugs—the formula showing the quantity of each ingredient to the extent required for labels.
3. For devices—a brief statement of the intended uses of the device.
4. Information in brief summary relating to side effects, contraindications, and effectiveness.
5. For specific devices where determined necessary, provide a full description of the components of the device.

In direct-to-consumer advertisements, the prominently printed statement "You are encouraged to report negative side effects of prescription drugs to the FDA. Visit www.fda.gov/medwatch or call 1-800-FDA-1088. If the advertisement is on the television or radio, there must be a clear, conspicuous, and neutral presentation regarding the drug name, conditions of use, side effects, and contraindications. Advertisements should be reviewed by the FDA, but do not require approval before dissemination.

Devics with an established name must also list it prominently under the same font requirements as drug labels unless no other nonproprietary name is listed. From a practical perspective, labeling for prescription devices that are used in health care facilities or healthcare professionals, or those used for in vitro diagnostic tests by healthcare providers or in blood establishments area allowed to be made available entirely electronically as long as it complies with other requirements and if requested, can be made available in paper form promptly and without additional cost.

2.5 Registration Requirement

All drug manufacturers and repackagers must register with the FDA [4]. If a company does not register, its products are considered misbranded. This requirement is not intended to regulate the practice of pharmacy or medicine and therefore, pharmacies are *not* required to register with the FDA for normal operations of dispensing prescription drugs pursuant to a valid prescription so long as they operate in compliance with federal, state, and local law and do not manufacture, prepare, compound, or process drugs or devices for resale other than in the regular course of business of dispensing. If a pharmacy does begin to compound or dispense beyond pursuance of a prescription, they must register. Every registered establishment is subject to inspection by the FDA.

Key Concept

Understanding when pharmacy registration is and is not required with the FDA.

No registration required—Jones Pharmacy receives a prescription from Dr. Gus for Mr. Smith for a compound. There is no commercially available, FDA approved medication that contains all of the ingredients that Dr. Gus believes is needed to treat Mr. Smith. Jones Pharmacy may prepare the compounded drug.

Registration required—Zill Pharmacy is located next door to a busy oncology practice that have many patients suffering from stomatitis due to chemotherapy. The pharmacy creates a unique recipe of "magic mouthwash" and prepares several batches each week. Physicians send patients specifically to Zill Pharmacy with prescriptions that list the drug as "Zill's Magic Mouthwash" rather than the individual ingredients or amounts in the compounded drug.

Key Concept

Key Provisions of the Food, Drug, and Cosmetic Act when Written In 1938.

- Formalized the FDA's authority over food, drugs, therapeutic devices, and cosmetics.
- Prohibited adulteration or misbranding for any drug introduced or intended for interstate commerce.
- Required registration for those involved in the drug chain supply—except for pharmacies and end users. If the company did not register, drugs were considered misbranded.
- Required proof of safety for new drugs before marketing.
- Required drugs to be labeled with adequate directions for safe use.
- Required warning label for habit forming drugs.

2.6 The Durham-Humphrey Amendment of 1951: The Prescription Drug Amendment

2.6.1 Overview of the Durham-Humphrey Amendment

After the passage of the FDCA, there arose a recognized need of pharmacists for better clarification about drugs required a prescription [7, 8]. The decision, including what factors should be considered, was primarily left to the discretion of the manufacturer [2]. Disagreements between pharmacists, physicians, and the FDA about this distinction quickly appeared [7, 8]. Two senators, who had previously practiced as pharmacists (Carl Durham and Hubert Humphrey Jr.), co-sponsored the Durham-Humphrey Amendment to address these concerns.

2.6.2 Criteria to Establish Prescription or Over-the-Counter Status

On of the major actions of the Durham-Humphrey Amendment was to separate the drugs into two classes: prescription and over-the-counter. The amendment specifically clarified what classified a drug as prescription or OTC status and gave final authority to make the determination to the FDA. Drugs that are habit-forming, potentially harmful, or are unsafe for self-medication and require a prescriber's supervision are considered prescription drugs.

Key Concept

The Durham-Humphrey Amendment outlines when a prescription drug could be dispensed.

1. Upon a written prescription by a licensed practitioner.
2. Upon an oral prescription from a licensed practitioner—which is promptly reduced to writing.
3. By refilling—if the refill is authorized on the original written or oral prescription.
4. By direct administration from the prescriber.

Originally, prescription drugs—often described as drugs that are habit-forming or potentially harmful in literature sources—were required bear a statement, or legend "Caution: Federal law prohibits dispensing without a prescription" on their labels [9]. This has since been shorten to the phrase **"Rx Only."** Packages containing prescription drugs (e.g., stock bottles) held in the pharmacy, whether dispensed directly to the patient or divided and placed in the pharmacy's prescription vials or bottles, must bear this phrase. If this statement is not on the label, the product is considered misbranded. Labels on vials or bottles dispensed to the patient are not required to have this phrase.

OTC drugs are those generally recognized by experts to be safe and effective for self-use, or without the need for supervision of a licensed practitioner [4]. They

Fun Fact
Prescription drugs have also been referred to as "legend drugs." This name comes from the requirement for these products to bear a "legend" or statement indicating they require a prescription in order to be dispensed.

have a wide margin of safety and positive benefit-to-risk ratio when used according to the labeling. Typically, they have a simple method of administration, such as oral or topical. Although not a rule, OTC products are often intended to alleviate symptoms rather than treat a disease or condition.

Interestingly, the Durham-Humphrey Amendment is the federal law most violated by pharmacists—even in compliance with state law. This is because a prescription drug, according to this law, cannot be dispensed without a valid prescription or authorized refill. However, several states, including Alabama, allow a pharmacist to provide limited quantities of a patient's chronic medication when there are no remaining refills, and the prescriber is not available to authorize a new prescription. Additionally, dispensing errors would be considered a violation of this law.

2.6.3 Minimal Information Requirements of the Prescription Label

The FDCA and related FDA regulations state a long list of information which must be included on a product's label as it comes from the manufacturer, repackager, or other source [4]. It is important to distinguish what information must appear on the original packaging label versus the label of the package that the patient ultimately receives. Drugs dispensed pursuant to a prescription are required to be labeled with certain information more relevant to the patient. Both federal and Alabama laws and regulations address the content of the prescription label. At the federal level, the Durham-Humphrey Amendment requires the following information to appear on the label of any prescription drug dispensed:

- Name and address of dispenser (i.e., pharmacy).
- Serial number of prescriptions.
- Date of prescription or its filling.
- Name of prescriber.
- Name of patient (if stated on prescription).
- Directions for use (if stated on prescription).
- Cautionary statements or warning labels (if stated on prescription).

2.7 The Kefauver-Harris Amendment of 1962: The Efficacy Amendment

2.7.1 Overview of the Kefauver-Harris Amendment

The Kefauver-Harris Amendment of 1962 derived, at least in part, from hearings held by Senator Estes Kefauver on the need to strengthen the FDCA and the weakness of the law [8, 10, 11]. These hearings had led to an early bill to amend the

FDCA to require drug efficacy, but disagreements about compulsory licensing and patents had stalled movement on that original bill [10]. The tragedy that revived discussions involved the drug thalidomide, a sedative drug with antiemetic effects (and at the time, not approved for use in the United States) which had caused thousands of babies to be born with teratogenic effects (mainly missing or abnormal limbs) [8, 11].

In general, the Kefauver-Harris Amendment requires proof of both of both efficacy and safety —through "adequate and well-controlled investigations"—before a new drug can be marketed [8, 10, 11]. It was the first federal law to require proof that a drug was effective. The law gave the FDA the authority to oversee the investigational process, including animal (now expanded to nonclinical) and human testing to ensure the process remained safe and ethical. Through the Drug Efficacy Study Implementation (DESI) program, a retrospective review of all drugs approved from 1938 to 1962 (which had only been required to prove safety before marketing) occurred and hundreds of drugs found to be ineffective were removed from the market [10, 11]. The extent of the FDA's oversight over drug testing and evaluation does not end upon the approval of a drug, as manufacturers are required to notify the FDA of adverse effects, including those not detected until after the drug is released commercially [11]. The law requires that all drugs have readable generic names and prohibited generic drugs from being sold as expensive medications under new trade names. Whereas the FDCA had previously authorized the FDA to inspect manufacturing facilities, the Kefauver-Harris Amendment mandates inspections every TWO (2) years to ensure compliance with good manufacturing practices (GMP) [11]. To ensure compliance with the mandate that drug advertising disclose arcuate information about efficacy and safety (i.e. must disclose side effects), transfer of regulatory authority over such advertising was given to the FDA [11].

Key Concept

Provisions of the Kefauver-Harris Amendment of 1962

- Required proof of safety and efficacy before marketing a new drug.
- Required an FDA review of efficacy for all drugs introduced 1938–1962 (Drug Efficacy Study Implementation or DESI).
- Established stricter FDA oversight over clinical trials.
- Mandated informed consent for clinical trial subjects.
- Transferred authority over prescription drug regulation from the Federal Trade Commission to the FDA.
- Required all drugs to have a readable generic name.
- Established good manufacturing practices (GMP) .
- Provided FDA with authorized access to records on manufacturer production and controls in order to verify GMP.

2.7.2 Understanding Drug Applications

Approval, regulation, and control of drugs in the United States is based on the New Drug Application (NDA) process which must be submitted and approved by the FDA before a drug can be commercially marketed [12]. Any and all information related to the drug, including (but not limited to) contents or ingredients, pharmaceutical science (e.g., mechanism, pharmacokinetics) information, production, packaging, data gathered during animal and human studies are part of the NDA. The purpose of the NDA is to give the FDA enough information to be able to determine if the drug is safe and effective for its proposed indication(s) (and if the benefits outweigh any risks), to evaluate if the proposed labeling is appropriate and what it should contain, and to assess whether the methods used in the manufacture of the drug and controls used to maintain the drug's quality are adequate to preserve the drug's identify, quality, purity, and strength [12].

In order to submit an NDA, clinical studies in humans are required. However, legally drugs must be FDA approved before they can be transported through interstate commerce. The FDA provides an exemption to this requirement through the Investigational New Drug (IND) process. Submission and approval of an IND is essentially permission to conduct studies in humans, and is about the time point where a new product changes legal status from a molecule to a new drug [13]. The IND (Table 3.3) should include all known information about the drug up until that point, including data from nonclinical studies (termed preclinical tests prior to 2022), essentially data from in vivo animal or acceptable nonclinical pharmacology and toxicology studies [12–14]. It should also contain all manufacturing information such as manufacturer identity, composition, stability, and controls for manufacturing, clinical trial protocols, investigator qualifications, and a commitment to IND regulations. The manufacturer, also referred to as a sponsor, must wait 30 calendar days to start any clinical trials. During this time, the FDA reviews the IND to ensure that no unreasonable risk is posed to study subjects. THIRTY (30) days after an IND submission, clinical studies may begin in humans (Table 3.4), unless the sponsor has been notified that such studies are prohibited [6, 15]. A treatment IND or emergency use IND may be submitted to obtain an investigational drug for a patient with a life-threatening condition where no alternative therapy is available or effective [4].

Upon completion of clinical studies, the NDA is submitted. The NDA is a comprehensive packet that contains every detail available to the sponsor about the drug to include all manufacturing information, the drugs pharmacologic properties and contents, data from preclinical and clinical testing, proposed labeling, proposed labeling, and any other related information. Once approved, the manufacturer may not make any change that affects information listed in the NDA without FDA approval [6]. This can range from changes in labeling (e.g., adding a new side effect) to a change in manufacturer location. To streamline this, a smaller application known as the supplemental NDA (SNDA), is submitted and focuses on the requested change to the original NDA. The final drug application is the abbreviated NDA (ANDA), which is submitted to obtain approval for generic drugs. The ANDA is discussed in more detail later in this chapter.

Table 3.3 Comparison of investigational new drug applications used in the drug approval process [12, 13]

	IND	Treatment IND	Emergency use IND
Purpose	To determine if a product is reasonably safe for initial testing in humans and if it exhibits pharmacologic activity worth pursuing additional development	To allow use of experimental drug with available data indicating efficacy for serious or immediately life-threatening conditions where there are no other comparable or satisfactory alternative treatment options	To allow use of an experimental drug in an emergency situation which does not allow time for IND submission or to allow use in patients who do not meet criteria for an existing protocol
Submitted to request	Permission for interstate transportation of an investigational drug for the purpose of conducting clinical studies in humans	Permission to give a promising investigational drug to a patient with serious or immediately life-threatening conditions outside of a clinical study	Single patient expanded access for an unapproved investigational drug for an individual patient
Application contents	Nonclinical data Manufacturing information Proposed clinical protocols Investigator qualifications Commitment to obtain informed consent, IRB review, and to adhere to IND regulations A summary of any previous human experience with the drug Description of possible risks and side effects	Expanded access form Completed by the physician	Specific Patient Expanded Access Form Treatment plan for investigational drug Letter of authorization from manufacturer Completed by physician Submitted to FDA
Comments	This can be for a new drug or for an approved product seeking a new indication or use in a new patient population	Treatment may begin 30 days after the application is received by the FDA or earlier if notified by FDA	Emergency requests may be made by calling the FDA and shipment and use may begin prior to the receipt of the written IND submission

FDA Food and Drug Administration, *IND* investigational new drug

Table 3.4 Comparison of new drug applications used in the drug approval process [6, 15]

	New drug application	Supplemental NDA	Abbreviated NDA
Purpose	A comprehensive packet of information submitted to obtain approval to market a new drug	To obtain approval for a change in information within an approved NDA	To obtain approval for a generic drug
Application contents	Labeling Pharmacology and toxicology Pharmaceutical and medicinal chemistry Manufacturing information including controls Nonclinical study data Clinical study data Pharmacokinetics and other pharmaceutical science information Microbiology (if applicable)	Information pertaining to the requested change	Labeling Pharmacology and toxicology Pharmaceutical and medicinal chemistry Manufacturing information including controls Bioequivalence data
Comments	Any change to information listed in the NDA for an approved drug requires FDA review and approval		

FDA Food and Drug Administration, *NDA* new drug application

2.7.3 The Drug Approval Process

The drug approval process in the United States takes years due to the intensive amount of research required to prove the drug is both safe for use in humans and effective with regards to its intended purpose(s) or use(s). Clinical studies in humans can begin 30 days after the IND is submitted to the FDA, unless the sponsor is informed that the studies are prohibited, but are conducted in phases of escalating patient enrollment to mitigate unknown safety risks that may occur during these trials (Fig. 3.1) [16]. This process may be repeated, at least in part, multiple times by a single product as attempts to determine safety and efficacy for new indications, in new patient populations, with new dosing, with new formulations, or other changes occur.

2.7.4 The Food and Drug Modernization Act of 1997 and the FDA Modernization Act 2.0

The Food and Drug Administration Modernization Act, also referred to as the Modernization Act, was initially passed in 1997 and was updated in 2022 with the FDA Modernization Act 2.0 [14–16]. The two laws amend the FDCA with respect to requirements of the drug approval process. The 1997 law was passed to improve the regulation of products governed by the FDCA. Specific to drugs, its provisions cover a broad depth of topics from labeling to clarification on misbranding and adulteration, but most modifications focus on requirements for drug approval and

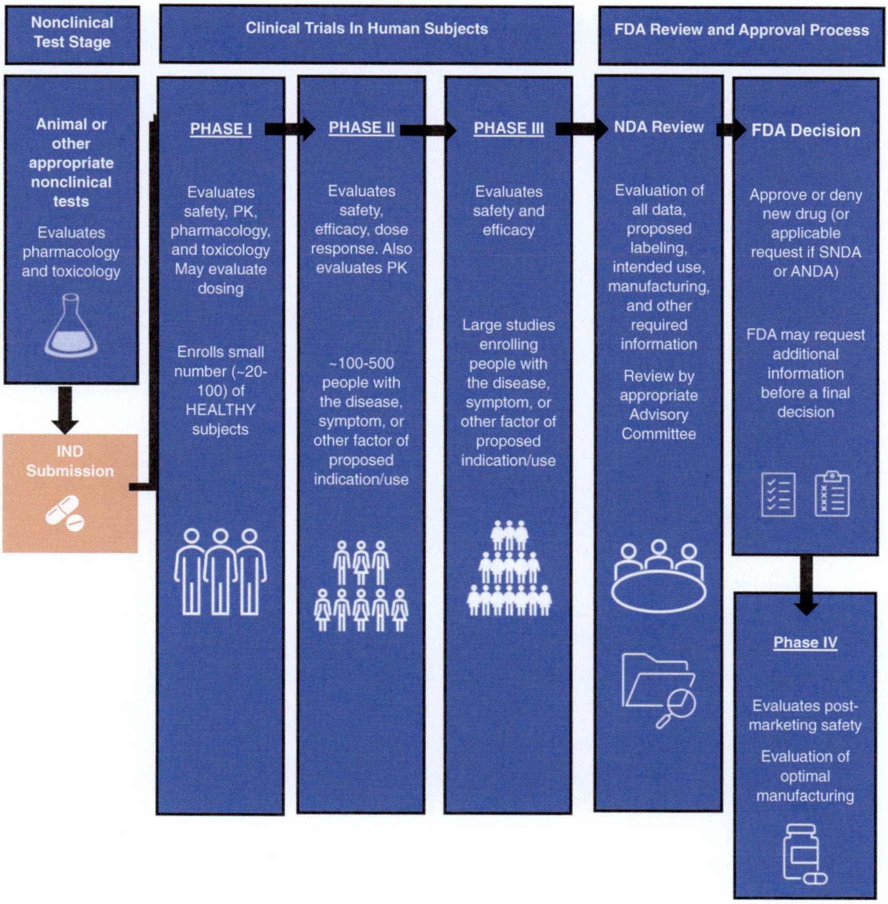

Fig. 3.1 Overview of the drug approval process in the United States

marketing [16]. It serves as the first reauthorization of the Prescription Drug User Fee Act of 1992 (discussed later in this chapter). It confides initiatives to bring biologic product regulation in concordance with drug regulations, codifies FDA practices and regulations intended to increase patient access to investigational drugs and devices and to accelerate the review of new medications directed toward unmet medical needs (Fast Track). Additional provisions included in the law are intended to improve the regulation of devices, including reducing or simplifying several regulatory obligations.

Key Concept

Important Actions of the Food and Drug Modernization Act of 1997 Regarding Drugs

- Replaces the required legend on prescription-only drugs to "Rx only."
- Removes requirement that certain products be labeled "Warning-May be habit forming."
- Defines when drug application fees are due, should be refunded, and are exempt.
- Includes provisions to facilitated increased enrollment and evaluation of pediatrics, women, and minorities in clinical trials.
- Introduces the "Fast Track" designation to facilitate development and expedite review of new drugs for serious conditions and unmet medical needs.
- Mandates a data bank of information on clinical trials for drugs intended for serious or life-threatening conditions.
- Declares that healthcare economic information provided to a formulary committee is not misleading or false if the information directly relates to an FDA approved indication for the drug and is based on competent and reliable scientific evidence.
- States that data from one clinical study and confirmatory evidence (obtained before or after such study) *may be* considered sufficient to establish effectiveness. (At the discretion of the FDA).
- Regulates new drug manufacturing changes and requires manufacturer validation on the effects of such changes.
- Permits clinical testing in humans to begin 30 days after the submission of an IND unless the sponsor has specifically been told that such trials will not be allowed.
- Modifies requirements of the NDA content and review process.
- Modifies requirements on the use of scientific advisory panels.
- Declares a when a compounded PET drug is adulterated.
- Mandates guidance on when abbreviated study reports can be submitted in lieu of full reports in an NDA.
- Allows a pilot of other small facility to be used to demonstrate drug or animal drug safety and effectiveness.
- Repeals certification requirements for insulin and antibiotics.
- Clarifies which provisions in the FDCA do not apply to a compounded drug.
- Requires postmarketing studies (i.e., Phase IV studies) and related reports.
- Requires a manufacturer who is the only producer of a drug, biologic, or device to notify the FDA when the product will cease being produced if the product is life supporting/sustaining or intended for the prevention of a debilitating disease/condition, has been approved under specified provisions, or was a product not originally derived from human tissue and replaced by a recombinant product. This information must be distributed to appropriate physician and patient organizations.

The FDA Modernization Act 2.0 is a much smaller law [14]. It allows for certain alternatives to traditional in vivo animal studies to be used in order to obtain IND approval and be able to move on to human testing. It further removes the requirement for animal studies in order to obtain a license for a biosimilar or other interchangeable product that is interchangeable with a biologic product. The law defines a nonclinical test as one conducted in vitro, in silico, *in chemico*, or a nonhuman in vivo test (i.e. animal test) that occurs before the clinical trial phase. This can include animal tests, non-animal tests, or human-biology based tests such as cell-based assays, microphysiological systems, or bioprinted or computer models.

2.8 Removing Drugs from the Market

Any product under the authority of the FDCA that is adulterated or misbranded when introduced into or held for sale after shipment into interstate commerce is subject to criminal penalties [4]. Such products may be seized or subject to recall [17]. Products that are seized are held in isolation pending court proceedings. Recalls occur when a product is removed from the market, a process which may occur on the manufacturer's initiative, at FDA request, or by FDA order [17]. The simplest is a market withdrawal, where a minor violation occurs which would not be subject to FDA legal action; the product can be removed completely or the violation can be corrected. More complicated recalls are separated into classes by severity.

- Class I—there is a reasonable probability that the use of or exposure to the product will cause serious health consequences or death.
- Class II—use of or exposure to a product may cause temporary or medically reversible adverse health consequences or where the probability of serious adverse health consequence is remote.
- Class III—use of or exposure to a product is unlikely to cause serious adverse health consequences.

2.9 National Drug Code

A National Drug Code (NDC) (Fig. 3.2) is a standardized numerical identifier defined in the FDCA as a set of numbers or characters used to uniquely identify every package or homogenous case of a drug [4]. The FDA requests that it appear on drug labels and on all drug labeling, but it is not required to be listed by law [6]. The NDC corresponds to a specific packaging of a particular product. The FDCA authorizes the NDC to be alphanumeric with up to 20 characters, but currently only 10–11 are used. However, in 2022, the FDA announced a proposed move to a uniform, 12-digit NDC because available 10-digit NDCs were being exhausted [18]. However, the move would not alter the overall format of the NDC. The NDC is divided into three segments. The first segment, known as the labeler code, is assigned

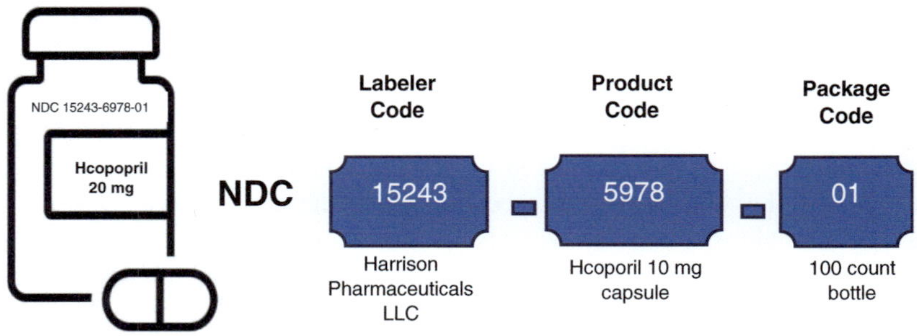

Fig. 3.2 Example of a national drug code

by the FDA [19]. It identifies the manufacturer of the product. The second segment is the product code which is specific for a drug, strength, dosage form, and formulation. The third segment is known as the package code and identifies the package size and type. The second and third segments are chosen by the manufacturer.

2.10 Compounded Drugs

A drug may be compounded for an individual prescription pursuant to the receipt of a valid prescription from a *licensed* prescriber as long as the compounding meets certain FDCA provisions.

1. Must be prepared by a licensed pharmacist in a State licensed pharmacy or Federal facility or by a licensed physician.
2. Prepared in limited quantities before the receipt of a valid prescription for an individual patient.
3. Is based on a history of the licensed pharmacist or physician receiving valid prescription orders for the compounding of the drug within an established relationship between the licensed pharmacist or physician and the individual patient for whom the prescription is written.
   (a) Alternatively, is based on an established relationship between the licensed pharmacist or physician preparing the compounded drug and the physician or other licensed practitioner who will write the prescription.

Compounded prescriptions must be prepared using bulk drug substances and other ingredients that conform to an official compendium designated by the FDCA [4]. If the compendium does not have a monograph for the compound, the drug substances must be components of approved drugs or appear on an approved list of products produced by a registered entity with a valid certificate of analysis. No drug which is commercially available in whole may be compounded. Furthermore, no drug which has been withdrawn or removed from the market for safety or efficacy concerns may be compounded.

The label of any compounded drug must included a statement such as "*This is a compounded drug*" or reasonable alternative that clearly indicates it is a compounded drug [4]. If prepared by an outsourcing facility, the label must also include:

- The outsourcing facility's name, address, and telephone number.
- The lot or batch number.
- Established name of the drug.
- Dosage form and strength.
- Statement on quantity or volume.
- Date the drug was compounded.
- Expiration date.
- Storage and handling instructions.
- The National Drug Code number (if available).
- The statement "Not for resale" for products distributed pursuant to a prescription.
- The statement "Office Use Only" for products distributed not distributed pursuant to a prescription.
- A list of active and inactive ingredients by established name and the quantity or proportion of each ingredient.

Containers of individual units of the drug (e.g., a plastic bag containing individual syringes of the drug) should also include this information. Additional information that should appear on containers includes directions for use, dose, and administration.

2.11 Medical Device Amendments of 1976

The original version of the FDCA limited the FDA's authority over medical devices to those which had entered interstate commerce and were deemed misbranded or adulterated. At the time, this was considered sufficient as devices were relatively simple. Over time, the introduction of more complex technology created a need for more oversight to ensure these medical devices were safe and effective. The Medical Device Amendments (MDA) of 1976 classify medical devices intended for use in humans based on safety and efficacy (Table 3.5) [20, 21]. The MDA authorizes a panel of experts to provide recommendations based on data as to what classification a device should be designated. Medical devices may only be sold and/or distributed pursuant to a prescription from a licensed practitioner. For Class II devices, the MDA authorizes a performance standard to be set. Because of the risk they pose, Class III devices require approval through an application process similar to the drug approval process in that safety and efficacy must be proven before the device is allowed to be marketed. Any device that presents a substantial deception or an unreasonable and substantial risk of illness or injury may be banned. The MDA provides the FDA with the authority to establish mandatory manufacturing methods (GMP) , inspect manufacturing facilities, and to seize any medical device in

Table 3.5 Medical device classification [20, 21]

Class	Description	Examples
Class I	Devices not purported to be for a use which is of substantial importance in supporting, sustain, or preventing impairment of human life or health AND Do not present a potential unreasonable risk of illness or injury AND General controls as defined are sufficient	Oral lubricant Examination gown Tongue depressor Bedpan Scale Manual stethoscope Elastic bandage
Class II	Devices where it is necessary to establish a performance standard to provide reasonable assurance regarding its safety and efficacy	Infusion pump Blood pressure cuff OTC pregnancy test Hemoglobin A1c Test System Many laboratory blood tests or assays Electrocardiograph
Class III	Devices where there is insufficient information to establish a performance standard to provide reasonable assurance regarding its safety and efficacy AND Are purported to be for a use which is of substantial importance in supporting, sustaining, or preventing impairment of human life or health OR Present a potential unreasonable risk of illness or injury	Pacemaker Implantable defibrillator Artificial heart valve Stent Cochlear implant Neurosurgical laser Contact lenses Hip prosthesis

OTC over-the-counter

violation of the law or adjacent regulations. There are also provisions regarding manufacturer registration, recordkeeping, reporting requirements, research funding, and education.

2.12 Other Impacts on the FDCA

Television advertisement for drugs must be submitted to the FDA for review at least 45 days prior to their dissemination [4]. Recommendations may be made based on information included on the drug's label, but approval for advertisements is not required and the FDA may not mandate any changes except in relation to the label. For example, if it is determined that the advertising would be false or misleading without a disclosure about a serious risk listed in the labeling, the inclusion of such information can be required.

2.13 Other Miscellaneous Amendments

Over the years, numerous other acts have been passed into law that have amended the FDCA. Certain larger acts important for the pharmacist to be familiar with and/or which may be evaluated by the MPJE are discussed later in this chapter. Overall, the FDCA is living legislation that continues to expand. The current law is over 920 pages with additional rules laid out in FDA regulations as authorized by the FDCA.

3 U.S. Adopted Names Council

In the United States, generic names follow a standardized classification of logical nomenclature that is based on pharmacologic or chemical relationships. The group which is responsible for the development of this nomenclature is the U.S. Adopted Names (USAN) Council [22]. The USAN Council is comprised one member each from the American Pharmacists Association, the American Medical Association, and the US Pharmacopeia Convention. Additionally, there is a member-at-large and a liaison from the FDA. The USAN Council is also the group responsible for assigning individual generic drug names to new chemical entities. In general, the company developing the drug applies for a generic name once the IND is active and clinical trials have started.

4 Poison Prevention Packaging Act of 1970

4.1 Overview of the PPPA

Prior to 1970, poisoning was considered the leading cause of injuries in children under 5 years [23]. The Poison Prevention Packaging Act (PPPA) of 1970 was enacted to protect children from accidental and/or unintentional ingestion of harmful products, including medications [24]. This law is unique in that authority over the law is given to the U.S. Consumer Product Safety Commission (CPSC) rather than the FDA. Drugs (prescription and OTC), household chemicals, and other hazardous products must use child-resistant packaging [25]. "Child resistant" specifically means that a child under 5 years of age would have significant difficulty opening or obtaining a toxic or harmful amount within a reasonable time (5–10 min in product testing) AND not difficult for normal adults to use properly [23, 26]. The most common form of this is a bottle, vial, or other package with a child-resistant cap. Product test is required to demonstrate child-resistance; no more than 20% of 200 children aged 42–51 months should be able to open the package while 90% of 100 adults ages 50–70 years should be able to open and close the package [23]. In addition to commercially available medications, oral drugs in clinical studies under an IND is also subject to the PPPA [23]. Although not formally part of the FDCA, failure to comply with PPPA requirements is considered misbranding.

► **Numbers of Importance** The PPPA was designed to protect accidental poisonings from occurring in children less than **FIVE (5)** years of age.

4.2 Products Exempt From the Child-Resistant Packaging Requirements

The products that fall under the authority of the PPPA were determined by a commission based on the degree or nature the hazard presents to children. All oral prescription and OTC drugs are included with certain exceptions or specific products (Tables 3.6 and 3.7) and those provided in sample packages by prescriber [26]. In general, inhaled products and those that are topically applied to the teeth or mouth do not require child-resistant packaging [23]. Additionally, medications dispensed for patient use in a hospital and other institutions (e.g., long-term care facilities) do not require special packaging [23].

Table 3.6 Medications exempt from child-resistant packaging requirements [26]

Effervescent aspirin tablets <15% aspirin	Potassium supplements ≤50 mEq/potassium/dosage unit
Sublingual nitroglycerine	Sodium fluoride ≤110 mg sodium fluoride or 50 mg elemental fluoride per package
Sublingual isosorbide dinitrate ≤10 mg/dose	Sodium fluoride ≤0.5% elemental fluoride
Chewable isosorbide dinitrate ≤10 mg/dose	Sacrosidase preparations in glycerol and water solution
Medroxyprogesterone acetate tablets	Pancrelipase tablets/capsules/powder without other substances
Cyclically administered oral contraceptives[a]	Hormone replacement therapy products that rely on activity of ≥1 progestogen or estrogen substances
Anhydrous cholestyramine in powder form	Unflavored aspirin powder

[a]In manufacturer's mnemonic dispenser pack and rely only on activity or ≥ 1 progesterone or estrogen substance

Table 3.7 Medication dispensed in packages exempt from child-resistant packaging requirements [26]

Medication	Dosage form	Maximum strength drug per package	Other requirements
Betamethasone	Tablets	12.6 mg	
Prednisone	Tablets	105 mg	No other substances included
Methylprednisolone	Tablets	84 mg	No other substances included
Erythromycin ethylsuccinate	Granules for oral suspension	8 gm erythromycin equivalent	
Erythromycin ethylsuccinate	Tablets	16 gm erythromycin equivalent	
Mebendazole	Tablets	600 mg	No other substances included
Colestipol	Powder	5 gm	No other substances included
Colesevelam hydrochloride	Powder	3.75 gm	

(continued)

Table 3.7 (continued)

Medication	Dosage form	Maximum strength drug per package	Other requirements
Conjugated estrogen	Tablets	32 mg	Dispensed in mnemonic packages with no other substances included
Norethindrone acetate	Tablets	50 mg	Dispensed in mnemonic packages with no other substances included
Sevelamer carbonate	Powder	2.4 grams	
Iron	Any	249 mg elemental iron or 0.025%	
Acetaminophen	Effervescent tablets or granules	15% acetaminophen	No other substances included
Acetaminophen—unflavored	Powder	13 grains/unit dose	No other substances included Not for pediatric packages

mg milligrams

4.3 Other Exemptions From the Child-Resistant Packaging Requirements

The law itself recognizes the burden that child-resistant packaging may put on older adults or disabled persons who are unable to open them. Prescription drugs may be provided with "easy open tops" or other non-child-resistant packaging when requested by the patient OR when directed specifically through the prescriber [25].

As such, it allows for the manufacturer of OTC drugs and nonmedicinal products are authorized to make available one single-size package in non-child-resistant packaging so long as it produces the same product in appropriate child-resistant packaging and that the product in non-child-resistant packaging be clearly labeled with the statement "This package for household without young children" or "Package Not-Child-Resistant" [25, 26].

4.4 Application of the PPPA to Substances That Are Not Medicinal

The requirements of the PPPA extend well beyond medications. There is a long list of products subject to the same requirements (Table 3.8) [26]. These products were selected based on the hazard risk posed to young children and must follow the same packaging requirements set forth in for medications.

Table 3.8 Nonmedicinal products exempt from child-resistant packaging requirements [26]

Furniture polish	Turpentine	Kindling	Illuminating preparations
Methanol	Sulfuric acid	Mouthwash	Glue removers with acetonitrile
Ethylene glycol ≥10%	Paint solvents	Fluoride	Permanent wave neutralizers
Imidazoline		Low-viscosity hydrocarbon products	

4.5 The Pharmacist's Responsibilities

The pharmacist plays a key role in ensuring compliance with the PPPA for prescription medications dispensed to patients. Oral prescription medications must be dispensed in child-resistant packaging unless it is except or if the pharmacist has received a request for non-child-resistant packing from the patient or prescriber [23]. Patients may provide a blanket request that all of their medications be placed in non-child-resistant packaging; however, a single request to dispense a specific prescription in non-child-resistant packaging should not indicate that such a blanket waiver request has been made. Patients who request non-child-resistant packaging have individual reasons for doing so. In patients who have made blanket requests, it is important that the pharmacist periodically confirm this preference with the patient or prescriber. The law itself does not require a written request; therefore, technically the request may be made verbally. The CPSC does recommend that requests for non-child-resistant packaging be in writing [23]. It is also important to recognize that the CPSC does not consider used plastic prescription bottles and vials to be in compliance with PPPA requirements and therefore refills should only be dispensed in new containers. On the other hand, the wear on class containers is not considered to undergo the same level of wear; they may be reused for refills so long as a new cap or closure is provided. Compliance with the PPPA allows pharmacist the opportunity to discuss appropriate handling and storage of medications with patients [24]. By doing so, pharmacists contribute to the efforts to protect children from potential dangers related to unintentional poisoning.

5 Federal Anti-Tampering Act

5.1 Overview of the FATA

In 1982, seven people in Chicago died as a result of taking acetaminophen laced with cyanide [27]. At the time, tamper-resistant packaging existed, but it was not required. The passage of the Federal Anti-Tampering Act (FATA) was a response to the tragedy [28]. Unlike most laws involving pharmacy, the FATA is part of the criminal code. The law makes it a federal offense to maliciously adulterate a drug, food, cosmetic, or other substances for the purposes of causing injury, death, or injury to a business reputation. It also makes it unlawful to maliciously convey false information on such an adulteration if fear of or actual injury or death occurs, or if there it results in a product recall.

5.2 Tamper-Evident Packaging

Tamper-evident are barriers to entry which would provide reasonable visible evidence that tampering has occurred if they are breached or missing. The term is also referenced as "tamper-resistant" within federal law and regulations but are essentially interchangeable. Both the FATA and FDA regulations govern this requirement [29]. All OTC drugs (for humans), cosmetic liquid oral hygiene products, vaginal products, contact lens solutions, and tablets to make such solutions must have tamper-resistant packaging. The exceptions to this mandate include insulin, throat lozenges, dermatologics, and dentifrices. All covered products must have ≥1 tamper-resistant feature, except for two-piece, hard gelatin capsules which are required to have ≥2 tamper-resistant features unless the capsules are sealed by tamper-resistant technology [29].

The packaging must be distinctive by design (such as aerosols) or employ identifying characteristics such as a pattern, trademark, or logo [29]. The product's label must contain a statement to alert people to the specific types of tamper-resistant feature(s) that should be present on the packaging and this statement must be placed in an area of that would be unaffected if the tamper-resistant packaging was removed or breached. Of note, aerosol products, ammonia inhalant in crushable glass ampules, and containers of compressed medical oxygen are not required to have this statement on their labels.

Key Concept

Common types of tamper-resistant packaging include transparent film wrappers, individual dose units (tablets or capsules) in sealed blister, strip packs, container bubble packs, heat shrink bands or wrappers, pouches that must be broken, seals, or cartons, breakable container caps, and metal cans.

6 The Orphan Drug Act

The twentieth century introduced a number of significant medical advancements. However, by the 1970s, experts began noticing that advances in therapeutics for uncommon conditions were not keeping the same pace [30]. The small patient populations for these diseases limited researchers ability to prove safety and efficacy under the standards of the time and financial return-on-investments for development. To address this need, the Orphan Drug Act was passed in 1983 [30–32].

The purpose of the Orphan Drug Act is to provide incentives for the development of drugs for "rare" diseases [31]. These disease had to be rare enough to facilitate market neglect [32].

▶ **Numbers of Importance** A "rare" disease affects less than **200,000** people in the United States OR one that occurs so infrequently that there is no reasonable expectation that the cost of developing and producing could be recovered from sales. The act specifically designates therapeutics intended to treat these diseases as orphan drugs.

Incentives offered for these Orphan Drugs include:

- 7 years of marketing exclusivity which begins *after* approval (and is independent of patent status)—unless the manufacturer cannot ensure availability of sufficient drug quantities.
- Provides tax credits and deductions for the cost of development and research—excluding amount funded by grants, contracts, or sources other than the manufacturer itself.
- Makes appropriations for grants or contracts to help companies defray the cost of research and development.
- FDA authorization to provide assistance in clinical study design.
- Allows for fast-track review.
- Only allows for approval of competitor products for the same indication if the competitor can prove therapeutic superiority (e.g., safer and/or more effective).

▶ **Numbers of Importance** Orphan drugs have **SEVEN (7)** years of marketing exclusivity after FDA approval.

Another incentive for the development and production of orphan drugs was implemented over a decade later. The law was amended by the Prescription Drug User Fee Act to waive user fees for orphan drugs.

Unrelated to pharmacy, but still included in the Act are provisions to appropriate money to study water quality of a reservoir in Massachusetts, develop tables to catalog the risk of radiogenic cancer from a given dose of ionizing radiation, develop assessments of the risk of thyroid cancer from Iodine 131. There are also multiple provisions regarding home health care.

▶ **Study Pro Tip** Many federal laws have additional provisions that are not directly applicable to pharmacy, medications, or pharmacy practice. These provisions are less likely or unlikely to appear on the MPJE.

7 Drug Price Competition and Patent Term Restoration Act of 1984: Hatch-Waxman Act

Although the FDCA allowed for generic drugs to be introduced into the market, very few generic drugs had actually become available by the 1980s. Patent law and regulations made generic approval a protracted, expensive, and unclear process [33]. Generic manufacturers were required to prove safety and efficacy, the investment of which some were uncertain would be recoverable. To complicate matters, these studies could not begin until the original brand-name patent had expired [33]. This was specifically highlighted in the case of *Roche Products Inc v. Bolar Pharmaceutical Co.* where the Supreme Court ruled that law at the time did in fact prohibit testing from starting until patent expiration. Subsequently, it would require approximately 2 years after patent expiration before a generic could become approved [33]. The Drug Price Competition and Patent Term Restoration Act of 1984, more commonly referred to as the Hatch-Waxman Act, was a law passed to circumvent these barriers in the generic approval process [34].

The Hatch-Waxman Act provides an outline for the ANDA approval process. In the ANDA, generic manufacturers are only required to demonstrate who the drug will be produced and prove that the drug is bioequivalent to the brand-name product. The Act provides something called "safe harbor" from patent infringement lawsuits to generic manufacturers during the time it is preparing the ANDA. This allows studies necessary to complete the ANDA to begin before the patent expires. The first company to file and have an ANDA approved is provided 180 days or generic marketing exclusivity and additional generic versions may not be introduced until afterward.

Manufacturers had incentive for minimizing the number of generics that became available. Prior to Hatch-Waxman, most of the patent-life of a brand-name drug occurred during the development and FDA approval process [33]. To address drug innovators' concerns, the Act provides *FIVE (5)* years exclusivity when the FDA approves a new chemical entity; during that time, a generic of the drug cannot be approved. Additionally, the drug's patent is extended by the duration of time it takes for the FDA to review the drug, therefore removing any punitive impact the approval process might have on the patent life. Only the patents provided to the FDA by the innovator and listed in the Orange book are extended.

Key Concept

The Hatch-Waxman Act requires a generic drug to prove bioequivalence. A drug is considered bioequivalent if there are no significant differences in the rate or absorption from the proprietary drug OR no difference in extent of absorption occurs, but there is an intentional difference in rate absorption that is considered medically insignificant and does not impact achievement of effective drug concentrations.

8 Prescription Drug Marketing Act of 1987

Our current supply chain is an intricate process where 90% of raw materials used in drug production are obtained from other countries [35]. Areas of weakness introduce opportunities for subpotent, adulterated, and counterfeit drugs reaching patients in the United States . Wholesale submarkets, sometimes referred to as the "gray market" or "diversion markets," have been known to contribute to the influx of these products [35]. The $75 billion counterfeit drug market accounts for approximately 10% of all medicines worldwide [35]. The Prescription Drug Marketing Act (PDMA) of 1987 amends the FDCA in a way to establish a legal framework for the effective and safe distribution of prescription medications. The Act was modified in 1992 by the Prescription Drug Amendments.

To reduce the risk of ineffective and unsafe medications in the market, the PDMA focuses heavily on the concept of reimportation. Once a prescription medication manufactured in the United States has been exported to another country, only that manufacturer may reimport it back into the country, except for emergency medical care [36]. It is important to understand the PDMA focuses on reimportation. Prescription medications may be imported in they were obtained abroad by an individual for personal use. Manufacturers may also purchase medications produced in an FDA-approved facility in a foreign country.

To further address weaknesses with the supply chain, the PDMA specifically addresses wholesalers. Any entity involved in the wholesale distribution of drugs which is not the manufacturer or the "authorized distributor" of record (defined as a distributor where the manufacturer has an "ongoing relationship" to distribute their products) is required to provide information before each wholesale distribution a dated list of each prior sale, purchase, or trade of the drug including the names and address of all parties involved. In general, hospitals and health care entities should not act as wholesalers. Wholesalers must be licensed by the States *from and into* which it is distributed [4]. The PDMA prohibits any drug purchased by a hospital (or similar health care entity) or donated or provided at a reduced price by a charity to them from being sold, purchased, or traded. The Act specifically defines "health care entity" as one that provides diagnostic, medical, surgical, dental, chronic, or rehabilitative care. Under this definition, a long-term care facility would qualify as a health care entity, but a community pharmacy does not. The law does allow for certain transactions within members of a group purchasing organization and to non-profit affiliates of the hospital.

Key Concept

It is important to understand what federal law considers to be a wholesaler. It is equally important to recognize what is not considered to be wholesale activities. The following are not considered to be wholesaler actions:

- Intracompany distribution.
- Distribution among hospitals or other health care entities under common control.
- Distribution for emergency medical reasons, including a public health emergency.
- Dispensing pursuant to a prescription.
- Distribution by a pharmacy in minimal quantities to a licensed practitioner for office use.
- Distribution by a charitable organization to a nonprofit affiliate to extent authorized by law.

- Purchase or acquisition by a hospital or other health care entity.
- Distribution by a manufacturer.
- Receipt or transfer of a drug by an authorized third-party logistics provider.
- Common carrier transporting drug.
- Distribution of a drug by an authorized repackager.
- Salable drug returns from a dispenser.
- Distribution of a collection of finished medical devices which may include a product or biological product in a medical convenience kit.
- Distribution of an intravenous (IV) drug intended to replenish fluids or electrolytes.
- Distribution of an IV drug used to maintain equilibrium of water and minerals, including dialysis solutions.
- Distribution of a drug intended for irrigation or sterile water.
- Distribution of a medical gas.
- Facilitating the distribution of a product through solely administrative services.
- Transfer of a product by a hospital or other health care entity (or at the direction of the facility) to a repackager for the purpose of repackaging the drug for use at the facility or facilities under common control.

The law acknowledges the risk that drug samples pose in misbranded, expired, and adulterated products finding their way to patients. Drug samples are defined as a unit of a drug that is not intended to be sold but intended to promote the sale of the drug [4]. As such, the PDMP bans the sale, purchase or trading of drug samples or coupons. Drug samples may only be distributed upon *written* request to licensed prescribers, hospital pharmacies, or other health care entities. These requests must contain the date, name, address, professional designation, and signature of the person making the request along with the identify and amount of sample requested. Manufacturers and distributors must keep a copy of these records for THREE (3) years. These samples may be stored in a hospital pharmacy at the request of a credentialed physician, but community pharmacies are prohibited from having samples onsite. Manufacturers and distributors are responsible for ensuring samples are stored in a manner that maintains stability, integrity, and effectiveness. Manufacturers and distributors must maintain a list of names and addresses of every representative who distributes samples along with a location of where samples are stored. Each year, an annual inventory of the samples in possession of every representative must be conducted. Records which document the distribution, destruction, or manufacture return of all samples must be stored for at least THREE (3) years.

9 Omnibus Budget Reconciliation Act of 1990 (OBRA-90)

An Omnibus Budget Reconciliation Act is enacted each year by Congress in order for the government to have a budget. What makes the Omnibus Budget Reconciliation Act of 1990 (OBRA-90) unique to pharmacy is that a very small portion of the law contains provisions that had a tremendous impact on pharmacy practice (Table 3.9) [37–39]. Technically, these provisions primarily are directed toward Medicaid patients, but practically they are often extended to all patients. The most impactful requirement was the **"Offer to counsel"** provision, where pharmacists must offer to counsel Medicaid patients on prescriptions. States, including Alabama, extended this counseling requirement to *all* patients. This provision had such a large impact on pharmacy practice, that many of OBRA-90's other provisions are not recalled as well. One important provision is the direction for states to create Drug Utilization (DUR) boards (composed of physicians and pharmacists) to manage medication purchasing and formulary decisions for state-funded healthcare (including Medicaid), to review prior medication use data and compare to target criteria, and to recommend and establish educational programs to improve compliance with target criteria [37]. In, Alabama, the DUR board evaluates use of medications already approved for use by Medicaid, while the Pharmacy and Therapeutics committee determines, based on scientific evident, which drugs can be considered "preferred" drugs and therefore covered under the plan. While "preferred" drugs are often generic, it may vary based on state, disease, and medication class. OBRA-90 allows the pharmacist to substitute for a preferred drug, assuming one is available in that state. To contribute to DUR activities, pharmacists are to participate in 3 key elements before a prescription is delivered: (1) Screen prescriptions before dispensing (Prospective DUR), (2) make the offer to counsel, and (3) document appropriately in the patient's record.

Table 3.9 Pharmacy provisions in OBRA-90 [37–39]

Patient counseling items	Prospective DUR	Patient record information
Drug name Intended use/expected action Route of administration/dosage form Dosage and schedule Common side effects—including how to avoid them and what to do if they occur Techniques for self-monitoring Proper storage Drug interactions Contraindications Refill information What to do if a dose is missed	Over and underutilization Therapeutic duplication Drug-drug interactions Drug-disease interactions Drug-allergy interactions Incorrect dose or duration Abuse or misuse	Patient's full name Address Telephone number Date of birth Gender Drug profile Pharmacist comments Chronic conditions Allergies or drug reactions

DUR drug utilization review

10 Prescription Drug User Fee Act of 1992

In the 1980's the average NDA review time was 29 months [40]. To provide the FDA more funding for the drug approval process, the Prescription Drug User Fee Act (PDUFA) was passed [40–42]. Within 6 years of passage, the approval process had decreased to 12 months [40]. There are three types of user fees authorized by the PDUFA:

- Application review fees paid for each drug/biologic application submitted.
- Establishment fees for each manufacturer facility—paid annually.
- Product fees—paid annually for each drug/biologic on the market.

The fees vary based on type with applications including clinical data carrying the highest fee and annual program fees being the lowest [42]. The law provides exemptions and waivers for drugs/biologics that treat rare (orphan) disease or unmet public health needs as well as those produced by small businesses.

The PDUFA must be renewed every 5 years [40, 41]. Subsequent revisions have added appropriations to increase post marketing (i.e., after FDA approval) monitoring of new products, apply user fees to monitoring of direct-to-consumer advertising and to improve the approval process for medical devices [40, 42]. The first reauthorization formally authorized the "Fast-Track" designation for drugs/biologics intended to address an unmet need [40]. This designation not only offers an opportunity for priority review, but provides applicants with increased engagement with the FDA early in the research and development process so that the applicant has a clear understanding of the trial design and data reporting that will be required.

Other provisions of the law and subsequent reauthorizations include a SIX (6) month marketing exclusivity extension for brand-name drugs when manufacturers conduct pediatric studies (regardless of outcome), authorizes advisory panels to provide recommendations on approval decisions, allows manufacturers to disseminate "scientifically sound," peer reviewed articles on off-label uses and pharmacoeconomic evaluations for on-label uses, and introduced the Risk Evaluation Mitigation Strategies (REMS) program for drugs with safety concerns.

11 Dietary Supplemental Health and Education Act of 1994

When the FDCA was enacted, supplements had been commercially available for over a decade [43]. Supplements were initially classified as foods, a status which was reaffirmed by Congress multiple times in the twentieth century. In the 1960s, the FDA began implementing rules about the standard identity of a vitamin or supplement, rules which were eventually overturned by courts. However, there continued to be growing concerns that the ingredients in supplements could be either unsafe or therapeutic in nature, making them inappropriate for marketing as a dietary supplement [43].

The Dietary Supplemental Health and Education Act (DSHEA) of 1994 was written to ensure that a wide variety of dietary supplements would be available. It establishes a definition of dietary supplements as those whose ingredients contained (1) vitamins and minerals, (2) amino acids, (3) herbs or botanicals, (4) other components of food, or (5) any combination of such ingredients [44]. Unlike medications, FDA approval of supplements is not required. Supplements containing "established ingredients" (defined as sold in the U.S. before 1994) do not require proof of safety and efficacy. Any supplement that has been developed since 1994 with new ingredients requires disclosure to and review by the FDA to ensure that the ingredients would be expected to be safe. The law bans the manufacture or sale of any dietary supplement that is *misbranded* or *adulterated* [44]. The DSHEA considers a supplemented to be adulterated, and therefore unsafe, if it presents a "significant or unreasonable risk of illness or injury" when used under ordinary conditions according to the product labeling. Additionally, product labels may not have false claims, particularly around structure/function statements. Though labels may indicate certain supportive statements (e.g., turmeric "supports immune health" or calcium "may reduce the risk of osteoporosis"), it cannot claim to prevent or treat any disease. To stress this, labels must bear the disclaimer "This statement has not been evaluated by the FDA. This product is not intended to prevent, cure, or treat any disease." Furthermore, the manufacturer must have evidence to substantiate any statement on the label and the FDA must be notified within 30 days that such a statement is being made. If any product is found to be in violation of these requirements after it reaches the market, the FDA has the authority to take action [45]. The FDA must be notified by the manufacturer regarding any serious issues, such as adverse events, associated with their supplement.

Key Concept
Supplements making therapeutic claims on the product labels without the disclaimer **"This statement has not been evaluated by the FDA. This product is not intended to prevent, cure, or treat any disease."** are considered *misbranded* under the DSHEA.

12 Health Insurance Portability and Accountability Act of 1996

The Health Insurance Portability and Accountability Act (HIPAA) of 1996 is one of the most recognized laws within modern pharmacy practice [46, 47]. In general, HIPAA sets minimum standards for the security and privacy of protected health information (PHI). The law applies to entities which submit claims electronically [48]. These are often referred to as "covered entities." The two major rules associated with HIPAA are referred to as The Privacy Rule and The Security Rule.

Key Concept
Protected health information includes any identifiable information for an individual that is transmitted or maintained in any form, including electronic media. This also applies to oral written forms of communication.

PHI must be kept confidential. Only the minimum amount of necessary information may be disclosed for the purpose of health care or payment. Discussion of PHI with a third-party individual or entity who is not involved with a patient's health care or healthcare payment is prohibited without the patient's consent. A common misunderstanding about The Privacy Rule is that no PHI can be disclosed without consent. In fact, HIPAA permits the communication of information between those who are actively engaged in the care of the patient. However, any information disclosed for the purpose of patient care and treatment should still conform to the necessary standard. For some situations, minimal PHI may need to be communicated while in others full PHI may require disclosure.

The Security Rule sets requirements pertaining to the security of PHI. Covered entities must ensure that electronic PHI is maintained in a way so as to assure confidentiality and integrity and safe from threats or hazards to its security. This includes ensuring that employees of the covered entity are compliant with the rule's requirements. If a patient complains about inappropriate disclosure of PHI, covered entities must investigate and, if necessary, take corrective steps. If unauthorized disclosure of PHI occurs, the covered entity must notify the patient and the Department of Health and Human Services Office for Civil Rights. Examples of PHI breaches within a pharmacy include:

- Another person overhearing a verbal discussion about PHI.
- Disposing of a patient's old prescription bottle in normal trash without taking efforts to hide PHI.
- Leaving password protected computer systems logged in while the user is away where unauthorized use by a different person can occur.
- Disclosing information about a patient's prescription medication to another person without the patient's consent.
- Accessing a patient's pharmacy record without a legitimate need or authorization.

13 Food and Drug Administration Amendment Act of 2007

The Food and Drug Administration Amendment Act (FDAAA) contains 11 titles (Table 3.10) on different legal and scientific issues relevant to the FDA [49, 50]. Its main purpose is to reauthorize major ways that the FDA activities are funded while at the same time it clarifies, expands, and reaffirms the FDA's authority over

Table 3.10 Summary of key provisions in the Food and Drug Administration Amendment Act [49, 50]

Title	Provisions
Title I—Prescription Drug User Fee Amendments of 2027	Reauthorizes the Prescription Drug User Fee Act Amends FDCA to include post-marketing safety activities in a drug application review Exempts certain orphan drugs from fees
Title II—Medical Device User Fee Amendments of 2007	Establishes or changes certain fees for medical devices Requires foreign country engaged in manufacturing medical device imported into the United States to register annually with FDA Reaffirms authority of accredited third parties to review premarket reports for medical devices and to make recommendations to FDA on device classification
Title III—Pediatric Medical Device Safety and Improvement Act of 2007	Requires description (if available) of any pediatric subpopulations that suffer from applicable condition on medical device applications
Title IV—Pediatric Research Equity Act of 2007	Requires a timeline for study in pediatric patients for any new drug or biologic or a waiver on why a pediatric formulation cannot be developed
Title V—Best Pharmaceuticals for Children Act of 2007	Amends certain FDCA requirements and provisions for pediatric studies Requires FDA to issue a public notice for any drug with a pediatric formulation developed and found to be safe and effective, but not introduced into the market within 1 year of approval
Title VI—Reagan-Udal Foundation	Establishes the Regan-Udal Foundation, a non-profit, to support the FDA's mission
Title VII—Conflicts of Interest	Bans membership on an FDA Advisory Committee by any person with a financial conflict of interest unless a waiver is granted to obtain specific expertise Prohibits waivers for financial COIs > $50,000 and limits financial waivers of $50,000
Title VIII—Clinical Trials Database	Expands clinicaltrials.gov and makes it publicly available.

(continued)

Table 3.10 (continued)

Title	Provisions
Title IX—Enhanced Authorities Regarding Post-Market Monitoring of Safety Drugs	Prohibits a "responsible person" from introducing into interstate commerce a new drug if that person is not complying with post-approval clinical trials or labeling changes Requires Phase IV studies Requires compliance with Risk Evaluation and Mitigation Strategy programs—where required Requires proposed REMS to include a timetable for assessment of strategy Establishes the Drug Safety Oversight Board Requires FDA to issue special guidance for antibiotic clinical trials Authorizes FDA to require review of TV advertisements for drugs before broadcast—but approval and implementation of FDA-issued recommendations are not required Requires approval of any food with an approved pharmaceutical product in it Requires standards to secure the drug supply chain against counterfeit, diverted, substandard, adulterated, misbranded, or expired drugs Requires standardization of NDC numbers for prescription drugs Requires certain information on NDA to be published on the FDA website Requires quarterly publication of a complete list of all approved generic drugs on the FDA website
Title X—Food Safety	Requires FDA to collect and post information regarding food recalls Requires FDA notification of potentially adulterated foods
Title XI—Other Provisions	Requires FDA to identify and periodically update clinically susceptible concentrations for antibiotics Amends Orphan Drug Act to reauthorize appropriations for grants and contracts to defray costs of development for drugs/devices/medical foods for rare diseases Requires contract with Institute of Medicine to study overall safety of genetic tests in order to improve oversite and regulation of these tests Creates a priority review program for neglected topical diseases and rare pediatric conditions

FDCA Food, Drug, & Cosmetic Act, *FDA* Food and Drug Administration, *NDA* new drug application, *REMS* risk evaluation and mitigation strategy, *TV* television medications and medical devices. The FDAAA reauthorizes the user-fee system which provides the FDA with a large portion of its revenues and budget. However, the FDAAA includes a variety of seemingly random provisions.

14 Drug Quality and Security Act of 2013

In 2012, there was an outbreak of meningitis that was traced to fungal contamination of compounded methylprednisolone acetate at a compounding center in New England [51–53]. Over 790 people developed fungal meningitis and 64 people died from what were supposed to be sterile injections. The pharmacist owner of the facility was sentenced to 8 years in prison. The public outcry from this tragedy lead to the passage of the Drug Quality and Security Act (DQSA) which was signed into law in November 2013 [54]. The law is separated into two sections or titles.

14.1 Title 1: Compounded Quality Act

Although not specifically an amendment to the FDCA, the Compounded Quality Act, or Title 1 does change section 503A of the FDCA [52]. Historically, section 503 allowed for compounding of medications and excepted compounding pharmacies from complying with the FDCA good manufacturing practices, labeling requirements, and FDA approval process. In 2002, The U.S. Supreme Court ruled that section 503A's prohibition on advertising for compounding products was unconstitutional, raising uncertainty about the validity of the section. Title 1 formally removes this wording from the section. It also removed the FDCA requirement that a prescription for a compounded drug be unsolicited. However, the Act does deem a compounded drug as misbranded if any advertising or promotion is false or misleading. The Act goes further to authorize the FDA to establish federal standards and registrations for compounding pharmacies, something that was primarily overseen by the states before. It is important to note that patient-specific compounding by traditional and small compounding pharmacies may continue to practice under other laws and regulations. Title 1 is primarily directed at large compounding facilities which prepare medications in bulk. Each large compounding facility, also referred to as an outsourcing facility, can register annually with the FDA. If the facility does not voluntarily register, it is subject to the same requirements as traditional manufacturers per the FDCA. While it must adhere to GMP, FDA approval of products is not required, and compounds may qualify for exemptions for adequate directions for use. These outsourcing facilities may only compound medications under the supervision of a licensed pharmacist or physician from a bulk ingredients list. Unlike traditional compounding pharmacies, outsourcing facilities are not required to have a patient-specific prescription. If a medication is already commercially available, it may only be compounded when on shortage. All outsourcing facilities are also subject to at-risk inspection schedules, if untoward trends are noted. Every SIX (6) months, these facilities must submit a report to the U.S. Secretary of Health and Human Services on what medications are being compounded by the facility and what, if any, adverse events have occurred. Based on this information, the Secretary is required to publish a list of drugs that are "demonstrating difficulty" in compounding and are reasonably likely to lead to an adverse effect.

Other major provisions set forth in Title 1 include:

- Requires an annual establishment fee for each outsourcing facility—and a reinspection fee.
- Prohibits the resale of a compounded drug labeled "not for resale."
- Requires state boards of pharmacy to submit to the Secretary any disciplinary action taken against a compounding pharmacy, recall of any compounded drug, or any concerns that a compounding pharmacy may be violating the Act.
- Requires the Comptroller Geneal to report on any pharmacy compounding and the adequacy of federal and state efforts to ensure the safety of these products.

14.2 Title 2: Drug Supply Chain Security Act

The Drug Supply Chain Security Act establishes requirements for a "track and trace" electronic system to follow prescription drugs intended for humans throughout the pharmaceutical supply distribution chain from "cradle to grave" [52, 55]. The intention of the Act is to protect patients from illegitimate drug products. All transactions must be documented and every manufacturer, wholesaler, dispenser/pharmacy, and repackager is held responsible for ensuring that they have all prior transaction information at time of transfer of ownership of the medication, that all trading partners are authorized. Each of these entities must implement a system to investigate and handle any products suspected of being illegitimate. The manufacturer or repackager must affix or imprint a product identifier on each package. The only exception to this identifier requirement are products required to have a standardized numerical identifier (e.g., NDC number) [56]. Any drug without this product identifier is deemed misbranded. In the event of a drug recall or when a suspected illegitimate product is suspected, applicable transaction documentation must be supplied (on request) to any appropriate federal or state official. Furthermore, manufacturers, wholesalers, and repackagers must verify any returned products before they can be further distributed.

15 Adhering to Federal and State Pharmacy Law

Federal pharmacy law and regulation primarily governs situations where drugs, biologics, devices, and other applicable products are transported within interstate commerce. Within these, there are a few references for individual state laws and regulations. One prominent example is the deference to the states for who is considered to be a licensed practitioner for the purpose of ordering a prescription medication. The day-to-day of most pharmacy practice activities are governed by individual states. It should not be assumed that there is consistency between the states. For example, the number of technicians that one pharmacist may supervise at a time varies from state to state. Where there is crossover in content, Federal and Alabama law and regulations are generally aligned. In any situation where one law or regulation is stricter, the rule of thumb is to abide by the stricter of the laws/regulations. A common scenario where this may occur involves controlled substances where a drug may be scheduled differently in Alabama than it is federally. The pharmacist should always apply considerations with the more stringent schedule to such a drug.

> **Study Pro Tip** If a question on the MPJE does not clearly indicate that it is asking about a state or federal law, always answer the question based on the stricter interpretation.

References

1. Tousley RD. The federal food, drug, and cosmetic act of 1938. *J Mark*. 1941;5(3):259-269.
2. Swann JP. FDA and the practice of pharmacy: prescription drug regulation before the Durham-Humphrey Amendment of 1951. *Pharm Hist*. 1994;36(2):55-70.
3. Commissioner O of the Sulfanilamide Disaster. *FDA*. Published online December 20, 2019. Accessed January 10, 2024. https://www.fda.gov/about-fda/histories-product-regulation/sulfanilamide-disaster
4. House of Representatives C. FEDERAL FOOD, DRUG, AND COSMETIC ACT, U.S. Code 21 §§ 301-399f (2022),. Published online January 5, 2023. Accessed January 10, 2024. https://www.govinfo.gov/app/details/USCODE-2022-title21/USCODE-2022-title21-chap9/summary
5. Lam C, Patel P. Food, Drug, and Cosmetic Act. In: *StatPearls*. StatPearls Publishing; 2023. Accessed January 10, 2024. http://www.ncbi.nlm.nih.gov/books/NBK585046/
6. CFR – Code of Federal Regulations Title 21. Accessed January 11, 2024. https://www.accessdata.fda.gov/scripts/cdrh/cfdocs/cfcfr/CFRSearch.cfm?fr=312.23
7. Hoge JF. The Durham–Humphrey Bill. *Food Drug Cosmet Law J*. 1951;6(2):135–141.
8. Commissioner O of the. Part III: Drugs and Foods Under the 1938 Act and Its Amendments. *FDA*. Published online March 15, 2019. Accessed January 11, 2024. https://www.fda.gov/about-fda/changes-science-law-and-regulatory-authorities/part-iii-drugs-and-foods-under-1938-act-and-its-amendments
9. THE DURHAM-HUMPHREY AMENDMENT. *J Am Med Assoc*. 1952;149(4):371. doi:https://doi.org/10.1001/jama.1952.02930210055017
10. Greene JA, Podolsky SH. Reform, regulation, and pharmaceuticals – the Kefauver-Harris Amendments at 50. *N Engl J Med*. 2012;367(16):1481–1483. doi:https://doi.org/10.1056/NEJMp1210007
11. Food and Drug Administration. Kevauver-Harris Amendments Revoulutionized Drug Development. *Consum Health Inf*. 2012;October: 1-2.
12. Research C for DE and. New Drug Application (NDA). FDA. Published February 15, 2022. Accessed January 11, 2024. https://www.fda.gov/drugs/types-applications/new-drug-application-nda
13. Research C for DE and. Investigational New Drug (IND) Application. FDA. Published November 14, 2023. Accessed January 11, 2024. https://www.fda.gov/drugs/types-applications/investigational-new-drug-ind-application

14. Sen Paul R [R K. S.5002 – 117th Congress (2021-2022): FDA Modernization Act 2.0. Published September 29, 2022. Accessed January 11, 2024. https://www.congress.gov/bill/117th-congress/senate-bill/5002
15. Center for Drug Evaluation and Research. Changes to an Approved NDA or ANDA, Guidance for Industry Revision 1 (2004). Published online 2004. Accessed January 11, 2024. https://www.fda.gov/regulatory-information/search-fda-guidance-documents/changes-approved-nda-or-anda
16. Sen, Jeffords JM [R V. S.830 – 105th Congress (1997-1998): Food and Drug Administration Modernization Act of 1997. Published November 21, 1997. Accessed January 11, 2024. https://www.congress.gov/bill/105th-congress/senate-bill/830
17. Affairs O of R. Recalls Background and Definitions. *FDA*. Published online December 26, 2019. Accessed January 11, 2024. https://www.fda.gov/safety/industry-guidance-recalls/recalls-background-and-definitions
18. Research C for DE and. Proposed Rule on Revising the National Drug Code Format. *FDA*. Published online December 27, 2022. Accessed January 11, 2024. https://www.fda.gov/drugs/drug-approvals-and-databases/proposed-rule-revising-national-drug-code-format
19. Research C for DE and. National Drug Code Database Background Information. *FDA*. Published online April 26, 2019. Accessed January 11, 2024. https://www.fda.gov/drugs/development-approval-process-drugs/national-drug-code-database-background-information
20. Rep. Rogers PG [D F 11. H.R.11124 – 94th Congress (1975-1976): Medical Device Amendments. Published March 9, 1976. Accessed January 12, 2024. https://www.congress.gov/bill/94th-congress/house-bill/11124
21. Food and Drug Administration. Product Classification. Published January 1, 2024. Accessed January 12, 2024. https://www.accessdata.fda.gov/scripts/cdrh/cfdocs/cfpcd/classification.cfm
22. United States Adopted Names Council. USAN Council. American Medical Association. Published January 8, 2024. Accessed January 9, 2024. https://www.ama-assn.org/about/united-states-adopted-names/usan-council
23. U.S. Consumer Product Safety Commission. Poison Prevention Packaging: A Guide for Healthcare Professionals. Published online 2005. Accessed January 10, 2024. https://www.cpsc.gov/s3fs-public/384.pdf
24. Bakshi A, Patel P. Poison Prevention Packaging Act. In: *StatPearls*. StatPearls Publishing; 2023. Accessed January 10, 2024. http://www.ncbi.nlm.nih.gov/books/NBK572141/
25. United States: Congress, United States: Congress. Poison Prevention Packaging Act of 1970. Published online August 14, 2008. Accessed January 10, 2024. https://www.govinfo.gov/app/details/COMPS-392
26. 16 CFR Chapter II Subchapter E – Poison Prevention Packaging Act of 1970 Regulations. Accessed January 10, 2024. https://www.ecfr.gov/current/title-16/chapter-II/subchapter-E
27. Rosette J. Tamper Evident Packaging: Law Enforcement and the Consumer | Office of Justice Programs. *FBI Law Enforc Bull*. 1992;61(9):16–19.
28. Rep. Sawyer HS [R M 5. H.R.1544 – 98th Congress (1983-1984): Federal Anti-Tampering Act. Published October 13, 1983. Accessed January 10, 2024. https://www.congress.gov/bill/98th-congress/house-bill/1544
29. Affairs O of R. CPG Sec. 450.500 Tamper-Resistant Packaging Requirements for Certain Over-the-Counter Human Drug Products. Published April 9, 2020. Accessed January 10, 2024. https://www.fda.gov/regulatory-information/search-fda-guidance-documents/cpg-sec-450500-tamper-resistant-packaging-requirements-certain-over-counter-human-drug-products
30. Swann J. The Story Behind the Orphan Drug Act. FDA. Published February 9, 2019. Accessed January 9, 2024. https://www.fda.gov/industry/fdas-rare-disease-day/story-behind-orphan-drug-act
31. Rep. Waxman HA [D C 24. H.R.5238 – 97th Congress (1981-1982): Orphan Drug Act. Published January 4, 1983. Accessed January 9, 2024. https://www.congress.gov/bill/97th-congress/house-bill/5238

32. Herder M. What Is the Purpose of the Orphan Drug Act? *PLoS Med*. 2017;14(1):e1002191. doi:https://doi.org/10.1371/journal.pmed.1002191
33. Robertson A. The Future of Patent Protection for Post-FDA-Approved Generics: A Look at the Federal Circuit's Incongruous Interpretations of the "Safe Harbor" Provision in 35 U.S.C. § 271(e)(1). *Seton Hall Circuit Rev*. 2014;10(2). https://scholarship.shu.edu/circuit_review/vol10/iss2/7
34. Sen. Hatch OG [R U. S.2748 – 98th Congress (1983-1984): Drug Price Competition and Patent Term Restoration Act of 1984. Published August 10, 1984. Accessed January 9, 2024. https://www.congress.gov/bill/98th-congress/senate-bill/2748
35. Cullen C, Stephens-Utne R. Prescription Drug Marketing Act. In: *StatPearls*. StatPearls Publishing; 2023. Accessed January 9, 2024. http://www.ncbi.nlm.nih.gov/books/NBK574533/
36. Rep. Dingell JD [D M 16. H.R.1207 – 100th Congress (1987-1988): Prescription Drug Marketing Act of 1987. Published April 22, 1988. Accessed January 9, 2024. https://www.congress.gov/bill/100th-congress/house-bill/1207
37. Sen. Sasser J [D T. S.3209 – 101st Congress (1989-1990): Omnibus Budget Reconciliation Act of 1990. Published November 8, 1990. Accessed January 9, 2024. https://www.congress.gov/bill/101st-congress/senate-bill/3209
38. Kentucky JCV BS Pharm, JD Professor, Department of Pharmacy Practice College of Pharmacy and Allied Health Professions Wayne State University Detroit, Michigan Joseph L Fink III, BS Pharm, JD Professor of Pharmacy University of Kentucky College of Pharmacy Lexington, Fink JL. OBRA '90 at Sweet Sixteen: A Retrospective Review. *US Pharm*. 2008;33(3):59–65.
39. Schatz R, Belloto RJ, White DB, Bachmann K. Provision of drug information to patients by pharmacists: the impact of the Omnibus Budget Reconciliation Act of 1990 a decade later. *Am J Ther*. 2003;10(2):93–103. doi:https://doi.org/10.1097/00045391-200303000-00004
40. Mitchell AP, Trivedi NU, Bach PB. The Prescription Drug User Fee Act: Much More Than User Fees. *Med Care*. 2022;60(4):287–293. doi:https://doi.org/10.1097/MLR.0000000000001692
41. Rep. Dingell JD [D M 16. H.R.5952 – 102nd Congress (1991-1992): Prescription Drug User Fee Act of 1992. Published September 24, 1992. Accessed January 9, 2024. https://www.congress.gov/bill/102nd-congress/house-bill/5952
42. Research C for DE and. Prescription Drug User Fee Amendments. FDA. Published December 15, 2023. Accessed January 9, 2024. https://www.fda.gov/industry/fda-user-fee-programs/prescription-drug-user-fee-amendments
43. Dickinson A. History and overview of DSHEA. *Fitoterapia*. 2011;82(1):5–10. doi:https://doi.org/10.1016/j.fitote.2010.09.001
44. Sen. Hatch OG [R U. S.784 – 103rd Congress (1993-1994): Dietary Supplement Health and Education Act of 1994. Congress.gov. Published October 25, 1994. Accessed January 9, 2024. https://www.congress.gov/bill/103rd-congress/senate-bill/784
45. Nutrition C for FS and A. Dietary Supplements. FDA. Published October 3, 2023. Accessed January 9, 2024. https://www.fda.gov/food/dietary-supplements
46. Rep. Archer B [R T 7. H.R.3103 – 104th Congress (1995-1996): Health Insurance Portability and Accountability Act of 1996. Published August 21, 1996. Accessed January 9, 2024. https://www.congress.gov/bill/104th-congress/house-bill/3103
47. Rights (OCR) O for C. HIPAA for Professionals. Published September 10, 2015. Accessed January 9, 2024. https://www.hhs.gov/hipaa/for-professionals/index.html
48. Figge HL. HIPAA: Privacy, Security, and Pharmacy Information Technology. *US Pharm*. 2011;36(11):79–81.
49. Wood SF, Perosino KL. INCREASING TRANSPARENCY AT THE FDA: THE IMPACT OF THE FDA AMENDMENTS ACT OF 2007. *Public Health Rep*. 2008;123(4):527–530.
50. Rep. Dingell JD [D M 15. H.R.3580 – 110th Congress (2007-2008): Food and Drug Administration Amendments Act of 2007. Published September 27, 2007. Accessed January 8, 2024. https://www.congress.gov/bill/110th-congress/house-bill/3580
51. Kastango ES. Lessons Learned from Compounding Tragedies. *Can J Hosp Pharm*. 2013;66(3):152–153.

52. Gabay M. The Drug Quality and Security Act. *Hosp Pharm*. 2014;49(7):615–676. doi:https://doi.org/10.1310/hpj4907-615
53. Affairs O of R. January 31, 2018: New England Compounding Center Pharmacist Sentenced for Role in Nationwide Fungal Meningitis Outbreak. *FDA*. Published online August 21, 2023. Accessed January 8, 2024. https://www.fda.gov/inspections-compliance-enforcement-and-criminal-investigations/press-releases/january-31-2018-new-england-compounding-center-pharmacist-sentenced-role-nationwide-fungal
54. Research C for DE and. Drug Supply Chain Security Act (DSCSA). FDA. Published December 13, 2023. Accessed January 8, 2024. https://www.fda.gov/drugs/drug-supply-chain-integrity/drug-supply-chain-security-act-dscsa
55. United States: National Archives and Records Administration: Office of the Federal Register. An act to amend the Federal Food, Drug, and Cosmetic Act with respect to human drug compounding and drug supply chain security, and for other purposes. Published online November 27, 2013. Accessed January 8, 2024. https://www.govinfo.gov/app/details/PLAW-113publ54
56. Research C for DE and. Title II of the Drug Quality and Security Act. *FDA*. Published online November 3, 2018. Accessed January 8, 2024. https://www.fda.gov/drugs/drug-supply-chain-security-act-dscsa/title-ii-drug-quality-and-security-act

4 Controlled Substances at the Federal and Alabama Level

Poisons and medicine are often the same substance given with different intents.

–Peter Mere Latham, nineteenth-century English physician and educator.

1 Introduction

The Controlled Substances Act (CSA) is enforced by the Drug Enforcement Administration (not "Agency" or "Association!") (DEA) . All legitimate handlers of controlled substances must be licensed by the DEA; these include manufacturers, distributors, physicians (and other clinicians), and pharmacies. As such, all transactions involving controlled substances are regulated (i.e., "controlled") in that they take place in a closed system, where controlled substances must be accounted for from the moment they are manufactured to the moment they are dispensed to a patient or otherwise destroyed (i.e., from "cradle to grave").

Key Concept
Manufacturers, distributors (wholesalers), physicians (and other clinicians), and pharmacies are licensed by the DEA, but *pharmacists* are not. Pharmacists in Alabama are licensed by the Alabama Board of Pharmacy. Unlike most states, Alabama requires pharmacists who wish to dispense controlled substances, to obtain a separate controlled substance license.

The DEA works with the Alabama Board of Pharmacy (ALBOP) to ensure that all controlled substances are prescribed, administered, and dispensed for *a legitimate medical purpose* in the *usual course of professional practice*. Examples of a "legitimate medical purpose" would be a podiatrist or a dentist providing pain

M. N. Bulloch et al., *Pharmacy Law in Alabama*,
https://doi.org/10.1007/978-3-031-84771-4_4

medication (i.e., hydrocodone) for a patient in need of analgesia. If either of these practitioners were to prescribe hydrocodone to a patient to prevent opioid withdrawal, this would not be considered a "legitimate medical purpose." An example of a medication being prescribed in the "usual course of practice" might include a psychiatrist prescribing methylphenidate for a patient with attention deficit hyperactivity disorder (ADHD). However, a dermatologist, even though they may have an MD degree, would not be expected to prescribe methylphenidate in the usual course of their professional practice. A pharmacist has a *corresponding responsibility*, along with the prescriber, to use due diligence in making sure that the medications they dispense are for a legitimate medical purpose and that the prescriber is operating within their usual course of professional practice. Any controlled substance prescription that is not issued for a legitimate medical purpose in the usual course of professional practice is not a valid prescription. The law does not require a pharmacist to fill a prescription of questionable or doubtful legitimacy. Any pharmacist who knowingly fills a fraudulent/invalid prescription has committed a felony offense.

2 Schedules of Controlled Substances

Controlled substances are categorized into five Schedules (Table 4.1). When it comes to learning what Schedule a controlled substance is in, it is important to first assess what you already do and do not know. For some medications, all drugs within that pharmacologic class are in the same Schedule (i.e., all benzodiazepines are in

Table 4.1 Examples of medications in Schedules 1–5 (C 1–5)

C 1	C 2	C 3	C 4	C 5
LSD Peyote MDMA (ecstasy) Kratom Phenibut Marijuana	Morphine Hydrocodone Hydromorphone Morphine Methadone Meperidine Oxycodone Fentanyl Codeine (as a sole ingredient) Amphetamine Methamphetamine Lisdexamfetamine Amobarbital Pentobarbital Secobarbital Glutethamide	Buprenorphine Butalbital Ketamine Anabolic steroids Benzphetamine Phendimetrazine Codeine combination products (i.e., codeine + acetaminophen); cannot contain more than 90 mg of codeine per dosage unit Paregoric (morphine 2 mg per 5 mL); cannot contain more than 50 mg of morphine per 100 mL or 100 g)	Benzodiazepines Carisoprodol Tramadol Phenobarbital Phentermine Diethylpropion	Gabapentin Pregabalin Ganaxolone Ezogabine Brivaracetam Lacosamide Lasmiditan Diphenoxylate 2.5 mg + atropine 25 mcg Difenoxin 0.5 or 1.0 mg + atropine 25 mcg Codeine-containing antitussive preps (not more than 200 mg codeine per 100 mL or 100 g) Opium antidiarrheal preps (not more than 100 mg opium per 100 mL or 100 g)

Schedule 4). For other drugs, it is more complex (i.e., barbiturates). It is also important to (1) appreciate medications that are rarely used and know what Schedule they are in and (2) be able to recognize both brand and generic names of all controlled substances, as MPJE questions may use these interchangeably.

2.1 Schedule 1 Medications

Schedule 1 medications do not have an accepted medical use, and they have the highest abuse potential compared to medications in Schedules 2–5. Even though marijuana (cannabis; THC) is legal for medical and/or recreational use in some states, it remains a Schedule I medication in Alabama. Kratom is an herbal preparation that is illegal in six states, including Alabama where it is in Schedule 1 [4]. Notably, Schedule 1 medications may be ordered and administered by DEA licensed investigators conducting research in animals or humans.

2.2 Schedule 2 Medications

Schedule 2 medications have the highest abuse potential among medications with an accepted medical use. Abuse of Schedule 2 medications may lead to severe psychological and physical dependence. As such, their use is more tightly restricted than medications in Schedules 3–5. Most potent opioid analgesics are in Schedule 2 if they are not part of a combination product. Certain sympathomimetic amines such as amphetamine and methamphetamine are Schedule 2 medications; however, other medications used for treating ADHD may not even be controlled substances (i.e., atomoxetine, viloxazine, clonidine, and guanfacine). It is important for the test taker to recognize and appreciate this information. Regarding the barbiturates, secobarbital, pentobarbital, and amobarbital are all Schedule 2 medications. This is noteworthy, as the barbiturates butalbital and phenobarbital are Schedule 3 and Schedule 4 medications, respectively. Lastly, the seldom-used medication glutethamide is a Schedule 2 medication.

2.3 Schedule 3 Medications

Schedule 3 medications have a lower potential for physical or psychological abuse than medications in Schedule 2. Anabolic steroids are Schedule 3 medications. As mentioned previously, butalbital is a Schedule 3 medication when combined with aspirin and caffeine (Fiorinal®). For reasons beyond the scope of this text, when butalbital is combined with acetaminophen (instead of aspirin) and caffeine (Fioricet®) it is not a controlled substance. With regard to opioids, all buprenorphine-containing products (with or without naloxone) are Schedule 3 medications. These include Suboxone®, Subutex®, and Sublocade®. Two anorexiants (i.e., "diet drugs") are in Schedule 3, these include benzphetamine (Didrex®) and phendimetrazine

(Bontril® and others). As will be discussed below, it is important to appreciate that two other anorexiants (phentermine and diethylpropion) are Schedule 4 medications. Lastly, codeine combination products used for analgesia (i.e., Tylenol #3®) are in Schedule 3, as is the morphine-containing antidiarrheal product, paregoric (Table 4.1).

► **Study Pro Tip** When preparing to take the MPJE, it would be wise to become familiar with both the brand and generic names of the anabolic steroids, appreciating that their generic names usually (but not always) end in "one."

2.4 Schedule 4 Medications

Schedule 4 medications have a lower potential for physical or psychological abuse than medications in Schedule 3. As previously noted, all benzodiazepines are in Schedule 4.

As noted above, phentermine and diethylpropion are in Schedule 4 (unlike phendimetrazine and benzphetamine, which are in Schedule 3), as is phenobarbital (unlike the other aforementioned barbiturates).

► **Study Pro Tip** (1) There are two benzodiazepines that do not end in "lam" or "pam"; these include chlordiazepoxide (Librium®) and clorazepate (Tranxene®) and (2) the combination product Librax®, which contains chlordiazepoxide 5 mg + clidinium 2.5 mg, is not a controlled substance. Again, familiarity with both brand and generic names of these medications is imperative.

2.5 Schedule 5 Medications

Schedule 5 medications have a lower potential for physical or psychological abuse than medications in Schedule 4. In some states, Schedule 5 medications can be purchased over-the-counter as long as certain rules and regulations are followed. In Alabama, all Schedule 5 medications require a prescription. Although not a federally Scheduled medication, gabapentin is a Schedule 5 drug in Alabama as of November 18, 2019. Notably, a number of codeine-containing cough syrups are in Schedule 5 (i.e., Robitussin AC®). It is important to recognize the difference in the amount of codeine allowed in Schedule 5 cough preparations versus Schedule 3 analgesic combination products. It is also worth noting, that when codeine is formulated as the sole active ingredient (i.e., not as part of a combination product), it is a Schedule 2 medication.

Key Concept
In Alabama, all Schedule 5 medications require a prescription.

3 Registration Requirements

3.1 Alabama Administrative Code

Any person or entity who actively *manufacturers, distributes,* or *dispenses* controlled substances (or any person or entity who proposes to engage in these activities) must obtain a registration from ALBOP This applies to *each individual pharmacy* and *each pharmacist* [5]. Each facility (manufacturer; wholesaler; distributor) must register/reregister every year, while each pharmacy and pharmacist must register/reregister during even-numbered years. If a person is not engaged in the manufacture, distributing, or dispensing of controlled substances (i.e., a pharmacist who works as an administrator for a college of pharmacy), they are not required to obtain this registration.

3.2 New Pharmacy Registration

Every pharmacy that stocks and dispenses controlled drugs, and all practitioners who store controlled drugs for prescribing and distributing must be registered with the DEA (Table 4.2). To register with the DEA as a new pharmacy, *DEA Form 224* must be filled out online. The pharmacy then receives a "Certificate of Registration," which is *DEA Form 223*. Form 223 must be kept at the pharmacy. *If an individual owns multiple pharmacies, each one must be registered with the DEA*. This is true for chain pharmacies as well; each one has their own DEA registration and hence their own DEA number.

Table 4.2 DEA forms

DEA form	Purpose
222	To order schedule 1 and 2 substances
224	A pharmacy fills out this form to apply for a new (initial) registration with the DEA
224a	A pharmacy fills out this form to *renew* their registration with the DEA
224b	Used by chain pharmacies ($\geq$ 50 stores) to renew DEA registration
223	Certificate of registration, showing that a pharmacy is registered with the DEA
107	Report theft of loss of listed chemicals (i.e., pseudoephedrine)
106	To report theft of less of controlled substances (and disposal receptacle)
41	To document the destruction of controlled substances
363	A practitioner fills this out to (initially) register as a narcotic treatment program
363a	A practitioner fills this out to *renew* as a narcotic treatment program
510	Used to apply for new (initial) registration application for domestic chemical registrations. Registration is required if a pharmacy wishes to distribute bulk quantities of scheduled licensed chemical products (SLCPs) (i.e., it allows them to become a chemical distributor)

3.3 Renewal of Pharmacy Registration

Each pharmacy must renew their DEA registration *every 3 years*. This is done by filling out Form *224a*. Hence, an individual fills out Form 224 to register a new pharmacy (i.e., the initial registration), and Form *224a to renew their registration.* Registrants must renew online *no earlier than 60 days* prior to the expiration date of their Certificate of Registration. If a person allows their registration to expire, they have one calendar month after the expiration date to get their license reinstated; if they fail to do so, they have to apply for a new DEA license (i.e., fill out Form 224). *If the pharmacy's registration expires, they must immediately stop all handling of controlled substances.*

3.4 Retail Chain Pharmacy Registration

In lieu of filling out a separate registration application for each of their pharmacies, a corporation that owns a chain of pharmacies may submit a single form: *DEA Form 224b*. The title of this form is *Retail Pharmacy Registration Affidavit for Chain Renewal*. The DEA requests that corporations with ≥50 retail pharmacy registrations enroll in the chain renewal program.

3.5 Change of Business Address and Termination of Registration

A "rule of thumb" to remember is that the DEA must always be notified regarding any type of change that impacts a pharmacy. This includes a change in address and termination of registration. If a pharmacy changes its location (i.e., address), the pharmacy should *first* request a "modification of registration"; this can be done online. The DEA will then issue the pharmacy an updated registration (which is of course, DEA Form 223). Similarly, if a pharmacy goes out of business, either completely or they stop handling controlled substances, they must inform the DEA. In addition, they must return all of their unused official order forms to their local DEA Registration Program Specialist. The DEA will also ask where required controlled substance records will be stored for the requisite 2-year period; these include inventory, prescriptions, and other documents.

3.6 Transfer of Business

Premise: a pharmacy registrant (i.e., transferring pharmacy or "seller") wishes to transfer its business operations to another pharmacy registrant (i.e., recipient pharmacy or "buyer"). The transferring pharmacy must submit detailed information (Table 4.3) either in person or by certified mail (not online) to the DEA Special

Table 4.3 Information that must be submitted to the DEA special agent in charge by the transferring pharmacy when one pharmacy transfers business to another

All pertinent information (i.e., name, address, and registration #) of both registrants—The "buyer" and the "seller"
Whether business will continue at the location of the "seller" or if a new location will be used by the "buyer." If a new location will be used, that address must be supplied to the DEA
The date on which the transfer of controlled substances will occur
On the date of transfer a complete controlled substance inventory must take place; it must include *drug name, strength,* and *quantity. This inventory requires an exact count of all scheduled medications*
This inventory serves as the *final inventory* of the "seller" (the pharmacy going out of business) and the *initial inventory* of the "buyer." A copy of this inventory must be kept by both pharmacies; a copy is not sent to the DEA
DEA form 222 must be used for the transfer of schedule 2 medications from one business to another
The transferring pharmacy (i.e., the "seller") tells the recipient pharmacy (i.e., "buyer") the exact quantity of all schedule 2 medications they have on hand. The "buyer" then fills out this exact information on DEA form 222, which is used to document the transfer. An electronic equivalent of DEA form 222 may be used instead of the paper form.
The "buyer" must keep all records of the transfer for 2 years; this includes executed DEA 222 forms, controlled substance invoices, controlled substance prescriptions, etc. The "seller" (transferor) is responsible for the accuracy of all records *before* the transfer/sale. The "buyer" (transferee) is responsible for the accuracy of all records *after* the transfer/sale

Agent in Charge of his/her area at least 14 days before the date of the proposed transfer.

3.7 Denial, Suspension or Revocation of Registration

A pharmacy may be denied a DEA registration if the DEA feels it is "inconsistent with the public's best interest." Also, the DEA has the authority to suspend or revoke a DEA registration for reasons, which might include (but are not limited) to the following: the registrant has (1) falsified information on the registration (2) been convicted of a felony involving a controlled substance or (3) had a pharmacy license suspended or revoked by a board of pharmacy in another state.

4 Ordering Controlled Substances

4.1 Ordering Schedules 1 and 2 Controlled Substances

Medications in Schedules 1 and 2 are ordered with an official paper order form, DEA Form 222, or the electronic equivalent, known as the Controlled Substance Ordering System (CSOS) . DEA Form 222 used to be a triplicate form, but as of October 20, 2021, it is a single sheet. DEA Form 222 (or CSOS) is required *for each distribution or transfer of a Schedule 1 or 2 medication.*

4.1.1 Obtaining DEA Forms 222

DEA Forms 222 are ordered through a secure electronic network or by contacting a DEA representative; these forms are issued in predetermined amounts in mailing envelopes. Any person (i.e., pharmacist in most cases) who is authorized/has power of attorney to order Schedule 1 or 2 medications, can order DEA Forms 222. Basically, the person ordering the forms provides the name, address, and DEA number of their pharmacy, and how many forms they would like sent to them. Each DEA Form 222 has an order form number and it contains the name, address, and registration number of the registrant, the authorized activity, and schedules of the registrant [4]. *The registrant cannot alter or change any of this information.*

4.1.2 Completing DEA Forms 222

There are specific rules that govern how DEA Form 222 must be filled out [6]. If the form is filled out incorrectly, the order cannot legally be filled by the supplier. There are four ways that DEA Form 222 may be filled out. By using a:

1. Typewriter.
2. Computer printer.
3. Pen.
4. Indelible pencil.

At the bottom of the form, the purchaser must fill in the number of lines completed in the space provided. The purchaser must also fill in the name and address of the supplier of the controlled substances in accordance with the instructions on the form. The supplier's DEA number may be entered by either the purchaser or supplier.

4.1.3 What to Do with DEA Forms 222 Once They Are Filled Out

After the purchaser completes DEA Form 222, they complete the following steps:

1. The purchaser makes a copy of the form and stores it in either paper or electronic form.
2. The purchaser sends the original form to the supplier, who stores it.
   - The supplier then fills out their section of DEA Form 222—*this includes the national drug code of the medications supplied, the number of bottles shipped, and the date shipped.*
   - The supplier makes a copy of this updated DEA Form 222 and sends the copy to the purchaser along with the medications that were ordered.
3. The purchaser receives the medication order along with the updated DEA Form 222. The purchaser fills in the final section of DEA Form 222—*this includes the number of packages received and the date received.*
4. *The purchaser takes the DEA Form 222 from Step 3 above, and attaches it to the DEA Form 222 copy from Step 1 above (either* via *paper or electronically); these forms are stored together by the purchaser for 2 years.*

4.1.4 Notifying the DEA of Transactions Involving Schedule 1 and 2 Medications

The DEA needs to know about all transactions involving Schedule 1 and 2 medications. So who is responsible for informing them, and how is this done? The answer is: *the supplier*. Suppliers who are wholesalers will be required to report transactions involving Schedule 1 and 2 medications to the DEA via the Automation of Reports and Consolidated Orders System (ARCOS). While wholesalers are required to use ARCOS for reporting transactions involving Schedule 1 and 2 medications, other entities, such as pharmacies and practitioners are usually not. For example, a dentist may wish to purchase Percocet (oxycodone/acetaminophen) from a local pharmacy for office administration. In this case, the dentist is the purchaser who fills out DEA Form 222 and the pharmacy would be the supplier. Since, in most cases, a pharmacy does not function as a supplier, it is not required to report disposition of Schedule 1 or 2 medications via ARCOS. *In which case, the pharmacy would be required to make a copy of the original DEA Form 222 and submit it to the DEA either by mail or email by the end of the month that the order was filled.*

> **Key Concept**
> Automation of Reports and Consolidated Orders System (ARCOS) is an automated reporting system that monitors the movement of Schedule 1 and 2 medications from when they were first manufactured through to the dispensing level (i.e., retail pharmacy; hospital pharmacy; practitioner). ARCOS is the means by which the DEA keeps track of Schedule 1 and 2 medications throughout the life cycle of the product (i.e., from the cradle to the grave).

4.1.5 Storing (Maintaining) DEA Forms 222 and Electronic Schedule 2 Orders

4.1.5.1 Paper Forms

DEA Forms 222 are always kept separately from all other records and they must be kept for 2 years. If a person has several registered DEA locations (i.e., they own multiple pharmacies), the executed DEA Forms 222 (and any related documents) must be stored at the address that is printed on the DEA Form 222. This does not include unexecuted DEA forms, which may be kept elsewhere.

4.1.5.2 Electronic Forms

As with paper DEA Forms 222, electronic forms DEA Forms 222 (along with any related documents) must also be stored separately from all other records; however, this does not mean that they have to be stored on a separate server. It simply means that electronic DEA Forms 222 have to be stored in a manner that allows them to be easily retrieved separately from all other records (i.e., they could be stored in a unique folder or on a specific hard drive). In fact, electronic DEA Forms 222 may be stored on a system at a location that differs from the registered location, as long as the records are readily retrievable.

4.1.6 Unaccepted and Defective Forms

A supplier must not fill an order if DEA Form 222 is not filled out correctly. Examples include forms that are not: complete, legible, properly prepared, or properly endorsed. Also, a defective DEA Form 222 cannot be corrected; a new form must be used. If a supplier determines that they cannot fill a DEA Form 222 order for any reason, they must return the original order form to the would-be purchaser and tell them why the order could not be filled. Note that *the supplier may refuse to fill an order for any reason* and they may simply state *"The order is not accepted."* If an order is not accepted by the supplier, the supplier sends the unfilled/rejected DEA Form 222 (either paper of electronic) back to the would-be purchaser. The purchaser then stores this form with a copy of the original (paper or electronic) DEA Form 222 that they submitted.

4.1.7 Power of Attorney to Sign DEA Forms 222

Only individuals who have been given special permission (i.e., power of attorney) may sign DEA Forms 222. Any registrant (it may help to think of this person as the pharmacy owner) may authorize one or more people to obtain (i.e., order) and execute (i.e., sign) DEA Forms 222. The person(s) granted power of attorney are not required to be located at the registered location.

4.1.7.1 Who Signs the Power of Attorney Form?

- The registrant, if an individual; a partner of the registrant, if a partnership; or an officer of the registrant, if a corporation.
- The person who is being granted power of attorney.
- The witnesses.

4.1.7.2 Other Items to Remember About Power of Attorney

- Any of the signees noted above may sign electronically or via "wet signature."
- Power of attorney can be revoked by the registrant.
- You only need to grant a new power of attorney if a new person completes the renewal of the DEA registration (i.e., the registrant changes).
- The power of attorney form is stored along with executed DEA Forms 222.

4.1.8 Canceling and Voiding DEA Forms 222

A purchaser may cancel an entire order or just part of an order. The purchaser must notify the supplier of the cancellation. The supplier must then indicate the details of the cancelation on the original DEA Form 222 that was sent by the purchaser. Specifically, the supplier must draw a line through any cancelled items, and print "cancelled" in the space provided for "number of items shipped."

4.1.9 Lost or Stolen DEA Forms 222

4.1.9.1 What to Do If an Unfilled DEA Form 222 Is Lost or Stolen

An "*unfilled DEA Form 222*" refers to *a form that was filled out but got lost or stolen prior to being filled by the supplier*; it *does not refer to blank DEA Forms 222*, which are discussed below under Sect. 4.1.9.2. If an unfilled DEA Form 222 is lost or stolen, the purchaser should execute another form (i.e., fill out a replacement form) and explain that the original order form was lost and the medication(s) were not received. The purchaser must store the copy of the original order form that got lost together with the replacement order form. If the supplier subsequently receives the original DEA Form 222 after they have filled a replacement order, they must write "not accepted" and return the form to the purchaser.

4.1.9.2 What to Do If Blank DEA Forms 222 Are Lost or Stolen

If blank DEA Forms 222 are lost or stolen, immediately report the loss/theft to the DEA Diversion Field Office. If these forms are later found, immediately report this information to the DEA Diversion Field Office.

4.1.9.3 What to Do If the Registration of any Purchaser Terminates (i.e. the Purchaser Dies or Goes Out of Business), or Is Suspended or Revoked

In any of these situations, the purchaser must return all unused DEA Forms 222 to the *Registration and Program Support Section.*

► **Study Pro Tip** It should be clear at this point that *all records pertaining to DEA Form 222 must be stored together*. As such, copies of any orders that are not accepted, cancelled, lost, stolen etc. will always be stored by the purchaser (typically a pharmacy) in proximity with the executed order (i.e., the order that is eventually filled). In other words, all documents that relate to the same order are stored together, as either paper copies or electronically. These records must be stored separately from other records, and readily retrievable at the location of the registrant. The same holds true for electronic orders for controlled substances. All electronic documents that pertain to the same order must be stored together (i.e., electronically linked) for 2 years.

4.1.10 Controlled Substances Ordering System (CSOS)

The CSOS system allows registrants who are permitted to order Schedule 1 or 2 controlled substances to do so electronically instead of using the paper DEA Form 222 if they so choose (i.e., using CSOS is optional) *(note: from this point forward only Schedule 2 drugs will be mentioned when referring to CSOS or DEA Forms 222 since Schedule 1 ordering is typically restricted to research settings)*. CSOS is the only electronic means of ordering Schedule 2 medications; it is not used to order Schedule 3–5 controlled substances.

4.1.10.1 CSOS Security

The CSOS system employs multiple electronic security measures including Public Key Infrastructure, which requires CSOS users to obtain a digital certificate, and a digital signature for ordering; these are issued by the Certification Authority under the direction of the DEA. It would behoove the test taker to remember the terms *Public Key Infrastructure*, *Digital Certificate*, and *Certification Authority* and their respective roles in maintaining a secure CSOS.

4.1.10.2 Who Can Obtain a CSOS Digital Certificate?

Anyone with power of attorney to sign DEA Form 222 is eligible to obtain a CSOS digital certificate. In addition, the person who signed the most recent DEA registration application and anyone authorized to sign the DEA registration application are also eligible to obtain a CSOS digital certificate.

4.1.10.3 Additional CSOS Information and Requirements

- The registrant must appoint a *CSOS Coordinator*. The CSOS Coordinator is responsible for all issues pertaining to digital certificates.
- A CSOS digital certificate is valid until the DEA registration expires (the digital certificate is approved under the DEA registration).
- If a digital certificate is revoked, this means the person can no longer order medications using the CSOS system. A digital certificate is revoked when (a) the holder of the certificate is no longer authorized to order Schedule 2 medications for the registrant (b) information on which the certificate is based changes or (c) the digital certificate has been lost, stolen, or compromised.
- The DEA has an E-Commerce Program website that provides additional information and details about the CSOS. The URL for this web page is: https://www.deaecom.gov/csosmain.html

4.1.10.4 Defective (Unacceptable) Electronic Orders

As with DEA Forms 222 that are incorrectly filled out, electronic orders that are defective in any way cannot be filled by the supplier. Examples of defective/invalid orders include, but are not limited to the following: required data fields have not been completed, the digital certificate has expired, the order is not signed using the digital certificate issued by the DEA, or the purchaser's key would not validate the digital certificate. Again, as is the case with invalid DEA Forms 222, if a supplier is unable to fill an electronic order, they must inform the purchaser why the order cannot be filled. Also, the supplier may refuse to fill an order for any reason, and if the supplier refuses to accept an order they may simply tell the purchaser that the order is not accepted. The purchaser must then electronically link this statement of nonacceptance with their original order and store them together for 2 years.

4.1.10.5 Canceling or Voiding an Electronic Record

As with DEA Forms 222, a supplier can void all or part of an electronic order. If part of an order is voided, this must be noted on the order by the supplier. If the entire order is voided, the supplier must make an electronic copy of the order, indicate "Void" on the order and return it to the purchaser. As you know by now, the purchaser links the voided order with the original electronic order and stores them together for 2 years. *Unlike the purchaser, the supplier is not required to keep a record of orders that are not filled.*

4.1.10.6 Lost Electronic Orders

Lost electronic orders are handled in basically the same manner as lost orders via DEA Form 222 (Sect. 4.1.9). If a purchaser determines that an electronic order has been lost, they must provide the supplier with a signed statement explaining the situation; this statement must include the unique tracking number of the order and the date of the lost order. If the purchaser creates a replacement order, they must electronically link this with a copy of their statement that the original order was lost. If a replacement order has been sent to the supplier by the purchaser, but in the meantime the lost order is found, the supplier must indicate that the "found" order is "not accepted" and return it to the purchaser. The purchaser then links this returned order to the record of the lost order and stores them together.

4.2 Ordering Schedule 3–5 Controlled Substances

The registrant (i.e., purchaser) must keep a receipt, typically an invoice (Table 4.4).

4.2.1 Storing Invoices/Receipts for Schedule 3–5 Orders

Invoices for Schedule 3–5 medications may be stored in one of two ways. They may be stored (1) *separately* from all other records of the registrant (this includes those pertaining to Schedule 2 medications or non-controlled medications) or (2) in such a way that the required information is *readily retrievable* from other business records of the registrant.

Table 4.4 Information that must be included on the receipt/invoice for Schedule 3–5 medications received by the pharmacy

1. Name of the medication
2. Each finished form [strength + dosage form (i.e., 10 mg tablets)]
3. The number of units of the finished form (i.e., number of bottles/containers)
4. Name, address, and registration number of the person from whom the units were acquired (you may think of this as the "supplier")
5. Name, address, and registration number of the person to whom the containers were distributed (you may think of this as the "purchaser")
6. Date the order was filled and the date the order was received and checked in. In accordance with Alabama state Board of Pharmacy (ALBOP) Administrative code chap. 680-X-3-0.09, *all receipts for controlled substances must be reviewed and approved by a pharmacist* (this could also be an intern operating under the direct supervision of a pharmacist) *who then signs the supplier's invoice* or similar such document.

5 Controlled Substance Inventory Requirements

The term "inventory" refers to an accurate and complete list of controlled substances possessed by the registrant. This list must be *written by hand, typewritten,* or *printed* (do not confuse this with the rules for filling out DEA Form 222 in Sect. 4.1.2!). *Inventories of Schedule 2 drugs are determined by an actual physical count* (i.e., their quantity is not estimated). In contrast, *inventories of Schedule 3, 4, and 5 medications may be estimated if there is an open bottle of 1000 dosage units (*i.e., *tablets or capsules) or less.* So then, if the bottle contains exactly 1000 dosage units, the quantity may be estimated. If the bottle contains more than 1000 dosage units, an exact count of the contents must be made. *Note that a DEA registrant's initial inventory must include an exact count of all controlled substances (Schedules 2–5) as discussed in Sect. 5.2.1 of this chapter.*

5.1 Storage of Inventory Records

Inventory records must be stored at the location site (typically, this means the pharmacy where the medications are kept) and kept for 2 years. *Schedule 2 inventory records are always kept separately from all other records, while Schedule 3–5 records may be stored separately from all other records or in a manner that allows them to be readily retrieved.* Note that these are basically the same requirements as those employed for storing invoices for Schedule 2 vs. Schedule 3–5 medications.

Key Concept
What is meant by "readily retrievable" with regard to Schedule 3–5 inventory information? Readily retrievable means that records can be easily separated from all other records in a reasonable time frame. This may be accomplished via an electronic recordkeeping system or via a paper inventory where certain items are noted with an asterisk, a red line, or other visual identifier.

5.2 Rules for Conducting Controlled Substance Inventories

5.2.1 New DEA Registrant

When a pharmacy is first issued a DEA registration, an actual physical count of all controlled substances (Schedules 2–5) must occur. If the registrant does not have any controlled drugs on hand, they must still make a record showing zero inventory. The following information must be included in the inventory:

1. Date of the inventory and whether it was taken at the start or close of business (i.e., before the store opened or after it closed).
2. Name of the drug, finished form, strength, exact count.

5.2.2 Recurring Inventory

Alabama requires that a controlled substance inventory be conducted every year on January 15th [7]. A detailed explanation of Alabama inventory requirements is included in Chap. 10, Sect. 2.1. During these annual inventories, medications in Schedules 3–5 may be estimated if they meet the conditions described above in Sect. 5. Schedule 2 medications always require an exact count.

5.2.3 Newly Scheduled Controlled Substance

Another situation that requires an exact count of a medication in Schedules 3–5, is if that medication is newly scheduled (i.e., it is switched from a noncontrolled legend drug to a scheduled drug). For example, on August 18, 2014, the DEA changed tramadol from a legend drug to a Schedule 4 medication. As such, all pharmacies were required to take an exact count inventory of tramadol at that time.

5.2.4 Inventory for Damaged, Defective, or Impure Substances

All controlled substances, regardless of their quality (i.e., whether or not they are damaged, defective, or impure) must be accounted for; hence this inventory requirement. Inventory of these items must include (1) the name of the substance, (2) the total quantity (to the nearest metric unit if a liquid, powder, ointment, etc. or the number of units in finished form [tablets or capsules]), and (3) the reason the pharmacy is holding onto the substance and whether or not the substance is capable of being used to manufacture a controlled substance in finished form.

5.2.5 Termination of Operation of a Pharmacy, Manufacturer, or Distributor Registered with the ALBOP

If a pharmacy, manufacturer, or distributor ceases to operate, they must conduct an inventory of all controlled substances in their possession within TEN (10) days of the time they stopped operating, and this inventory must be furnished to the ALBOP [8]. The ALBOP must also be informed as to the final disposition of all controlled substances on hand when operations terminated. If a pharmacy terminates its operation due to the death of the pharmacist/owner, then the next of kin of that pharmacist has 30 days (instead of 10 days) to provide this information. If a manufacturer or distributor is located outside of Alabama, but is licensed to distribute controlled substances within Alabama, they must also provide ALBOP with (1) a final controlled substances inventory and (2) an explanation of what was done with the controlled substances on hand (i.e., their final disposition).

- **Numbers of Importance** If a pharmacy, manufacturer, or distributor ceases to operate, they must conduct a final inventory of all their controlled substances within 10 days and furnish it to the ALBOP.
- If a pharmacy terminates its operation due to the death of the pharmacist/owner, the next-of-kin must submit a final inventory of all their controlled substances within 30 days and furnish it to the ALBOP

6 Recordkeeping Requirements

6.1 Required Records

Each pharmacy must maintain complete records of all controlled substances that enter and leave its possession. These records provide "cradle to grave" (i.e., from manufacture to dispensing) accountability of said controlled substances and reduce potential for diversion. Several of the controlled substance records that each pharmacy must maintain for TWO (2) years have been discussed individually earlier in this chapter. They are listed collectively here and should be easily recognizable (Table 4.5).

6.2 Central Recordkeeping

If a DEA registrant desires to store shipping and financial records (not executed order forms) at a central location (instead of their registered location) they can ask the DEA in writing for permission to do so. Unless permission is denied by the DEA, the registrant can start storing records at a central location FOURTEEN (14) days after the DEA receives the request.

6.3 Prescription Records for Controlled Substances

There are 2 options for storing controlled substance prescriptions; they are shown below. These records must be readily retrievable and maintained for TWO (2) years (Table 4.6).

Table 4.5 Controlled substance records that must be maintained by each pharmacy

Executed (i.e., filled) DEA forms 222 or their electronic equivalent (via CSOS)
Signed power of attorney authorization form
Invoices/receipts for schedule 3, 4, and 5 medications
Initial and annual inventory records
Records of any controlled substances *distributed* (not dispensed). This includes sales to other registrants, returns to vendors, and distributions to reverse distributors. This may not be applicable to all pharmacies
Records of controlled substances *dispensed* (i.e., prescriptions—Paper and electronic)
Records of the theft or loss of controlled substances if applicable (DEA form 106)
Records of controlled substances destroyed (DEA form 41)
DEA registration certificate (DEA form 223)
Self-certification certificate and logbook (or electronic equivalent) as required under the *combat methamphetamine epidemic Act of 2005*, which tracks the sale of pseudoephedrine (discussed under Section 13 of this chapter)
Suspicious orders report system (SORS). All DEA registrants that distribute controlled substances to other DEA registrants are required to use this online system to report suspicious controlled substance orders (as required by the SUPPORT ACT). *If a pharmacy does not distribute controlled substances to other DEA registrants, SORS reporting will not be applicable*

Table 4.6 The two (2) options for storing controlled substance prescriptions

Option 1: prescriptions are stored in THREE (3) separate files: 1. Schedule 2 prescriptions 2. Schedule 3, 4, and 5 prescriptions 3. Noncontrolled prescriptions Option 2: Prescriptions are stored in two (2) separate files: 1. Schedule 2 prescriptions 2. Schedule 3, 4, and 5 prescriptions *plus* non-controlled prescriptions where schedule 3, 4, and 5 prescriptions are readily retrievable. One way of making these controlled substance prescriptions "readily retrievable" is to place a red "C" stamp on them. However, this is not necessary as long as the pharmacy has an electronic record keeping system that assigns prescription numbers, making it possible to retrieve each prescription and identify the prescriber's name, drug dispensed, and date filled

6.4 Electronic Prescription Records

If a prescription is created, signed, transmitted, and received electronically, then *all records related to that prescription must be retained electronically* (i.e., the pharmacy cannot maintain a mix of paper and electronic records for the same prescription). In addition to being readily retrievable and maintained for TWO (2) years, *electronic records must be easily rendered into a format that is readable*. In other words, the pharmacy's computer system must be able to print out or transfer these electronic records in a format that is legible to DEA officers. Also, electronic prescription records must be sortable by (1) prescriber name, (2) patient name, (3) drug dispensed, and (4) date filled. You may wish to remember this as: *date*, *doctor*, *drug*, and *dude* (i.e., *patient*).

7 Prescription Requirements

A prescription is an order for a medication which is dispensed to or for an ultimate user. It *is not* an order for a medication meant to be dispensed for immediate administration (i.e., as occurs in a hospital setting). A prescription for a controlled substance must contain specific information (Table 4.7).

Familiarity with a sample controlled substance prescription (Fig. 4.1) is an easy way to recall its necessary components.

Alabama Board of Medical Examiners Administrative Code: 540-X-4.06 also states that a prescription must be written in ink, indelible pencil, typewritten, or printed on a computer printer [9]. The prescription must be *manually signed* (i.e., a "wet signature") *by the practitioner on the date it is written*. A practitioner is not allowed, under any circumstances, to "pre-sign blank prescription pads" and make them available to employees or support personnel nor are they allowed to mechanically or photostatically reproduce their signature on a prescription (i.e., it cannot be rubber stamped or photocopied). A practitioner/prescriber may authorize an agent who acts on their behalf, to perform a limited role in communicating a controlled substance prescription to a pharmacy (it may help to think of a nurse calling in a

Table 4.7 Information required on a controlled substance prescription

Prescriber's name, address, DEA number, and signature
Patients full name and address
Drug name, strength, quantity, dosage form, and directions for use
Date issued (cannot be pre- or postdated)
Number of refills if applicable
According to the *Alabama Board of Medical Examiners Administrative Code: 540-X-4.06*, every written prescription for a controlled substance must contain 2 signature lines. Under one signature line shall be printed, "*dispense as written*" under the other signature line shall be written, "*product selection permitted*." The prescriber lets the pharmacist know whether generic substitution is permitted by signing the appropriate line

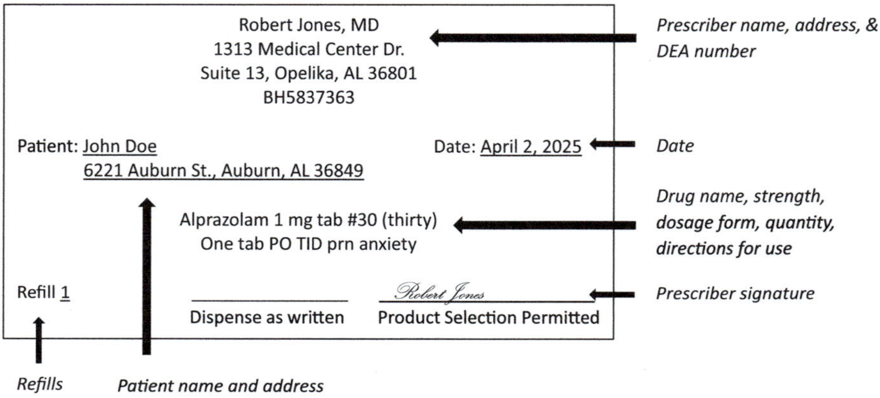

Fig. 4.1 Sample prescription for a controlled substance

prescription to a pharmacy on behalf of a physician). However, the practitioner is not allowed to delegate to an agent the authority to issue a prescription for a controlled substance. In other words, *it is the practitioner (and not the agent) who determines that there is a legitimate medical need to prescribe a controlled substance*. After determining this need, the practitioner may ask the agent to perform the following functions on their behalf:

- *The agent may prepare a written prescription for the practitioner to sign*. It is still the practitioner's responsibility to ensure that, in their usual course of practice, the prescription is written accurately (i.e., it contains all the required elements of a controlled substance prescription) and is for a legitimate medical purpose.
- *The agent may telephone or FAX a prescription to a pharmacy for a Schedule 3, 4, or 5 medication on behalf of the practitioner*. For telephone prescriptions, the practitioner must prepare a valid oral prescription ahead of time for the agent to communicate to the pharmacy.
- *A prescriber cannot delegate (to an agent) which type of medication to prescribe, nor its dosage, dosage form or allotted refills*.

The DEA recommends that practitioners make a list of agents authorized to act on their behalf, and the scope of any such authorizations. This list may be shared with pharmacies that receive regular communications from the agent. Of note, the agent acting on behalf of the practitioner is not required to register with the DEA.

7.1 Individuals Permitted to Issue a Prescription for a Controlled Substance

The following individuals are authorized to issue prescriptions for controlled substances:

- Physician (MD, DO).
- Dentist (DDS, DMD).
- Podiatrist (DPM).
- Veterinarian (DVM).
- Mid-level practitioner (Physician's Assistant [PA] , Certified Registered Nurse Practitioner [CRNP] and others).
- Other registered practitioners may be authorized to prescribe controlled substances by the jurisdiction in which they are licensed to practice. This would include a practitioner who is employed by a hospital (i.e., it may be useful to think of a resident physician) and is operating in their normal course of business where *the practitioner does not have their own DEA number but is operating under the DEA registration of the hospital*. Typically, the practitioner will have a code that identifies them, and they will include this code, along with the DEA number of the hospital, on any controlled substance prescriptions that they issue.
- A practitioner may not issue a prescription to obtain controlled substances to subsequently dispense to their patients. For example, a practitioner may not write a prescription for tramadol and state "for office use" on the prescription. If a practitioner wishes to obtain medication for office use, they must use either DEA Form 222 for Schedule 2 medications or an invoice for Schedule 3–5 medications.

7.1.1 The Following Practitioners, Employed by the U.S. Federal Government, Are Authorized to Prescribe Controlled Substances but Are Exempted from DEA Registration

- A member of the Public Health Service (PHS).
- Member of the Federal Bureau of Prisons.
- Military practitioners (Army, Navy, Marine Corps, Air Force, and Coast Guard).

In lieu of a DEA number, practitioners employed by any of the governmental organizations listed above must include their *Branch of service* (i.e., U.S. Army) and their *service identification number* on any controlled substance prescriptions they issue. If a federal government practitioner wishes to maintain a private practice, they must register with the DEA.

7.2 Electronic Prescriptions (E-Prescribing)

DEA regulations allow practitioners to write prescriptions for controlled substances electronically; they also allow pharmacies to receive, dispense, and store these prescriptions electronically.

7.2.1 Requirements for Electronic Prescribing of Controlled Substances

Stated simply, software used by the prescriber must communicate accurately with software used by the pharmacy such that the pharmacy's software recognizes the prescriber's digital signature and imports and archives all required information needed for a controlled substance prescription. In addition, software used by the prescriber and the pharmacy must:

- Be audited by a third party to ensure that the pharmacy software accurately and consistently imports, stores, and displays all information that is required for controlled substance prescriptions (Fig. 4.1). This includes the ability to include notes or phrases required on a prescription in certain situations, such as "Authorization for Emergency Dispensing."

> **Study Pro Tip** Always remember that any information required for a controlled substance prescription written on paper is also required for an electronic controlled substance prescription.

- The auditor provides a report of its findings to the pharmacy who then has it approved by the DEA.
- Check to ensure that the prescriber's digital certificate is valid (which ensures that the prescriber's signature is valid). *To clarify further, the prescriber must digitally sign the electronic prescription using their cryptographic key; the pharmacy software must in turn apply the prescriber's public key to confirm that the prescription was signed.*
- The pharmacy software must also be capable of performing automated internal audits and providing reports.

7.2.2 Preventing "Double Filling" of a Controlled Substance Prescription

If a pharmacist receives a paper or oral prescription that indicates it was originally transmitted to the pharmacy electronically, the pharmacist must check the pharmacy's records to ensure the prescription was not already filled and dispensed. If a pharmacist receives a paper or oral prescription that indicates it was originally transmitted electronically to a different pharmacy, the pharmacist must check with that pharmacy to ensure the prescription was not already filled and dispensed. In either case, if the prescription was already filled electronically, it should not be filled again. By exercising due diligence in these situations, the pharmacist makes sure that a controlled substance prescription is not accidentally filled twice.

7.3 Construction of a Valid DEA Number for Practitioners

Pharmacists are responsible for making sure that any controlled substance prescriptions they fill are written by practitioners who are legally authorized by the DEA to write such prescriptions. One means of meeting this responsibility is knowing how to assess a DEA number to determine whether it is valid.

- **The first letter of DEA numbers** for physicians, veterinarians, dentists, and podiatrists will begin with *A*, *B*, or *F*, whereas DEA numbers for mid-level practitioners Mid-level practitioners (MLP) (such as physician assistants etc.) will begin with *M*.
- ***The second letter of DEA numbers*** is nearly always the first letter of the registrant's last name.
- **Steps to verify a DEA number.**
  1. Add the first, third, and fifth digits of the number.
  2. Add the second, fourth, and sixth digits of the number, and multiple the sum by 2.
  3. Add the numbers together (from 1 and 2 above), and the right most digit should be the same as the last digit of the DEA number.

Key Concept

How to validate a DEA number:

Example: Validate the DEA number of Dr. Robert Jones, MD. His DEA number is.

BJ2243551

Step one: 2 + 4 + 5 = 11

Step two: 2 + 3 + 5 = 10 x 2 = 20

Step three: 11 + 20 = 31

The last digit of the DEA number matches the last digit of the number from step three, indicating that Dr. Jones has a valid DEA number

7.4 Registration Requirements for Mid-level Practitioners

Mid-level practitioners (MLP) are registered and authorized by the DEA and the state in which they practice. Common examples of MLPs include nurse practitioners, nurse midwives, nurse anesthetists, clinical nurse specialists, physician assistants (PAs) and optometrists. MLPs may apply for their own DEA number in Alabama.

7.5 Schedule 2 Controlled Substances

Prescriptions for Schedule 2 medications must either (1) be written and manually signed by the practitioner or (2) submitted as an electronic prescription that meets all requirements of an electronic controlled substance prescription.

7.5.1 Expiration

There is no time limit within which a Schedule 2 medication must be filled after it is signed by the practitioner. This may seem counterintuitive, since Schedule 3 and 4 medications expire 6 months after the date on which they are written (as will be discussed later in Sect. 7.5.5.2). Nonetheless, the pharmacist should check with the patient to make sure that they still need the medication. In addition, the quantity of the medication must be consistent with its use for a legitimate medical purpose; however, *there is no law limiting the amount of a Schedule 2 substance that can be prescribed* (although insurance companies typically impose quantity limitations).

7.5.2 Oral Prescribing of Schedule 2 Medications

An oral prescription for a Schedule 2 medication is only allowed in 3 specific emergency situations, all of which involve patients from a unique population (noted below). In other words, an emergency oral prescription for a Schedule 2 medication is not an option for a "regular patient." An emergency situation occurs when (1) the patient has an immediate need for the medication and (2) an alternate medication, which is not a Schedule 2 drug, is not an option. An emergency oral prescription for a Schedule 2 medication may be called in by telephone for:

1. A resident of a *long-term care facility.*
2. A patient receiving *hospice services.*
3. A patient receiving *home healthcare services.*

Of note, the practitioner must call the prescription in themselves; they cannot have an agent make the call on their behalf. The quantity of the oral prescription should be commensurate with the "amount adequate to treat the patient" but *not more than a 72-hour supply*. The pharmacist taking the oral prescription must immediately write down all of the required information, and take reasonable measures to ensure that the order is from a registered practitioner. *The prescriber must provide the pharmacy with a hard copy of the prescription within 7 days of the oral order. This hard copy must have written on its face, "Authorization for Emergency Dispensing" and the date of the oral order*. If the hard copy is delivered via United States mail, it must be postmarked within 7 days of the oral order. Once the pharmacist receives the hard copy of the prescription, they must attach it to the oral prescription and store both items together.

7.5.3 Issuance of Multiple Schedule 2 Medication Prescriptions

Although it is not lawful for a Schedule 2 medication to be refilled, a practitioner may issue multiple Schedule 2 prescriptions (Fig. 4.2) as long as the following conditions are met:

- *The patient may not receive more than a 90-day supply of medication.* This usually consists of 3 prescriptions, each for a 30-day supply. However, this is not a requirement (i.e., the practitioner could write 9 prescriptions, each for a 10-day supply if they so wished).
- *The current date is written on each of the prescriptions.* None of the prescriptions are post-dated.
- The prescriber typically intends for the *first prescription to be filled immediately, followed sequentially by the other prescriptions (typically prescriptions 2 and 3 if each prescription is for a 30-day supply).* On each prescription, other than the first one, *the practitioner must indicate in the directions, the earliest date that the prescription may be filled.*

It must be noted that just because practitioners have the option of writing multiple prescriptions for Schedule 2 medications, they are by no means required to do so. In fact, prior to deciding to prescribe multiple Schedule 2 prescriptions for a patient, a practitioner must first conclude that doing so will not create an undue risk of diversion or abuse. As a point of clarification, if a practitioner is writing multiple Schedule 2 prescriptions on the same date as described above, there is a 90-day supply limit. However, if writing a single prescription for a patient for a Schedule 2 medication, there is no limit on the quantity or day supply that the practitioner may prescribe. Finally, the *"Do not fill before"* date is firm, and cannot be moved up to accommodate a holiday or any other circumstance.

7.5.4 Faxing Schedule 2 Prescriptions

There are 4 situations in which a prescription for a Schedule 2 medication may be faxed. In 3 of the situations, the faxed prescription serves as the prescription of record, in one situation it does not. The situations are as follows:

1. A practitioner can fax in (to a pharmacy) a written and signed prescription for a Schedule 2 medication *so that the pharmacist can fill the prescription prior to the patient's arrival.* However, the patient must bring in the original written prescription and give it to the pharmacist. The pharmacist then reviews the original prescription to make sure it is the same as the one that was faxed. After the pharmacist makes this confirmation, the faxed prescription is destroyed and the original prescription (that the patient brought in) serves as the prescription of record. The purpose of allowing this process is to save time for the patient.

a

Thomas G. Hartwig, MD, FCP
1331 EAMC Medical Center
Suite 21, Opelika, AL 36801
BH5837363

Patient name: John Doe
6221 Lakeshore Drive, Opelika, AL 36801

Date: April 2, 2025

Methylphenidate ER 20 mg #30
Take one tablet once daily in the a.m.

Refill: 0

Dispense as Written

T. G. Hartwig, MD
Substitution Permitted

b

Thomas G. Hartwig, MD, FCP
1331 EAMC Medical Center
Suite 21, Opelika, AL 36801
BH5837363

Patient name: John Doe
6221 Lakeshore Drive, Opelika, AL 36801

Date: April 2, 2025

Methylphenidate ER 20 mg #30
Take one tablet once daily in the a.m.
Do not fill before May 2, 2025

Refill: 0

Dispense as Written

T. G. Hartwig, MD
Substitution Permitted

c

Thomas G. Hartwig, MD, FCP
1331 EAMC Medical Center
Suite 21, Opelika, AL 36801
BH5837363

Patient name: John Doe
6221 Lakeshore Drive, Opelika, AL 36801

Date: April 2, 2025

Methylphenidate ER 20 mg #30
Take one tablet once daily in the a.m.
Do not fill before June 2, 2025

Refill: 0

Dispense as Written

T. G. Hartwig, MD
Thomas G. Hartwig, MD, FCP

Fig. 4.2 (**a**–**c**) Multiple Schedule 2 prescriptions each written on the same day and filled sequentially (**a**, **b**, then **c**)

2. *The patient is receiving hospice care*; the faxed prescription serves as the prescription of record.
3. *The patient is residing in a long-term care facility*; the faxed prescription serves as the prescription of record.
4. *The Schedule 2 medication is to be compounded for the direct administration to a home infusion patient by parenteral, intravenous, intramuscular, subcutaneous, or intraspinal infusion*. You may wish to remember it like this: *"A Schedule 2 medication to be prepared and given to a home infusion patient through a needle for immediate administration."*
5. *Alabama Administrative Code: 680-X-3.09* indicates that a Schedule 2 prescription may be faxed by an agent of the prescriber. In addition to including the prescriber's signature on the prescription (in addition to all other legally required information on a Schedule 2 prescription) *the fax must also contain the signature of the agent.*

► **Study Pro Tip** There tends to be confusion between the rules of when a Schedule 2 prescription can be *transmitted by fax* and when a Schedule 2 prescription can be *called in by telephone*. These two situations are compared and contrasted here:

When a schedule 2 prescription (RX) may be transmitted by fax	
Situation	*Does the Fax serve as the RX of record?*
Hospice patient	Yes
Long-term care facility patient	Yes
RX for home infusion patient for immediate parenteral administration	Yes
Fax to a pharmacy prior to a patient's arrival	No
When a schedule 2 prescription (RX) may be called in by telephone[a]	
Situation	
Hospice patient	
Long-term care facility patient	
Home healthcare patient	

[a]Must be an emergency; cannot exceed a 72 hr. supply; the practitioner must supply a hard copy of the prescription to the pharmacy within seven (7) days of the telephoned order

7.5.5 Schedule 3–5 Controlled Substances

7.5.5.1 Original Prescriptions

Prescriptions for medications in Schedules 3–5 may be presented to the pharmacy as a(n) (1) signed paper prescription, (2) prescription called in by telephone, (3) electronic prescription, or (4) fax of a signed paper prescription. In accordance with *Alabama Administrative Code: 680-X-3.10, any faxed order, by an agent of the prescriber, must also contain the signature of that agent* (this is the same as the rule for faxed Schedule 2 prescriptions). Also, a pharmacist may only fill a faxed controlled substance prescription that is *transmitted from the practitioner's office* or a *long term care facility*. Finally, the receiving fax machine *must be located in the prescription department* of the pharmacy.

7.5.5.2 Refills

- *Schedule 3 and 4 medications may be refilled a maximum of 5 times within 6 months of the date it is written*. The prescription expires after 5 refills or 6 months from the date written, whichever comes first.
- When a refill of a Schedule 3 or 4 medication occurs, the following information must be recorded: the *pharmacist's initials*, *date of the refill*, and the *quantity of drug refilled*. This is automatically done by the vast majority of pharmacy computer systems. Prior to the advent of computer systems in pharmacies, when refilling a prescription, the pharmacist would pull the original hard copy of the prescription and write this required information on the back of it.

7.5.5.2.1 Electronic Recordkeeping of Schedule 3 and 4 Medications

As mentioned above, instead of manually recording refill information on the back of each paper prescription, *the storage and retrieval of refill information may be carried out* via *electronic means* (i.e., *by the pharmacy computer*). All information related to the prescription must be retrievable. This includes the prescription number; patient name and address; original date filled; name, address and DEA number of the practitioner; name and quantity of the medication; directions for use and medication dosage form; number of authorized refills; complete refill history with dates and medication quantities. *With regard to all controlled substances, the pharmacy computer must be capable of printing a refill audit trail for any specific patient, practitioner, medication, date, pharmacist, or prescription number. The pharmacy's computer system must be capable of providing this printout within 48 hours of a request*. This information must be stored for at least 2 years from the original date of dispensing.

7.5.5.2.2 Documentation Requirements

- If the pharmacy's computer system provides a printout of all the Schedule 3 and 4 prescriptions refilled that day, each pharmacist who refilled those prescriptions must sign the printout, verifying that the information on the printout is accurate. *This must be completed within 72 hours of the date the refills were dispensed.*
- If the pharmacy's computer system does not provide a printout, then the pharmacy must maintain a bound log book or a separate file in which each pharmacist who dispensed Schedule 3 and 4 drugs that day signs their name, attesting that the refill information entered into the computer that day was accurate for those medications.
- If the pharmacy's computer system is inoperable for a period of time the pharmacy must have a backup system in place to document and store refill information. This contingency plan must ensure that all refills are valid and quantities dispensed are correct. Once the computer is functioning again, the refill information from the "down period" must be entered into it.

7.5.5.3 Transferring Prescriptions in Schedules 3–5

A pharmacy that is registered by the DEA may transfer a controlled substance prescription (Schedules 3–5) to another DEA-registered pharmacy on a one-time basis. However, an original prescription that has not been filled yet, cannot be transferred from one pharmacy to another. In other words, if a physician's office calls in a prescription to your pharmacy for a controlled substance (i.e., lorazepam) and the patients asks you to call it over to a different pharmacy closer to their home, this is not allowed because the prescription has not yet been filled. If the prescription had been filled once, it could legally be transferred to the other pharmacy (assuming enough time had passed to allow the medication to be refilled).

Transfers are subject to the following rules:

- *The prescription may be transferred one time within a six-month period.* If a Schedule 3–5 medication is transferred from Pharmacy A to Pharmacy B, then all subsequent refills must be obtained from Pharmacy B prior to the prescription's expiration 6 months from the date it was written. However, this rule does not apply to pharmacies operating on the same computer system (see below).
- *Pharmacies operating within the same computer system* (i.e., *all pharmacies within the same chain) may transfer refills without limit*—until the prescription runs out of refills or it expires SIX (6) months from its original date. For example, a patient may get all 5 of their phenobarbital refills, a Schedule 4 medication, from 5 different pharmacies within the same chain since they all use the same "real-time" computer system.
- *When a refill for a Schedule 3–5 medication is transferred between pharmacies, the transfer must be made between two licensed pharmacists.* This may also include licensed interns, as interns in Alabama are able to perform the same functions as pharmacists as long as they are under the direct observance of a pharmacist.
- The pharmacist who is transferring the prescription must perform the following steps:
  - Pull the original paper prescription (if it was written on paper) and write "VOID" on its face.
  - On the back of the prescription, the transferring pharmacist shall record their full name (not initials); the full name (not initials) of the pharmacist receiving the transfer; the name, address, and DEA number of the pharmacy receiving the transfer.
  - For an electronic prescription, bring up the prescription on the computer, indicate that the prescription has been transferred, and electronically record the same information (noted above) that would be recorded manually on a paper prescription.
- The pharmacist who is receiving the transferred prescription must perform the following steps:
  - Write "TRANSFER" on the face of the prescription, and reduce to writing everything that is required on a controlled substance prescription. In addition, the pharmacist must record the following information: original date that the

prescription was written; date that the prescription was first filled; original number of refills allowed on the prescription; original prescription number at the transferring pharmacy; number of valid refills remaining on the prescription; dates and locations of previous refills; name, address, and DEA number of the transferring pharmacy; pharmacist's full name (not initials) who is transferring the prescription.

Key Concept

Review of controlled substance original prescriptions (RXs) and refills
Original RXs for schedule 2 medications may be conveyed via:
Paper RX
Electronic RX
Faxed RX in limited situations (see Chap. 4, Sect. 7.5.4)
Oral RX in limited emergency situations
Original RXs for schedule 3–5 medications may be conveyed via:
Paper RX
Orally transmitted RX (i.e., telephoned RX)
Faxed RX
Electronic RX
Options for refill RXs for schedule 2 medications
Not applicable—Schedule 2 medications are not refillable
Options for refill RXs for schedule 3 and 4 medications
A maximum of five (5) refills are allowed within six (6) months of the date the RX was originally written
Options for refill RXs for schedule 5 medications
Schedule 5 medications may be refilled "as authorized by the prescriber"; however, if the RX is partially filled (i.e., the quantity dispensed is less than the full quantity prescribed by the practitioner), then the RX expires 6 months after the date the RX was originally written

8 Dispensing Requirements

8.1 Prescription Labels

The following information is required on the label of a controlled substance medication in Schedules 2–5:

- Prescription number.
- Patient name.
- Prescribing practitioner's name.
- Pharmacy name and address.
- Name of medication, quantity, and directions for use.
- Number of refills if applicable (never applicable for Schedule 2 medications).
- Cautionary statements (i.e., auxiliary labels) if applicable or required.

- The following statement, which is typically preprinted on most pharmacy labels, must be included: *"CAUTION: Federal law prohibits the transfer of this drug to any person other than the patient for whom it was prescribed."*

If the prescription is filled at a central fill pharmacy, the central fill pharmacy must affix a label to the medication package that shows the retail pharmacy's name and address (i.e., the address where the patient dropped off and is picking up the prescription) along with a unique identifier (such as the DEA number of the central fill pharmacy) that specifies the central fill pharmacy that filled the prescription.

The pharmacist must *dispense* the medication to the patient themselves or to a member of the patient's household (a designee authorized by the patient is probably also acceptable, such as a non-live-in caretaker). If the drug is not going to a patient or their representative, then it is being *distributed* not dispensed.

8.2 Partial Filling of a Schedule 2 Prescription

There are 2 situations where a Schedule 2 prescription may be partially filled: (1) The pharmacy does not have enough medication on hand to provide the full quantity that was prescribed and (2) The patient or the prescribing physician requests that the prescription be partially filled.

8.2.1 When the Pharmacy cannot Provide the Full Quantity of the Schedule 2 Prescription. In This Case the Pharmacist Must:

- *Note the quantity dispensed on the front of the prescription (or electronically, as the case may be).*
- *Dispense the remaining quantity to the patient within 72 hours.* If the pharmacy is unable to supply the remaining quantity within 72 hours, the pharmacist must notify the prescribing practitioner and let them know the situation, because no further quantity may be dispensed beyond 72 hours without a new prescription. Of note, *the patient is not required to pick up the medication from the pharmacy within this 72-hour period.*

8.2.2 The Patient or the Practitioner Requests That the Schedule 2 Prescription Be Partially Filled (Which Is Allowed Through the Comprehensive Addiction and Recovery Act of 2016 [CARA]) in this Case, the Following Rules Apply

- The total quantity dispensed in all partial fillings must not exceed the total quantity prescribed.
- *The remaining quantity of the prescription must be filled within 30 days of the original date of the prescription* EXCEPT *if the patient resides in a long-term care facility (LTC) or has a terminal illness, in which case the remainder of the prescription must be dispensed within 60 days of the original date of the*

prescription. If the patient resides in a LTC facility or is terminally ill, the pharmacist must document this on the face of the prescription.

- For each partial filling, the pharmacist must record (in most cases on the pharmacy computer system; if not, then on the back of the prescription) the date of the partial filling, quantity dispensed, remaining quantity authorized to be dispensed, and the identification of the dispensing pharmacist.

Numbers of Importance

Scenario	Number to know
A pharmacy is unable to provide the full quantity of a schedule 2 medication because they do not have the full amount in stock. So they dispense a partial quantity to the patient	The pharmacist must notify the prescriber, write "partial fill" on the face of the RX (or electronic equivalent), and dispense the remainder of the prescription within *72 hours*
The patient or the prescriber requests that a schedule 2 prescription be partially filled, and the patient *does not* reside in a long-term care facility or have a terminal illness	The remaining quantity must be filled within *30 days* of the date the RX was written
The patient or the prescriber requests that a schedule 2 prescription be partially filled, and the patient resides in a long-term care facility or has a terminal illness	The remaining quantity must be filled within *60 days* of the date the RX was written. Also, the pharmacist must document on the face of the RX that the patient resides in a long-term care facility or has a terminal illness

8.3 Partial Filling of Schedule 3–5 Prescriptions

- Partial fillings are allowed for medications in Schedules 3–5 as long as partial fillings are recorded in the same manner as refills (typically electronically).
- *Each partial filling counts as a refill.* So, even if there are dosage units remaining after 5 refills (and it is within 6 months), the prescription is no longer valid, and those remaining dosage units are forfeited.
- The total quantity dispensed in all partial fillings must not exceed the total quantity prescribed.

8.4 Delivery of Controlled Substances to Persons in Other Countries

- Even if a controlled substance is dispensed pursuant to a legitimate prescription in the U.S. , it cannot be delivered or shipped outside of the country without proper authorization.
- In order to legally send controlled substances out of the country, the sender must register with the DEA as an exporter or they must obtain the necessary permits.

9 Security Requirements

9.1 Pharmacy Employees

A DEA registrant (such as a pharmacy) cannot employee someone, and give them access to controlled substances, if they have been previously convicted of a felony related to controlled substances or they previously applied for a DEA registration and their application was denied, revoked, or surrendered for cause (with "surrendered for cause" meaning that the person most likely chose to give up their registration or application before it was taken away because they did something illegal with regard to controlled substances). If a registrant (i.e., pharmacy) feels strongly that they wish to hire someone who meets the above criteria, they may ask the DEA Diversion Control Division for a waiver. However, the DEA would not consider a waiver unless there are valid reasons to believe that drug diversion is unlikely to occur if the person in question is hired.

9.2 Pharmacy Burglary, Robbery, or Theft with Significant Loss of Controlled Drugs

The pharmacist should take the following action when a burglary, robbery, or theft occurs at their pharmacy where there is significant loss (addressed below) of controlled drugs. These steps should be documented in writing and completed within 24 hours of the event:

- Call the police and file a report.
- *Directly* notify the DEA Diversion Field office within 1 day of the event. This means that the pharmacist at the store where the robbery occurred must make the notification (i.e., corporate headquarters does not make the call to the DEA).
- *File DEA Form 106* with the DEA (available online). The pharmacy keeps a copy of this form for 2 years. If, upon further investigation, it is determined that no theft occurred, the pharmacist should notify the DEA in writing.
- Send the following to the ALBOP: (1) a copy of the police report and (2) a copy of DEA form 106 by email or by fax (U.S. mail is not an option) [10].
- If the theft is committed by a licensed or registered member of the ALBOP (i.e., a pharmacist or technician, respectively), the pharmacist must report their name and license number to the ALBOP State Drug Inspector assigned to the area where the pharmacy resides.
- If the theft/robbery/burglary does not involve controlled substances, do not notify the DEA; instead, *notify the ALBOP State Drug Inspector* assigned to the area where the pharmacy resides.

▶ Study Pro Tip What constitutes a "significant loss" of controlled substances?

The term "significant loss" is not defined in the CSA; therefore, the registrant must use their best judgment when determining what represents a significant loss. What would be considered a significant loss for a retail pharmacy may not be considered a significant loss for a hospital or manufacturer. Also, note that small losses over an extended period may indicate diversion and therefore constitute a significant loss. Additional considerations are whether the "missing" drug is likely to be abused (is Percocet® missing or is Lomotil® missing?). Other considerations are whether the loss(es) appear to be associated with the presence of a particular employee or whether the loss appears to be random or associated with a specific time period.

9.3 In-transit Loss or Theft of Controlled Substances

If all or part of an order containing controlled substances does not reach the purchaser, it is the supplier who is responsible for reporting the loss to the DEA using DEA Form 106. Conversely, if the purchaser signs for the order, the purchaser has taken custody of the medications and is responsible for notifying the DEA.

9.3.1 In-transit Loss Involving a Central Fill Pharmacy

A Central Fill Pharmacy fills prescriptions (including prescriptions for controlled substances) on behalf of retail pharmacies with which it has a contractual agreement or with pharmacies who share a common owner. Central fill pharmacies often use a courier service to deliver filled prescriptions to the retail pharmacies with which they contract. Central fill pharmacies are discussed in more detail in Sect. 12. In such cases, if there is an in-transit loss of controlled substance medications, the Central fill pharmacy is responsible for notifying the DEA. Conversely, a retail pharmacy may employ a courier service to retrieve (pick-up) filled prescriptions from the Central fill pharmacy. In such cases, if there is an in-transit loss of controlled substance medications, the retail pharmacy is responsible for notifying the DEA. In other words, the entity (either the central fill pharmacy or the retail pharmacy) who employs the courier to deliver/pickup medications is the one responsible for notifying the DEA of any in-transit loss of controlled substances.

9.4 Breakage or Spillage of Controlled Substances

Neither the CSA nor the DEA provides regulations that specifically address breakage or spillage of controlled substances; however, they do offer the guidance discussed below:

9.4.1 Witnessed Breakage or Spillage of a Controlled Substance

Witnessed breakage or spillage of a controlled substance does not constitute a loss because it can be accounted for (i.e., the medication is not "lost" if multiple people saw it spill onto the floor after a glass bottle was dropped). These types of incidents do not require that the DEA be notified (again, because no "loss" occurred).

9.4.1.1 If the Drug *Is Not* Recoverable (i.e., It Is Spilled on the Floor)

If the drug is not recoverable, the registrant should document the circumstance of the event in their records on *DEA Form 41*, which is used for recording the destruction of controlled substances. The form should be *signed by two individuals* who can testify that the breakage or spillage occurred.

9.4.1.2 If the Drug *Is* Recoverable

If the drug is recoverable (i.e., the pharmacy has a number of broken tablets of a controlled substance [i.e., Norco®]). In this case there are three options that the pharmacist can choose:

- Promptly *destroy the remaining drug* (i.e., broken tablets, if that is the case) using an onsite method of destruction that is in accordance with federal and state laws. "Destroyed" means that the controlled substance is *non-retrievable*.
- *Send the contents to a reverse distributor*. If the drug is a Schedule 2 medication, the reverse distributor fills out DEA Form 222 with the name and quantity of the medication it will be receiving from the pharmacy. Once the reverse distributor destroys the controlled substance(s) the reverse distributor is responsible for submitting a DEA Form 41 to the DEA. DEA Form 41 is *not* used to document the transfer of controlled substances from the pharmacy to the reverse distributor.
- Contact the local DEA Diversion Control Office and ask for assistance in disposing of the controlled substance. There is never a situation where drugs are to be forwarded to the DEA unless the registrant has received prior approval.

9.5 Robberies and Burglaries Involving Controlled Substances

The Controlled Substance Registration Protection Act of 1984 (CSRPA), which was enacted to protect DEA registrants against certain crimes, identifies specific conditions where the federal government gets involved in the investigation of controlled substance burglaries or robberies.

10 Transfer or Disposal of Controlled Substances

10.1 Transfer of Controlled Substances to the Original Supplier or the Manufacturer

In the event of a medication recall, the recalled medication is typically returned to the entity from which it is obtained (i.e., the supplier or manufacturer). If a pharmacy transfers (sends back) Schedule 3–5 controlled substances to either the original supplier or the manufacturer they must maintain a written record showing the information below (note that this is the same information that would be included on an invoice for Schedule 3–5 substances):

- The date of the transaction.
- Name, strength, dosage form, and quantity of controlled substances.
- Name, address, and DEA number of the supplier or manufacturer where the drugs are being sent.

If Schedule 2 medications are being shipped, DEA Form 222 must be prepared to document the transfer. In this case, the supplier or manufacturer would prepare DEA Form 222 because they are receiving the drug from the pharmacy. The pharmacy would contact the supplier or manufacturer ahead of time and tell them the names and quantities of the Schedule 2 medications.

11 Authorized Collectors

11.1 The Secure and Responsible Drug Disposal Act

The Secure and Responsible Drug Disposal Act was signed into action in 2010. The purpose of this act was to give ultimate users or their representative the ability to lawfully dispose of unwanted controlled substances as a means of preventing diversion. This act gave the following entities authorization to collect controlled substances, via mail-back programs or onsite collection receptacles, from ultimate users: manufacturers, distributers, reverse distributors, narcotic treatment programs, hospitals/clinics with an on-site pharmacy, and retail pharmacies. A general rule is that collection receptacles must be kept securely within a building (i.e., not outside as a "dropbox" would function) in an area that can be readily monitored by employees.

- A retail pharmacy or a clinic/hospital pharmacy can become an authorized collector of controlled substances by modifying their DEA registration. In other words, they do not need to get a new registration, they simply modify their current registration at no cost.

- A retail pharmacy that is authorized as a collection location must maintain its collection receptacle so that it is (a) securely inside the location, (b) in the vicinity where controlled substances are stored, (c) viewable from the pharmacy counter.
- A hospital/clinic with an onsite pharmacy that is authorized as a collection location must maintain its collection receptacle in an area that is regularly monitored by employees. The receptacle cannot be located in an area where emergency or urgent care is provided (presumably due to chaos and traffic that might make it possible for someone to remove drugs from the receptacle without being noticed).
- A long-term care facility that is authorized as a collection location must maintain its collection receptacle securely in an area that is regularly (i.e., routinely) monitored by LTC facility employees. A LTC facility employee may dispose of controlled substances into a collection receptacle on behalf of a patient. This should ideally be done immediately, but it must be done within THREE (3) business days of discontinuation of use. This typically occurs when a patient's medication has been discontinued, they have been discharged, or they are recently deceased.

► **Study Pro Tip** With regard to DEA Form 222, remember that *it is always the entity receiving the Schedule 2 medication(s) that fills out DEA Form 222*. This could be (1) a pharmacy that is ordering Schedule 2 medications from a supplier—perhaps the most common scenario, (2) a pharmacy that is conducting its initial inventory where it is taking over the inventory—including Schedule 2 drugs—of a pharmacy going out of business, or (3) a practitioner, reverse distributor, supplier, or manufacturer who will be receiving Schedule 2 medications from a pharmacy.

11.2 Authorized Collection Activities

- Ultimate users (i.e., patients) in lawful possession of controlled substances (Schedules 2–5) can drop them off in a receptacle of an authorized collector; *this does not include street drugs or other dangerous or illicit substances*.
- *Ultimate users may comingle non-controlled drugs with controlled drugs* when depositing medications into receptacles (i.e., it is OK for a patient to drop off ibuprofen with alprazolam).
- Ideally, controlled substances should be dropped off in their original container, although it is not possible to enforce this.
- Once controlled substances are deposited into a receptacle they are not inventoried. In other words, they are not counted, sorted, or otherwise handled. This is why these collection receptacles are so closely guarded—because if anyone removed medications from one of these receptacles there would be no way of knowing what was missing!

11.3 The Collection Receptacle and Inner Liner

- The collection receptacle consists of an outer secure container with a removable inside liner.
- The collection receptacle must be securely fastened to a permanent structure so that it cannot be removed, and it must be locked.

11.3.1 The Outer Container

- The outer container of the collection receptacle must have a sign indicating that only Schedule 2–5 drugs may be added (with an exception for comingled non-controlled drugs).
- The outer container of the collection receptacle has a small opening that allows contents to be added to the inside liner but not removed. The small opening must be locked when an employee is not present. An exception to this rule pertains to collection receptacles at narcotic treatment programs. At a narcotic treatment program, the receptacle is located in a room that does not contain any other controlled substances, and it remains locked with controlled access. Note that this is essentially the "opposite" of where receptacles are stored in a retail pharmacy (i.e., in direct proximity to controlled substances).

11.3.2 The Inner Liner

- Important requirements govern the installation, removal, and general handling of the inner liner (Table 4.8).

11.3.2.1 Installation and Removal

- When the inner liner of the receptacle is installed or removed, two employees of the authorized collector must do the job—*Why is this so?* Again, recall that the drugs inside the inner liner are never inventoried, so nobody knows if something

Table 4.8 Key requirements for the inner liner

It must be tamper-evident
It must be sealable immediately upon removal (so that its contents are never emptied or even touched)
It must be tear-resistant, waterproof, and have its size clearly marked on it
It must contain a unique number (i.e., a serial number) so that it can be tracked. If inner liners were not tracked via serial numbers it would be easy for an entire bag to "go missing"
The contents within the inner liner must not be viewable from the outside
Access to the inner liner shall be restricted to employees of the collector (not the establishment where the receptacle resides, such as retail pharmacy employees)
As with installation and removal, the inner liner must be sealed by two employees of the collector
The sealed liner must not be opened, X-rayed, analyzed, or otherwise penetrated by anyone
All liner information (serial number; size; address and DEA number of the location etc.) is recorded when the liner is installed, when it is removed and sealed, when it is transferred to storage, and when it is transferred from storage for destruction. Note that *an inner liner may only be stored at a LTCF for THREE (3) days* before it is taken away for destruction. The names of the employees performing these activities are recorded as well

goes missing. Having two people install/remove inner liners reduces the chance of diversion.

- For installation or removal of an inner liner from a collection receptacle at an LTC facility either two employees of the authorized collector must do the job, or it must be carried out by one employee of the authorized collector and one supervisor level employee of the LTC facility (i.e., a charge nurse).

> **Study Pro Tip** Record keeping for inner liners involves recording every step of their existence, starting with their installation and ending with the destruction of their contents. In this sense, inner liners are similar to controlled substances in that they are tracked "from cradle to grave."

12 Other Pharmacy Operations

12.1 Central Fill Pharmacy

As explained in Chap. 9 and in Sect. 9.3.1 of this chapter, a central fill pharmacy fills prescriptions (including prescriptions for controlled substances) on behalf of retail pharmacies with which it has a contractual agreement or with pharmacies who share a common owner.

12.1.1 Recordkeeping

- Both the central fill pharmacy and the retail pharmacy must keep records that document the disposition (incoming and outgoing) of all controlled substances.
- Regarding controlled substances, a central fill pharmacy must maintain the same records and employ the same security measures as a retail pharmacy.

12.1.2 Operations

- Some retail pharmacies also perform central fill activities. In such cases, the retail pharmacy does not have to get a separate DEA registration (their DEA registration as a retail pharmacy is sufficient).
- Central fill pharmacies are permitted to fill new prescriptions for controlled substances and to refill prescriptions for controlled substances.
- Both the central fill pharmacy and the retail pharmacy have a corresponding responsibility to make sure that all prescriptions for controlled substances are written for a legitimate medical purpose by a practitioner in their usual course of practice.
- Prescription information is provided by the retail pharmacy to the central fill pharmacy.
- Schedule 2–5 prescriptions may be distributed electronically (including by fax) from the retail to the central fill pharmacy.

- For electronic prescriptions for controlled substances, the following information must be transmitted: (a) The name, address, and DEA of the central fill pharmacy to which the prescription has been transmitted (this makes sense because they are the ones actually filling the prescription); (b) name of the pharmacist (not initials) at the retail pharmacy who is transmitting the prescription; (c) the date of transmittal.
- For paper prescriptions for controlled substances, the following information must be written on the face of the prescription: "CENTRAL FILL." The prescription must also contain the (a) name, address, and DEA of the central fill pharmacy to which the prescription has been sent to be filled (b) name of the pharmacist (not initials) at the retail pharmacy who is transmitting the prescription; (c) the date of transmittal. Note that the prescription being sent/transmitted to the central fill pharmacy must contain the same information regardless of how it is transferred.
- The retail pharmacy is responsible for making sure that a controlled substance prescription has all of the required information included on it (see Sect. 7 of this chapter). The retail pharmacy must keep the original prescription for 2 years from the date it was last filled (not 2 years from the date written or the date first filled).
- After the central fill pharmacy fills the prescription, they send the medication back to the retail pharmacy. The retail pharmacy keeps a record of receipt from the central fill pharmacy. This receipt must contain (a) the date, (b) method of delivery (i.e., contract carrier and private courier), and (c) the name of the retail pharmacy employee who signed for the delivery.
- The central fill pharmacy must (a) keep a copy of the prescription (either in electronic form or a faxed paper copy), (b) record the date they received the prescription, (c) date(s) that the prescription is filled or refilled, and (d) the name of the pharmacist filling the prescription. The central fill pharmacy must also keep a record of the date the filled prescription was returned to the retail pharmacy (i.e., both the central fill and the retail pharmacy keep records documenting the transmittal and return of prescriptions).
- The central fill pharmacy must attach a label to the package they are sending back to the retail pharmacy. Note that this is not the label that goes on the prescription bottle. Think of this as the label that is stapled to the bag when you pick up a prescription. This label must contain the following information: (a) date the prescription was filled (b) prescription number (c) name of the patient (d) name of the prescriber (e) the retail pharmacy's name and address (this may seem counterintuitive, that the central fill pharmacy would attach a receipt with the retail pharmacy's name and address on it) (f) a unique identifier, indicating that the prescription was filled at a central pharmacy; this "unique identifier" can be the DEA number of the central fill pharmacy (g) directions for use and cautionary statements if any.

12.2 Automated Dispensing Units (ADU) at Long-Term Care Facilities

An ADU is a mechanical unit that stores and dispenses medications; this also includes packaging, counting, and labeling the medications. These units are managed remotely by a retail pharmacy, which keeps records of all transactions. The DEA allows a retail pharmacy to register at the site of the LTC facility. Some retail pharmacies may have ADUs at multiple LTC facilities. If so, these retail pharmacies are allowed to store most records required for these sites/units at the retail pharmacy or at another central location approved by the DEA. If a retail pharmacy wants to operate an ADU at a LTC facility, they need to contact the DEA Office of Diversion Control to get instructions on how to register. Additional rules and regulations regarding ADUs that do not pertain specifically to controlled substances are discussed in detail in Chap. 13.

12.3 Emergency Kits for LTC Facilities

Emergency kits differ from ADUs and stat cabinets. It is easy to confuse rules and requirements when it comes to these methods of medication storage. Appendix H of the Pharmacist's Manual: An Informative Outline of the Controlled Substances Act lists guidelines for emergency kits at long-term care facilities.

For an institutional facility, such as a LTC facility, that does not have a pharmacy in it, drugs may be provided (for use by authorized personnel) via emergency kits located at the facility. Additional rules and regulations regarding emergency kits that do not pertain specifically to controlled substances are discussed in detail in Chap. 13.

12.4 Opioid Addiction Treatment Programs: Methadone

Practitioners who wish to dispense methadone (a Schedule 2 drug) for opioid maintenance and detoxification must (a) obtain a separate DEA registration as a Narcotic Treatment Program (NTP) via DEA Form 363 and (b) get approval and certification by the Center for Substance Abuse Treatment (CSAT) within the Substance Abuse and Mental Health Services Administration (SAMHSA) of the U.S. Department of Health and Human Services. Note that the practitioner (a person) must become registered as a Narcotic Treatment Program (a program), which may strike some as odd wording.

- *Any practitioner who is authorized by the DEA to prescribe controlled substances may prescribe methadone for pain.* The practitioner only needs to register as an NTP if they wish to prescribe methadone for opioid maintenance or detoxification.

12.5 Opioid Addiction Treatment: Buprenorphine +/– Naloxone

The following medications are each used for opioid maintenance and/or detoxification: buprenorphine + naloxone sublingual film (Suboxone®), buprenorphine sublingual tablets (Subutex®), and buprenorphine extended- release injection for subcutaneous use (Sublocade®). Each of these products is a Schedule 3 medication. These medications may also be used for the treatment of pain. There used to be limitations and restrictions on which practitioners could prescribe buprenorphine-containing products. However, this has recently changed so that any prescriber who is registered with the DEA to prescribe controlled substances may prescribe buprenorphine (with or without naloxone) for the opioid maintenance and/or detoxification, or for pain.

12.5.1 Alabama Requirements

- *Phoning in a buprenorphine prescription to a pharmacy:* if a buprenorphine prescription is being used to treat pain, it may be phoned into a pharmacy. If it is being used for opioid maintenance or detoxification, it cannot be phoned in unless the prescriber obtains a HIPAA release from the patient. If the patient brings in a paper prescription for a buprenorphine-containing prescription, a HIPAA release is not required [11].
- Alabama requires the following counseling points be shared with the patient when buprenorphine-containing products are dispensed: (a) warn of risk of overdose when combined with other agents that cause central nervous system (CNS) depression (i.e., benzodiazepines and alcohol) (b) warn of the risk of operating heavy machinery or driving while taking buprenorphine (c) instruct the patient to notify their prescriber about other medications they may be taking or may take in the future [12].
- An Alabama pharmacist may fill an out-of-state prescription for a buprenorphine-containing product if they feel the prescription is being filled out of state for a legitimate reason (i.e., the patient is deployed, is traveling for work, or is on vacation). The pharmacist must still take all necessary steps to ensure that the prescription is being filled for a legitimate medical purpose in the practitioner's normal course of practice.

12.6 Delivery of a Controlled Substance to an Administering Practitioner: When a Pharmacy Delivers a Controlled Substance to an Administering Practitioner, the Following Conditions Must Be Met

- The pharmacy must deliver the controlled substance to the address that is on the practitioner's DEA certificate of registration.

- The controlled substance must be administered for the purpose of opioid maintenance or detoxification and it must be administered by injection or implantation (i.e., Sublocade®).
- The prescription must be written for a specific patient and the practitioner must administer the drug to that patient within 14 days of receiving it from the pharmacy.
- The prescribing practitioner or the practitioner who administered the controlled substance (this could be the same person) must maintain complete and accurate records of all controlled substances received, administered, or otherwise disposed of.

12.7 Controlled Substance Distribution by a Pharmacy: The "Five Percent Rule"

A pharmacy that is registered to dispense controlled substances may also *distribute* controlled substances to another pharmacy or a practitioner (who then dispenses the medications to patients). The *Five Percent Rule* states that the *total number of dosage units* (for simplicity sake, you may think of these as "tablets," although they may include other dosage forms as well) of all controlled substances *distributed* (i.e., sent to another pharmacy or practitioner for subsequent dispensing) *may not exceed five percent of the total number of dosage units* dispensed *and* distributed *by the pharmacy during a calendar year* (Fig. 4.3).

12.7.1 Additional Conditions that Apply to the "Five Percent Rule"

- The pharmacy or practitioner receiving the controlled substance(s) must be licensed by the DEA to dispense controlled substances.
- The distributing pharmacy and the recipient (either another pharmacy or a practitioner) must each record the transaction(s) in accordance with DEA requirements (remember, this will be DEA Form 222 or electronic equivalent for Schedule 2 drugs, and most likely an invoice for Schedule 3–5 drugs). Also recall that the distributing pharmacy, acting as the "supplier" in this situation, keeps the original copy of the DEA Form 222.

$$\frac{\text{Units Distributed}}{\text{Units Distributed} + \text{Units Dispensed}} \times 100 = \text{Percent Distributed}$$

"Units" refers to the number of controlled substance dosage units.
"Percent Distributed" must be less than 5%; if this number exceeds 5% at any time during the calendar year the pharmacy must register as a distributer

Fig. 4.3 Five percent rule

12.8 United States Postal Service Requirements for Mailing Controlled Substances

Authorized handlers of controlled substances (i.e., manufacturers, suppliers, pharmacies and anyone else approved by the DEA) may lawfully send them through the mail as long as either the mailer (sender) or the addressee (recipient) is registered by the DEA or exempt from DEA registration.

12.8.1 Guidance from the U.S. Postal Service on Mailing Controlled Substances

- The package must not be outwardly dangerous.
- The inner package must be marked and sealed in accordance with the CSA.
- The outer package must be securely wrapped in a plain wrapper. *In other words, in order to deter diversion, the package should not publicize the fact that it contains a controlled substance.*

12.9 Patients Bringing Medications from Home to the Hospital

If a patient is admitted to a hospital via an ambulance and (a) there are no family members present and (b) they have controlled substance medications with them, it is the DEA's position that:

- If the practitioner treating the patient at the DEA-registered hospital feels it would be medically appropriate for them to continue taking the controlled substance, the hospital can secure the controlled substance with the patient's belongings in their hospital room (i.e., in a small safe for example). In this case, the hospital does not take possession of the controlled substance, so no unlawful distribution (by the patient to the hospital) takes place.
- If the practitioner treating the patient at the DEA-registered hospital feels it would NOT be medically appropriate for them to continue taking the controlled substance, or if it is the hospital's policy not to allow patients to bring controlled substances into the hospital, then the hospital has the following options:
- The hospital can give the drug to a relative of the patient who can take the drug home or deposit it into a receptacle at the hospital (if the hospital is an authorized collector of controlled substances).
- The hospital can provide the patient's relative with an empty mail-back package, so that they can mail the controlled substance to a DEA-registered reverse distributor.
- If the patient does not have a friend or relative who can take the controlled substance, the hospital may contact local law enforcement and ask them to dispose of the medication.

13 Combat Methamphetamine Epidemic Act (CMEA) of 2005

The CMEA includes requirements that must be followed by regulated sellers of List 1 chemicals (ephedrine, phenylpropanolamine [PPA], and pseudoephedrine), since these chemicals can be used in the illegal manufacture of methamphetamine. Because ephedrine and PPA are no longer available in the U.S, these requirements apply exclusively to the retail sale of the over-the-counter product, *pseudoephedrine* (Sudafed®). *"Regulated seller"* refers to a *retail distributor* (typically a pharmacy, but also a mobile retail vendor).

13.1 Scheduled Listed Chemical Products (SLCPs)

SLCPs are a new category of products that include ephedrine, phenylpropanolamine [PPA], and pseudoephedrine. SLCPs refer only to non-prescription (over-the-counter) products. These products (and again, we're really only talking about pseudoephedrine and all of its salts and isomers) are subject to specific rules regarding their sale. Pseudoephedrine can only be sold by a pharmacy that is licensed by the ALBOP (i.e., it cannot be sold by a gas station or smoke shop) and it must be stored behind the counter or in a locked cabinet (also discussed in Chap. 10).

13.1.1 Identification Requirements

- Regulated sellers of pseudoephedrine must check the identity of purchasers and keep a log (written or electronic) of each sale that includes: *date, time,* and *quantity of pseudoephedrine sold* and the *purchaser's name, address*, and *signature.*
- The seller must also check the identification (ID) of the purchaser and verify that the name on the ID is consistent with the name recorded in the log book. Valid forms of ID include a/an:
  - Valid driver's license (not expired!)
  - US or foreign passport.
  - State ID card.
  - Uniformed Services identification.
  - Alien registration receipt care or permanent resident card.
  - Employment authorization document that contains a photograph.

13.1.2 Age Requirement

In Alabama, a person must be at least 18 years old to purchase pseudoephedrine [13].

13.1.3 Recordkeeping (Log Book Requirements)

The following requirements must be followed with regard to the log book in which SLCP sales are recorded:

- Can be written or electronic.
- Must be kept for at least 2 years.
- Must include a notice to purchasers that entering false information in the log book may lead to criminal penalties.

13.1.4 Quantity of Pseudoephedrine That Can Legally Be Purchased

- The maximum amount of pseudoephedrine that can be purchased during a calendar day is 3.6 grams.
- The maximum amount of pseudoephedrine that can be purchased in a 30-day period is 7.5 grams.
- If a person purchases no more than 60 mg of pseudoephedrine (i.e., a single sale unit-dose package), the log book requirement does not apply.

13.1.5 Training Required to Sell SLCPs (Pseudoephedrine)

Regulated sellers of SLCPs) are responsible for training their employees in all of the requirements pertaining to the sale of pseudoephedrine. This includes a *Self-Certification process* that must be completed by all employees who sell pseudoephedrine; this process certifies to the DEA that the training has occurred. The training must be completed *annually* and can be done from any computer. The seller must maintain records showing that their employees have undergone self-certification training.

13.1.6 Loss or Theft of SLCPs) (Pseudoephedrine)

Report loss orally to the DEA office as soon as possible, and file a written report of losses using DEA Form 107 within FIFTEEN (15) days of becoming aware of the loss.

13.1.7 Distribution of Bulk Quantities of SLCPs) (Pseudoephedrine)

If a pharmacy wishes to distribute bulk quantities of SLCPs they must register with the DEA as a chemical distributor using online *DEA Form 510*.

14 Ryan Haight Online Pharmacy Consumer Protection Act of 2008

The purpose of the Ryan Haight Act is to combat rogue Internet sites that unlawfully dispense controlled substances. The act applies to all controlled substances from all Schedules. Specifically, the Ryan Haight act states that *It is against federal law to deliver, distribute, or dispense a controlled substance by means of the Internet unless the pharmacy is registered by the DEA as an online pharmacy*. To be registered as an online pharmacy, the pharmacy would have to have a modification to their standard DEA registration, indicating that they are authorized to operate as an online pharmacy. A pharmacy that violates the Ryan Haight Act is subject to criminal penalties.

14.1 Definition of an Online Pharmacy

An online pharmacy is any person, entity, or Internet site, in the United States or abroad, that knowingly delivers, distributes, or dispenses a controlled substance by means of the Internet. Reworded for simplicity, an online pharmacy is any web site that purposely sells (or offers to sell) a controlled substance to someone who places an order for it. This also includes (a) the person who operates such a website, (b) any person who pays a practitioner to write prescriptions for controlled substances for customers of such a website, (c) any person who pays a pharmacy to fill prescriptions for controlled substances that were issued to customers of such a web site, (d) any pharmacy that knowingly fills prescriptions for controlled substances that were issued to customers of such a website, (e) any person who sends an email that offers to sell a controlled substance or a prescription for a controlled substance in a manner not authorized by the act, and (f) any person who sends an email that directs buyers to a website operating in violation of the act. As you can see, an online pharmacy may be defined in many ways, and these definitions can be confusing. To summarize, any time a website or email is used to issue controlled substance prescriptions, fill controlled substance prescriptions, distribute controlled substances, or advertise the sale of controlled substances, where the pharmacy is not registered by the DEA as an online pharmacy, the Ryan Haight Act has been violated.

14.2 Notification Requirements

Thirty days before offering a controlled substance for sale on the Internet, an online pharmacy must notify the DEA, and the state boards of pharmacy in all states where they plan to sell/deliver controlled substances. Notification of the DEA is achieved by completion of the Application for Modification of Registration for Online Pharmacies. The online pharmacy must certify to the DEA that they have given notice to the state boards of pharmacy in the states where they plan to distribute controlled substances (which they do separately).

14.3 How to Register as an Online Pharmacy

First, the would-be online pharmacy must be registered with the DEA via a standard registration. Then, the pharmacy can apply (online) to modify their registration at no cost. If the modification is approved, the DEA issues a modified DEA registration certificate with the new business activity, listed as "*online pharmacy.*" Notably, the online pharmacy can still function as a retail pharmacy, and it does so under the same DEA number.

14.4 State Licensure Requirements

When pharmacies complete the *Application for Modification of Registration for Online Pharmacies*, they have to certify that they are in compliance with all state laws. An online pharmacy must list the states in which it is licensed, and it can only dispense medications to patients residing in those states.

14.5 Online Pharmacy Website Requirements

- When a pharmacy applies to modify its DEA registration to become an online pharmacy, it must state the following on its website's home page:
  "In accordance with the controlled substance act and the DEA regulations, this online pharmacy has made the notifications to the DEA administrator required by 21 U.S.C. 831 and 21 CFR 1304.40."
- Once a pharmacy receives approval to operate as an online pharmacy, it must display a declaration on its website's homepage that it is in compliance with the requirements of 21 U.S.C 831 with respect to the delivery and sale of controlled substances.
- An online pharmacy is required to post *Internet Pharmacy Site Disclosure Information* on the homepage of each Internet site it operates. This information must be posted in a clear and visible manner and state the following:
  - Name and address of the pharmacy as it appears on the DEA registration.
  - Pharmacy's telephone number and email address.
  - Name of the pharmacist in charge, professional degree, state(s) of licensure, and phone number.
  - A list of states where the pharmacy is licensed to dispense controlled substances.
  - Certification that the pharmacy is registered to dispense controlled substances via the Internet.
  - Name, address, phone number, professional degree, and states of licensure of any practitioner who has a contractual relationship to provide medical evaluations or issue prescriptions for controlled substances, through referrals from the website or at the request of the owner or operator of the website, or any employee or agent thereof.
  - The following statement must be displayed on the website:
    "This online pharmacy is obligated to comply fully with the Controlled Substances Act and DEA regulations. As part of this obligation, this online pharmacy has obtained a modified DEA registration authorizing it to operate as an online pharmacy. In addition, this online pharmacy will only dispense a controlled substance to a person who has a valid prescription issued for a legitimate medical purpose based upon a medical relationship with a prescribing practitioner. This includes at least one prior in-person medical evaluation in accordance with section 309 of the Controlled Substances Act

(21 U.S.C. 829), or a medical evaluation via *telemedicine in accordance with section 102(54) of the Controlled Substances Act (21 U.S.C. 802(54)).*"

14.6 Reporting Requirements

- Each online pharmacy must submit a report to the DEA, detailing the amount of each controlled substance dispensed by the pharmacy during the previous *calendar month* (notice it does not say "the previous 30 days").
- A detailed report is required if *EITHER* (1) ONE HUNDRED (100) or more prescriptions for controlled substances (Schedules 2–5) were filled during the previous calendar month *OR* (2) FIVE THOUSAND (5000) or more dosage units of controlled substances (Schedules 2–5) were dispensed during the previous calendar month. If either of these criteria are met, the pharmacy must generate a report that includes the *total amount of controlled substances dispensed by any means* (this includes Internet transactions, mail-order transactions, face-to-face transactions, etc. The report does not have to specify the means of dispensing).
- The report is due on or before the 15th of each month, and reports are kept for TWO (2) years. These reports are required for all pharmacies that have a modified DEA registration that authorizes them to operate as an online pharmacy, regardless of whether or not they dispense any controlled substances by means of the Internet that month.
- If neither of the criteria in Sect. 14.7 are met, a report is still required. The report simply indicates a "negative response" for the previous calendar month.

▶ **Numbers of Importance** An online pharmacy must submit a report to the DEA, detailing the quantity of each controlled substance they dispensed (either via online prescriptions or prescriptions filled in the retail setting) *if one of the following conditions are met*:

The pharmacy filled 100 or more controlled substance prescriptions in the previous calendar month. This includes all schedules (i.e., 2–5).

The pharmacy filled 5000 or more dosage units of controlled substances in the previous calendar month. This includes all schedules (i.e., 2–5).

The report is due on or before the 15th of each month, and reports are kept for TWO (2) years.

14.7 Prescription Requirements

- Definition of a valid prescription: it must be written for a legitimate medical purpose in the usual course of professional practice *by a practitioner who has conducted at least one in-person medical evaluation of the patient*. An exception would be a practitioner who is covering for another practitioner (i.e., the "in-person" medical evaluation would not be required in that situation).

- A pharmacy website is *exempted* from the definition of an online pharmacy if its Internet-facilitated activity relating to controlled substances is limited to filling new and/or refilling controlled prescriptions in Schedule 3–5 *IF*: (a) the pharmacy dispensing the controlled substance prescription has previously dispensed that prescription to the patient (i.e., the "original prescription") other than by means of the Internet *and* the pharmacy contacts the practitioner who issued the original prescription and asks them for authorization to fill it again. This is confusing at first because it appears to be stating that all pharmacies who use the Internet for new or refill prescriptions are exempt from registering as an online pharmacy. The *key* to understanding this exemption, is that the "new" prescription referred to in the above statement is indeed technically new; however, it is for a (controlled) medication *that the patient has received previously by means other than the Internet*, and the pharmacy is asking the same prescriber who wrote the original prescription to "re-new" (not refill) it once again.

References

1. United States. Drug Enforcement Administration. Office of Compliance and Regulatory Affairs. (1980). Pharmacist's manual : an informational outline of the Controlled Substances Act of 1970. Washington, D.C: U.S. Dept. of Justice, Drug Enforcement Administration. 2022 Edition. chrome-extension: //efaidnbmnnnibpcajpcglclefindmkaj. https://www.deadiversion.usdoj.gov/GDP/(DEA-DC-046R1)(EO-DEA154R1)_Pharmacist's_Manual_DEA.pdf (accessed July 12, 2024)
2. Alabama State Board of Pharmacy (ALBOP) Administrative Code Chapter 680-X-3.
3. Alabama Uniform Controlled Substances, and the Alabama Board of Medical Examiners Administrative Code Chapter 540-X-4 Controlled Substances Certificate
4. Hartley C 2nd, Bulloch M, Penzak SR. Clinical Pharmacology of the Dietary Supplement Kratom (Mitragyna speciosa). J Clin Pharmacol. 2022 May;62(5):577–593. doi: https://doi.org/10.1002/jcph.2001. Epub 2022 Jan 5. PMID: 34775626
5. ALBOP Administrative Code Chapter 680-X-3.01
6. Using DEA Form 222 to order controlled substances. University of Minnesota, Driven to Discover. https://hsrm.umn.edu/department-environmental-health-safety/lab-research-safety/controlled-substances/purchasing/using (accessed July 12, 2024)
7. Alabama Administrative Code: 680-X-3.08
8. Alabama Administrative Code 680-X-3-.06
9. Alabama Board of Medical Examiners Administrative Code: 540-X-4.06
10. Alabama Administrative Code 680-X-3-.07
11. Code of Federal Regulations, Title 42, Subchapter A, Part 2
12. Alabama Board of Pharmacy, Frequently Asked Questions: https://albop.com/frequently-asked-questions/#medications (accessed July 12, 2024)
13. Code of Alabama §20-2-190

The Structure of Pharmacy Practice in Alabama

5

Opiferque per Obem dictor (I am called for help throughout the world)

—Motto of the Worshipful Society of Apothecaries.

1 Pharmacy in Alabama

The practice of pharmacy, including the operation of pharmacies, is considered a matter of public health, safety, and welfare in the state of Alabama [1]. The laws, rules, regulations, and policies that govern pharmacy in this state all have that central consideration at their core. The Alabama State Board of Pharmacy was officially established by the state legislature in 1887 [2]. It was intended that the board would resemble the demographics of the pharmacy profession in the state. Alabama laws are categorized by title and chapter numbers. The board is officially given the authority to carry out and enforce Title 34, Chapter 23, also known as the Practice of Pharmacy Act 205, and Title 20, Chapter 2, the Alabama Uniform Controlled Substance Act [3].

It is important to remember that pharmacy is governed by both state and federal rules and regulations. With a few exceptions, most laws and rules on the actual practice of pharmacy is left to the states to regulate. There are topics that are covered at both the federal and state level; in Alabama, these areas are generally in alignment with one another. While federal and state law and rules can differ in depth and stringency, they do not oppose one another.

M. N. Bulloch et al., *Pharmacy Law in Alabama*,
https://doi.org/10.1007/978-3-031-84771-4_5

2 The Alabama Board of Pharmacy

2.1 The Alabama Practice of Pharmacy Act

The Alabama Practice of Pharmacy Act (Practice Act) outlines what the Alabama Board of Pharmacy is (ALBOP), who may serve on the board, how it operates, what authority the board has, what responsibility it is entrusted with, and the process for judicial appeal or disputes of ALBOP actions [4]. While much of the Practice Act is broad in scope, the law is quite specific on some aspects related to the ALBOP. An important aspect of the ALBOP is that it allows the practice of pharmacy within the state to be directed by those within the profession. This is an essential foundational principle for any profession and ensures that pharmacy will always be overseen with those who are committed to its best interests and to the health and welfare of our patients.

2.2 Composition of the Alabama Board of Pharmacy

As of the begining of 2025, the ALBOP is composed of FIVE (5) members who represent different practice settings within pharmacy (Table 5.1) [3, 5]. The members have staggered five-year terms with one seat changing each year. To ensure fresh perspectives on the ALBOP, no member may serve two terms consecutively, but there is nothing to prohibit a pharmacist from serving on the ALBOP multiple times, in nonconsecutive terms. All candidates must have had an *active* Alabama pharmacist

Table 5.1 Membership on the Alabama Board of Pharmacy [3, 5]

	Nominated by	Specific nomination requirements	Seat obtained by
Hospital pharmacy	Alabama Society of Health System Pharmacists		Governor appointment
Independent community pharmacy	Alabama Pharmacy Association (APA)	Only APA members who practice at an independent pharmacy participate in the nomination process	Governor appointment
Chain pharmacy	Alabama Pharmacy Association	A "Chain" is considered any retail pharmacy employing ≥40 full-time pharmacists Candidates must be employed full-time by a chain pharmacy for ≥3 years Only APA members who practice at a chain pharmacy participate in the nominating process	Governor appointment
At-large or non-designated—TWO (2) positions	Alabama Pharmacy Association		Pharmacist vote

license for at least FIVE (5) years and must be *actively* engaged in the practice of pharmacy. Members must continue to practice (e.g., remain employed) while serving on the Board.

Key Concept
In order to serve on the Alabama Board of Pharmacy, a person must be an ACTIVE pharmacist. They must have an active Alabama pharmacist license AND actually practicing pharmacy and/or pharmacy administration in the state throughout their board term.

Each January, the ALBOP meeting includes four returning members and one new member. THREE (3) members of the ALBOP are appointed by the Governor to fill seats that represent a particular practice setting [5]. The Governor appoints ONE (1) person from a slate of three (3) candidates nominated by specific state pharmacy organizations (which are mentioned in the law by name) the year prior to that seat becoming vacant. These three designated seats represent *independent* pharmacy, *hospital* pharmacy, and *chain* pharmacy and the person who is appointed to the seat should work in that practice setting. Of note, the law does not specify that the independent pharmacy seat must be held by a pharmacy owner, only that the person must work at an independent community pharmacy. Typically, though not required, the designated organization announces the names of the candidates whose names will be submitted to the Governor midyear; this then allows the Governor the remainder of the year to interview the candidates and make an official decision and nomination.

The remining two members of the ALBOP represent pharmacists at-large, may be filled from a pharmacist from any practice setting and are voted on by pharmacists with an active Alabama license [5]. The year prior to an at-large seat vacancy, the Alabama Pharmacy Association forms a nominating committee of five (5) pharmacist members who receives nominations and narrows a list of candidates to two names. These two candidates are required by the Practice Act to prepare a biographical sketch of 150 words or less, including their most recent practice experience, which is included on the ballots. Ballots are distributed to everyone with an active pharmacist license in Alabama by a third party (a company contracted to conduct the vote). Voting must begin by September 1 and be received by October 1. A simple majority is required to win the seat.

An ALBOP member may elect to step down at any time during their five-year term [5]. Otherwise, the only way a board member may be removed by the board is if the Governor removes them for proven charges of inefficiency, incompetency, immorality, or professional misconduct. If a vacancy occurs for an unexpired term, it is filled in the same manner as required based on the type of seat (Governor appointment or elected). The person selected to step into a vacant seat is then a member of the ALBOP for an entire 5 years (rather than just the remaining duration of the unexpired term).

▶ Numbers of Importance There are FIVE (5) pharmacist members of the Alabama Board of Pharmacy.
Each member serves a FIVE (5) year term.

▶ **Study Pro Tip** It is reasonable for the MPJE in many states to test on the composition of the Board of Pharmacy.

A pharmacist appointed by the Alabama Governor or elected by their peers to the ALBOP must take an oath or affirmation within 30 days before a "properly qualified officer" that they will "faithfully and impartially" perform the duties of the office. Traditionally, the oath is administered by a standing member of the ALBOP. The oath/affirmation is then filed with the Alabama Secretary of State [5]. For the next 5 years, unless they steps down or is removed from office (for egregious actions) by the Governor, that pharmacist will serve the profession and direct its course in the state of Alabama.

2.3 The Roles and Responsibilities of the Alabama Board of Pharmacy

The ALBOP is required by the Practice Act to meet at least THREE (3) times per year; in actuality, the board meets monthly [6]. Per the Practice Act, the board members determine where the meeting will take place. Most meetings take place at the ALBOP building in Hoover, Alabama but occasionally a meeting may be held elsewhere if something requiring a change of venue comes up. At least 30 days before each meeting, a notice must be posted to the public. These meetings are open to the public and may be attended in-person or virtually (the link to attend virtually is posted on the ALBOP website prior to the meeting). For a meeting to be held, a quorum of three members must be present. At the last regular meeting of the calendar year, the members elect officers amongst themselves for the following year [5]. These positions include president, vice-president, and treasurer, and each position is a one-year term [5]. A member can serve in a specific officer position for consecutive terms but may not serve in any one role for more than two (2) years throughout the entire five (5) year term. The president leads all board meetings; if the president is absent, the vice president presides [6]. Because ALBOP members may live across the state, the law allows compensation for them while they are performing their duties.

The only ALBOP officer who is not a board member is the secretary [5] The secretary is a paid position performed by the same person who serves as the ALBOP executive officer [6]. The secretary cannot be a board member nor be employed by a board member. While the ALBOP members are only present for meetings, the office has a staff who handle board designated activities such as licensing. As the executive officer, the secretary is the person who oversees the day-to-day operations of the ALBOP office, including record keeping, finances, and other activities necessary.

Key Concept

The ALBOP secretary has certain specific tasks outlined in the Practice Act:

1. Make, keep, and be in charge of all ALBOP records and documents.
2. Collect and record all fees.
3. Receive and respond to all board communication.

2.4 Powers and Authority Given to the Alabama Board of Pharmacy

The Practice Act gives the ALBOP specific powers and responsibilities. It recognizes that a primary goal of health care is to prioritize patient safety and wellness, and in that regard identifies the ALBOP as the best entity to determine what practice of pharmacy does just that (Table 5.2) [7, 8]. Overall, these items broadly give the ALBOP authority over pharmacy related matters within the state. Some of these are undertaken by the board members themselves, while others may be designated to board staff. The law importantly grants the ALBOP and its members immunity from liability under state and federal antitrust laws for any rule it makes and adopts that is anticompetitive, but with a clearly demonstrated and documented effect on public safety and wellness.

In general, the ALBOP has authority of the practice of pharmacy in Alabama. This includes both tangible resources as the actual pharmacy and human resources such as those who work within the pharmacy. The ALBOP also holds authority over laws involving the medications themselves including their manufacture, production, packaging, repackaging, sale, and distributions. This oversight is extended to relevant chemicals and poisons which may or may not be recognized or approved as drugs. This includes not only the products themselves, but labeling, recordkeeping, and other relevant parts of the medication use process.

The Practice Act is vague and broad in some areas; it simply grants the ALBOP the authority to regulate an area. In other areas, the law is more detailed and specific. This is an important point; it is much easier for the ALBOP to change a rule than it is to have the Practice Act, or another law changed, amended, or removed by the state legislature. The ALBOP may adopt a rule that supplements or clarifies a statutory (law) definition, but no rule may conflict with a law or statute that defines the practice of pharmacy [8]. When there is something specifically laid out by Alabama or federal law, the ALBOP must work within those boundaries. For example, the Practice Act grants the ALBOP the ability to determine what the requirements for pharmacy licensure are. However, it also says that the ALBOP may only grant pharmacy licensure to people who graduate from colleges and schools of pharmacy approved by the ALBOP. Therefore, unless the Alabama legislature amends, removes, or replaces that portion of the law, the ALBOP cannot create a rule that would allow a person who has not graduated from a college or school of pharmacy to obtain a pharmacist license.

Table 5.2 Powers and duties designated to the Alabama Board of Pharmacy by the Practice Act [7–9]

Power	Comments
To adopt rules about what *records and reports* must be created and stored by pharmacies regarding handling/ preservation of drugs themselves and prescription dispensing	
Set the standards and requirements for any of the licenses or permits it is authorized to issue	The ALBOP determines what qualifies a person or entity can obtain a permit or license
To make and adopt rules that regulate how licensees practice pharmacy	
To prohibit unlicensed people from practicing pharmacy	
To set rules and regulations on sanitation that are consistent with state health regulations	
To employ staff necessary for the board to perform its duties (e.g., clerical help, attorneys, chemists, agents)	
To employ state drug investigators necessary to enforce the Practice Act	This includes a position defined in the law as "Chief Drug Investigator" who is the head state drug investigator
To adopt other rules and regulations necessary to administer and enforce the Practice Act	
To investigate violations of the Practice Act of any other law related to the practice of pharmacy	
To issue subpoenas and require attendance of witnesses at a hearing and production of any evidence (e.g., papers, books, and records) related to the revocation, suspension, or probation of any license	
To administer oaths related to ALBOP duties	
To create an annual written report of all receipts and disbursements for the Governor and the "State Pharmaceutical Association," including the names of all people or entities who were issued a license to practice or permit during that year	"State Pharmaceutical Association" refers to the "Alabama Pharmacy Association"
To enforce other state laws involving pharmacy	There are other laws outside of the Practice Act that pertain to the practice of pharmacy This includes, but is not limited to, all laws involving controlled substances This law allows the ALBOP to work with other law enforcement agencies to enforce any law pertaining to the practice of pharmacy
To conduct hearings to investigate alleged violations of the Practice Act or subsequent rule or regulation which may result in the revocation, suspension, or probate of a license or permit	The law limits the ALBOP financial penalties to a maximum of $1000 per violation The ALBOP may also start other legal proceedings necessary (e.g. work with law enforcement for a person's arrest and prosecution)

(continued)

Table 5.2 (continued)

Power	Comments
Upon request, provide a copy of a certified copy of a license, permit, or copy of a board rule or regulation	The law specifically directs this task to the ALBOP secretary This law allows for an unspecified fee to be collected by the secretary to provide the requested information If the information is to be used in a court or legal proceeding, the certified copy of a license, permit, or rule is considered appropriate evidence
To acquire real property	"Real property is immovable property, such as a building The ALBOP can acquire real property by gift, grant, purchase, condemnation or other methods Example: This power gives the ALBOP the power to purchase and own a building from which to operate

A copy of any rule or regulation to be adopted must be electronically mailed to every Alabama registered pharmacist at least TEN (10) days before it becomes effective [7]. The ALBOP must also provide a printed copy of its rules and regulations when it receives a written request by an Alabama pharmacist; however, all of the Board's rules, regulations, and policy statements are located on the ALBOP website and on the Alabama Legislative Services Agency website, which houses the Alabama Administrative Code.

Key Concept
The Alabama Board of Pharmacy cannot make a rule or policy that conflicts with state or federal law.

▶ **Study Pro Tip** The MPJE does not ask test takers to distinguish between what concepts are defined by law and which are defined by administrative rules and regulations. The test assumes the test taker views all of them with equal weight.

When the board is investigating a matter, it gathers evidence in a similar manner that would occur for a criminal investigation [9]. The Practice Act designates the state Attorney General as the board's attorney, but also allows the board to employ other lawyers, which the ALBOP does. Subpoenas issued by the ALBOP have the same weight as a court of law. If a person is subpoenaed as a witness for an investigation, they are entitled to be paid witness fees and reimbursed for travel and mileage expenses [7]. The ALBOP has the authority to issue sanctions and fines. Any party affected may appeal an ALBOP ruling to the circuit court of the country where they aggrieved party resides or in the county where the ALBOP headquarters is, as long as they file the appeal within 30 days of receipt of the ALBOP ruling or order [10] Currently, the ALBOP headquarters is in Shelby County. This means that a pharmacist from Cullman who disagrees with a sanction placed on them by the ALBOP can file an appeal in the circuit court of either Cullman or Shelby counties.

While the ALBOP has substantial legal weight and authority, the authority to prosecute a crime in criminal court is given to the district attorney of the judicial circuit where the offense is alleged to have occurred, or if relevant, to the appropriate federal prosecutors [9]. The ALBOP is required to assist and furnish any evidence it may have in any of these types of prosecutions. The source of any information with respect to law violations can only be revealed to the court [11]. Finally, in order to prevent unlawful pharmacy-related activities by those outside of the profession, the ALBOP is authorized to bring action in its own name to the circuit court for an injunction for any person or entity who is not licensed or permitted by the ALBOP, but who is violating the Practice Act [12]. This provision protects against unscrupulous activity that could harm public health and welfare. For example, if the ALBOP is made aware of a non-licensed person compounding a product in their home and selling it as a medication, they can take legal action with the court to force the person to stop.

► **Important Concept** The Practice Act extends the ALBOP's authority beyond the Practice Act and related rules and regulations. The board also enforces state laws on controlled substances and state laws on drug purity and strength as they relate to the pharmacy. Generally, the board works with other law enforcement agencies in this regard.

As an example: If John, a licensed pharmacist, is alleged to be distributing opioids without a prescription from the pharmacy inventory, the ALBOP is authorized to conduct an investigation, gather all necessary evidence, and hold a hearing on the matter.

It is important to understand that while the ALBOP may investigate a matter, other law enforcement and the State Board of Health are also authorized to enforce laws on controlled substances. An ALBOP investigation and action does not prevent administrative judicial proceedings from these other entities from taking place.

► **Important Concept** Each year, the ALBOP is required to provide an annual report to the Governor and the "State Pharmaceutical Association". There is no actual "State Pharmaceutical Association" that exists and operates in the state of Alabama. To fulfill this requirement, the ALBOP provides this report at one meeting each year for both the Alabama Pharmacy Association and the Alabama Society of Health System Pharmacists.

Fun Fact
The current ALBOP headquarters is located in Shelby County Alabama.

3 The Structure of Pharmacy in Alabama

When one first glances at the lists of laws, rules, regulations, and policies related to pharmacy in Alabama, it can seem overwhelming. However, when taken collectively, there are not as many actual legal dictates than it first appears, and most fall within a few large categories: requirements for pharmacy personnel, licensing and permits, prescribing and dispensing, recordkeeping, controlled substances, and policies and procedures. There are miscellaneous ones that do not fit within these categories mixed in, but many do. The broad, and sometimes vague, nature of the pharmacy law, rules, and regulations in Alabama provide the pharmacist with a respectful degree of professional autonomy in the practice of the profession.

The structure of pharmacy centers around pharmacy personnel, which in Alabama includes the supervising pharmacist, the pharmacist, pharmacy technician, extern, and/or intern—whose ultimate mission is to provide safe and effective medications and treatments to patients who need them. Most of the laws and rules directing this process in Alabama are described within other chapters in this book.

4 The Importance of the Supervising Pharmacist

The supervising pharmacist takes on the full weight of responsibility for pharmacy operations at the pharmacy for which they are assigned in that role (Table 5.3) [13] EVERY pharmacy must be under the direct supervision and control of a pharmacist who works in that pharmacy and who is licensed by the ALBOP. Likewise, the ALBOP must know the name of the designated supervising pharmacist at every pharmacy. When a pharmacist begins *and* stops working as a supervising pharmacist, the PHARMACIST must notify the ALBOP. The online form can be found on the ALBOP website. The pharmacist has TEN (10) days from the time they start or stop working in this role to complete the form. It is equally important that the public

Table 5.3 Responsibilities of the supervising pharmacist In Alabama [13]

Supervising pharmacy personnel
Ensure all pharmacy personnel licenses and registrations are in good standing with ALBOP
Maintain accurate records of all prescription medications received and dispensed
Maintain security of the pharmacy and its contents
Ensure only ALBOP registered pharmacists provide professional consultations with patients or physicians
Ensure only ALBOP registered pharmacists (or supervised interns) accept telephone prescriptions (including those left on voicemail)
Operate the pharmacy in a clean and orderly manner
Ensure pharmacy is operated at all times with good pharmaceutical practices
Maintain inspection records provided by the ALBOP or its staff
When discrepancies are identified by the ALBOP or its staff, submit to the ALBOP in writing steps taken or proposed to eliminate the discrepancy within 15 days of notice
Ensure compliance with the Alabama Pharmacy Practice Act, the Rules of the ALBOP, and the Alabama Controlled Substances Act (and other applicable laws and rules)
The word "pharmacy" specifically applies to the prescription department

know who the supervising pharmacist is. For this reason, Alabama requires the name of the supervising pharmacist must be placed in a conspicuous place in the prescription department so that it can be clearly seen by the public.

The supervising pharmacist must work (be on duty) at least 50% of the hours that the pharmacy is open OR at least THIRTY (30) hours per week—whichever is less. The permit holder (e.g., the pharmacy owner) is responsible and accountable for making sure that the supervising pharmacist works the required number of hours. Because of the enormous responsibility that this person holds, a pharmacist may not serve as supervising pharmacist for more than one pharmacy. The ALBOP *may* not deem it supervising multiple pharmacies if the pharmacist is supervising a pharmacy and an institutional pharmacy which is open less than FIFETEEN (15) hours per week, or a noninstitutional pharmacy that is open no more than the minimum hours allowed by ALBOP. This provision allows for practical and economic supervision over small practices which would otherwise not be able to afford to meet the requirement.

Alabama does recognize that there may be times when the permit holder rather than the supervising pharmacist may be the one at fault for a law or rule violation. In such cases, the ALBOP will absolve the supervising pharmacist from responsibility and hold the permit holder accountable. Because of the tremendous responsibility placed on the supervising pharmacist, Alabama prohibits any person or entity from subverting the authority of the supervising pharmacist by impeding the management of the pharmacy in compliance with state and federal law and regulations. For example, a corporate pharmacy owner cannot force a supervising pharmacist to allow a pharmacy technician whose Alabama registration has expired to continue to work in the pharmacy. Attempts at impeding the lawful operation of a pharmacy may result in charges being filed against the permit holder.

While it is the pharmacist's responsibility to notify the ALBOP when they start or stop such a role, the permit holder has its own requirements when the supervising pharmacist either leaves employment or steps down from the administrative role. The permit holder has TEN (10) days to provide the ALBOP with an action plan for designating another supervising pharmacist. They do not have to have a replacement supervising pharmacist in place during these 10 days, just a plan. The plan itself can last up to NINETY (90) days. If a new supervising pharmacist has not been appointed by this time, the ALBOP may close the pharmacy until one is appointed. At times, a supervising pharmacist may take a temporary leave of absence, but not permanently stop their role. For example, the supervising pharmacist may take parental leave at the birth or adoption of a new baby or require an extended absence to recover from surgery. When there is a temporary absence of the supervising pharmacist greater than THIRTY (30) days, the permit holder must designate a temporary supervising pharmacist and notify ALBOP of the person's name and time period when they will fill that temporary role. This notification must occur prior to the appointment being made. The permit holder must also inform the ALBOP when the original supervising pharmacist returns from the absence.

5 When to Notify the ALBOP

There are specific times when the ALBOP must be contacted. Unless otherwise stated, it is the responsibility of the pharmacist to provide these notifications. Many of the notifications must be done in writing, thought the ALBOP may have forms that meet the requirement. Do not assume that someone else, such as an employer, will notify the ALBOP on your behalf.

1. *Change of employment*—must be submitted in writing within TEN (10) days of change in employment [14].
   (a) Notice must contain pharmacist name, license number, pharmacy formally employed (where you are leaving), and the name of the pharmacy currently employed (i.e., your new position). If you are not starting a new position, you would only notify them that you are leaving your former position.
2. *Change in supervising pharmacist*—the "Notice of Change in Supervising Pharmacist" form must be submitted to the ALBOP within TEN (10) days of assuming the duties of the supervising pharmacist [13].
3. *Stopping work as a consultant pharmacist*—the "Consultant Application" must be submitted to the ALBOP when applying to be a consultant pharmacist. This application has a line for the name and address of the nursing facility where services will be provided (if applicable). When the pharmacist stops providing consultant services, the ALBOP must be notified within TEN (10) days [15].
4. *Change of pharmacist, intern, or technician contact information*—this information is changed on the ALBOP website. There is no time requirement attached to this change.
5. *Change of pharmacy employer*—this information is changed on the ALBOP website. There is no time requirement attached to this change.
6. *Change in control of ownership*—must be reported to the ALBOP in writing within TEN (10) days of occurrence [16]. There is a change of ownership application form on the ALBOP website which may be used, but it is not electronically submitted like other forms can be.

6 Violating the Alabama Practice of Pharmacy Act

The practice of pharmacy by a pharmacist, technician, or intern, requires a valid licensed issued by the ALBOP. The operation of a pharmacy, manufacturer, wholesaler, or distributor, or other related entity requires an ALBOP issued permit. It is understood that any person or entity which holds a valid license or permits does so with the awareness that all pharmacy laws and rules must be followed and upheld [17]. Additionally, it is understood that no licensee or permit holder would knowingly allow someone else to violate one of these laws or rules. Some laws and rules have penalties listed in the rule or law itself should they be violated, but many do not. If a rule or a law is not associated with a specific penalty, the consequences of violating it are covered in general by a section of the Practice Act. Violations of pharmacy related laws and rules are considered misdemeanor offenses. If found guilty, the convicted person or entity can face a fine of up to $1000 and potentially incarcerated for up to 12 months for each offense. The pharmacy professional should clearly understand that if they become aware of a violation, they are expected to stop, deter, or report the violation to the appropriate authorities, such as ALBOP.

Key Concept
If a person was aware that a violation of pharmacy law or rules was occurring and did not act to stop, deter, or report it, that person can face similar consequences as the one who actually committed the violation. For example, a pharmacist who knowingly allows a person who is not registered with the ALBOP to work in a pharmacy as a pharmacy technician would be considered to have also violated the law.

References

1. *Ala. Code. § 34-23-2 (1966).*
2. ABOUT US. Alabama Board of Pharmacy. Accessed June 17, 2024. https://albop.com/about-us/
3. *Alabama State Board of Pharmacy Administrative Code, Chapter 680-X-1-.01 Oragnization. § 680-X-1-.01 (1982 and Rev 2019).*
4. *Ala. Code. § 34-23-1-187 (1966 and Rev 2024).*
5. *Ala. Code. § 34-23-90 (1966 and Rev 2022).*
6. *Ala. Code. § 34-23-91 (1966 and Rev 1993).*
7. *Ala. Code. § 34-23-92 (1966 and Rev 2017).*
8. *Ala. Code. § 34-23-92.1 (1966 and Rev 2016).*
9. *Ala. Code. § 34-23-93 (1966).*
10. *Ala. Code. § 34-23-94 (1966 and Rev 2019).*
11. *Alabama State Board of Pharmacy Administrative Code, Chapter 680-X-2-.03 Practice of Pharmacy § 680-X-2-.3 (1982 and Rev 2021).*
12. *Ala. Code. § 34-23-12 (1966).*
13. *Alabama State Board of Pharmacy Administrative Code, Chapter 680-X-2 Practice of Pharmacy. § 680-X-2-.12 (1982 and Rev 2021).*
14. *Ala. Code. § 34-23-10 (1966).*
15. *Alabama State Board of Pharmacy Administrative Code, Chapter 680-X-2 Practice of Pharmacy. § 680-X-2-.08 (1982 and Rev 2021).*
16. *Ala. Code. § 34-23-30 (1966 and Rev 2023).*
17. *Ala. Code. § 34-23-13 (1966).*

6 Education Requirements to Obtain and Maintain a Pharmacist License

Continuous learning is the minimum requirement for success in any field.

—Brian Tracy.

1 Pharmacist License Application

1.1 Application Process

Anyone pursuing a pharmacist license in the state of Alabama must file a pharmacist application with the Alabama Board of Pharmacy (ALBOP) at least 30 days prior to taking the North American Pharmacist Licensure Examination® (NAPLEX®) [1]. The application may be completed and submitted online on the ALBOP's website (albop.com) in the Forms and Applications section [2].

1.2 Application Components

Each pharmacist's application must be accompanied by an examination and application registration fee [1].

1.3 Application Fees

Applicants seeking pharmacist licensure must pay a fee (Table 6.1). All fees are nonrefundable [3].

M. N. Bulloch et al., *Pharmacy Law in Alabama*,
https://doi.org/10.1007/978-3-031-84771-4_6

Table 6.1 Pharmacist application fees [4]

Application	Fee ($)
New/renewals	100
Duplicate license	10
Late penalty fees (per month)	10
Non-disciplinary late renewal fee for January 1–January 30	1000
50 years of licensure	25
Reciprocity exam and score transfer	300

2 Qualifications

Each applicant who desires to engage in the practice of pharmacy within Alabama must meet the following qualifications to receive a pharmacist license [1]:

- Be a citizen of the United States or if not a citizen of the United States, legally present in the United States with appropriate documentation from the federal government.
- Be at least NINETEEN (19) years of age.
- Possess good moral character.
- Hold a professional degree from a division, school, college, or a university department of pharmacy practice recognized by the Alabama Board of Pharmacy.

3 Practical Training Program

Each applicant seeking pharmacist licensure in Alabama must complete a practical training program that has been approved by the ALBOP. This training program is referred to as an externship/internship and experiential rotations by colleges and schools of pharmacy. All interns/externs who are enrolled in a college or school of pharmacy pursuing the academic and experiential training requirements required for licensure are to apply for a permit with the ALBOP. Interns/externs who are absent from school for more than two consecutive semesters or three consecutive quarters are not considered enrolled. The college or school of pharmacy is required to notify the ALBOP within 10 days of a student's status change.

The intern/extern applying for the permit will undergo a criminal background check upon initial application. The applicant is to pay the fee for the background check. The permit expires on December 31 of odd-numbered years. The cost for the initial and renewal permit is $50. If an intern/extern does not pay the renewal fee by December 31 of odd-numbered years, the permit becomes null and void. The permit is required before an intern/extern may perform duties in a pharmacy.

A minimum of 1500 internship/externship hours under the supervision of a registered preceptor is required for pharmacist licensure. Four hundred (400) of the hours are to be completed after completing the requirements of the second professional year of pharmacy school and must be completed in a traditional pharmacy setting where the emphasis is on the medication distribution process, prescriptions, and medical supplies. The college or school of pharmacy will certify to the ALBOP that the intern has completed 1100 internship hours plus any traditional hours. The ALBOP will accept internship hours from preceptors who are approved by the college or school of pharmacy. A preceptor may supervise up to three interns/externs at one time. If an applicant for pharmacist licensure has less than the required 1500 internship/externship hours, they may still take the licensing examination as long as they meet all other requirements. Upon successfully passing the examination, they are to file an affidavit attesting that they have completed the required training prior to being issued a pharmacist license [5].

▶ **Numbers of Importance** A minimum of 1500 internship/externship hours under the supervision of a registered preceptor is required for pharmacist licensure in the state of Alabama.

Key Concept

Four hundred (400) of the required hours for pharmacist licensure are to be completed after completing the requirements of the second professional year of pharmacy school and must be completed in a traditional pharmacy setting where the emphasis is on the medication distribution process, prescriptions, and medical supplies.

4 Examinations

4.1 North American Pharmacist Licensure Examination

Each pharmacist applicant must pass the National Association of Boards of Pharmacy (NABP) North American Pharmacist Licensure Examination® (NAPLEX®). The NAPLEX® is designed to assess the applicant's knowledge of general pharmacy practice. It is a six-hour examination comprised of 225 questions [6]. If the applicant fails the examination on the first attempt, the applicant has up to 3 years to complete and pass the examination, up to a third attempt. If the applicant fails the third attempt, the applicant is eligible for one additional attempt (fourth attempt) but only after satisfactorily completing additional preparation as instructed by the ALBOP.

An applicant may be denied access to complete the examination if the applicant has violated the Code of Alabama Title 24 Chapter 23. If the applicant has been expelled from an examination for any of the below reasons, the applicant will not be allowed to complete the examination, and the applicant will not be able to apply to take the examination during the same calendar year of the offense or the following year [1].

- Cribbing.
- Cheating.
- Other dishonest conduct.

The applicant must receive a passing score on the NAPLEX® for licensure. The regulations state that applicants must receive a general average score of 75, but results are now communicated to applicants as either pass or fail instead of a numerical score [7].

4.2 Alabama Multistate Pharmacy Jurisprudence Examination

Each applicant must pass the NABP Alabama Multistate Pharmacy Jurisprudence Examination® (MPJE®). The MPJE is state-specific and is designed to assess the applicant's knowledge of the rules and regulations in the state in which they are seeking licensure. It is a two-and-a-half-hour examination comprised of 120 questions. Applicants are allowed up to five attempts to successfully pass the examination per state [8]. The applicant must receive a passing score on the Alabama MPJE® for licensure. The rules state that applicants must receive a score of 75, but results are now communicated to applicants as either pass or fail instead of a numerical score [7]. Additional information regarding the MPJE® is discussed in Chap. 21.

5 Reciprocity

A pharmacist license may be issued in Alabama without an applicant completing an examination in the case of reciprocity [1, 9]. This program is known as the Electronic License Transfer Program (eLTP) and allows pharmacists who are licensed in one state to transfer their existing pharmacist license to one or more states [10]. In this instance, the applicant must submit documentation showing they have completed an examination and have been licensed to practice pharmacy in another state. The applicant must also be of good moral character and temperate habits. The requirements for the state(s) in which the applicant is currently licensed must meet NABP's requirements [1]. The following steps must be successfully completed for a pharmacist with an existing license to reciprocate their license to Alabama [10]:

1. Complete the eLTP application (located on the NABP website).
2. Apply to take the Alabama MPJE® (on the NABP website).
3. Complete the Alabama pharmacist application (on the ALBOP website). Make sure to select "Reciprocity" when filling out the application.
4. NABP will generate the applicant's name as a candidate requesting eligibility to take the Alabama MPJE.

5. Once ALBOP grants the applicant's eligibility to take the Alabama MPJE, NABP will send the applicant an authorization to test (ATT) number. Once the applicant has received the ATT, the applicant may schedule the MPJE.
6. Once the applicant completes and passes the Alabama MPJE, the ALBOP will schedule an interview with the applicant.
7. The applicant will meet with at least two ALBOP members for an interview.
8. The ALBOP will grant the applicant reciprocal licensure and provide the applicant with an Alabama pharmacist license.

Once the applicant has received an Alabama pharmacist license, they must maintain their license in the state of original licensure [11].

6 Score Transfer

An additional way a pharmacist license may be issued in Alabama without an applicant completing an additional NAPLEX is in the case of a score transfer [12]. Applicants have two opportunities to indicate they wish to have their score transferred to another state. The first is when they initially purchase the NAPLEX. Once the applicant is granted eligibility to take the examination, they can purchase a score transfer. NABP charges a fee of $75 per score transfer. The second option for purchasing a score transfer is after an applicant takes the NAPLEX. The applicant has up to 89 days after taking the examination to purchase a score transfer [13]. Once the applicant has transferred their NAPLEX score, they still must take the Alabama MPJE and participate in an oral interview with the ALBOP. The applicant must provide documentation that they hold a pharmacy degree from a program recognized by the ALBOP [12].

7 Expiration and Renewal of Certification

Pharmacists' licensure expires on December 31 of even-numbered years. To maintain licensure, pharmacists must pay a biennial (every two years) renewal fee. The fee must not be less than $25 and not more than $150. This fee is due on October 31 of even-numbered years and is considered late after December 31 of even-numbered years. If a pharmacist fails to pay the biennial renewal fee by the deadline (December 31 of even-numbered years), then they must pay a late penalty of $10 per month. If the license has lapsed for greater than 5 years, then the license may only be reinstated after an examination by the ALBOP. Pharmacists who hold life certificates to practice pharmacy do not have to pay renewal fees [14].

8 Continuing Education Requirements

Each pharmacist must complete a total of THIRTY (30) continuing education (CE) hours each license renewal period to maintain licensure. SIX (6) of the 30 hours must be live CE hours. If a pharmacist has only been licensed for one full calendar year, they are required to complete FIFTEEN (15) hours of CE to renew their license. At least three of the hours must be live CE hours. If a pharmacist has been licensed for less than one full calendar year, they are not required to complete any hours of CE to renew their license.

It is each pharmacist's responsibility to keep a record of CE hour completion. The ALBOP randomly audits pharmacists' CE documentation, and the pharmacist must provide documentation of the hours completed within 30 calendar days of the request by the ALBOP. Failure to maintain the CE hours requirement or submit the requested documentation within 30 calendar days to the ALBOP will result in a fine for the first offense.

A pharmacist may submit a written request to the ALBOP asking for a waiver or an extension of time to complete the CE hours requirement. The ALBOP may grant the request given it is of good and sufficient cause. The ALBOP may require the pharmacist to submit documentation necessary to decide whether to grant the waiver or extension.

If a pharmacist allows their license to lapse for at least one and up to 5 years, they are required to provide documentation they have completed 15 CE hours for each lapsed calendar year to have their license reinstated. At least three of the hours per year must be live CE hours. If a pharmacist allows their license to lapse for more than 5 years, in addition to the ALBOP examination requirement previously mentioned, the ALBOP may require the pharmacist to complete any amount of CE hours it deems appropriate in order for the pharmacist's license to be reinstated [15].

► **Numbers of Importance** Each pharmacist must complete a total of 30 CE hours each license renewal period (two years) to maintain licensure.

Six of the 30 hours must be live CE hours.

If a pharmacist has only been licensed for one full calendar year, they are required to complete 15 hours of CE to renew their license. At least three of the hours must be live CE hours.

If a pharmacist has been licensed for less than one full calendar year, they are not required to complete any hours of CE to renew their license.

9 Reporting Place of Employment

All pharmacy candidates who are working as a pharmacy intern or extern must report the name of their pharmacy employer to the ALBOP. This information must be reported within TEN (10) days of employment. Additionally, if they must report any changes in employment, these changes must be reported within TEN (10) days [16].

▶ **Numbers of Importance** All interns and externs must report the name of their pharmacy employer to the ALBOP within TEN (10) days of employment and within TEN (10) days of an employment change.

10 Licensure of Graduates of Foreign Colleges and Schools of Pharmacy

If an applicant for pharmacist licensure in Alabama is a graduate of a foreign school of college of pharmacy, they must comply with all the aforementioned requirements. To receive a license, they must do the following [17]:

- Obtain a Foreign Pharmacy Graduate Equivalency Committee Certification and provide it to the ALBOP.
- Pass the Alabama MPJE®.
- Complete a practical training program as previously outlined.
- Demonstrate to the ALBOP they can effectively communicate in English.

The guidelines for reciprocity apply to graduates of foreign colleges and schools of pharmacy if they possess a pharmacist license in another state [17].

References

1. Ala. Code. § 34-23-51 (1975, rev. 2021) Available from: https://alison.legislature.state.al.us/code-of-alabama
2. Alabama Board of Pharmacy. Forms and applications [Internet]. 2024 [cited 2024 Apr 16]. Available from: https://albop.com/forms/
3. Alabama State Board of Pharmacy Administrative Code, Chapter 680-X-2 Practice of Pharmacy. § 680-X-2-.34 (2006 and rev. 2013)
4. Alabama Board of Pharmacy. License fees [Internet]. 2024 [cited 2024 Apr 16]. Available from: https://albop.com/license-fees/
5. Alabama State Board of Pharmacy Administrative Code, Chapter 680-X-2 Practice of Pharmacy. § 680-X-2-.16 (1984 and rev. 2022)
6. National Association of Board of Pharmacy. NAPLEX [Internet]. 2024 [cited 2024 Jul 1]. Available from: https://nabp.pharmacy/programs/examinations/naplex/
7. Alabama State Board of Pharmacy Administrative Code, Chapter 680-X-2 Practice of Pharmacy. § 680-X-2-.02 (1982 and rev. 1995)
8. National Association of Board of Pharmacy. MPJE [Internet]. 2024 [cited 2024 Jul 1]. Available from: https://nabp.pharmacy/programs/examinations/mpje/
9. Alabama State Board of Pharmacy Administrative Code, Chapter 680-X-2 Practice of Pharmacy. § 680-X-2-.17 (1984 and rev. 1997)
10. National Association of Board of Pharmacy. Electronic licensure transfer program [Internet]. 2024 [cited 2024 Apr 16]. Available from: https://nabp.pharmacy/programs/licensure/licensure-transfer/
11. National Association of Board of Pharmacy. General requirements for licensure transfer [Internet]. 2024 Mar 7 [cited 2024 Apr 16]. Available from: https://nabp.pharmacy/wp-content/uploads/Licensure-Transfer-General-Requirements.pdf

12. Alabama State Board of Pharmacy Administrative Code, Chapter 680-X-2 Practice of Pharmacy. § 680-X-2-.29 (1999 and rev. 2012)
13. National Association of Board of Pharmacy. How do I add a NAPLEX score transfer? [Internet]. 2024 [cited 2024 Apr 29]. Available from: https://nabp.pharmacy/help/how-do-i-add-a-naplex-score-transfer-if-i-have-applied-for-the-naplex-but-have-not-sat-for-the-examination/
14. Ala. Code. § 34-23-52 (1975, rev. 2021) Available from: https://alison.legislature.state.al.us/code-of-alabama
15. Alabama State Board of Pharmacy Administrative Code, Chapter 680-X-2 Practice of Pharmacy. § 680-X-2-.36 (2006 and rev. 2022)
16. Alabama State Board of Pharmacy Administrative Code, Chapter 680-X-2 Practice of Pharmacy. § 680-X-2-.10 (1975 and rev. 1982)
17. Alabama State Board of Pharmacy Administrative Code, Chapter 680-X-2 Practice of Pharmacy. § 680-X-2-.38 (2006)

Pharmacy Technicians in Alabama 7

Alone we can do so little; together we can do so much.

–Helen Keller

1 Registration

To become a pharmacy technician in Alabama, an individual must register with the Alabama Board of Pharmacy (ALBOP). The registration process involves the applicant completing an online application, uploading a copy of their driver's license, providing a current photograph, and undergoing a background check. There is a $60 application fee, a $40 background check, and a $4 service fee. All fees are nonrefundable [1].

If a pharmacy technician experiences a change in employment, the technician is required to notify the ALBOP of the change. The notice must occur in writing and contain the following information [2]:

- Pharmacy technician name.
- Technician registration number.
- Former employer pharmacy's name.
- Current employer pharmacy's name.

An individual may not be granted pharmacy technician registration if the ALBOP receives evidence regarding the applicant and their behavior (Table 7.1).

M. N. Bulloch et al., *Pharmacy Law in Alabama*,
https://doi.org/10.1007/978-3-031-84771-4_7

Table 7.1 Grounds for pharmacy technician not to receive pharmacy technician registration [2]

Applicant does not possess good, moral character
Applicant has willfully violated provisions of or rules or regulations associated with the Code of Alabama Title 34 or the Alabama Uniform Controlled Substances Act
Applicant has engaged in threatening behavior to the public's health, safety, or welfare
Applicant has been convicted of a felony or misdemeanor that involves moral turpitude. According to the Merriam-Webster definition, moral turpitude is "an act or behavior that gravely violates the sentiment or accepted standard of the community" [3]
Applicant has been convicted of a felony or misdemeanor that involves a drug-related offense related to a controlled substance
Applicant has been convicted of a crime or offense that demonstrates the applicant is unable to engage in the duties of a pharmacy technician to protect the public's health and safety
Applicant tried to obtain pharmacy technician registration by dishonest means
Applicant has violated a law related to narcotics sale or dispensing
Applicant is unable to perform pharmacy technician duties due to illness, inebriation, drug misuse, narcotics, alcohol, chemicals, other substances, or mental or physical condition
Applicant has had pharmacy technician registration, license or permit suspended, revoked, or put on probation in another state
Applicant received an order to meet with the ALBOP and refused to appear
Applicant was dishonest to the ALBOP

2 Training Program

All applicants who apply for pharmacy technician registration on or after January 1, 2020 are required to complete an ALBOP-approved training program. This training program must be completed within the first SIX (6) months of registering, and the pharmacy technician must submit evidence documenting completion of the training program to ALBOP within TEN (10) days of completion. Both the pharmacy technician and the pharmacy where the technician is employed are required to keep documentation of completion of the training program for at least TWO (2) years from the date of completion.

Failure of the pharmacy technician to complete the training program within the instructed timeframe, furnish documentation to the ALBOP, or keep documentation for the required 2 years may result in sanctions against the pharmacy technician, the Supervising Pharmacist at the pharmacy technician's employment, and/or the pharmacy permit holder of the pharmacy technician's employer [2].

► **Numbers of Importance** Pharmacy technicians must complete an initial training program within the first SIX (6) months of registering, and they must submit evidence documenting completion of the program to ALBOP within TEN (10) days of completion.

The pharmacy technician and the pharmacy where the technician is employed are required to keep documentation of completion of the training program for at least TWO (2) years from the date of completion.

3 Role of Pharmacy Technicians

3.1 Pharmacy Technician to Pharmacist Ratios

A pharmacy technician must be under the direct supervision of a licensed pharmacist to perform pharmacy functions or be present in the pharmacy's prescription area. In addition to the pharmacy technician, the licensed pharmacist is responsible and liable for the pharmacy technician's actions [1]. In the retail and institutional pharmacy settings, for each full-time pharmacist on duty, the following ratios to pharmacy technicians exist:

- FOUR (4) pharmacy technicians if TWO (2) of the technicians are certified.
- THREE (3) pharmacy technicians if ONE (1) of the technicians is certified.
- TWO (2) pharmacy technicians if neither of the technicians are certified.

However, a pharmacy may employ pharmacy technicians to perform supervised tasks that do not require professional judgment [2].

Key Concept

For each full-time pharmacist on duty, the following ratios to pharmacy technicians exist:

- FOUR (4) pharmacy technicians if TWO (2) of the technicians are certified.
- THREE (3) pharmacy technicians if ONE (1) of the technicians is certified.
- TWO (2) pharmacy technicians if neither of the technicians are certified.

3.2 Functions Pharmacy Technicians Cannot Perform

The ALBOP has developed guidelines regarding functions pharmacy technicians cannot perform to protect public health (Table 7.2).

Table 7.2 Functions pharmacy technicians cannot perform [2]

Communicate any medical, therapeutic, clinical, or drug information orally or in writing
Communicate any information on a patient's profile orally or in writing that requires professional judgment
Document the receipt of a controlled substance into inventory
Accept a new prescription by oral communication
Transfer a prescription to another pharmacy orally
Read a prescription to another person
Provide a prescription to a patient that has not been verified for accuracy by a licensed pharmacist
Perform medication counseling to a patient
Perform a drug utilization review
Perform any task that requires a pharmacist's professional judgment
Perform any task that would violate any federal, state, or local pharmacy regulations

3.3 Miscellaneous

Pharmacy technicians are required to wear a name tag that identifies them as a pharmacy technician while they are working at a pharmacy [2].

4 Registration Expiration, Renewal, and Reinstatement

Pharmacy technician registration expires on December 31 of odd-numbered years. To maintain registration, pharmacy technicians must pay a biennial renewal fee ($60). This fee is due on October 31 of odd-numbered years and is considered late after December 31 of odd-numbered years. If a pharmacy technician fails to pay the biennial renewal fee by the deadline (December 31 of odd-numbered years), then the technician registration becomes null and void. A pharmacy technician's registration can be reinstated if the technician pays a late penalty. The late penalty is $20 for each lapse year of registration [2].

Key Concept

Pharmacy technician registration expires on December 31 of ODD-numbered years.

Pharmacist registration expires on December 31 of EVEN-numbered years.

5 Continuing Education Requirements

Each pharmacy technician must complete THREE (3) continuing education (CE) hours annually or a total of SIX (6) CE hours biennially each registration renewal period to maintain registration. ONE (1) hour per year or a total of TWO (2) of the 6 h must be live CE hours. If a pharmacy technician has only been registered for one full calendar year, they are required to complete THREE (3) hours of CE to renew their license. At least ONE (1) of the 3 h must be live CE hours. If a pharmacy technician has been registered for less than one full calendar year, they are not required to complete any hours of CE to renew their registration [2] A pharmacy technician may request an extension to complete the CE requirements from the ALBOP. Failure to complete the CE requirements will result in disciplinary action by the ALBOP [1].

Pharmacy technicians are responsible for maintaining accurate documentation for completion of CE requirements for a period of 2 years. If the ALBOP requests this information, the technician must submit the documentation within 30 calendar days. The ALBOP randomly audits CE documentation, and failure to maintain compliance with completion of required CE or submitting falsified documentation to the ALBOP may subject the pharmacy technician to nondisciplinary administrative penalty. For a first violation, the penalty may be $25–$100 and to be determined by the ALBOP.

If a pharmacy technician allows their registration to lapse for at least one calendar year but no more than five calendar years, they are required to complete three CE hours for each lapsed year. If they have allowed their registration to lapse for more than five calendar years, the ALBOP determines how many CE hours they will need to complete [4].

> **Numbers of Importance** Each pharmacy technician must complete THREE (3) continuing education (CE) hours annually or a total of SIX (6) CE hours biennially each registration renewal period to maintain registration.
>
> ONE (1) hour per year or a total of TWO (2) of the 6 h must be live CE hours.
>
> If a pharmacy technician has only been registered for one full calendar year, they are required to complete THREE (3) hours of CE to renew their license. At least ONE (1) of the 3 h must be live CE hours. If a pharmacy technician has been registered for less than one full calendar year, they are not required to complete any hours of CE to renew their registration.

6 Revocation or Suspension of Registration; Probation

The ALBOP may revoke or suspend a pharmacy technician's registration for reasons including but not limited to the following [5]:

- Willfully violating the Code of Alabama or the Alabama Uniform Controlled Substances Act or any associated rule or regulation.
- Committing an action that threatens the public health, safety, or welfare.
- Conviction of a felony or misdemeanor involving moral turpitude or drugs (legend or controlled substance).
- Obtaining a pharmacy technician registration through fraudulent means.
- Violating the laws and regulations relating to the sale or dispensing of drugs, including narcotics and legend drugs.

References

1. Ala. Code. § 34-23-131 (1975, rev. 2017) Available from: https://alison.legislature.state.al.us/code-of-alabama
2. Alabama State Board of Pharmacy Administrative Code, Chapter 680-X-2 Practice of Pharmacy. § 680-X-2-.14 (1982 and rev. 2022)
3. Merriam-Webster. (n.d.). Moral turpitude. In Merriam-Webster.com legal dictionary. Retrieved May 9, 2024, from https://www.merriam-webster.com/legal/moral%20turpitude
4. Alabama State Board of Pharmacy Administrative Code, Chapter 680-X-2 Practice of Pharmacy. § 680-X-2-.37 (2006 and rev. 2012)
5. Ala. Code. § 34-23-132 (1975, rev. 1996) Available from: https://alison.legislature.state.al.us/code-of-alabama

The Pharmacy

8

Pharmacists are the most accessible healthcare provider as nearly 90% of Americans live within five miles of a community pharmacy, and patients visit a pharmacy almost twice as often as they visit a physician [1, 2].

1 Pharmacy Permits

1.1 Initial Pharmacy Permit

All pharmacies must register to receive a permit with the Alabama Board of Pharmacy (ALBOP). This includes community pharmacies, hospital pharmacies, and any other establishment that sells, compounds, or dispenses drugs. Additionally, this rule applies to any entity that provides pharmacy services to patients who live in the state of Alabama. The application for a permit must be submitted to the ALBOP at least THIRTY (30) days prior to the business opening. Pharmacies are not allowed to open for business until they are registered with and inspected by the ALBOP and have received their permit. The following information must be submitted on the permit application:

- Ownership information.
- Licensed pharmacists' names.
- Licensed pharmacists' license numbers.
- Pharmacy location.
- Other information as required by the ALBOP.

If the pharmacy has multiple locations that are owned by the same owner, separate applications must be submitted for each pharmacy, and separate permits must

M. N. Bulloch et al., *Pharmacy Law in Alabama*,
https://doi.org/10.1007/978-3-031-84771-4_8

be obtained. If the pharmacy is owned by a corporation, the permit will be issued in the corporation's name [3].

► **Numbers of Importance** A pharmacy permit application must be submitted to the ALBOP at least THIRTY (30) days prior to the pharmacy opening.

1.2 Pharmacy Services Permit

In Alabama, one may apply for a pharmacy services permit from the ALBOP for the limited purpose of pharmacists and pharmacy technicians providing pharmacy services to patients. The pharmacy services permit holder must designate a pharmacist to be the Supervising Pharmacist who will be on site and responsible for maintaining compliance standards. Pharmacy services permits can be granted for both in-state pharmacies as well as out-of-state pharmacies. The ALBOP has additional requirements set forth that out-of-state pharmacies must meet to receive a permit (Table 8.1).

In addition to the application for the pharmacy services permit, all applicants (in state and out of state) must submit a policy and procedure manual for the ALBOP to review and approve. At a minimum, the policy and procedure manual must include the following information:

- Pharmacy's hours of operation.
- The name of the pharmacist who has been designated as the on-call pharmacist. The on-call pharmacist's responsibilities include responding to requests that cannot be addressed remotely. For example, if a patient's physician has an urgent request for information regarding the patient that cannot be provided by the pharmacists who are providing services through remote order processing, the on-call pharmacist would be responsible for responding to the request.
- Procedures in case there is downtime.
- Details regarding the process for identifying and responding to any medication errors that occur as a result of remote order processing.

Table 8.1 Out-of-state pharmacy requirements [4]

Complete an out-of-state pharmacy services application
Pay a fee determined by the ALBOP
The pharmacy services permit will become void on December 31 of even-numbered years
Submit documentation from the applicant's home state that verifies that the pharmacy license in the home state is valid and in good standing
Designate someone who is a resident of the state of Alabama as the resident agent
If the applicant has plans to operate with remote order processing but not the shipping, mailing, or delivering of medications to an Alabama citizen, the applicant must also maintain compliance with the following requirements:
All requirements set forth by the state of Alabama pertaining to controlled substances
All requirements set forth by the state of Alabama pertaining to drug product selection laws
ALBOP requirements for data submission pertaining to volumes of orders processed

- The system that will be used to ensure the quality of remote order processing (both initially and continuing).
- How the site plans to maintain compliance with HIPAA requirements.

Lastly, a pharmacist must be designated as the supervising pharmacist. The supervising pharmacist will be responsible for ensuring that the site maintains compliance with all rules and regulations, including the technician-to-pharmacist ratios [4].

1.3 Display of Permit

The permits and licenses issued by the ALBOP to pharmacists working in a pharmacy must be prominently and conspicuously displayed in the pharmacy's prescription area. The location of the permits and licenses must be readily observable by the public who enter the pharmacy [5].

1.4 Changes in Ownership or Pharmacists

If there are ever any changes in pharmacy ownership or licensed pharmacists, the changes must be reported to the ALBOP within TEN (10) days of the change. If a licensed pharmacist's employment is terminated, the pharmacy owner must notify the ALBOP upon this termination. If the pharmacy owner is not a licensed pharmacist and the licensed pharmacist has been terminated, further operation of the pharmacy in the absence of a licensed pharmacist is prohibited. The pharmacy owner has THIRTY (30) days to comply with this rule. If the owner is a licensed pharmacist and dies, the owner's next of kin has THIRTY (30) days to comply this with rule. If there is not a licensed pharmacist on duty, no prescriptions are allowed to be filled [3].

▶ **Numbers of Importance** Changes in pharmacy ownership or licensed pharmacists must be reported to the ALBOP within TEN (10) days of the change.

1.5 Renewal

Pharmacy permits must be renewed biennially on even-numbered years. All permits are due on October 31 of even-numbered years and will become null and void on December 31 of even-numbered years. If there are ever any changes in pharmacy ownership or licensed pharmacists, they must be reported to the ALBOP within TEN (10) days of the change [3].

Key Concept

Pharmacy permits must be renewed biennially (every 2 years) on EVEN-numbered years. All permits are due on October 31 of EVEN-numbered years and will become null and void on December 31 of EVEN-numbered years.

1.6 Fees

The ALBOP provides cost information regarding pharmacy permits and pharmacy services permits (Table 8.2) [6, 7].

Table 8.2 Pharmacy permit fees [6, 7]

Application	Fee ($)
In-state pharmacy permits	
New	200
Renewals	100
Change in pharmacy ownership	250
Late fee	25
Nonresident pharmacy permits	
New	750
Renewals	400
Change in pharmacy ownership	250
Late fee	25
In-state pharmacy services permit	
New	200
Renewal	100
Change in pharmacy ownership	250
Late fee	25
Out-of-state pharmacy services permit	
New	750
Renewal	400
Change in pharmacy ownership	250
Late fee	25
Nondisciplinary Late Renewal Fee if renewal is received January 1–January 30	
Retail, institutional, nonresident pharmacies, and pharmacy services permit	1000
Pharmacy controlled substance permits, including retail, institutional, and nonresident pharmacies	500

2 Hours of Operation

For community pharmacies specifically, the pharmacy must be open a minimum of TWENTY (20) hours per week. A pharmacy may request an exception or waiver from the ALBOP in cases of special circumstances. A representative of the pharmacy must meet with the ALBOP before an exception or waiver is granted. The pharmacy's daily hours of operation must be clearly displayed on a sign that is located either at the main entrance of the building or near the prescription department. The sign shall include block letters that are at least ONE (1) inch in height [8].

> **Numbers of Importance** Community pharmacies must be open for a minimum of TWENTY (20) hours per week.

3 Supervising Pharmacist

Each pharmacist must designate one pharmacist as the supervising pharmacist. The supervising pharmacist is responsible for only one pharmacy and must practice at that pharmacy. If a pharmacist is supervising a pharmacy and an institutional pharmacy that is open less than 15 hours per week, the pharmacist is not considered to be supervising more than one pharmacy. Additionally, if a pharmacist is supervising a pharmacy and another pharmacy that is open less than the minimum number of hours allowed by the ALBOP, the pharmacist is not considered to be supervising more than one pharmacy. The supervising pharmacist must be on duty at the pharmacy a minimum of 50% of the hours the pharmacy is open or at least THIRTY (30) hours per week, whichever is less.

Within TEN (10) days of assuming the supervising pharmacist role, the supervising pharmacist must notify the ALBOP by completing the "Notice of Change of Supervising Pharmacist" form. The supervising pharmacist's name must be clearly displayed to the public in the pharmacy's prescription department. Within FIFTEEN (15) days of assuming the supervising pharmacist role, the supervising pharmacist must take an inventory of the pharmacy's controlled substances. Additionally, the supervising pharmacist has specific roles and responsibilities (Table 8.3) [9].

If the pharmacy permit holder violates any rules or regulations, the ALBOP may hold the permit holder responsible and not the supervising pharmacist. The pharmacy permit holder is responsible for ensuring that the supervising pharmacist is working the designated number of hours necessary to satisfy the ALBOP's requirement as well as the requirement to renew the pharmacy's permit. If the supervising pharmacist is no longer employed at the pharmacy or no longer wishes to serve as the supervising pharmacist, the permit holder must notify the ALBOP within 10 days. The permit holder must submit an action plan designating another pharmacist as the supervising pharmacist. If this plan exceeds 90 days, the permit holder is in violation of operating the pharmacy without a supervising pharmacist, and the ALBOP may require the pharmacy to close until a supervising pharmacist can assume the role. If a supervising pharmacist is temporarily absent for more than

Table 8.3 Supervising pharmacist roles and responsibilities [9]

Supervising the pharmacy personnel, including ensuring that all pharmacy personnel's licenses and registrations are current and in good standing order with the ALBOP
Maintaining accurate prescription records
Maintaining the prescription department's security
Ensuring that only licensed pharmacists provide professional consultation with patients and/or physicians
Ensuring that only licensed pharmacists accept telephone prescriptions
Operating the pharmacy in a clean and orderly manner
Maintaining inspection records provided by the ALBOP. The supervising pharmacist must notify the ALBOP of any discrepancies within 15 days of discovery
Ensuring the pharmacy is operated under good pharmaceutical practices at all times by ensuring compliance with all rules and regulations set forth in the Pharmacy Practice Act, Rules of the ALBOP, and the Controlled Substance Act
Notifying the ALBOP within 10 days of terminating the supervising pharmacist role by completing the "Notice of Change of Supervising Pharmacist" form

30 days, the permit holder must designate a temporary supervising pharmacist and notify the ALBOP of the person's name and how long they anticipate them serving in this role. The permit holder must notify the ALBOP prior to the temporary pharmacist assuming this role. The permit holder must notify the ALBOP when the original supervising pharmacist returns from their absence [9].

► **Numbers of Importance** The supervising pharmacist must be on duty at the pharmacy a minimum of 50% of the hours the pharmacy is open or at least THIRTY (30) hours per week, whichever is less.

Within TEN (10) days of assuming the supervising pharmacist role, the supervising pharmacist must notify the ALBOP by completing the "Notice of Change of Supervising Pharmacist" form.

4 Absence of Pharmacist

4.1 Absence of Licensed Pharmacist Supervising an Assistant

In a situation where there is a licensed pharmacist who is supervising an assistant and the pharmacist leaves the premises, the pharmacy must post a sign on the prescription counter that includes the pharmacist's name, the hours in which the pharmacist will be away from the pharmacy, and the pharmacist's contact information including address and telephone number. If the pharmacist has designated another pharmacist as an alternate supervising pharmacist, then the sign must include that pharmacist's name, address, and telephone number. The supervising pharmacist must be able to return to the pharmacy within THIRTY (30) minutes of being summoned [10].

4.2 Temporary Absence of Pharmacist

The purpose of this rule is to provide pharmacists with breaks and meal periods. If the pharmacy has one pharmacist on duty, the pharmacist may temporarily leave the pharmacy area for breaks and meal periods without closing the pharmacy. The pharmacist has the right to decide whether to remove pharmacy technicians, interns, and externs from the pharmacy during their temporary absence. This decision is based on whether they believe the security of the pharmacy's controlled substances will be maintained during their absence. The pharmacist may choose to close the pharmacy during their absence, and in this case, they should remove pharmacy technicians, interns, and externs from the pharmacy. While the pharmacist is absent from the pharmacy, prescription medications may be provided to patients but only if the medications are new or refill medications that the pharmacist had previously verified and determined that the prescriptions did not warrant a pharmacist's consultation.

During the pharmacist's temporary absence and if the pharmacist has allowed them to remain in the pharmacy, pharmacy technicians, interns, and externs may continue to perform duties according to rules that are deemed nondiscretionary. When the pharmacist returns to the pharmacy, they must review the pharmacy technicians', interns', and externs' work. A pharmacist may be temporarily absent from the pharmacy for no more than THIRTY (30) minutes. In addition, the pharmacist must remain within the facility during this temporary absence and be readily available in case of an emergency. The pharmacy must have written documentation in the site's policies and procedures that outline the process for the management of the pharmacy area during the temporary absence of the pharmacist for breaks and meals [11].

▶ **Numbers of Importance** A pharmacist may be temporarily absent from the pharmacy for no more than THIRTY (30) minutes.

5 Pharmacy Requirements

5.1 Prescription Department

All pharmacies other than hospital pharmacies must adhere to prescription room area requirements. The pharmacy area must be a minimum of 240 square feet. This area includes the prescription compounding area, prescription dispensing area, and the area in which restricted drugs are sold. The prescription compounding counter's surface must be at least 24 inches in width. The size of the pharmacist's workspace depends on the number of pharmacists that are present in the pharmacy. If there is one pharmacist present, there must be at least 16 square feet of unobstructed working space. If there are two pharmacists present, there must be at least 24 square feet of unobstructed working space. The floor aisle where the pharmacist is located must extend the entire length of the prescription compounding counter and be clear and unobstructed for at least 36 inches from the working side of the counter [12].

All licensed pharmacies, including institutional pharmacies' satellite pharmacies, are to have on hand the latest edition of "Facts and Comparisons" or another reference material (book or electronic media). Additionally, they are required to have both hot and cold running water in the prescription area. Community pharmacies must also have an exempt narcotic register. Lastly, pharmacies should have any additional technical equipment needed to support its level of practice. The example provided in the rules is that pharmacies that prepare intravenous products need to have a hood [13].

▶ **Numbers of Importance** The pharmacy area must be a minimum of 240 square feet.

The prescription compounding counter's surface must be at least 24 inches in width.

If there is one pharmacist present, there must be at least 16 square feet of unobstructed working space. If there are two pharmacists present, there must be at least 24 square feet of unobstructed working space.

The floor aisle where the pharmacist is located must extend the entire length of the prescription compounding counter and be clear and unobstructed for at least 36 inches from the working side of the counter.

5.2 Consultation Area

Each pharmacy must have a private consultation area in which the pharmacist can communicate with patients regarding their medications and other pertinent information (Fig. 8.1) [14]. This rule is in response to the patient counseling standards details in the Omnibus Budget Reconciliation Act of 1990 (OBRA '90). OBRA '90 required pharmacists to offer counseling to Medicaid patients [15]. Regarding the size of the consultation area, it must be large enough to accommodate the pharmacist and patient. The consultation area must be a dedicated space to providing patient care and counseling and not simply a storage room for pharmacy-related products. The patient must be able to access the consultation area from the outside of the pharmacy area and must be private to sound as well as viewing by unauthorized people. The consultation area must be located away from the pharmacy's checkout area and located in an area that does not disrupt the flow of the pharmacy traffic or present any barrier to communicating with the patient.

Fig. 8.1 Private consultation area in a pharmacy. (Source: Lena McDowell)

If the pharmacy opened after January 1, 1997, the pharmacy must be in compliance prior to receiving a permit. Any pharmacy that is relocated after this date must be in compliance. All pharmacies must be in compliance by the date of January 1, 2005 [14].

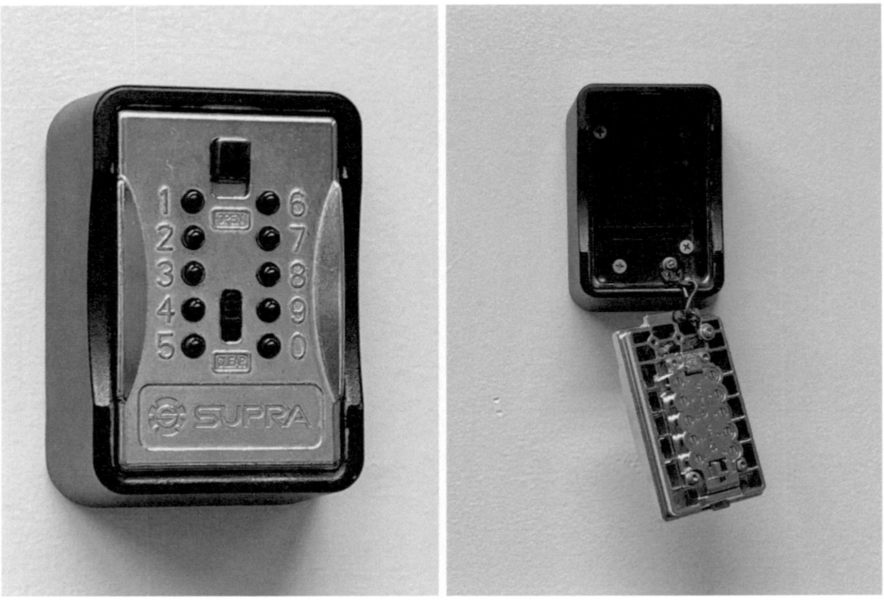

Fig. 8.2 Knox box closed and open. (Source: Lena McDowell)

6 Pharmacy Access

While a pharmacy is not open for business, it must remain enclosed and securely locked. There is an exception during a pharmacist's temporary absence from the pharmacy (see Chap. 8, Sect. 3.2). Registered pharmacists who have been designated by the pharmacy licensee must always have the pharmacy keys or alternate controlled access device in their possession. The pharmacy owner may designate one person who is not a registered pharmacist to have possession of the pharmacy keys or alternate controlled access device. The supervising pharmacist must agree to this person having access to the pharmacy keys. The pharmacy owner must have a signed agreement with the person who is not a registered pharmacist that they have designated pharmacy access to and must submit the agreement to the ALBOP. The ALBOP must review and approve the agreement prior to the person receiving keys or other access to the pharmacy.

If local rules require that access to the pharmacy via keys or other controlled access be made available to first responders to maintain compliance with the fire code, the pharmacy owner must execute a signed agreement with the official who possesses the highest rank within the organization that requires access. A copy of the agreement must be submitted to the ALBOP for review and approval before the owner provides access to a key or other access device to the official. A Knox Box (Fig. 8.2) or alternate method for accessing the key or other access device must have a tamper protection system that is connected to an alarm system. This system must be in working order and set up so that the pharmacy owner or supervising pharmacist is notified if there is an attempt to remove the key or other access device by any unauthorized person.

In the case where the pharmacist does not have access to the pharmacy's prescription area when the entire store is closed, the owner should have an established plan which grants the pharmacist access to the prescription area in case of an emergency [16].

7 Central Prescription Filling

Per the ALBOP Administrative Code, central prescription filling is "the filling of a new or refilling of a prescription drug order by one pharmacy licensed by the Alabama State Board of Pharmacy at the request of another pharmacy licensed by the Alabama State Board of Pharmacy for delivery to the patient or patient's agent, pursuant to the lawful order of a practitioner" [17].

7.1 Operational Standards

A pharmacy may outsource the filling of a prescription drug order to another pharmacy given the two pharmacies:

- Share the same owner.
- Execute a written agreement stating the services to be provided and responsibilities of each pharmacy.
- Share a common computer system or have the technology for the two pharmacies to share information required to fill the prescription drug order.
- Have presented a presentation to and been approved by the ALBOP.

For the remainder of this section, the two pharmacies will be referred to as the filling pharmacy, the pharmacy that fills the prescription drug order, and the dispensing pharmacy, the pharmacy that delivers the prescription drug order to the patient or ultimate user. The supervising pharmacist at the filling pharmacy must ensure the pharmacy uses appropriate shipping processes to maintain the drug's stability, potency, and security throughout the delivery process. If a prescription drug order that has been filled is not picked up, the drug must be returned to the dispensing pharmacy's inventory. There is the stipulation that Schedule I and II controlled substance medications may not be centrally filled. Neither the filling pharmacy nor the dispensing pharmacy may accept the return of any unused portions of filled prescriptions.

Any pharmacy who engages in outsourcing prescription drug orders to be filled by a central pharmacy must notify patients prior to outsourcing their prescriptions. The pharmacy may notify patients by providing a one-time written notice or by displaying a sign containing this information in the pharmacy. The information must include the name of the pharmacy or network of pharmacies that may fill the prescription drug orders [17].

7.2 Prescription Labeling

In addition to the federal and state labeling requirements, the filling pharmacy must include a unique identifier of the filling pharmacy as well as the name and address of the dispensing pharmacy on the prescription drug order label. The label should clearly indicate which pharmacy filled the prescription drug order. The example statement provided in the rules is: "Filled by ABC Pharmacy for WYZ Pharmacy" [17].

7.3 Records

In addition to adhering to the recordkeeping rules, there is certain information that the dispensing and filling pharmacies must document and maintain. The dispensing pharmacy must keep a record of the date on which the request to fill the prescription drug order was made. Additionally, it must document the date on which the prescription drug order was received from the filling pharmacy and the person who accepted the delivery. The filling pharmacy must keep records that track the prescription drug order throughout the entire process, including transmission, filling, dispensing, and delivery. The records must include the name, initials, or identification code for each pharmacist or pharmacy technician who performed the aforementioned steps in process. The filling pharmacy must also maintain records that include the date the prescription drug order was shipped to the dispensing pharmacy, the name and address of the dispensing pharmacy where the prescription drug order was shipped, and the delivery method [17].

7.4 Policies and Procedures

The filling and dispensing pharmacies shall develop and keep a policies and procedures manual on site and have it readily available for inspection. The manual should outline the specific responsibilities of each pharmacy and include each pharmacy's name, address, telephone number, and license and registration numbers. Specific policies and procedures should be included for the following [17]:

- "Notifying patients that their prescriptions may be outsourced to another pharmacy for centralized prescription filling and the name of that pharmacy;
- Protecting the confidentiality and integrity of patient information;
- Dispensing prescription drug orders when the filled order is not received or the patient comes in before the order is received;
- Complying with federal and state laws and Rules;

- Operating a continuous quality improvement program for pharmacy services designed to objectively and systematically monitor and evaluate the quality and appropriateness of patient care, pursue opportunities to improve patient care, and resolve identified problems.
- Annually reviewing the written policies and procedures and documenting such review."

8 Remote Work

Per the ALBOP Administrative Code, "remote pharmacy work means performing the practice of pharmacy while not physically located within a permitted pharmacy or facility" [18]. There are several stipulations for being able to perform remote pharmacy work, including that pharmacists must be an employee of certain entities (Table 8.4) [18].

The remote location must be located within the United States or United States territories. Additionally, the remote location must have the capability to allow the pharmacist to securely access the pharmacy or facility's system. Both the Health Insurance Portability and Accountability Act and the Health Information Technology for Economic and Clinical Health Act must be followed in order to protect health information data. Pharmacists who engage in remote pharmacy work must be able to perform their responsibilities in the same manner (i.e., same level of competence, attention, and proficiency) as if they were physically located in the pharmacy or facility. If a pharmacist who is engaged in remote pharmacy work changes employment, their access to the pharmacy or facility's system needs to be revoked as they will no longer be engaged in remote work for the site.

The regulations outline activities that are not permitted through remote pharmacy work. Those activities include [18]:

- Final product verification.
- Storing, packaging, and/or labeling of prescription drugs.
- Dispensing of a prescription.
- Receiving of hard copy prescriptions.
- Duplicating, downloading, transferring, or removing part of the pharmacy or facility's database.
- Performing remote pharmacy work for more than one location of a pharmacy or facility.

Table 8.4 Pharmacist employers for remote work [18]

ALBOP-permitted pharmacy or facility
Alabama Department of Public Health-regulated facility
Alabama Department of Insurance-regulated facility
Physician's office

9 Pharmacy Off-Site Order Entry

Per the ALBOP Administrative Code, "off-site order entry pharmacy means a pharmacy which has a valid permit issued by the Board to process legend and controlled substance prescriptions that remotely accesses another pharmacy's electronic data base from outside the pharmacy in order to process prescription drug orders, provided the pharmacy establishes controls to protect the privacy and security of confidential records." [19] Certain activities are allowable as part of off-site order entry (Table 8.5) [19].

Performing a drug regimen review is allowable as part of off-site order entry, but what exactly does this involve? This process involves reviewing a prescription drug order and a patient's profile for allergies, contraindications, dose and route of administration, directions for use, potential duplicate therapy, drug interactions (with other drugs or food), and proper utilization, including both overutilization and underutilization.

Before a pharmacy may engage in off-site order entry, either the supervising pharmacist or the pharmacy permit holder must submit a written request to the ALBOP requesting off-site order entry. This request must be made at least THIRTY (30) days prior to the pharmacy initiating off-site order entry. Accompanying the request, the supervising pharmacist or the pharmacy permit holder will submit a policy and procedure manual. This manual outlines the participating pharmacies' responsibilities and must be retained and available for inspection at all pharmacies involved in off-site order entry. Additionally, the following information must be included:

- Name, address, and telephone number of all pharmacies involved in off-site order entry.
- Policy and procedure for maintaining patient confidentiality.
- Policy and procedure for meeting compliance with HIPAA requirements.
- Procedure for documenting the name, initials, or identification code and specific activities of the pharmacist or pharmacy technician who performed a task and the pharmacy in which the task was performed.
- Procedure for tracking the prescription drug order throughout the entire dispensing process.
- Procedure for reviewing the policies and procedures annually and documentation of the review.

Table 8.5 Allowable off-site order entry activities [19]

Interpreting or clarifying prescription drug orders
Entering prescription drug order information
Transferring prescription drug order information
Performing a drug regimen review
Obtaining refill authorizations
Obtaining substitution authorizations
Performing therapeutic interventions
Providing clinical drug information regarding a patient's prescription

The pharmacist involved in off-site order entry is responsible for ensuring compliance with the policies and procedures. The pharmacist or pharmacy technician working directly under the pharmacist may only enter prescription drug orders from a pharmacy that is a duly licensed pharmacy. In order for two pharmacies to engage in off-site order entry, the pharmacist must share the same electronic file (or have the appropriate technology to allow access to information), share the same owner, or enter into a written agreement stating the services to be provided and responsibilities of each pharmacy. Both pharmacies must have permits issued by the ALBOP and be in good standing. Additionally, retail pharmacies engaged in off-site order entry are required to be located within TWENTY-FIVE (25) miles of each other.

If an institutional facility is involved in off-site order entry, it may not have an average daily census of over 75 beds or an in-house pharmacy that is available 24 hours a day 7 days a week. Institutional pharmacies may in cases of emergency engage in off-site order entry. They must provide emergency policies and procedures to the ALBOP that contain the definition of emergency, identify security measures, and outline processes for maintaining HIPAA compliance. The pharmacy must notify the ALBOP within 72 hours of enacting the emergency plan and the anticipated duration of the emergency plan. The pharmacy must also notify the ALBOP once the emergency has ended.

Working from home, a call center, or from a portable computer outside of a pharmacy is strictly prohibited. Any task completed by a pharmacy technician must be verified by the pharmacist who is present onsite before transferring the prescription drug order to another pharmacy or dispensing it to a patient.

Similar to remote order entry, the initials of the pharmacist who entered the data must be present on the prescription drug order's label. Also, patients must be notified that the pharmacy may outsource off site prescription order entry to another pharmacy. This notification must be provided to patients before outsourcing their prescription and include the name of the pharmacy to which the prescription may be outsourced. The notification may either be provided through a onetime written notice or a sign in the pharmacy that displays this information.

Both pharmacies involved in off-site order entry must keep records that document the name, initials, or identification code of the pharmacist or pharmacy technician who performed each task in the prescription drug order process. This information must be kept for at least 2 years from the date of entry. The information may either be stored separately at each pharmacy or in a shared electronic file as long as the system can produce a printout of the tasks performed by each pharmacy team member. Hard copy prescription drug orders must be able to be readily retrieved. Each prescription drug order, including the original hard copy prescription and the scanned image, can only be assigned one prescription number [19].

Specifically for off-site vaccine order entry processing, a licensed pharmacist or a registered pharmacy technician and/or intern under the supervision of a licensed pharmacist, may access the pharmacy's electronic database remotely to process vaccinations. The pharmacy must have controls in place to protect patients' privacy and security. The processing is limited to the following:

- Interpreting or clarifying vaccine orders.
- Data entry of the vaccine order information.
- Performing drug regimen review.
- Providing clinical vaccine information concerning a patient's immunizations.

Off-site vaccine order entry processing does not include order entry or dispensing for any drugs, including legend drugs and controlled substances. Off-site order entry processing for vaccines must occur in real time at the remote location where the vaccines are being administered. Any technology used to facilitate off-site vaccine order entry processing must be returned to the pharmacy once order entry has been completed so that it can be securely stored. If any records are generated as part of the off-site vaccine order entry process, they must be securely stored at the pharmacy for a minimum of 2 years [20].

Key Concept

Before a pharmacy may engage in off-site order entry, either the supervising pharmacist or the pharmacy permit holder must submit a written request to the ALBOP requesting off site order entry. This request must be made at least THIRTY (30) days prior to the pharmacy initiating off-site order entry.

In order for two pharmacies to engage in off-site order entry, the pharmacist must share the same electronic file (or have the appropriate technology to allow access to information), share the same owner, or enter into a written agreement stating the services to be provided and responsibilities of each pharmacy. Retail pharmacies engaged in off-site order entry are required to be located within TWENTY-FIVE (25) miles of each other.

10 Mail Order Pharmacy

All pharmacies engaged in shipping, mailing, or delivering prescription drugs and/or devices to Alabama residents must be registered and obtain a mail order permit with the ALBOP. Each nonresident mail order pharmacy must designate an Alabama resident as the agent of record for service of process. For a mail order pharmacy to receive a permit, they must comply with certain requirements (Table 8.6) [21].

All mail order pharmacies must comply with rules and regulations regarding controlled substances in the state of Alabama, even if they differ from federal rules and regulations; drug product section; labeling prescriptions dispensed; and medication quantities to be dispensed. These nonresident pharmacies must develop a policy and procedure manual and provide it to the ALBOP. The manual must detail normal delivery protocols and time and the procedure for instances when a patient's medication is unavailable at the nonresident pharmacy or the delivery will be delayed beyond the normal delivery time. Additionally, the manual must explain the pharmacy's plan for addressing delivering medications to patients during cases of

Table 8.6 Mail order pharmacy requirements [21]

Possess registration in the state in which the pharmacy is located and maintain good standing
Maintain dispensing records of legend drugs and/or devices dispensed to Alabama patients
Provide requested information to the ALBOP
Maintain pharmacy hours that allow for the timely dispensing of drugs to Alabama patients, and provide access for patients to consult with a licensed pharmacist about their medications
Provide patients with toll-free telephone consultations with a pharmacist at the pharmacy who has access to the patient's records. Ensure the telephone number is visible on the medication label
Designate a supervising pharmacist who is licensed in the state of Alabama and who will be responsible for ensuring the pharmacy permit holder complies with all rules and regulations. If there is a change in the supervising pharmacist, the pharmacy permit holder must notify the ALBOP by submitting the "Notice of Change of Supervising Pharmacist" form. If the pharmacy permit holder does not appoint another pharmacist as the supervising pharmacist, they must notify the ALBOP within 10 days with an action plan to designate another pharmacist as the supervising pharmacist. The action plan must not exceed 90 days or else the pharmacy permit holder will be in violation of operating a pharmacy without a supervising pharmacist. The ALBOP may require that the pharmacy close until a supervising pharmacist is appointed

acute illness whether via delivery courier or an alternative method to ensure the patient receives the medication as soon as possible. Lastly, the manual must also address the plan for instances when the patient has not received the medication via delivery and is out of the medication. The pharmacy must have a policy for ensuring the patient receives the medication in the interim while the medication is being mailed [21].

Key Concept

All pharmacies engaged in shipping, mailing, or delivering prescription drugs and/or devices to Alabama residents must register and obtain a mail order permit with the ALBOP. Each nonresident mail order pharmacy must designate an Alabama resident as the agent of record for service of process.

11 Prescription Drug Disposal

Pharmacies that receive, collect, or dispose of controlled substances from ultimate users or people entitled to dispose of prescription drugs must comply with the Secure and Responsible Drug Disposal Act of 2010. Ultimate users are people who have lawfully obtained and who possess medications for their own use or for the use of a member of the person's household. It can also refer to medications for an animal owned by the person or member of the person's household. A person entitled to dispose of prescription drugs refers to someone who is lawfully able to dispose of a deceased person's prescription drugs if the deceased person was an ultimate user and died while in possession of the drugs.

The pharmacy must obtain authorization from the DEA to be a designated collector and submit this documentation to the ALBOP within 10 days of receiving it. Pharmacies that receive, collect, or dispose of noncontrolled substances from patients should follow the same requirements as for controlled substances with the exception that they do not have to receive authorization from the DEA. The pharmacy must notify the ALBOP if it ceases to collect medications from patients [22].

References

1. Berenbrok, L. A., Tang, S., Gabriel, N., Guo, J., Sharareh, N., Patel, N., Dickson, S., & Hernandez, I. (2022). Access to community pharmacies: A nationwide geographic information systems cross-sectional analysis. *Journal of the American Pharmacists Association: JAPhA, 62*(6), 1816–1822. https://doi.org/10.1016/j.japh.2022.07.003
2. Valliant, S. N., Burbage, S. C., Pathak, S., & Urick, B. Y. (2022). Pharmacists as accessible health care providers: quantifying the opportunity. *Journal of managed care & specialty pharmacy, 28*(1), 85–90. https://doi.org/10.18553/jmcp.2022.28.1.85
3. Ala. Code. § 34-23-30 (1975, rev. 2022) Available from: https://alison.legislature.state.al.us/code-of-alabama
4. Alabama State Board of Pharmacy Administrative Code, Chapter 680-X-2 Practice of Pharmacy. § 680-X-2-.41 (2012 and rev. 2013)
5. Ala. Code. § 34-23-70 (1975, rev. 2022) Available from: https://alison.legislature.state.al.us/code-of-alabama
6. Alabama Board of Pharmacy. License fees [Internet]. 2024 [cited 2024 May 31]. Available from: https://albop.com/license-fees
7. Alabama State Board of Pharmacy Administrative Code, Chapter 680-X-2 Practice of Pharmacy. § 680-X-2-.48 (2010 and rev. 2022)
8. Alabama State Board of Pharmacy Administrative Code, Chapter 680-X-2 Practice of Pharmacy. § 680-X-2-.31 (2005 and rev. 2013)
9. Alabama State Board of Pharmacy Administrative Code, Chapter 680-X-2 Practice of Pharmacy. § 680-X-2-.12 (1982 and rev 2021)
10. Alabama State Board of Pharmacy Administrative Code, Chapter 680-X-2 Practice of Pharmacy. § 680-X-2-.06 (1982)
11. Alabama State Board of Pharmacy Administrative Code, Chapter 680-X-2 Practice of Pharmacy. § 680-X-2-.28 (2001 and rev 2002)
12. Ala. Code. § 34-23-71 (1966, rev. 2022) Available from: https://alison.legislature.state.al.us/code-of-alabama
13. Alabama State Board of Pharmacy Administrative Code, Chapter 680-X-2 Practice of Pharmacy. § 680-X-2-.04 (1982 and rev. 2020)
14. Alabama State Board of Pharmacy Administrative Code, Chapter 680-X-2 Practice of Pharmacy. § 680-X-2-.27 (1995 and rev 1996)
15. Patient counseling—a pharmacist's responsibility to ensure compliance. Centers for Medicare and Medicaid Services. 2014. Cited on 2024 May 31. Available from: https://www.cms.gov/files/document/patientcounselingbooklet111414pdf
16. Alabama State Board of Pharmacy Administrative Code, Chapter 680-X-2 Practice of Pharmacy. § 680-X-2-.11 (1982 and rev 2012)
17. Alabama State Board of Pharmacy Administrative Code, Chapter 680-X-2 Practice of Pharmacy. § 680-X-2-.30 (2003 and rev. 2019)
18. Alabama State Board of Pharmacy Administrative Code, Chapter 680-X-2 Practice of Pharmacy. § 680-X-2-.49 (2023)
19. Alabama State Board of Pharmacy Administrative Code, Chapter 680-X-2 Practice of Pharmacy. § 680-X-2-.39 (2009 and rev. 2021)

20. Alabama State Board of Pharmacy Administrative Code, Chapter 680-X-2 Practice of Pharmacy. § 680-X-2-.47 (2009 and rev. 2021)
21. Alabama State Board of Pharmacy Administrative Code, Chapter 680-X-2 Practice of Pharmacy. § 680-X-2-.07 (1982 and rev. 2023)
22. Alabama State Board of Pharmacy Administrative Code, Chapter 680-X-2 Practice of Pharmacy. § 680-X-2-.42 (2013 and rev. 2013)

Legal Requirements Related to the Prescription and Related Items

9

I wondher why ye can always read a doctor's bill an' ye niver can read his purscription.

–Finley Peter Dunne

1 Key Definitions

1. Central Prescription Filling—filling of a new prescription or refill by a pharmacist licensed by the Alabama State Board of Pharmacy (ALBOP) at the request of another pharmacy licensed by the ALBOP for delivery to the patient/patient's agent pursuant to a lawful order from a prescriber [1]
2. Certified Registered Nurse Practitioner (CRNP)—an advanced practice nurse with additional training and certification that has a collaborative practice agreement with a collaborating physician [2, 3]
3. Certified Nurse Midwife (CNM)—an advanced practice nurse with advanced knowledge and skills specific to the management of women's health including pregnancy, childbirth, postpartum period, care of the newborn, family planning, and other gynecological issues that has a collaborative practice agreement with a collaborating physician [2, 3]
4. Dispense—to sell, distribute, administer, leave with, give away, dispose of, deliver, or supply a medication to the ultimate user or their agent.
5. Drug Regimen Review—evaluation of prescription orders and patient profiles for allergies, contraindications, reasonable dose, route of administration, and directions for use, duplication, interactions, or proper utilization [4]
6. Off-Site Order Entry—a process where a pharmacy with a valid permit from the ALBOP process prescription orders. Activities may include interpreting or clarifying prescription orders, data entry, transferring of prescription orders, drug regimen reviews, obtaining authorization for refills or substitutions, therapeutic interventions, or providing clinical drug information. Off-site order entry does not include dispensing [4]

M. N. Bulloch et al., *Pharmacy Law in Alabama*,
https://doi.org/10.1007/978-3-031-84771-4_9

7. Off-Site Order Entry Pharmacy—a pharmacy with a valid permit from ALBOP to process prescription and controlled substance prescription that remotely accesses another pharmacy's electronic database from outside the pharmacy in order to process prescription drug orders [5]
8. Physician Assistant—a licensed and registered healthcare professional who performs medical services under the supervision of a physician [2, 3]

2 Legal Guidance on Prescribing in Alabama

When a prescriber wishes for a patient to be dispensed a medication that is not available over the counter, they write a prescription or a medication order that outlines what medication the patient should receive and how they should take or administer the medication. This prescription is then presented or transmitted to the pharmacy for review and dispensing. Prescribing requirements is one area of pharmacy law that can have significant variation from state to state. All prescribing must comply with any federal laws and regulations which are discussed in more detail in Chap. 3. Alabama laws and rules regarding prescribing and the prescription are found both within the Code of Alabama and the Alabama Administrative Code, but not all of them are located under the "pharmacy" heading. Some are located within other professions (for example, medicine) or from state agencies other than the ALBOP.

3 Authorized Prescribers in Alabama

3.1 Scope of Practice and Related Prescribing

Alabama regulates prescribing according to the type of healthcare provider and according to medication schedule (Table 9.1). In general, all authorized prescribers are allowed to prescribe noncontrolled substances, Schedule IV, and Schedule V

Table 9.1 Authorized prescribing by clinicians in Alabama

	Noncontrolled	Schedule II	Schedule III	Schedule IV	Schedule V	Methadone (for pain)
Physician (MD or DO)	Yes	Yes	Yes	Yes	Yes	Yes
Dentist	Yes	Yes	Yes	Yes	Yes	Yes
Physician assistant	Yes	Restricted	Yes	Yes	Yes	Restricted
Nurse Practitioner	Yes	Restricted	Yes	Yes	Yes	Restricted
Optometrist	Yes	No	Yes—96 h supply	Yes	Yes	No
Podiatrist	Yes	Yes	Yes	Yes	Yes	Yes
Veterinarian	Yes	Yes	Yes	Yes	Yes	Yes
Midwife	Yes	Restricted	Yes	Yes	Yes	Restricted

medications. Schedule II, Schedule III, and methadone prescribing is more limited. Table 9.1 references methadone prescribing only for pain and does not impact any federal or state restrictions on methadone prescribing for substance abuse. Optometrists (Doctor of Optometry or OD) have the most restrictions on prescribing; they may not prescribe any Schedule II medications for any reason, and they may not prescribe any controlled medication containing hydrocodone. Prescribing restrictions on Physician Assistants, Nurse Practitioners, and other physician extenders are covered more in Sect. 3.2.

Prescribers should only prescribe medications within their scope of practice [6] This may have some variation. While technically, physicians may specialize in certain area (e.g., cardiology, internal medicine, and surgery), physicians in Alabama are not legally restricted by pharmacy law or rules in what types of medications they may prescribe, except under certain medication-specific circumstances described elsewhere in this book [6] It is important to understand while both ophthalmologists and optometrists specialize in the care of the eye, ophthalmologists are physicians and are not subject to the same prescribing restrictions as optometrists, who possess a Doctor of Optometry degree. Nonphysician and nonphysician extender prescriptive authority is limited to their narrower scope. Optometrists should limit prescribing to medications necessary for the examination and treatment of diseases of the eye, and podiatrist (Doctor of Podiatry) prescribing should be limited to the care of the feet, toes, and heels. A prescription issued by a dentist should relate to the care of teeth, gums, and the mouth. A veterinarian should only prescribe medications for animals.

Key Concept

In Alabama, pharmacists may refuse to fill or refill a prescription if the pharmacist believes it is not in the patient's best interest, if it would be harmful to the patient, or if there is a question regarding the validity of the prescription. This effectively means that a pharmacist cannot be forced or compelled to fill any prescription.

▶ **Study Pro Tip** When studying what medications each clinician is authorized to prescribe, it may be easier to remember what medications they cannot prescribe.

A prescriber's Drug Enforcement Administration (DEA) registration is terminated when the person passes away, stops professional practice, discontinues the business, surrenders the registration, or "ceases legal existence" [7]. The ALBOP has stated that legitimate prescriptions written before a prescriber's death may be filled after the death for up to a maximum of 30 days' supply with no refills. Prescribing or dispensing controlled substances to oneself, to a spouse, child, or parent is not allowed, except in exceptional and/or emergency circumstances. Pharmacists should notify the Alabama Board of Medical Examiners (ALBME) if this occurs. The same restriction on prescribing to oneself or family does not apply to noncontrolled substances legally, although there may be ethical concerns with the practice. Pharmacists should use their professional judgment on whether to fill such prescriptions [8, 9].

3.2 Prescribing by Physician Extenders

Physician Assistants (PA) and Nurse Practitioners (NP) are the two most common types of physician extenders in Alabama. A Certified Nurse Midwife (CNM) is a physician extender who focuses on women's health, including gynecology and obstetrics. The types of medications that they are authorized to prescribe are listed in Table 9.1, but more specific details are controlled by their respected state oversight agencies. There may be specific restrictions on their ability to prescribe noncontrolled medications, but it is not considered the responsibility of the pharmacist to enforce those restrictions. As discussed above, it is reasonable to expect physician extender prescribing to be limited to their specialty and scope of practice. Unlike physicians, physician extenders are specifically banned from prescribing for themselves or immediate family members [2, 3] In addition to standard requirements of a prescription, they must identify the name, address, and telephone number of their supervising physician.

Key Concept

Physician Assistants, Nurse Practitioners, and Certified Nurse Midwives must have a Qualified Alabama Controlled Substance Certificate (QACSC) to prescribe Schedule III–V medications and a Limited Purpose Schedule II Permit (LPSP) to prescribe Schedule II medications. Both are issued by the Alabama Board of Medical Examiners.

3.2.1 Prescribing of Schedule III–V Medications by Physician Extenders

It is important to be aware of additional restrictions on controlled substance prescribing for these clinicians that may not exist in other states. Physician extenders may prescribe Schedule III–V medications only if they have been issued a Qualified Alabama Controlled Substance Certificate (QACSC) and are limited to those agents listed on a formulary submitted to and approved by the ALBME [2, 3, 10].

The QACSC is an annual certificate specific to each collaborative registration agreement. Legally, only medications listed on the ALBME formulary can be prescribed by the physician extender, but practically it may be difficult for the pharmacist to know the details of that formulary. A new prescription for the Schedule III–V medication is limited to a 30-day supply and may only be reissued (refilled) by the collaborating/supervising physician [11] If a patient was initially issued a prescription for the Schedule III–V medication by the physician AND the patient is maintained on a stable dose, the physician extender may prescribe a 30-day supply with two refills (a 90-day supply total). In addition to a DEA registration, clinicians with a QACSC will have a QACSC registration number (assigned by the ALBME) that should be listed on all prescriptions for controlled substances.

> **Numbers of Importance** 30—physician extenders may prescribe a maximum 30-day supply of a new prescription for any controlled medication (Schedule II–V). Only the collaborating physician may reissue or refill the prescription.

> **Numbers of Importance** 90—physician extenders may prescribe a 30-day supply with up to two refills of a Schedule III–V medication that was initially prescribed by the collaborating physician and the patient takes as a chronic/maintenance medication, for a maximum of 90-day supply.

3.2.2 Prescribing of Schedule II Medications by Physician Extenders

In order to prescribe Schedule II medications, physician extenders must have a valid Limited Purpose Schedule II Permit (LPSP) issued by the ALBME [12, 13] The LPSP is similar to the QACSC with the obvious exception that it only applies to Schedule II medications. The ALBME maintains a submitted and approved LPSP formulary for each prescriber. According to the ALBME, this list is *not* all-inclusive but rather a list of *examples* that the prescriber is authorized to prescribe. An LPSP number must be included on all prescriptions issued under the permit. A LPSP is only issued to clinicians with a DEA number and a QACSC. Therefore, a physician extender could not have authorization to prescribe Schedule II medications without first receiving authorization to prescribe other controlled substances.

How much of a Schedule II medication that a physician extender may prescribe depends on whether the medication is short-acting or long-acting. Prescriptions for short-acting Schedule II medications written under an LPSP are limited to a 30-day supply. If the prescription was a new medication for the patient, it may only be reissued by the collaborating physician. This is similar to what is required for Schedule III–V medications under a QACSC, except that the physician must see and exam the patient before reissuing a prescription for the Schedule II medication. If a medication was initially prescribed by the collaborating physician, the physician extender may issue one prescription for a 30-day supply, after which the patient must see and receive a prescription from the physician.

Long-acting Schedule II medications may only be prescribed under a LPSP for patients in nursing homes, rehabilitation facilities, within an oncology practice, or receiving hospice or palliative care services [13] Even to those patients, the physician extender may only issue prescriptions for medications that are considered maintence doses. New prescriptions and any dose escalations must be issued by the physician. As an example, a nursing home patient who has been treated with the same dose of a transdermal fentanyl patch for a year may be issued a valid prescription from a Physician Assistant. However, that same clinician may not increase the dose of a patient's oxycodone extended-release tablets.

3.3 Healthcare Professionals Who Are Not Allowed to Prescribe in Alabama

Prescribing authorization varies from state to state. There are many healthcare professionals, including those with doctoral degrees, who do not have prescribing privileges in the state of Alabama. The following professionals are not allowed to prescribe medications themselves:

- Pharmacist (except according to an approved collaborative practice agreement).
- Psychologist and doctor of psychology.
- Physical therapist.
- Occupational therapist.
- Chiropractor.
- Registered or licensed practical nurse.
- Doctor of naturopathy.
- Doctor of homeopathy.
- Other provider not specifically authorized to prescribe in Alabama.

While these professionals may not be allowed to prescribe themselves, they may be authorized to communicate a prescription from an authorized prescriber as the prescriber's designee. For example, a registered nurse in a physician's office may call a pharmacy and verbally communicate a prescription on behalf of the physician. The order itself should be specified by the prescriber, and the person acting as a designee should not act independently.

4 Prescribing in Alabama

4.1 Methods of Prescribing

Alabama does not differ from most other states in the ways in which a prescriber can transmit a prescription order to a pharmacy. Chapter 12 discusses medication orders in a hospital, a health system, or a pharmacy providing services to a nursing facility. In the outpatient setting, a prescriber can send a prescription as a valid written prescription order form, orally via telephone (to include leaving a voicemail), by fax, or through an authorized electronic transmission. Prescriptions may also be transferred from one pharmacy to another. Each method of prescribing has its own considerations that the pharmacy professional should be familiar with, some of which may be unique to the state of Alabama.

4.2 Requirements of the Prescription

What information must be included in a prescription order may differ slightly depending on whether the medication is a noncontrolled or controlled substance

Table 9.2 Requirements of prescription orders [16–19]

	Federal requirements (controlled substances)	Alabama requirements		
		Noncontrolled	Schedule III–V	Schedule II
Patient name	YES	YES	YES	YES
Patient address	YES	NO	YES	YES
Date the original prescription was written	YES	YES	YES	YES
Medication name and strength (if needed, dosage form)	YES	YES	YES	YES
Quantity	YES	NO	YES	YES
Directions for use	YES	YES	YES	YES
Total number of refills authorized (if any)	YES	YES	YES	Not applicable
Prescriber's name	YES	YES	YES	YES
Prescriber's signature	YES	NO	YES	YES
Prescriber's address	YES	No	YES	YES
Prescriber's DEA number	YES	NO	YES	YES
Prescription number (assigned by the pharmacist)	NO	YES	YES	YES
Any additional information deemed essential	YES	YES	YES	YES

(Table 9.2). The prescription itself can only use the English or Latin language generally used by medical and pharmacy professionals [14]. Any prescription written using a different language or using non-Latin characters is not valid.

All written prescription blanks issued by a prescriber in Alabama must contain two different signature lines [15]. By signing on one line, the prescriber indicates that only the name of a medication written should be dispensed. Though not always the case, this usually refers to a brand name medication. Signing on the other line indicates that product selection is permitted.

Key Concept

Not every state has the requirement for two signature lines on a prescription blank to indicate whether the prescription should be dispensed as written or if product selection is permitted, allowing the pharmacist to substitute a cheaper, but therapeutically and pharmacologically equivalent drug—usually referring to a generic drug.

A prescription must be for a *single* patient. For example, a pediatrician may not write the same prescription for siblings on the same prescription blank; each person should have their own order. Alabama allows a prescription blank to contain more than one prescription, but only one side of the paper may be used. Multiple pages with a single signature are not permissible.

Key Concept
Written prescriptions (including faxed prescriptions) can include orders for multiple medications on the same paper, but only the front of the paper may be used, and each piece must be signed by the prescriber.

Alabama law specifically prohibits prescription blanks used by prescribers from containing an imprint of the name or address of any pharmacy, pharmacist, or anyone registered with the ALBOP [14].

4.2.1 Information That Must Be Provided on Prescription Orders

Each state has specific requirements regarding what information must be provided on a prescription order. Table 9.2 compares the federal and state requirements for noncontrolled and controlled medications. Federal law requires certain information on prescriptions for controlled substances not mandated by Alabama specifically. However, state law generally requires prescriptions to meet federal requirements, so by default, those items must be included. Paper prescriptions, including those transmitted to the pharmacy by fax, for controlled substances should be manually signed in the same way that a prescriber would sign any other legal document [16] This is a handwritten signature—it should not be a computer-generated signature. Federal law explicitly states that a pharmacist is liable for any controlled prescription that they fill which was not prescribed according to DEA regulations [16].

Prescriptions for Schedule III–V medications used for detoxification or maintenance treatment of addiction must include the identification number issued by the program administrator [16] If the prescription is for gamma-hydroxybutyric acid (GHB), it must include a notation from the prescriber of the medical need for the drug [16].

Most prescribers are familiar with the information required on a prescription. However, there are provisions in the law about what can be done if the pharmacist receives a prescription that is missing certain domains or some domains are incorrect (such as a patient's address). The patient's name, the medication prescribed (except for generic substitution), and the prescriber's signature can never be added or changed [20]. The pharmacist may add or change a patient's address after verifying it with the patient. Other missing information can be documented only after oral consultation with the prescriber [20]. For Schedule III–V medications, this includes the dosage form, strength, drug quantity, directions for use, or issue date. If the prescription for the Schedule III–V medications is missing the prescriber's signature, the pharmacist can obtain a new oral prescription from the prescriber and discard the unsigned one.

Allowable additions or changes to prescriptions for Schedule II medications are less clear. In 2022, The Drug Enforcement Agency issued a guidance document indicating that the agency was reviewing the issue and would be drafting new regulations [21]. Until those regulations are written and approved, pharmacists are expected to adhere to state requirements. In Alabama, any change authorized for a

Schedule III–V prescription may be made to a prescription for a Schedule II medication.

4.3 Acceptable Methods for Receiving a New Prescription

4.3.1 Paper Prescriptions

The concept of the prescription originally referred to a medication written on paper and presented to a pharmacy for dispensing. Many laws and rules relate to the concept of a physically written prescription, and specific information must be included on the document (Table 9.2). A prescriber may only write medication orders for one person on a single prescription blank. More than one noncontrolled medication may be prescribed on a single side of the prescription blank. Information must be written with ink or indelible pencil (e.g., cannot be edited), by typewriter, or printed on a computer printer [16]. Prescriptions for controlled substances should be manually signed by the prescriber in the same way they would sign a legal document.

4.3.2 Prescriptions Given Orally and/or via Telephone

Oral prescriptions were first authorized by the Durham-Humphrey Amendment to the Food, Drug, and Cosmetic Act but are also authorized by Alabama law [14, 17]. It may be given face-to-face, directly by telephone, or left verbally on the pharmacy's voicemail system. Once received, it must be promptly reduced to writing and filed by the pharmacist. "Reduced to writing" can mean literally written out—generally on a pharmacy prescription blank—or directly entered into the pharmacy's computer system. According to Alabama law, only a licensed pharmacist or registered intern may accept an oral prescription of any nature [14].

Oral prescriptions are only permitted for Schedule II medications in emergency situations [16]. Only a quantity adequate to treat the patient during the emergency period may be prescribed and dispensed, and the pharmacist must follow other requirements for oral prescriptions. If the pharmacist is unfamiliar with the prescriber, they must make a reasonable effort to determine that the person is an authorized prescriber. Within 7 days of authorizing an emergency oral prescription, the prescriber must provide (in person or postmarked) the dispensing pharmacist with a written prescription which must contain the phrase "Authorization for Emergency Dispensing" and the date or the oral order on the face. The pharmacist must attach the paper prescription to the oral emergency prescription that had been reduced to writing at the time received. If the prescription is transmitted electronically, the pharmacist must annotate the record of the electronic prescription with the original authorization of the oral order. If a written or electronic prescription is never received by the pharmacist from the prescriber for an emergency oral order, the pharmacist must notify the DEA.

Key Concept

An oral prescription contains the same information required on a paper prescription, except that the pharmacist is the one writing out the information. Instead of a prescriber signature, the prescriber's name is noted.

4.3.3 Faxed Prescriptions

A facsimile machine is an electronic device that sends a copy of an image to a receiver over a telephone line. These machines are still used in pharmacies and in other business, though less often after the introduction of electronic prescribing (e-prescribing). However, it remains a viable method for the pharmacy to receive a prescription, and the pharmacy professional should be aware of what is and is not permissible with this machine. The same allowances and boundaries placed on other methods of prescribing may or may not apply to faxed prescriptions.

To ensure security and confidentiality, the machine that the pharmacy uses to receive faxed prescriptions must be physically located in the pharmacy area and/or department [18, 22]. This means that a store cannot have a fax machine in a front office accessible by non-pharmacy employees where prescriptions are sent. Faxed prescriptions are treated in a similar manner as paper copy prescriptions; each is assigned a pharmacy-specific prescription number and maintained in pharmacy records for minimum 2 years.

4.3.3.1 Noncontrolled and Schedule III–V Medications

A prescription for a noncontrolled or Schedule III–V medication may be sent to the pharmacy via a fax machine so long as it contains all of the information required by federal and state law and rules [18, 22]. This includes refill authorizations. If the prescription is intended for a long-term care (LTC) patient, such as those receiving hospice or in nursing facilities, it must be signed by the prescriber and (if applicable) by the designated person who is actually faxing the prescription to the pharmacy. This requirement appears in the Alabama Uniform Controlled Substances Code but has a stipulation that effectively applies to any prescription medication sent for a LTC patient.

4.3.3.2 Schedule II Medications

A prescription for a Schedule II medication may be faxed to a pharmacy to begin the filling process but may not be dispensed to the patient until the original (paper) *manually signed* prescription is given to the pharmacist for review [16]. There are limited situations where a faxed copy of a Schedule II medication prescription may serve as the original copy, and they are described below. The rules and provisions below in the Alabama Administrative Code mirror federal regulations [16, 18, 22].

1. A Long-Term Care Patient.

   A prescription for a LTC patient, which includes those in nursing facilities or hospice patients, can be sent via fax from the prescriber to the pharmacy [18,

22]. Upon receipt, the pharmacist should verify that the fax received is from the machine of the authorized person who sent it. The facsimile (faxed version) received by the pharmacy serves as the original prescription and should be filed appropriately. All other information required to be on a prescription for a Schedule II medication (see Chap. 4 for details) must appear on the facsimile including the prescriber's signature. If someone other than the prescriber actually sends the fax (e.g., an authorized nurse in a physician's office), their signature must also appear on the fax.

2. Home Infusion and/or Intravenous Pain Therapy Patient.
   A prescription for a Schedule II medication that must be compounded for direct administration for a patient receiving home infusion therapy by the *parenteral, intravenous, intramuscular, subcutaneous*, or *intraspinal* infusion may be faxed by the prescriber or authorized agent to the pharmacy, and the facsimile serves as the original prescription [18, 22]. Because this provision does not authorize the use of faxed prescriptions for any other dosage form other than the ones specified above, the pharmacy setting where this is permitted is limited. This provision is in alignment with federal regulations [16]

4.3.4 Electronic Prescriptions and E-prescribing

Sending a prescription electronically from a prescriber directly to the pharmacy has become a common method of prescribing; some clinicians, both prescribers and pharmacists, have never practiced when this practice was not possible.

All electronic prescriptions (e-prescriptions) must comply with laws and regulations regarding prescriptions and recordkeeping in general. They must include the patient's name and address, medication, strength per dose, directions for use, the prescriber's name, or authorized agent [16, 23]. The network used to transmit the prescription must be approved by the ALBOP [23]. Transmissions must ensure appropriate security and authenticity. This includes the following:

- An electronic signature process that enables the pharmacy to confirm the identity of the prescriber.
- Date and time stamp.
- Transmitting system identifier.
- Prescriber internal sender identification.
- Pharmacy internal receiver identification.

Prescriptions for controlled substances may be sent electronically [16]. When Alabama first implemented its e-prescribing rule, the DEA had not yet implemented its own regulations on the subject. The Alabama rule states that e-prescribing for controlled substances would only be permissible once the DEA regulations were in place, and those regulations must be complied with [23]. Since that time, the DEA has issued rules which are generally consistent with the ALBOP [16].

4.4 Dispensing by Internet Pharmacies

Internet pharmacies are an expanding type of practice setting. A pharmacist who works for an Internet pharmacy must make every reasonable effort to ensure that any order received has been issued for a legitimate medical purpose by an authorized prescriber pursuant to a valid patient–practitioner relationship before the pharmacist may dispense the medication [24]. This requirement must be done regardless of how the prescription is transmitted to the pharmacy.

4.5 Prescription Expirations

It is a common misunderstanding that prescriptions are legally no longer valid after 12 months from the date written. In some states, this is true. However, in Alabama, prescriptions for noncontrolled, Schedule II, and Schedule V medications do not have an expiration date, so long as the other requirement for the prescription is valid. Some insurance or managed care payers may not cover the cost of the prescription after a certain time period, and patients should be aware of any limitations their healthcare coverage imposes. There are no specific Alabama state laws or rules for Schedule III–IV medications, but federal law mandates that prescriptions for Schedule III–IV medications expire 6 months after the date written or after five refills, whichever occurs first [16]. While a prescription may still be "legally" valid, the Alabama pharmacist may use clinical judgment in determining whether the medication prescribed months or years previously should be filled and dispensed to the patient. It is possible that there has been a change in the patient's clinical and functional status, comorbidities, and/or other medications, and a medication that would have been safe and appropriate on the date written is no longer optimal and potentially harmful.

4.6 Prescription Refills

When a prescription is refilled, the date of the refill must appear on the prescription or in a permanent prescription record book—an electronic record is acceptable [14]. When a prescription is written for a medication where the concept of refills is legally allowable (medications except for Schedule II agents), the prescriber should indicate the number of refills authorized. The designation "Refill PRN" (i.e., refill as needed) is legally acceptable for noncontrolled medications in Alabama (in compliance with other refill restrictions), but the medication should only be refilled in quantities commensurate with the dosage scheduled. For example, if the original prescription was written for 30 tablets for a 30-day supply, a refill may not provide 60 tablets for a 60-day supply.

Schedule III–V medications may be refilled up to five times within 6 months of the date the prescription was written [16]. Refills are through any permissible method of prescription transmission. There must be an annotation on either the original paper prescription or in the electronic prescription record each time the medication is refilled. Using the prescription number, certain information must be readily retrievable, including (1) the name and dosage form, (2) date filled or refilled, (3) quantity dispensed, (4) initials of the dispensing pharmacist for each refill, and (5) the total number of refills for that prescription. If the pharmacist simply initials and dates the back of the prescription, or annotates the electronic prescription record, it is considered that the full-face amount of the prescription has been dispensed.

► **Numbers of Importance** Schedule III–V medications may be refilled up to five times within 6 months of the date the original prescription was issued

4.6.1 Emergency Prescription Refills

Emergency prescription refills involve medications necessary for the maintenance or control of a chronic condition where interruption in therapy could result in harm. At times, patients on these medications run out of supply and have no (additional) refills authorized. It can take time to obtain refill authorization from the prescriber, particularly if the issue arises after business hours, on a weekend, or during a holiday. Technically, these types of refills are not permitted based on the definition of a prescription outlined in the Durham-Humphrey Amendment [17, 25]. However, both Alabama law and the Alabama Administrative Code allow the pharmacist to dispense emergency refills under specific circumstances [26, 27] (Table 9.3). The dispensing pharmacist must create a written order that contains all required prescription information with the addition of the phrase "Emergency Fill" [26, 27]. The pharmacist must notify the prescriber of the emergency dispensing within 24 hours [26, 27]. An emergency refill on a medication may only be issued once in a 12-month period, and the pharmacist must inform the patient or representative that the refill is being provided without prescriber authorization and that a prescription will be necessary before any additional medication can be dispensed [26].

Table 9.3 Criteria for dispensing of emergency prescription refills in Alabama [26, 27]

Criteria
A refill authorization from the prescriber cannot be readily obtained
Only one refill containing up to a 72 h supply—or the smallest dispensable package size—of the medication may be dispensed
The medication cannot be a Schedule II medication
The medication is essential to the maintenance of life or continuation of therapy for a chronic condition
There is a record of a prescription at the pharmacy, or the pharmacist has been given proof of a prescription filled within the last 90 days for the patient

4.7 Special Considerations for Prescribing Medications for Weight Loss in Alabama

The ALBME administers rules that regulate prescribing medications for weight loss [28]. These rules primarily focus on the use of controlled substances. Schedule II medications, specifically amphetamines, amphetamine-like anorexic medications, sympathomimetics, or any related medication cannot be prescribed for weight control, loss, or reduction, or the treatment of obesity. Any authorized prescriber may prescribe, dispense, or administer a noncontrolled medication for this purpose, but only a licensed physician may prescribe a Schedule III–V medication. Prescriptions may be written or sent to the pharmacy electronically but are specifically prohibited from being telephoned into the pharmacy as an oral prescription. Patients must meet certain criteria listed in the rule (Table 9.4).

The medication may be prescribed for a maximum of 35 days' supply, after which the patient must be examined by the physician or a physician extender. If continued use of the medication is warranted, the physician may prescribe another 35-day supply. Should the physician determine that the patient requires the medication for an extended period of time, the patient must be reevaluated before each new 35 day-supply is issued. In short, these prescriptions cannot be written with authorized refills.

Prescribing noncontrolled medications, such as a GLP-1 agonist, for weight reduction or obesity has restrictions that the general prescription of noncontrolled agents for other indications does not have. The first prescription may not contain any refills because the patient must be reevaluated after the initial course of therapy has been finished. Subsequent prescriptions may contain five refills which are valid for 6 months after the date on which the prescription is written and issued.

Key Concept

Rules governing refills of noncontrolled substances for weight reduction mimic rules for refilling Schedule III–V medications for indications other than weight loss. Beginning with the second prescription, up to five refills may be authorized and used within 6 months from the date on which the prescription was written.

Table 9.4 Required patient criteria for prescribing Schedule III–V medications for weight loss, reduction, or control [28]

Meets ≥1 body size criteria
BMI ≥ 30 kg/m2
BMI > 25 with ≥1 comorbidity factor
Measurable body fat content ≥25% of total body weight for males and ≥ 30% for females
Abdominal girth ≥40 inches for males or ≥ 35 inches for females
No history of illicit drug or alcohol abuse
No documented contraindications

4.8 Prescription Transfers Between Pharmacies

Transfer of prescription information is allowed so long as the communication of information occurs between licensed pharmacists or interns/externs under the direct supervision of a licensed pharmacist [29] Table 9.5 lists information that must be recorded by the transferring and receiving pharmacy for the prescription [16, 29]. Noncontrolled prescriptions may technically be transferred as often as there is remaining medication authorized on the order. Controlled substances may only be transferred one time [16]. For Schedule II medications, this type of transfer would generally be for an electronically prescribed medication that has not yet been filled and dispensed. The transfer of Schedule III–V includes all remaining authorized refills.

Prescriptions may also be transferred electronically [29] In fact, if a prescription for a controlled substance was originally electronically prescribed, it may only be transferred to another pharmacy in electronic form [16] The transferring pharmacy must provide the receiving pharmacy with all of the original prescription information, the total number of refills and/or quantity of medication remaining, and the name and address of the pharmacy from which the prescription was transferred (e.g., transferring pharmacy). When the receiving pharmacy creates an electronic record for the prescription, it must include the transferring pharmacy's name and the original prescription information. The word "transfer" must be added to the electronic prescription at the receiving pharmacy [16].

All records of prescription transfers must be maintained for at least 2 years from the date of transfer at both the transferring and receiving pharmacy [16].

Table 9.5 Information that must be communicated and documented during oral prescription transfers [16, 29]

	Transferring pharmacist	Receiving pharmacist
Date of transfer	YES	YES
Name of pharmacist/intern/extern transferring the information	YES	YES
Name of pharmacist/intern/extern receiving the information	YES	NO
Name and address of the pharmacy to where the prescription is being transferred (e.g., receiving pharmacy)	YES	NO
Name and address of the pharmacy from where the prescription is being transferred (e.g., transferring pharmacy)	NO	YES
Date the original prescription was issued	NO	YES
Medication name and strength	NO	YES
Directions for use	NO	YES
Total number of refills and/or quantity remaining	NO	YES
Prescribing practitioner's name	NO	YES
Date of last fill by the transferring pharmacy	NO	YES
Any other information deemed essential	NO	YES

> **Study Pro Tip** Most pharmacy records are required to be kept and stored for at least 2 years. There are a lot of different types of records that must be stored. When studying, make note of any records where the required time period is different from the 2-year requirement. It will be easier to remember.

5 Dispensing Medications in Alabama

5.1 Requirements of Prescription Labels

When the law, rule, or regulation refers to prescription labels, it means the label that is placed on a container that is dispensed to the patient (Table 9.6). These are not the same requirements that a manufacturer must comply with when labeling a stock bottle of a medication. Prescription labels are expected to comply with all federal and state requirements (Fig. 9.1) [30] This means that any item not addressed by Alabama law or regulation that is required by a federal law or regulation must still appear on the label. The information outlined in Table 9.6 lists what items are required by Alabama to appear on a prescription label. It is important to note that this is the minimum information that should appear; additional information may be added at the pharmacist's discretion.

Some medications, including but not limited to compounded medications, are mixtures containing more than one ingredient. If the mixture has a "common given name"—a name readily associated with the mixture—only that name must be indicated on the prescription label in the drug name space [30]. Though not specifically stated in the rules, the name should be unique to that particular mixture of ingredients. Names such as "Magic Mouthwash" would not fit this definition because there are hundreds of different recipes and mixtures that are colloquially referred to as "Magic Mouthwash," and which of the ingredients were included in the compound cannot be known without listing them out.

Not all mixtures have a broadly recognized name; some may even be a unique compilation from an individual prescriber. If the label allows, it is good pharmaceutical care to list out the individual ingredients. Sometimes, this is not possible

Table 9.6 Items required to appear on the label of a prescription dispensed to a patient [17, 30]

Alabama requirements	Federal requirements
Pharmacy name and address Medication name Strength per dosage unit Prescriber's direction for use Any additional factual information deemed essential for proper storage, handling, safety, or use of the medication	Pharmacy name and address Serial number of prescription Date filled Patient name Prescriber name Prescriber's direction for use Applicable warning labels

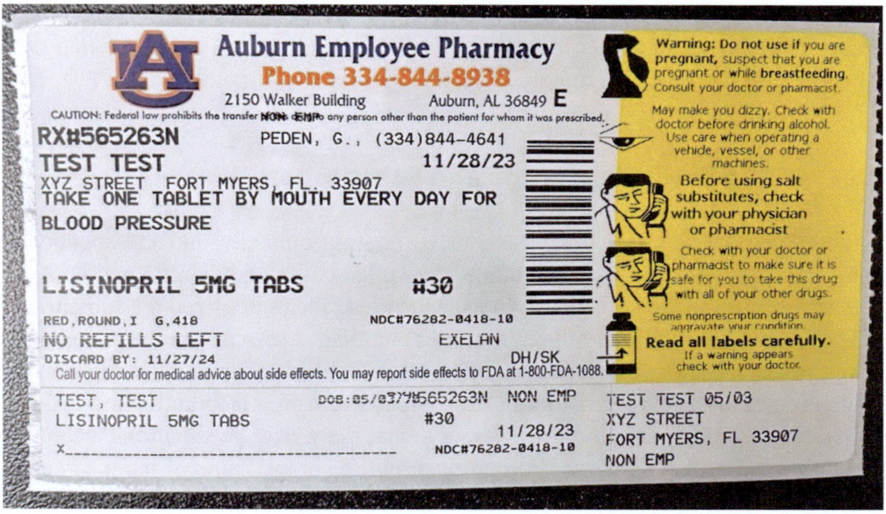

Fig. 9.1 Example of a prescription label. (Source: Greg Peden, PharmD, Executive Director, Auburn University Harrison College of Pharmacy Clinical Affairs and Outreach)

because of the number of ingredients in the mixture. When this occurs, the term "Prescriber's Mixture" can be used on the prescription label [30].

In Alabama, the medication name and dosage can be excluded from the prescription label at the prescriber's request [30]. There are various reasons why this may occur such as clinical research or treatment of patients with compliance concerns. While not required legally, it is a good practice to obtain documentation of the request in writing and keep it on hand.

Labels for medications administered to hospitalized patients have certain exclusions to prescription label requirements [30, 31]. Directions for use may be (and usually are) excluded from labels because medication administration records are used to provide this information to nursing staff administering the medications. Individual unit dose units or floor stock medications are often controlled using "proof-of-use" sheets rather than labels on each product, and therefore the institutional name does not have to appear on these products.

5.1.1 Labels on Over-the-Counter Products

Labels for over-the-counter (OTC) medications are governed by federal law and regulations. The requirements for these labels are discussed in depth in Chap. 3. These requirements assume that the product is being used for self-care outside of medical supervision. However, there will be times when a prescriber will write a prescription for a medication with OTC status. There may be a variety of reasons why a prescriber would do this. For example, a patient's insurance may cover the medication if it is prescribed. The prescriber may also use the prescription as a method for underscoring the importance of the medication in the patient's pharmacotherapy profile. If an OTC medication is prescribed, and the patient elects to have it filled and dispensed rather than purchasing it in its commercial container, the pharmacist should attach a prescription label to the dispensed container that contains the same information required of a noncontrolled substance.

5.2 Drug Product Selection and Substitution

A pharmacist may select a less expensive pharmaceutically and therapeutically equivalent drug product which contains the same active ingredient(s) and is of the same dosage form and strength, so long as the prescriber authorized the substitution [15] This is most commonly thought of as a pharmacist selecting a cheaper generic drug product when the prescriber listed the brand name drug on the prescription, but it also is permissible to substitute a less expensive different brand name product containing the exact same product. Though rare, there may be situations where the prescriber writes for a generic drug product, but the brand name of the medication is cheaper, and the pharmacist may dispense the less expensive brand; this provision would apply to this situation as well. In the same manner, a pharmacist may substitute a less expensive interchangeable biologic product for a brand name biological product [32] However, the law specifically bans biologic therapeutic substitution for Medicaid recipients if the Alabama Medicaid Agency has determined that the prescribed biologic is lower in net cost to the agency.

> **Study Pro Tip** There are places in pharmacy law and rules that use the term "drug" and others where the term "medication" is used. When referring to FDA-approved or investigational products, consider the two terms to be interchangeable.

Key Concept

With drug product selection and substitution, the intended active ingredient, dosage form, and strength of the prescription are dispensed. If a physician prescribes "Lipitor 40 mg" (tablets) and indicates substitution is permissible, the pharmacist may dispense "Atorvastatin 40 mg" (tablets). Substituting a completely different medication is not allowed by this rule. In the previous example, the pharmacist is not permitted to substitute a different statin.

> **Study Pro Tip** It is not necessary, for the purposes of studying for the MPJE, to know which biologic products Alabama Medicaid requires brand name dispensing for. The agency has special contracts and agreements with different manufacturers which may allow the agency to pay a lower cost for a brand name than it could pay for the product that would otherwise be substituted. The law only mentions Medicaid by name, and this exclusion does not apply to any other payer.

On a written or faxed prescription, a prescriber provides this authorization by signing on the appropriate prescription line on the prescription order information [15, 32]. When sending an oral, electronic, or e-faxed prescription, the prescriber should instruct the pharmacist whether drug or biologic substitution may occur or not, and the pharmacist notes the instructions on the file copy of the prescription. A pharmacist (or their designee) is required by law to inform the patient or patient's agent before dispensing an interchangeable biologic product [32] The pharmacist must also notify the prescription that a different biologic product was substituted and which one (including name and manufacturer) was actually dispensed within 24 h (excluding Sunday and federal holidays). Yes—the prescriber notification of a substituted biologic is required even when the prescriber signed or indicated that the authorization was permissible. The pharmacist may notify the prescriber via electronic message using the electronic prescribing system connecting the pharmacy and prescriber's office, by telephone or fax. In contrast, notifying either the patient or the prescriber is not required for traditional (i.e., nonbiologic) medication products. The pharmacist records on the prescription order the name and manufacturer or distributor of the product that was actually dispensed.

An important exclusion to this law involves *hospitals*. For many reasons, hospitals do not obtain and store every possible medication that is commercially available. Hospitals maintain a formulary or a list of drugs that the hospital will use for patient care. When medications within a drug class are considered therapeutically similar by the institution's medical staff, the hospital may only place a limited number, or even one, on the formulary for use. For example, MBC hospital may select pantoprazole as its formulary proton pump inhibitor (PPI). Any time a prescriber orders any PPI at the hospital, the MBC pharmacy will dispense pantoprazole.

5.3 Counseling Requirements

Chapter 3 discusses counseling requirements according to federal law, particularly OBRA-90. Shortly after the federal bill was passed, Alabama implemented rules on counseling [33] Patients must be offered counseling for all NEW prescriptions and, where appropriate, for refill prescriptions. Note that the rule does not say that counseling itself must be provided but only that an offer to counsel must be provided. This offer can be made either by the pharmacist or the pharmacist's designee orally in a face-to-face communication and can be made to either the patient or the patient's representative. If the pharmacist determines that an oral, face-to-face offer is inappropriate or unnecessary, the offer to counsel can be made in written communication, by telephone, or another manner that the pharmacist determines to be appropriate. This offer to counsel is considered a standard of care practice; if a pharmacist is ever involved in civil or criminal issues involving counseling, they should be able to provide evidence that the offer to counsel was indeed provided. A printed statement must be included with each prescription dispensed that lists the pharmacy's telephone number in case the patient has questions about their medications.

To be able to provide this counseling, the pharmacist must appropriately review each new medication (and where appropriate, each refill) for information of importance. Alabama specifically requires that the information below be reviewed, but this list should be considered to be a minimum expectation and not an all-inclusive list [33].

- Therapeutic duplication.
- Drug-disease contraindications.
- Drug-drug interactions.
- Incorrect dosage.
- Incorrect duration.
- Drug allergy interactions.
- Clinical abuse and/or misuse.

Counseling can be provided by the pharmacist or supervised intern [33] The rule specifically lists the following items that the pharmacist may discuss. However, this list is neither mandatory nor all-inclusive.

- Name and description of the medication.
- Dosage form.
- Dose.
- Route of administration.
- Duration of therapy.
- Special directions, precautions for preparation, administration, and use by the patient.
- *Common severe* side effects, adverse effects, interactions, or therapeutic contraindications.
- Techniques for self-monitoring.
- Proper storage.
- Refill information.
- What the patient should do if they miss a dose.

5.3.1 Private Consultation Areas for Counseling

Every pharmacy which dispenses medications directly to patients must have a private area dedicated to patient consultation (Fig. 9.2) [34]. In fact, the ALBOP will not issue a pharmacy permit unless a new pharmacy is in compliance with this rule. Closed door pharmacies, such as a home-infusion pharmacy that does not dispense medication to the pharmacy directly, do not require a private consultation area which is practical since there are no patients who enter the building to consult with. The consultation area must be large enough to accommodate the participants and should be entirely dedicated to patient care. These areas cannot be used to store merchandise or other items when not being used for its intended purpose. The patient must be able to access the area from outside the pharmacy area without having to go through the pharmacy area or a stockroom. It should provide privacy in terms of both sound and viewing from others. The area should not be placed near the

Fig. 9.2 Private consultation area in a pharmacy. (Source: Lena McDowell)

register, checkout areas, or other places where the flow of traffic would restrict privacy and patient communication.

5.3.2 Charging Fees for Counseling

Though not specifically authorized, the Alabama Administrative Code states that there is nothing to prohibit a pharmacist from charging and/or being reimbursed for patient counseling [33]. If the pharmacist does charge, the fee for counseling must be identified on an itemized bill.

5.4 Central Prescription Filling

Most outpatient prescriptions in Alabama are filled by the traditional community pharmacy model. However, Alabama allows central pharmacy filling so long as the two pharmacies involved have the same owner or have a written contract/agreement that lists the services provided and the responsibilities and accountabilities of each pharmacy which must comply with all other federal and state laws and regulations (Fig. 9.3) [1]. Pharmacies wishing to participate in central pharmacy filling must present their request and receive authorization from the ALBOP. There must be a common electronic file or technology that allows access to sufficient information

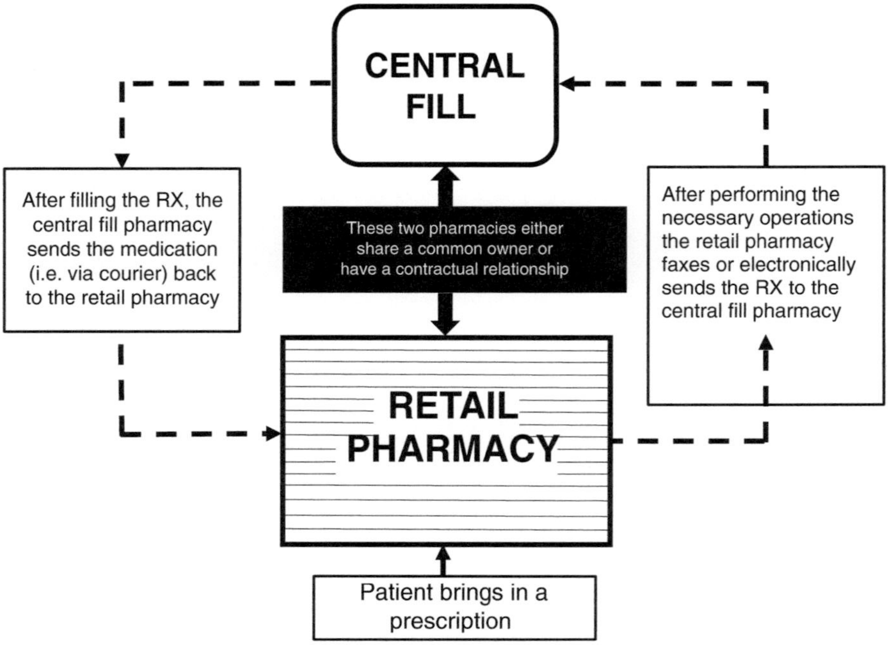

Fig. 9.3 Central fill process

necessary to fill or process the medication order. The pharmacy that fills the prescription will be referred to as the "filling pharmacy," and the pharmacy that ultimately dispenses the medication to the patient/patient's agent will be termed "dispensing pharmacy."

Pharmacies participating in central pharmacy filling must notify patients that prescriptions may be outsourced to another pharmacy. This notice must provide the name of the filling pharmacy. If the pharmacy is part of a network under common ownership where any of the network pharmacies could potentially fill the prescription (such as a chain pharmacy), the notice should state that fact. This notice can be provided either as a one-time written notice or through using a sign at the pharmacy.

Central prescription filling is only permissible for noncontrolled and Schedule III–V medications. In addition to other prescription label requirements, the filling pharmacy must place on the prescription label a "unique identifier" of the filling pharmacy as well as the dispensing pharmacy's name and address. The label should also indicate which pharmacy filled the prescription. A simple statement such as "Filled by Zebra Pharmacy for Lion Pharmacy" is acceptable.

It is the responsibility of the supervising pharmacist of the filling pharmacy to ensure that adequate storage or shipment containers and shipping processes are used to maintain medication stability and potency. Appropriate packaging material and/or devices must be used to maintain the appropriate temperature range to ensure the integrity of the medication throughout the delivery process. These shipping containers must be sealed so that they would show evidence of opening or tampering if it were to occur. Once a medication has been filled and transported to the dispensing pharmacy, it cannot be returned to the filling pharmacy. If the prescription is not picked up by the patient/patient's agent, it should be placed into the dispensing pharmacy's inventory.

Records may be kept in an alternative data retention system, such as a data processing system or direct imaging system so long as they contain all of the information required on the annual record and both pharmacies can produce an audit trail for prescription filling and dispensing.

The dispensing pharmacy's records must list the date that the request for filling was transmitted to the filling pharmacy, the date the filled prescription was received by the dispensing pharmacy, and the name of the person accepting that delivery. The filling pharmacy records must track the prescription order throughout the filling process and identify the names (which may be stated names, initials, or identification codes) and specific activities of each pharmacist or pharmacy technician involved in the process to include transmission, filling, dispensing, and delivery. Their records should also list the date that the prescription was shipped to the dispensing pharmacy, the name and address where the medication was shipped, and the method of delivery.

There must be policies and procedures (which must be reviewed annually with documentation) that direct how patients are notified of central pharmacy filling, protecting patient privacy, compliance with laws and regulations, and how a medication will be dispensed if the filled prescription is not received at all or if the patient arrives before it is received by the filling pharmacy. The policies and procedures should also outline a continuous quality improvement program.

5.5 Off-Site Order Entry

In Alabama, off-site order entry is permissible with approval by the ALBOP [4]. Off-site order entry is when a pharmacy accesses another pharmacy's electronic database from outside the pharmacy in order to process prescription drug orders. Activities involved are listed in the Key Definitions section of this chapter but does not include the actual dispensing of the medication. There must be established controls to protect the privacy and security of all confidential records. The supervising pharmacist must submit a written request to the ALBOP for off-site order entry at least 30 days before the off-site order entry may begin. This request must be accompanied by a policy and procedure manual (Table 9.7). Any modification to the activities, policies, or procedures contained in an approved request must be approved by the ALBOP before being implemented.

In order for a pharmacy to utilize another pharmacy for off-site order entry, the pharmacies must share a common electronic system or have appropriate technology to allow access to sufficient information or required to process a nondispensing function (similar to what is required for central prescription filling). The pharmacies must either have the same owner or have a written contract/agreement that outlines

Table 9.7 Information required in a policy and procedure manual for Off-Site Order Entry [4]

An outline of the responsibilities of each pharmacy
Name, address, and telephone number for each pharmacy involved in off-site order entry
Policies and procedures for patient confidentiality and full HIPAA compliance
Policies and procedures for the maintence of appropriate records to identify the name(s), initials, or identification code(s) and specific activity(ies) of each pharmacist or pharmacy technician who performed any processing and the pharmacy where the processing occurred
Policies and procedures for a mechanism for tracking the prescription order during each step of the process
Policies and procedures to ensure each pharmacist involved in the off-site order process is responsible for ensuring compliance and potential consequences for disciplinary actions for failing to do so
Specification that an Alabama-licensed pharmacist or pharmacy technician working under the direct supervision of a pharmacist shall enter prescription orders at a location that is permitted by the ALBOP
Compliance with federal and state laws and regulations
Procedures for an annual review of the policies and procedures for needed modification with documentation of the review

the services to be provided and the responsibilities and accountabilities of each pharmacy in compliance with federal and state laws and regulations.

There are specific boundaries for off-site order entry. It will only be approved under the following circumstances:

- Community pharmacies are located within 25 miles or one another.
- An institutional facility must have a maximum average daily census of 75 beds AND be without an in-house 24 h pharmacy available 7 days a week.
- Any pharmacy technician function must be verified by the on-site pharmacist prior to transfer to other pharmacy or dispensing to the patient.

Any pharmacies who do not meet the above parameters, but who still want to utilize the off-site order entry, must provide their request as a presentation to the ALBOP. These presentations are often conducted at ALBOP meetings.

Patient confidentiality and HIPAA compliance must be observed. The rule specifically prohibits prescription processing from being conducted outside the physical premises of a pharmacy permitted by the ALBOP. This ban includes work from home, call centers, and work from portable or handheld computers not physically in an Alabama-permitted pharmacy. A hard copy prescription must be readily retrievable. Only one prescription number may be assigned and only in relation to the actual dispensing of the medication.

5.5.1 Institutional Pharmacy Off-Site Order Entry

Off-site order entry is generally associated with either community pharmacies or institutional pharmacies with a small census (less than 75 bed average census) without an in-house pharmacy available at all times. However, institutional pharmacies may institute off-site order entry in certain emergency situations [4]. The institutional pharmacy has to anticipate that they might need to implement emergency off-site order entry and plan for the need ahead of time. There must be emergency policies and procedures created and approved by ALBOP. These policies and procedures must define what "emergency" means to the institutional pharmacy. There must be identified processes and security measures for off-site entry to occur outside the institution's physical location and procedures that ensure HIPAA compliance. If the emergency plan is implemented, the institutional pharmacy must notify the ALBOP within 72 h and inform the ALBOP how long they anticipate the emergency plan to last. The ALBOP should be notified again when the use of emergency actions end.

Key Concept

Off-site order entry approval for community pharmacies and small hospitals (without in-house pharmacies available at all times) must be given by the ALBOP before utilized, but afterward, the ALBOP must only be notified if any detail in the original request changes. Larger institutional pharmacies must either present their request directly to the ALBOP or only use off-site order entry during emergency situations which follow previous Board-approved procedures. When emergency actions are used, the institutional pharmacy must notify ALBOP within 72 h and again when the emergency use of off-site order entry stops.

5.6 Remote Work by Pharmacists

Remote pharmacy work occurs when the practice of pharmacy is performed outside of the physical premises of an Alabama-permitted pharmacy or facility [35]. It is permissible when performed by a pharmacist who is employed by a pharmacy permitted by the ALBOP, a facility permitted by the ALBOP or regulated by the Alabama Department of Public Health or the Alabama Department of Insurance, or by a physician's office. Because of this, a pharmacist may not perform remote work for multiple pharmacies or facilities under the remote work rule. The work must occur in a location within the United States or territories that are equipped with secure access to the information system. There must be controls to protect confidentiality and integrity of protected health information, and all activities must comply with state and federal law and regulations. When a pharmacist is no longer employed by the pharmacy under which remote work is authorized, they should no longer be able to access the information system or perform remote work. Remote work must be performed at the same level of competence, attention, and proficiency as that done by a pharmacist physically present in the pharmacy.

Just as long as the rules allowing remote work are rules outlining what activities are prohibited in relation to remote work. Prohibited activities are described below.

- Product verification and dispensing—except for immunizations, final product verification or dispensing or a prescription from a location outside of or other than the permitted pharmacy is not allowed. (Final product verification or dispensing is covered by other sections such as central prescription filling.)

- A hard copy prescription may not be received outside the premises of a permitted pharmacy.
- The facility's database may not be physically or electronically duplicated, downloaded, transferred, or removed from the electronic database.

Key Concept

Remote pharmacy work, off-site order entry, and central prescription filling all refer to parts of the practice of pharmacy conducted away from the pharmacy where a medication is dispensed. Off-site order entry involves parts of the prescription filling process up to, but NOT including, final product verification or the dispensing process. Handling of the drug product does not occur. This portion is completed at the dispensing pharmacy. In contrast, central prescription filling does involve final product verification and selection, though it occurs at a separate pharmacy from where the actual dispensing occurs. Remote pharmacy work is a catchall for other activities involved in the practice of pharmacy. Although not specifically specified in the rule, this type of work generally involves work beyond prescription processing and dispensing, such as clinical pharmacy activities or work with prior authorizations (among others).

6 Recordkeeping and Record Storage

Pharmacies must maintain patient medication profiles for each patient [33] The pharmacist (or designee) should make a reasonable effort (verbally or in writing) to obtain this information and at minimum should include:

- Patient name.
- Age.
- Gender.
- Address and phone number.
- Individual patient history—to include a list of prescription medications and devices.
- Pharmacist comments.

6.1 Prescription Files and Storage

As mentioned in other sections of this chapter and in other chapters of this book, the pharmacy must add a prescription number to each prescription, and it must follow a mandatory process [36]. The prescriptions are numbered consecutively in the order

Table 9.8 Information required to be stored by computer systems regarding prescriptions and refills in Alabama [36]

Original prescription	Refills
Original prescription number Prescriber name Full patient name and address Date issued (written) Date dispensed (if different from date issued) Medication name Medication strength Medication dosage form Quantity dispensed Total number of refills authorized (including if zero) Prescriber DEA and Alabama-controlled substances number (for controlled substances only) Identification of the dispensing pharmacist	Medication name Date of all refills Quantity originally dispensed Quantity dispensed for *each* refill Total number of refills dispensed to date for the specific prescription order For Schedule III–V medications—documentation that refill information is correct

dispensed. A prescription with the number 540123 indicates that the pharmacy—since it opened—dispensed 540,122 medications prior to that one. This number system is unique to *each* physical pharmacy location. If XYZ Drugs operates a store in Warrior Alabama and in Livingston Alabama, each store will have its own number series.

Prescription files must be kept by the pharmacy for at least 2 years and stored in the order or compounding or dispensing [14]. Each prescription file must contain the initials of the pharmacist who compounded and/or dispensed the medication, the pharmacy-assigned prescription number, and the date that the medication was dispensed.

Before computers, paper files had to be physically stored for retrieval. To improve efficiency and reduce space requirements, Alabama allows pharmacies to use computer systems to store and retrieve original prescription orders (Table 9.8) [36].

Each week, the pharmacy should produce a printout listing all new and refill prescription activity for the pharmacy during that time period [36]. This is separate from the required printout for controlled substance refill data (discussed in Sect. 5.1.1). This report includes data for all prescriptions, regardless of noncontrolled or controlled, and includes dispensing data for new, original prescriptions. These printouts should be kept in a separate binder for at least 2 years.

6.1.1 Special Requirements for Records Regarding Controlled Substances

All pharmacy computer systems must be able to produce a printout of any and all refill data [36]. The report must contain the (1) prescriber name, (2) patient name and address, (3) quantity dispensed for each refill, (4) date each refill was dispensed, (5) identification of the dispensing pharmacist, and (6) the original prescription number. Reports should be able to provide a refill-by-refill audit trail that can be focused on any medication (by generic or brand name), strength, and dosage form.

If a physical copy is not stored on-site at the pharmacy, the central recordkeeping location must provide the printout to the pharmacy within 2 business days.

When a Schedule III–V medication is refilled, the pharmacist must document that the information entered into the computer system from an original prescription order is correct [36]. This must be done for each refill of the medication. This documentation can be done in one of two authorized ways:

1. Computer system hard copy printout—a daily paper printout that lists the day's controlled substance refill data.
   - The pharmacist must verify the information and date and sign it.
   - The report must be available from the computer system within 72 hours of the refill date. Many systems are capable of same-day report printing.
2. Maintenance of a bound logbook (or separate file)—each individual pharmacist involved in dispensing of Schedule III–V medication refills signs a statement each day (they were involved) attesting that the refill information entered into the computer on that day was reviewed by them and is correct.

This documentation should be kept for at least 2 years [36]. If the pharmacy uses the printout method, the printouts should be stored in a separate binder.

When a pharmacy experiences computer software downtime, there must be a procedure used to document refills of Schedule III–V medications which ensures that (1) refills are authorized, (2) not exceeding the maximum number of refills authorized, and (3) that all appropriate data are retained for computer entry as soon as the system is available for use again [36].

6.2 Storage of Records

The laws and regulations addressing the storage of records are discussed in more detail in Chap. 11. Most records must be stored, either on-site or readily retrievable, for at least 2 years.

6.3 Inspections by Authorized Agency and Law Enforcement Personnel

State and federal agencies employ investigators and agents whose role is to ensure federal and/or state laws and regulations on pharmacies and medications are followed. State drug investigators employed by the ALBOP, DEA agents, and local law enforcement officers are just some of the people with whom pharmacy personnel may engage in this regard.

The ALBOP employs state drug investigators, most of whom are assigned to a specific region of the state (Fig. 9.3). Many pharmacists come to know their region's investigator. In order to be employed by the ALBOP as a state drug investigator, the person must submit proof to the ALBOP of good moral character, and the ALBOP must determine that the applicant has sufficient knowledge of the laws pertaining to pharmacy practice and law enforcement in order to carry out investigator duties [37]. Each investigator serves an apprenticeship for a minimum of 6 months and posts a bond of $2000 on the faithful performance of their duties.

By Alabama law, these state drug investigators have the authority to inspect medications, drug products, domestic remedies which are manufactured, packaged, packed, made, sold, offered for sale, exposed for sale, or kept for sale in Alabama [37]. In short, they have access to anything medication related within the state. They may enter, *during business hours*, and inspect any Alabama pharmacy or other place where medications, drug products, or proprietary medicines are manufactured, packaged, packed, made, sold, offered for sale, or kept for sale, whether or not licensed by the ALBOP. Investigators are authorized by law to inspect all records, shipping tickets, or any document pertaining to the transfer of medications or drug preparations, from or to hospitals, pharmacist, wholesalers, manufacturers, or any other place where drugs or drug preparations are kept or stored. This includes, but is not limited to, inspection of all prescription files, prescription record books, poison registers, exempt narcotic registers, and any other prescription-related record. They must comply with restrictions on search and seizures placed on other law enforcement officers but may issue citations for any violation of laws, rules, or regulations, and if necessary, institute criminal proceedings for the violation(s). Investigators are tasked with taking possession of all revoked or suspended pharmacy-related licenses and permits which have not been voluntarily surrendered to ALBOP. State drug investigators only have authority over entities overseen by the ALBOP.

The pharmacy is required to produce any prescription file when legally required [14]. At any time, the prescriber, the ALBOP, or ALBOP investigators should be allowed to inspect a file [14]. ALBOP inspectors and DEA agents must be provided any requested daily printout of controlled substance refill data [36]. If the pharmacy does not have a physical copy on-site, the central recordkeeping location must send it to the pharmacy within 2 business days (Fig. 9.4).

Key Concept

If an Alabama state drug investigator arrives at your pharmacy, they have the right to inspect any aspect of the pharmacy, its operations, or its records. They have the authority of any other law enforcement officer. If they find violations of federal or state pharmacy laws or rules, they can start a process that can lead to ALBOP review and/or criminal proceedings, depending on the violation.

Key Concept

Law enforcement officers, including (but not limited to) state drug investigators and DEA agents, may expect to be allowed entry into the pharmacy during business hours. There is no legal requirement for a pharmacist to provide entry outside of business hours.

Fig. 9.4 Alabama state drug inspectors. (Source: Marilyn Bulloch)

References

1. Alabama State Board of Pharmacy Administrative Code, Chapter 680-X-2 Practice of Pharmacy. § 680-X-2-.30 (2003 and Rev 2019).
2. Alabama Board of Medical Examiners Administrative Code, Chapter 540-X-7 Prescriptions and Medication Orders – Physician Assistants § 540-X-7 (1998 and Rev. 2021).
3. Alabama Board of Medical Examiners Administrative Code, Chapter 540-X-8 Prescriptions and Medication Orders by Certified Registered Nurse Practitioners § 540-X-8 (1996 and Rev. 2021).
4. Alabama State Board of Pharmacy Administrative Code, Chapter 680-X-2 Practice of Pharmacy. § 680-X-2-.39 (2009 and Rev. 2021).
5. Alabama State Board of Pharmacy Administrative Code, Chapter 680-X-2 Practice of Pharmacy. § 680-X-2-.39 (2009 and Rev 2021).
6. Alabama Board of Pharmacy. PRESCRIPTIVE AUTHORITY OF HEALTH PROFESSIONALS IN ALABAMA. Alabama Board Of Pharmacy. Published June 30, 2015. Accessed May 31, 2024. https://albop.com/prescriptive-authority/
7. 21 CFR 1301.52 – Termination of registration; transfer of registration; distribution upon discontinuance of business. Accessed June 7, 2024. https://www.ecfr.gov/current/title-21/part-1301/section-1301.52
8. Alabama Board of Pharmacy. FREQUENTLY ASKED QUESTIONS. Alabama Board Of Pharmacy. Accessed May 31, 2024. https://albop.com/frequently-asked-questions/
9. Alabama Board of Medical Examiners Administrative Code, Chapter 540-X. § 540-x- (1996 and Rev. 2024).
10. Alabama Board of Medical Examiners Administrative Code, Chapter 540-X-18 Qualified Alabama Controlled Substances Registration Certificate (QACSC) for Certified Registered Nurse Practitioners (CRNP) and Certified Nurse Midwives (CNM) § 540-X-8 (2013 and Rev. 2024).
11. Alabama Board of Medical Examiners. Qualified Alabama Controlled Substances Certificate (QUCSC) (Schedules III-V) Prescribing Protocol. Published online July 21, 2021. Accessed May 31, 2024. https://www.albme.gov/uploads/pdfs/QACSC-LPSPprotocol.pdf
12. Alabama Board of Medical Examiners Administrative Code, Chapter 540-X-20 Limited Purpose Schedule II Permit (LPSP) § 540-X-20 (2014 and Rev. 2023).
13. Alabama Board of Medical Examiners. Limited Purpose Schedule II (LPSP) Prescribing Protocol. Published online July 21, 2021. Accessed May 31, 2024. https://www.albme.gov/uploads/pdfs/QACSC-LPSPprotocol.pdf
14. Ala. Code. § 34-23-70 (1966, Rev. 2018).
15. Ala. Code. § 34-23-8 (1966, Rev 2019).

16. 21 CFR Part 1306 – Prescriptions. Accessed June 3, 2024. https://www.ecfr.gov/current/title-21/chapter-II/part-1306?toc=1
17. House of Representatives C. FEDERAL FOOD, DRUG, AND COSMETIC ACT, U.S. Code 21 §§ 301-399f (2022). Published online January 5, 2023. Accessed January 10, 2024. https://www.govinfo.gov/app/details/USCODE-2022-title21/USCODE-2022-title21-chap9/summary
18. Alabama State Board of Pharmacy Administrative Code, Chapter 680-X-3 Alabama Uniform Controlled Substances § 680-X-3 (1982 and Rev. 2020).
19. Alabama State Board of Pharmacy Administrative Code, Chapter 680-X-2 Practice of Pharmacy. § 680-X-2-.45 (2020).
20. Alabama State Board of Pharmacy Policy 20100825. Published online August 25, 2010. https://albop.com/oodoardu/2021/04/AUGUST-2010-Schedule-II-Prescription-Changes-FAQ-.pdf
21. Drug Enforcement Administration. Changes Pharmacists May Make to Schedule II Paper Prescriptions. Guidance Document. Published online October 18, 2022. https://www.deadiversion.usdoj.gov/GDP/(DEA-DC-063)(EO-DEA257)_Changes_to_a_Prescription_Guidance_-_Final.pdf
22. Alabama State Board of Pharmacy Administrative Code, Chapter 680-X-3 Alabama Uniform Controlled Substances. § 680-X-3-.10 (1999).
23. Alabama State Board of Pharmacy Administrative Code, Chapter 680-X-2 Practice of Pharmacy. § 680-X-2-.32 (2006 and Rev 2021).
24. Alabama State Board of Pharmacy Administrative Code, Chapter 680-X-2 Practice of Pharmacy. § 680-X-2-.33 (2006 and Rev 2020).
25. THE DURHAM-HUMPHREY AMENDMENT. Journal of the American Medical Association. 1952;149(4):371. doi:https://doi.org/10.1001/jama.1952.02930210055017
26. Alabama State Board of Pharmacy Administrative Code, Chapter 680-X-2 Emergency Prescription Refills. § 680-X-2-.26 (1993 and Rev. 2023).
27. Ala. Code. § 34-23-75 (1991, Rev. 2023).
28. Alabama Board of Medical Examiners Administrative Code, Chapter 540-X-17 Guidelines and Standards for the Utilization of Controlled Substances for Weight Reduction § 540-X-20 (2012 and Rev. 2023).
29. Alabama State Board of Pharmacy Administrative Code, Chapter 680-X-2 Practice of Pharmacy. § 680-X-2-.45 (2020).
30. Alabama State Board of Pharmacy Administrative Code, Chapter 680-X-2 Practice of Pharmacy. § 680-X-2-.13 (1982).
31. Alabama State Board of Pharmacy Administrative Code, Chapter 680-X-2 Practice of Pharmacy. § 680-X-2-.22 (1990 and rev. 2022). Accessed April 18, 2024. https://albop.com/oodoardu/2022/08/PHARM-680-X-2-.22-proposed-.pdf
32. Ala. Code. § 34-23-8.1 (2019).
33. Alabama State Board of Pharmacy Administrative Code, Chapter 680-X-2 Practice of Pharmacy. § 680-X-2-.21 (1991 and Rev 1999).
34. Alabama State Board of Pharmacy Administrative Code, Chapter 680-X-2 Practice of Pharmacy. § 680-X-2-.27 (1995 and Rev 2024).
35. Alabama State Board of Pharmacy Administrative Code, Chapter 680-X-2 Practice of Pharmacy. § 680-X-2-.49 (2023).
36. Alabama State Board of Pharmacy Administrative Code, Chapter 680-X-2 Practice of Pharmacy. § 680-X-2-.15 (1982 and Rev 1997).
37. Ala. Code. § 34-23-3 (1966, Rev. 2017).

The Medications

10

Medicine is the restoration of discordant elements; sickness is the discord of the elements infused into the living body.

–Leonardo da Vinci

1 Introduction

Since the Pure Food and Drug Act of 1906, numerous additional acts, laws, codes, statutes, and rules have been implemented that attempt to ensure the safe and effective use of medications [1]. Many of these regulatory efforts apply specifically to controlled substances, are enforced by the Drug Enforcement Administration (DEA), and are discussed in Chap. 4. However, unscheduled (noncontrolled) prescription drugs, also known as legend drugs, are also subject to formal regulations. These regulations impact all entities that handle prescription drugs including manufacturers, wholesale distributors, repackagers, third-party logistics providers, and of course pharmacies and practitioners.

2 Inventory

2.1 Annual Inventory

Alabama law states that every pharmacy must conduct a complete inventory *once each year on January 15* [2]. However, a pharmacy can request that this date be changed by petitioning the Alabama Board of Pharmacy [ALBOP]. If approved by the ALBOP, the annual inventory may be conducted on any fixed date that does not vary by more than 6 months from the annual date that would otherwise apply. Reasons why a pharmacy might want to conduct their yearly inventory on a date other than January 15 are (1) the owner owns multiple pharmacies, and they would

M. N. Bulloch et al., *Pharmacy Law in Alabama*,
https://doi.org/10.1007/978-3-031-84771-4_10

like all of their inventory dates to coincide. For example, let us consider a pharmacist who owns two pharmacies and recently acquired a third. The inventory date for their first two pharmacies, which they previously negotiated with the ALBOP, is May 15. As such, the owner will likely ask the ALBOP for permission to conduct the annual inventory for their most recently acquired store on May 15 as well and (2) the initial inventory was conducted on a date different from January 15, and the pharmacy would like to keep their annual inventory date the same as their initial inventory date. Consider a pharmacy that was purchased in December, and its initial inventory was conducted on December 9. The pharmacy will likely ask permission to conduct their annual inventory on December 9. Otherwise, they would have to conduct their first annual inventory on January 15, which is less than 2 months after their initial inventory.

2.2 Inventory When a Pharmacy Is Newly Registered

The pharmacy must indicate in their business records (1) whether the inventory was taken at the opening or closing of business (i.e., before the store opened or after it closed), (2) the date of the inventory, and (3) the signature of the person who conducted the inventory. If the pharmacy commences business (i.e., opens their pharmacy) with no controlled substances on hand, they must indicate this on their initial inventory [2].

2.3 Inventory Records for Drug Manufacturers, Wholesale Distributors, Repackagers, and Third-Party Logistics Providers

All permitted entities (i.e., drug manufacturers, wholesale distributors, repackagers, and third-party logistics providers) that store, receive, and/or distribute drugs must maintain inventories and records of all transactions regarding the receipt and distribution of drugs in compliance with Drug Supply Chain Security Act (DSCSA) standards. These inventories and records must be made available for inspection by authorized personnel for a period of 2 years. All permitted entities must allow authorized personnel (i.e. Federal, State, and Municipal law enforcement, as well as the ALBOP) to inspect their premises and audit their records and written operating procedures at reasonable times. Records that are kept at the inspection site, or that can be immediately retrieved electronically, must be readily available for inspection. If the records are kept at a central location (i.e., not at the inspection site) and are not electronically retrievable, they must be made available for inspection within 2 working days of a request by authorized personnel. These records must include (a) the source of the drugs (i.e., where they came from), (2) the name and quantity of each drug, (3) the principal address of the seller/transferor, (4) the address from where the drugs were shipped, and (4) the dates the drugs were received or shipped [3].

3 Storage of Prescription Drugs

3.1 Storage Within a Pharmacy

All prescription drugs must be stored within the prescription department and/or storage room. The storage room, which is typically accessed through the pharmacy, must not be accessible to the general public [4]. This makes sense, as the general public should not be able to access prescription medications. Pharmacies must not dispense or distribute any medications that have been adulterated in any manner [5]. In addition, prescription drugs may only be dispensed pursuant to the prescription of a licensed practitioner; this includes new prescriptions as well as refills. However, pharmacies may still legally return prescription drugs to suppliers or sell/transfer prescription drugs to other entities who are licensed to possess them [4].

3.2 Storage of Extemporaneously Compounded Medications

Compounded products prepared in anticipation of a prescription may be prepared in "reasonable amounts," and they must be appropriately labeled with the following: (1) a complete list of ingredients, (2) preparation date, (3) beyond use date, and (4) batch or lot number. These products must be stored in a clean, dry place in accordance with their composition and stability requirements [6, 7].

3.3 Drug Distribution and Control Within a Pharmacy

The pharmacist in charge (PIC) is directly and personally responsible for all activities and operations at the pharmacy within their institution. This includes making sure that all functions and activities of pharmacy technicians are personally supervised by a registered pharmacist (this does not include tasks that do not require professional judgment, such as dusting shelves, etc.). The PIC must establish written procedures for the safe and efficient distribution of drugs at their facility. These written procedures must be updated annually and kept on hand for inspection by the ALBOP [8].

3.4 Recall Procedure Requirements

The PIC must develop a recall procedure that can be quickly activated to notify medical staff and pharmacy about all drugs affected by the recall, so that these drugs can be immediately returned to the pharmacy for proper disposition and to ensure that no patients receive the recalled medications.

3.5 Storage and Distribution by Manufacturers, Wholesale Distributors, and Repackagers

Wholesalers, manufacturers, and repackagers must adhere to written policies and procedures with regard to the storage of medications. Any entity that stores drugs (i.e., they repackage drugs or hold drugs that will later be sold) must store them under proper conditions with regard to lighting, ventilation, temperature, sanitation, and humidity. Also, storage facilities must be free from infestation by insects, rodents, birds, or vermin of any kind. In other words, drug manufacturers and distributors must store drugs under clean and secure conditions free from bugs and animals. If a drug has a particular storage requirement (i.e., it must be refrigerated), then that drug must be stored in accordance with that requirement. If a drug does not have specific storage requirements, it may be stored at a controlled room temperature, as defined in an official compendium. The temperature of the storage area must be regularly monitored and documented [3].

3.5.1 Storage of Quarantined Medications

A separate quarantined storage section must be provided for drugs that are (1) deteriorated, outdated, misbranded, or otherwise adulterated or (2) drugs that are in immediate or sealed secondary containers that have been opened (i.e., think of drugs that are in the process of being repackaged from larger containers into smaller ones) [3].

3.5.2 Incoming and Outgoing Medication Shipments

All incoming and outgoing drug shipments must be visually inspected for identity and to prevent the acceptance or distribution of contaminated or damaged products [3]. This basically means that incoming and outgoing shipments should be looked over to make sure that they appear to be in good shape.

4 Medication Samples

4.1 Purpose, Distribution, Handling, and Storage

Medication samples are not intended to be sold; they are intended to promote the sale of a drug. “Starter packs” provided by drug company representatives are not considered to be samples. The prescriber (it may be helpful to think of a physician practicing out of their office) must submit a written request for medication samples on an approved form. This form must be filled out each time samples are provided. Drug sample receipts must contain five elements:

1. Name and address of the requesting prescriber.
2. Name and address of the hospital or care facility (i.e., doctor’s office).
3. Name, address, and title of the person acknowledging delivery of the samples (i.e., the person “signing for the delivery”).

4. Proprietary name (i.e., brand name) of the drug, its strength, quantity, and lot number.
5. Date of delivery.

Lastly, medication samples must be stored and handled in a manner that ensures that they remain intact, stable, and effective. In other words, they must be kept free from contamination, deterioration, and adulteration [9, 10].

5 Repackaging Medications for Residential Care Patients

Sometimes, residential care patients are not allowed to have bottles of medications in their rooms; therefore, the residential care facility hires a retail pharmacy to repackage each patient's medications into unit doses [11]. The pharmacy that wishes to engage in repackaging must possess a current retail pharmacy permit to package, relabel, and store any noncontrolled legend drug for a patient residing in a residential care facility, which does not have a pharmacy located on its premises. Of note, any retail pharmacy (chain or independent) with the appropriate permit can engage in this service. It is important to remember that *this service can only be provided for noncontrolled drugs* at care facilities without a pharmacy on site.

Key Concept

- Repackaging of medications for residential care patients may be conducted by a pharmacy with a *current retail pharmacy permit.*
- Only *noncontrolled substances* may be repackaged under this service.

6 Disposal of Prescription Drugs

An "ultimate user" is a person who lawfully possesses a prescription drug, which may or may not be a controlled substance, and is therefore entitled to dispose of it [12]. The medication may have been prescribed for the ultimate user, a member of their family, or an animal they own. Pharmacies that wish to become a collector of medications, including both controlled and noncontrolled prescriptions drugs, must register with the DEA, as explained in detail in Chap. 4. There are essentially three main options for individuals who wish to relinquish or destroy their unwanted, expired, or unused medications. These include: (1) community take-back programs and collection receptacles (see Chap. 4, Section 11); (2) flushing medications down a toilet after consulting the FDA's "flush list"; and (3) mixing medications with an unpalatable substance [12, 13].

6.1 Community Take-Back Programs and Collection Receptacles

As discussed in Chap. 4, a pharmacy can take back medications for purposes of disposal if they are registered with the DEA as an "authorized collector." A pharmacist can never redispense medications after they have left the control of the pharmacy because once a medication leaves the pharmacy, there is no way to ensure that it has not been contaminated or adulterated in some manner. Local law enforcement or city government may be able to provide information on take-back opportunities.

6.2 Flushing Medications Down a Toilet

The FDA maintains a "flush list" of medications that can safely be flushed down a commode [14]. While it is important to appreciate that an FDA "flush list" exists, it is not important to know the medications on this list for the MPJE.

6.3 Mixing Medications with an Unpalatable Substance

Medications may be mixed with an unpalatable substance such as cat litter, coffee grounds, or dirt. During this process, tablets should not be crushed nor should capsules be opened. The mixture should be placed in a sealed plastic bag and thrown out in the trash. Identifiable information should be removed from discarded pill bottles [15].

7 Behind the Counter Drugs

7.1 Pseudoephedrine and Ephedrine

Pseudoephedrine is a Scheduled Listed Chemical Product (SLCP) whose sale is regulated by the DEA. Federal laws pertaining to the sale of pseudoephedrine are discussed in detail in Chap. 4. Briefly, in Alabama, pseudoephedrine must be sold by a licensed pharmacy and kept behind the counter. A person may purchase no more than 3.6 g of pseudoephedrine per calendar day and no more than 7.5 g per 30 days [16]. Anyone purchasing pseudoephedrine must be at least 18 years of age and provide a valid, unsuspended driver's license or nondriver ID card issued by one of the 50 states. A U.S. Uniformed Services Privilege and ID card or a US or foreign passport are also acceptable forms of identification. Dietary supplements containing ephedrine were banned by the U.S. Food and Drug Administration (FDA) in 2004 [17].

7.2 Insulin and Syringes

Insulin may be sold in Alabama without a prescription. It is stored behind the counter in a pharmacy in accordance with product labels from all three U.S. insulin manufacturers, which recommend that insulin be stored in a refrigerator at approximately 36 °F to 46 °F [18]. While a few states continue to require a prescription in order to purchase syringes, Alabama does not. Nonetheless, a pharmacist maintains the right to refuse to sell syringes if they feel they will not be used appropriately [19].

▶ **Numbers of Importance** Alabama and Federal pseudoephedrine purchase limit per calendar day: 3.6 g.
Alabama pseudoephedrine purchase limit per 30-day period: 7.5 g.

> **Key Concept**
> Although there is a federal pseudoephedrine purchase limit of 9 g per 30-day period, the limit in Alabama is lower at 7.5 g. The stricter (e.g., lower) limit must be followed.

8 Theft and Loss of Drug Requirements

8.1 Pharmacies

A detailed account on how to deal with theft or loss of controlled substances is covered in Chap. 4. Briefly, the pharmacy must notify the Field Division Office of the DEA and the ALBOP immediately upon recognizing the theft or significant loss of any controlled substance. The pharmacy must also file a report with local police and complete DEA Form 106 (see Chap. 4). In Alabama, four copies of a report describing the loss/theft must be made. The pharmacy must keep a copy for its records and forward two copies (the original and a duplicate copy) to the Field Division Office of the DEA and provide one copy to the ALBOP. If the loss/theft is committed by a licensed or registered member of the ALBOP (i.e., a pharmacist or technician, respectively), the pharmacist must report their name and license number to the ALBOP State Drug Inspector assigned to the area where the pharmacy resides. If the theft/robbery/burglary does not involve controlled substances, do not notify the DEA; instead, *notify the ALBOP State Drug Inspector* assigned to the area where the pharmacy resides [20].

8.2 Wholesale Drug Distributors and Private Label Distributors

Wholesale drug distributors and *private label distributors* must create and follow written policies and procedures. The policies and procedures must address (1) incoming and outgoing medications, and medications lost to theft; records of the disposition of these medications must be retained for 2 years; (2) how the distributor will handle any crisis that affects security or operation, such as a natural disaster or a strike; (3) how outdated, damaged, deteriorated, adulterated, or misbranded drugs will be segregated from other drugs before they are returned to the manufacturer or destroyed; (4) that the oldest stock of the drug product will be distributed first; an exception to this rule may be implemented if appropriate and temporary; and (5) how recalls (i.e., an FDA recall) and market withdrawals will be handled [3].

References

1. 21 U.S.C. I – Federal Food And Drugs Act Of 1906
2. Alabama Administration Code: 680-X-3.08
3. Alabama Administration Code: 680-X-2-.23
4. Alabama Code § 34-23-70-I
5. Alabama Code § 34-23-9
6. Alabama Code § 34-23-150
7. Alabama Code § 34-23-159
8. Alabama Administration Code: 680-X-2-.18
9. 503 [d] Federal Food Drug and Cosmetic Act
10. 21 CFR 203.32
11. Alabama Code § 34-23-76
12. Administration Code: 680-X-2-.42
13. 21 CFR §1317.40
14. Drug disposal: FDA's flush list for certain medicines. U.S. Food and Drug Administration. https://www.fda.gov/drugs/disposal-unused-medicines-what-you-should-know/drug-disposal-fdas-flush-list-certain-medicines
15. Disposal of unused medicines: what you should know. U.S. Food and Drug Administration. https://www.fda.gov/drugs/safe-disposal-medicines/disposal-unused-medicines-what-you-should-know
16. Alabama Code § 20-2-190
17. NIH national Center for Complementary and Integrative Health. Ephedra. https://www.nccih.nih.gov/health/ephedra#:~:text=The%20U.S.%20Food%20and%20Drug,the%20United%20States%20in%202004
18. Information Regarding Insulin Storage and Switching Between Products in an Emergency. U.S. Food and Drug Administration. https://www.fda.gov/drugs/emergency-preparedness-drugs/information-regarding-insulin-storage-and-switching-between-products-emergency#:~:text=According%20to%20the%20product%20labels,expiration%20date%20on%20the%20package.
19. Frequently Asked Questions. Alabama Board of Pharmacy. https://albop.com/frequently-asked-questions/
20. Alabama Administration Code: 680-X-3.07

Records and Inventory Requirements 11

If it wasn't documented, it wasn't done.

–John L. Colaizzi R.Ph., PhD

1 Pharmacy Records

There are a variety of records which pharmacies, pharmacy professionals, and pharmacy entities are required to maintain and store in case they need to be inspected or utilized later. Because of how many records and documents that are created and encountered in the course of operating a pharmacy, some content discussed in this chapter has been reviewed in other chapters within this book. In most cases, the records do not have to be located physically on-site, a feat that might be impossible for pharmacies who have been in business for a long time. But in all cases, the records must be *readily retrievable* (something which is given a specific timed definition with some records) when they are requested by authorized people.

The pharmacy's supervising pharmacist is responsible for ensuring that accurate records of all prescription medications received and dispensed are appropriately maintained, but all of those who work in a pharmacy environment must comply with the requirements [1]. These records are subject to inspection by the Alabama Board of Pharmacy (ALBOP) (and staff). When a discrepancy is found in the records, the supervising pharmacist has 15 days to submit—in writing—steps taken or proposed to eliminate the discrepancy.

2 Computers for Recordkeeping

While the pharmacy is required to maintain records of prescription files, a computerized system can be used for the storage and retrieval of these records (Table 11.1) [2]. This mitigates space concerns and constraints for storing paper records. The

M. N. Bulloch et al., *Pharmacy Law in Alabama*,
https://doi.org/10.1007/978-3-031-84771-4_11

Table 11.1 Information that must be available in a computerized system used to store prescription records in Alabama pharmacies [2]

Original prescription	Refills
Original prescription number Prescriber's name Patient's full name and address Date of original prescription written Date of original prescription dispensed Medication name Medication strength Medication dosage form Quantity dispensed Total number of refills authorized by the prescriber Identification of the dispensing pharmacist For controlled substances—prescriber's DEA registration number and Alabama controlled substances number	Medication name Date of all refills Quantity dispensed originally Quantity dispensed on each refill Identification of the dispensing pharmacist for the original dispensing Identification of the dispensing pharmacist for each refill Total number of refills dispensed to date for the order

system must be able to retrieve, by prescription number, key information from the prescription record.

3 Storage of Prescription Files

All prescription files must be kept by the pharmacy for at least 2 years from the date the prescription was dispensed [3]. To facilitate record inspection, each prescription must contain the initials of the pharmacist who compounded and/or dispensed it, the prescription number, and the date of dispensing [4].

4 Reports of Pharmacy Dispensing

The pharmacy must be able to produce a printout report illustrating a week's dispensing activity for new and refill prescriptions [2]. This report should contain information for all medications dispensed, including noncontrolled and controlled medications, and is stored in a dedicated binder. These reports must be maintained for at least 2 years from the week of dispensing.

5 Special Reports of Controlled Substance Dispensing

A special report is required to showcase refill data on Schedule III–V medications that were dispensed [2]. This is a *daily* report. If the pharmacy's system provides a hard-copy printout, the document must be verified, dated, and signed by the pharmacist. Many pharmacies print this document out at the end of the business day; the computer system has 72 h from the date of dispensing to make it available for printing. The document must contain the prescriber's name, patient name and address, quantity dispensed on each refill, date of each refill dispensing, name or identification code of the dispensing pharmacist, and the original prescription order. As an alternative to this printed document, the pharmacy may maintain a separate bound logbook or separate file which lists each individual pharmacist who is involved in the controlled substance refill dispensing signs their name attesting that all refill information entered into the computer on that day was reviewed by them and is correct.

If the pharmacy elects to use the logbook method, the computer system must still be capable of producing a printout of refill data when necessary or requested to provide a refill-by-refill audit train for any specified strength and dosage form of a controlled substance when requested by name (brand, generic, or both) [2]. Many systems allow the document to be printed by the pharmacy, but some may not. In either instance, the computer system's central recordkeeping location (i.e., software company, corporate office, or similar entity) must be able to send the printout to the pharmacy within two business days. If a state drug inspector employed by the ALBOP, a Drug Enforcement Administration (DEA) special agent, or compliance investigator requests a copy of the printout, the pharmacy should verify the printout transmittal capability of its system by documentation (e.g., a postmark).

6 Compounding Records

All records related to compounding prescriptions are retained for the same amount of time for any other prescription record [5]. If the compound includes any controlled substance, the record must comply with the requirements of the controlled substance records. The prescription, including a hard copy or computer information, must indicate that the prescription should be compounded.

7 Mail Order Prescription Records

Pharmacies not located in the state of Alabama, but who supply Alabama patients with medications or medical devices via mail, are referred to as "Nonresident Pharmacies" [6]. These pharmacies must be registered in good standing in the state where they are located. The pharmacy should maintain in readily retrievable form records of prescription medications or devices dispensed to Alabama patients. The pharmacy must also produce the required Policy and Procedure Manual when requested.

8 Records Related to Central Prescription Filling

Two pharmacies involved in central prescription filling are required to either share the same computer system or have technology that allows access necessary to fill or process an order (Table 11.2) [7]. Records may be maintained in an alternative data retention system (e.g., data processing system and direct imaging system) as long as

Table 11.2 Requirements of records related to central prescription filling [7]

Dispensing pharmacy	Filling pharmacy
Date request for filling transmitted to filling pharmacy Date-filled prescription was received by dispensing pharmacy Name of person at dispensing pharmacy accepting delivery of the filled prescription	Date the prescription was shipped to dispensing pharmacy Name and address where the prescription was shipped Method of delivery

the records contain all information required on the annual record; both the filling and dispensing pharmacy must comply will all laws and rules related to the maintenance of records and can produce audit trail of all prescriptions filled or dispensed by the pharmacy.

9 Records Required by Pharmacy-Related Entities Who Handle Medications

All permitted manufacturers, wholesalers, repackagers, and other non-pharmacy-related entities that handle medications must establish and maintain inventories and records of all transactions that show the receipt, distribution, and/or other disposition of the drugs [8]. These inventories and records must be available for inspection and photocopying by authorized personnel for at least 2 years. They may be kept on-site or immediately retrieved by a computer or other electronic means. If records are kept at an off-site location and not electronically retrievable, they must be made available within two working days of the request. At minimum, the records should contain the following information:

- The source of the medications—to include the name and principle address of the seller or transferor and the address of the location from where the medications were shipped.
- The identity and quantity of the medications received/distributed/disposed.
- The dates of receipt/distribution/disposition.

Additional requirements for these permittees are discussed in Chaps. 10, 11, and 16.

10 Pharmacy Permits and Licenses

The most basic record of a pharmacy is the pharmacy's permit to legally operate and the licenses and permits of its employees to legally work and practice within the dispensing area. The permits and licensure certificates issued by ALBOP to each pharmacist employed at the pharmacy must be *prominently* and *conspicuously* displayed in the pharmacy [9].

10.1 Miscellaneous Pharmacy Records and Documents

When an owner of a pharmacy designates one unregistered (i.e., nonpharmacist, such as a store manager) to have a key, controlled access device, or other method access to the pharmacy, there must be a signed agreement with that person [10]. A copy of the agreement must be submitted to the ALBOP for approval before the key or access is provided. The owner does not have to create the signed agreement; ALBOP has forms available for this purpose. If a local municipality's Fire Code requires that a key or access to the pharmacy be made available to First Responders, the owner must execute a signed agreement with the highest-ranking official of the agency to be provided access, which must be submitted to the ALBOP for approval before access is given.

10.2 Continuing Education Records

The pharmacist or the pharmacy technician is responsible for maintaining records of continuing education (CE) courses attended and completed [11, 12]. These records should be maintained for at least 2 years after the date attended. Many of these records are submitted and kept by a system called CPE Monitor which is operated by the National Association of Boards of Pharmacy (NABP) [13]. Prior to the release of CPE Monitor, the CE provider gave the attendee a copy of proof of activity completion which was kept for renewal purposes. Today, the CE provider submits attendance certification to the CPE Monitor system where it is added to the person's record, and paper documentation is no longer required. CPE Monitor primarily stores CE activities which are Accreditation Council for Pharmacy Education (ACPE)- approved; activities which are only approved for CE credit by the ALBOP or other non-ACPE-approved providers may not be submitted and stored to this system. The ALBOP is able to view CE credit earned on the CPE Monitor system. However, if it requests information on CE completion, a copy of this record along with any documentation for non-ACPE-approved CE should be submitted to the board within 30 calendar days of the request [11, 12].

▶ **Study Pro Tip** Test takers should be familiar with the rules regarding continuing education (CE), including (1) how many hours are required per year/cycle, (2) how many live hours are required, (3) requirements for special licenses, and (4) how long these records have to be maintained. The test may ask about requirements for either a pharmacist, a pharmacy technician, or both. Each state has different requirements for CE, and Alabama's rules may be very different from another state where the MPJE is being tested.

11 Controlled Substance Records

There are many different records that are required in association with controlled substances. Those are described in more detail in Chap. 4. Below are requirements not otherwise covered in this chapter that are specific to these products.

- All receipts of controlled substances by a pharmacy must be reviewed and approved by a pharmacist who documents their approval by signing the invoice or similar document [14].
  - Every amount of a controlled substance must be accounted for from manufacture through dispensing. By signing the invoice or document, the pharmacist is confirming what the pharmacy received and how much.
- Manufacturers, wholesalers, and distributors who sell, furnish, give away, or dispose of Schedule I–V medications or precursor agent to a registrant who is not another manufacturer or wholesaler must provide the ALBOP with legible copies or records and reports required by the DEA concerning increases in purchases or high or unusual volumes purchased by pharmacies within 30 days [15].
  - Those who supply the pharmacy with the medications are often the first to become aware when unusual changes in prescribing and dispensing habits occur. Although a high or increase in purchase volume may be due to legitimate medical needs, it may also be a signal of illicit prescribing or diversion.

12 Inspection of Records by Law Enforcement and State Drug Inspectors

One of the main reasons that pharmacies must maintain records is in case they need to be reviewed or inspected by law enforcement or by a state drug investigator employed by the ALBOP. There are differences in legal authority between local law enforcement, DEA agents, and state drug investigators. Depending on the reason for wanting to inspect the pharmacy or records, local law enforcement officials may require a warrant, while DEA agents and state drug investigators have much broader access to the pharmacy. While they are still subject to the same restrictions as any other law enforcement official related to search and seizure, Alabama law gives the state drug inspectors the power to inspect any medicine, drug, drug product, or domestic remedy, which is manufactured, made, packaged, packed, sold, offered for sale, exposed for sale, or kept for sale within Alabama [16]. In addition to the products themselves, state drug inspectors may inspect all records or documents in the pharmacy. They are required to report to the ALBOP any violations of pharmacy law or regulations they encounter, and if necessary, they are authorized to issue citations or even start criminal proceedings.

13 Records Involved in an Audit

The Pharmacy Audit Integrity Act requires a pharmacy benefit manager (PBM) who is conducting an audit of a pharmacy to provide the pharmacy with at least 2 weeks' notice prior to an on-site audit [17]. The PBM must provide a list of material that is copied or removed during the audit; if the requested information is not on-site, the pharmacy must produce them within 30 days. The PBM is limited to auditing up to 150 prescriptions, where refills are not considered a separate prescription.

References

1. Alabama State Board of Pharmacy Administrative Code, Chapter 680-X-2 Practice of Pharmacy. § 680-X-2-.12 (1982 and Rev 2021).
2. Alabama State Board of Pharmacy Administrative Code, Chapter 680-X-2 Practice of Pharmacy. § 680-X-2-.15 (1982 and Rev 1997).
3. Ala. Code. § 34-23-70 (1966, Rev. 2018).
4. Alabama State Board of Pharmacy Administrative Code, Chapter 680-X-2 Practice of Pharmacy. § 680-X-2-.05 (1982).
5. Ala. Code. § 34-23-158 (2003).
6. Alabama State Board of Pharmacy Administrative Code, Chapter 680-X-2 Practice of Pharmacy. § 680-X-2-.07 (1982 and Rev 2023).
7. Alabama State Board of Pharmacy Administrative Code, Chapter 680-X-2 Practice of Pharmacy. § 680-X-2-.30 (2003 and Rev 2019).
8. Alabama State Board of Pharmacy Administrative Code, Chapter 680-X-2 Practice of Pharmacy. § 680-X-2-.23 (1990 and Rev 2024).
9. Ala. Code. § 34-23-70 (1966, Rev. 2018).
10. Alabama State Board of Pharmacy Administrative Code, Chapter 680-X-2 Practice of Pharmacy. § 680-X-2-.11 (1982 and Rev 2012).
11. Alabama State Board of Pharmacy Administrative Code, Chapter 680-X-2 Practice of Pharmacy. § 680-X-2-.36 (2006 and Rev 2022).
12. Alabama State Board of Pharmacy Administrative Code, Chapter 680-X-2 Practice of Pharmacy. § 680-X-2-.37 (2006 and Rev 2022).
13. National Association of Boards of Pharmacy. CPE Monitor. Accessed June 14, 2024. https://nabp.pharmacy/programs/cpe-monitor/
14. Alabama State Board of Pharmacy Administrative Code, Chapter 680-X-3 Alabama Uniform Controlled Substances. § 680-X-3-.09 (1996).
15. Alabama State Board of Pharmacy Administrative Code, Chapter 680-X-3 Alabama Uniform Controlled Substances. § 680-X-3-.05 (1989 and Rev. 1996).
16. Ala. Code. § 34-23-3 (1966, Rev. 2017).
17. Ala. Code. § 34-23-184 (1912, Rev. 2018).

Laws on Health System and Institutional Pharmacies 12

Take care of the patient and everything else will follow.

–Dr. Thomas Frist Sr

Key Definitions

1. Hospital—an institution that cares and treats the sick and injured, is licensed by the Alabama State Board of Health, and is authorized to be entrusted with the custody of drugs and medications, with the professional use of drugs and medications being under the direct supervision of a medical practitioner or pharmacist [1].
2. Nursing facility—a business that provides housing, meals, and care to sick or disabled patients who require daily or more frequent medical care, nursing care, or rehabilitation services [2].
   (a) May be more commonly known by the terms "nursing home," "long-term care facility," "skill nursing facility," or other similar names.
3. Repackager—a person who purchases or acquires a drug, medicine, chemical, or poison from a manufacturer or distributor for the purpose of bottling, labeling, or otherwise repackaging for sale or distribution [1].
   (a) This definition does not apply to a licensed physician whose activity occurs as part of their professional practice.
4. State Board of Health—term used throughout the law and administrative code. This.

refers to the Alabama Department of Public Health.

M. N. Bulloch et al., *Pharmacy Law in Alabama*,
https://doi.org/10.1007/978-3-031-84771-4_12

▶ **Study Pro Tip** The ALBOP has a specific regulation in the administrative code (Chapter 680-X-2 Practice of Pharmacy) that is titled "Institutional Pharmacies." This is only one of multiple sources of health system pharmacy law and regulation. Not all regulations that impact health system pharmacy practice are written and administered by the ALBOP. Other agencies, such as the Alabama Department of Public Health, have important rules and regulations that must be adhered to with equal attention.

1 Health System Pharmacy Law

There are relatively few laws, rules, and regulations specifically directed toward health system and institutional pharmacies in the state of Alabama. Most enacted are directed toward pharmacy practice in hospitals, long-term care facilities, or other health system practice settings. A health system or institutional pharmacy *must still adhere to all other applicable laws, rules, and regulations relating to general pharmacy practice* at the federal and state levels. This chapter will focus on those that are explicitly targeted toward the health system. It is important to understand that there are laws that impact the practice of institutional pharmacy within Alabama that are found in statutes other than the Pharmacy Practice Act. Similarly, state agencies other than the Alabama Board of Pharmacy (ALBOP) may administer rules or regulations that impact pharmacy practice in the state.

▶ **Study Pro Tip** Earlier chapters explain the requirements of general pharmacy practice and operation requirements. These requirements must still be followed in the health system setting. When studying those requirements, consider how they may be applied in different pharmacy practice settings.

1.1 General Pharmacy Law in the Health System

While this chapter primarily focuses on laws and rules specific to the health system, there are certain requirements of pharmacy overall that still apply to the health system. Unless the law or rules provide exemption, pharmacies are still expected to comply with all other requirements.

▶ **Study Pro Tip** When studying for the MPJE, keep in mind that the test is designed to evaluate your knowledge of pharmacy law across all settings. Do not assume that the test will predominantly cover laws and rules for one setting over another. Failing to know laws and regulations for more specific practice settings—including those discussed in this chapter—could very easily cause you to fail the MPJE.

It is the ADPH rather than the ALBOP that requires hospitals to provide pharmaceutical services through a pharmacy directed by a licensed pharmacist or a drug storage area under "competent" supervision [3]. Hospitals must employ an adequate number of personnel to meet the pharmaceutical service needs of their patient population. This may include full-time, part-time, or consulting pharmacists. As discussed later in this chapter, the ADPH also requires nursing facilities to provide medications and pharmacy services under the direction of a licensed pharmacist. Whereas most hospitals employ their own pharmacist(s), most nursing facilities contract services with a separate pharmacy.

1.2 Hospital Pharmacy Permits

Hospital pharmacies are required to have a permit issued by the ALBOP which is renewed every *EVEN*-numbered year. When a facility wishes to open a new pharmacy or establish new pharmacy services, there must be an application submitted to the ALBOP at least 30 days prior to the pharmacy opening. If a health system operates more than one facility, each facility must obtain its own pharmacy permit. For example, a health system whose main hospital is in Birmingham, but who operates a smaller hospital in a rural area, must obtain separate pharmacy permits for each facility. There are fees related to hospital pharmacy permits (Table 12.1). The ALBOP is authorized to set the fee within a minimum and maximum range. If a permit has not been renewed by December 31 of an even-numbered year, there is a penalty fee of $25 per month that must be paid in addition to the usual renewal fee.

> **Numbers of Importance** 30
> An application for a new pharmacy or new pharmacy services must be submitted to the ALBOP at least 30 days prior to opening.

When the hospital or entity where pharmacy services are performed is owned by a corporation, the permit is issued in the name of the corporation. Only licensed pharmacists may practice pharmacy. In any pharmacy, if the owners or operators are not licensed pharmacists, they must notify the ALBOP immediately when the

Table 12.1 Fees associated with pharmacy permits

	Minimum fee	Maximum fee
New pharmacy permit application	$100	$200
Pharmacy permit renewal	$50	$150
Transfer of ownership	$150	$400
Out-of-state pharmacy or entity where pharmacy services are performed	$750	$2000
Renewal of out-of-state pharmacy or entity where pharmacy services are performed	$400	$750

termination of employment of licensed pharmacists occurs; if there are no licensed pharmacists, the permit is surrendered. This requires special consideration for health system pharmacies. Because most health system pharmacies have more than one licensed pharmacist employed, the facility does not need to surrender its permit nor cease operations when one person's employment at the facility stops. This provision is in place to ensure that no pharmacy (regardless of setting) operates without a licensed pharmacist. However, this provision could apply to small and rural facilities who may not have multiple full-time licensed pharmacists employed.

1.3 Change in Licensed Pharmacists

Any change in licensed pharmacists working at the pharmacy must be reported to the ALBOP in writing within 10 days of the change [2, 4]. It is the pharmacist's responsibility to report this change to the ALBOP.

1.4 Adherence to the FDA Guidelines in the Drug Quality and Security Act

All pharmacies, including those in the health system, must comply with the Food and Drug Administration guidelines in the Drug Quality and Security Act [5]. This is because the pharmacy is part of the supply chain for drugs and products used for medicinal purposes.

> **Numbers of Importance** 10
> A pharmacist has 10 days to report change of employment to ALBOP.

2 Managing Pharmacies

Any pharmacy located in a hospital, skilled nursing home, or other related institution in Alabama is required to be under the supervision of a licensed pharmacist [6]. The pharmacy responsible for supplying prescribed medications to a licensed healthcare facility is referred to as the "managing pharmacy" [7]. The managing pharmacy may be an institutional pharmacy that operates as a department of the facility. A great example of this type of managing pharmacy is the Department of Pharmacy within a hospital. However, a managing pharmacy does not have to be part of the facility from a business perspective. Some facilities, particularly those whose size and budget are not sufficient for operating their own pharmacy, utilize the services of an outside pharmacy with a current ALBOP pharmacy permit. Any pharmacy acting as a managing pharmacy must be physically located in Alabama. The drug or medicine room of a facility that does not operate its own pharmacy must be under the direct supervision and direction of either a consulting pharmacist or a licensed physician member of the medical staff [6].

3 Institutional Pharmacies

3.1 What Is an "Institutional Pharmacy"?

The term health system pharmacy can be applied broadly across multiple different pharmacy practice settings. An institutional pharmacy is more specifically defined by the ALBOP, a physical portion of a licensed healthcare facility which is engaged in the (1) compounding, (2) dispensing, (3) and distribution of drugs, devices, or other materials and the provision of services to prevent, diagnose, or treat injury, illness, or disease [7]. The definition also requires the institutional pharmacy to have an institutional pharmacy permit. To qualify under this definition, the pharmacy must be in a licensed healthcare facility, which is defined as a (1) hospital that is licensed by the Alabama Department of Public Health or (2) a Federally Qualified Health Center.

3.2 Undesignated Facilities

There are "institutions" that operate and provide care that are not classified by the Alabama Department of Public Health (ADPH) as a skilled nursing home, maternity home, home for the aged, domiciliary institution, or other institution. Because these "nursing homes" are not true licensed facilities, but often private homes, any medication used for patients must be obtained from a pharmacy in the same manner as any outpatient prescription is dispensed [6]. The only prescription drugs that may be onsite in these settings are within an emergency kit (described later in this chapter), as authorized by the ADPH.

3.3 Responsibilities of the Institutional Pharmacy's Supervising Pharmacist

Every institutional pharmacy must have a supervising pharmacist who is licensed to practice in Alabama [7, 8]. Much like in the community setting, the supervising pharmacist is responsible for all activities and operations of the institutional pharmacy. The supervising pharmacist's name must be placed in an exposed place in the prescription area where it is clearly visible to the public. It is acceptable for this to be placed in the secured pharmacy area rather than in the general hallway of the facility. Because of the degree of responsibility associated with being a supervising pharmacist, they may only supervise one pharmacy. There is an exception to this rule. The supervising pharmacist may be responsible for an additional institutional pharmacy if that pharmacy is open less than 15 h per week. The supervising pharmacist is required to actually work at the pharmacy they are responsible for. They must be present at least 30 hours per week or 50% of the pharmacy's operating hours, whichever is less.

The ALBOP must be aware at all times of who is responsible for a pharmacy's operations. When a new person takes over the role of a facility's supervising pharmacist, the *pharmacist* must notify the ALBOP of the change within 10 days using the dedicated "Notice of Change of Supervising Pharmacist" form. Within 15 days of assuming responsibility, the supervising pharmacist must inventory all of the pharmacy-controlled substances. When the pharmacist ceases duties as a supervising pharmacist, they must notify the ALBOP within 10 days using the same notification form. Separately, the *facility* must notify the ALBOP when a pharmacist stops serving as a supervising pharmacist within the same 10-day period. This submission requires an action plan for designating another supervising pharmacist. The action plan is authorized for up to 90 days. No pharmacy may go more than 30 days without a supervising pharmacist. If the facility is searching for a new supervising pharmacist to hire, or if the supervising pharmacist takes an extended, but not permanent, leave of absence (lasting longer than 30 days), a temporary supervising pharmacist must be named. The facility must notify the ALBOP of the pharmacist's name and period of the temporary appointment. If the supervising pharmacist was on a leave of absence, the facility must inform the ALBOP of the pharmacist's return to work.

Key Concept

It can be tricky to sort out who is responsible for notifying the ALBOP about the facility's supervising pharmacist.

The PHARMACIST is responsible for notifying the ALBOP when they start and permanently stop the role of supervising pharmacist. This provision only applies to permanent appointments and is not required of a pharmacist assuming a temporary assignment.

The FACILITY is responsible for notifying the ALBOP when a supervising pharmacist permanently ceases the role of supervising pharmacist.

The FACILITY is responsible for notifying the ALBOP when it names a temporary supervising pharmacist in the absence of a permanent supervising pharmacist.

If applicable, the FACILITY is responsible for notifying the ALBOP when a supervising pharmacist returns from an extended absence.

▶ **Numbers of Importance** 10

The ALBOP must be notified within 10 days of any change in the supervising pharmacist.

▶ **Numbers of Importance** 15

A newly appointed supervising pharmacist has 15 days to complete an inventory of the pharmacy-controlled substances.

The supervising pharmacist must ensure that the pharmacy complies with all general pharmacy laws and provisions that are applicable to any pharmacy setting. Many of those responsibilities may be found in earlier chapters of this book. Below are responsibilities that are *specific* to the institutional setting.

- Establish written policies and procedures for:
  - The safe and efficient distribution of drugs and provision of institutional pharmacy services.
  - The use and/or storage of a patient's own medications (received at a community pharmacy) while the patient is at the facility.
  - Use and/or storage of a patient's own medication supply.
  - Returning all drugs that have been recalled (by the manufacturer, Food and Drug Administration (FDA), or other appropriate entity) to the pharmacy for proper disposal.
- Verify that any pharmacist engaged in sterile product compounding has a valid ALBOP parenteral certification [9].

3.4 Drug Distribution and Control Within Institutional Pharmacies in Alabama

Every institutional pharmacy is required to have established and written policies and procedures that detail how drugs and pharmacy services are provided within the facility. These operational policies and procedures must be kept on hand for inspection by the ALBOP if requested. It is expected that these policies and procedures will be followed and enforced to ensure safe pharmacy practice and medication use.

3.4.1 Patient's Home Medications Brought to the Institutional Pharmacy

Institutions are responsible for ensuring the quality and necessity of any medication dispensed to a patient while at their facility. The easiest way to do this is to establish a policy that only allows hospital-dispensed medications, with rare exceptions. Some patients arrive at the hospital with medications dispensed from an outpatient pharmacy. These medications should not be used if the institutional pharmacy has the medication, or an alternative deemed acceptable by the designated committee (such as a Pharmacy and Therapeutics Committee) available for dispensing from the pharmacy. Medications should be given to an *adult* member of the patient's immediate family so that they can remove them from the facility. If no such family member is available, the medications should be stored according to the institutional pharmacy's policy. This standard also prevents a patient from inadvertently taking the medication dispensed by the facility and their home medication concurrently and risking toxicity. Occasionally, a patient may be prescribed a medication that the institutional pharmacy does not have and/or cannot obtain in a reasonable time period. There are many reasons that this may occur: the medication may be uncommon, expensive, or there may be too many versions to designate acceptable alternatives. For example, a patient with a rare disease may be taking an expensive medication that is only distributed by a single centralized pharmacy. In such cases where the provider caring for the patient deems that continuing the medication while in the facility is medically necessary, the patient's own stock of medication may be used.

Key Concept

Some patients are prescribed medications that are not kept in stock or are unable to be obtained by institutional pharmacies. The hospital may dispense the patient's own supply of medication as long as there is an *order* by an authorized prescriber at the facility for the medication and the medication has been *verified* for authenticity (a task commonly performed by a pharmacist). Once verified, the patient's supply of medication is taken and stored in a designated, secure space. It is administered by the nurse (or other appropriate clinician) at the time(s) designated by the medication order. When the patient is discharged from the facility, the medication supply is returned to them.

3.4.2 Investigational Drugs for Inpatient Use

Many licensed health facilities participate in clinical research. Some research is internal to the institution, and some research is external, where the facility serves as a clinical trial site for a larger study. Any investigational drug intended for inpatient use must be stored in and dispensed from the pharmacy. All information related to these investigational drugs should also be maintained in the pharmacy.

3.4.3 Allowance of Formularies

Hospitals in Alabama are authorized by the ALBOP and required by the ADPH to establish and use a formulary or drug list [3, 10]. This helps facilitate efficiency, control costs, and reduce medication errors. As a result, the hospital is unlikely to keep every potential medication in stock. A committee, such as a Pharmacy and Therapeutics Committee, determines what medications will be available for use in the hospital. When it is determined that medications within a particular class can be acceptably interchanged, only select agents will be stocked and administered. Other entities such as accrediting bodies may have additional requirements governing the formulary system, but they are outside the scope of this book.

3.4.4 "Emergency" Dispensing by Institutional Facilities

The term "Emergency" with regards to dispensing by an institutional pharmacy is not the same concept as emergency dispensing in the community pharmacy. In the community, this type of dispensing relates to a person who requires a medication but does not have any remaining authorized refills. It is a very different situation in the institutional setting, and the term "emergency" may not be the best terminology here, but it is the one used by the ALBOP. Emergency dispensing by an institutional pharmacy is permissible for bulk medications intended for single patient use (e.g., an inhaler) or any medication deemed necessary with approval from the ALBOP. When written, this rule was envisioned to apply to medicines such as an inhaler or insulin pen used in a setting such as an emergency room; these medications have multiple doses in the container but cannot be reused for a different patient. Obviously, this type of medication use occurs with inpatients as well; while the original vision may have been the emergency room setting, there are no restrictions for other institutional settings. For example, a hospital could discharge a patient with an albuterol inhaler which the patient has been using while hospitalized, that still has remaining doses in the container, and for which the prescriber intends for the patient to continue to use after leaving the hospital. When emergency dispensing occurs with institutional pharmacies, the label applied to the medication must include:

- The name and address of the facility dispensing the medication.
- Directions for use.
- Drug name as dispensed.
- Strength per dosage unit.
- Any additional truthful information that is considered essential for the proper storage, handling, safety, and/or usage of the medication.

It is generally accepted that it is up to the pharmacist's professional judgment to determine what, if any, "additional information" is required for the medication label.

4 Drug Storage Systems, Cabinets, and Kits

Larger hospitals often provide continuous pharmacy services 24/7, but not all licensed healthcare facilities have a pharmacy attended by a pharmacist at all times. Smaller facilities with an on-site institutional pharmacy may only have pharmacist coverage at set times. Nursing facilities and other facilities utilizing a managing pharmacy do not typically have an on-site pharmacist whose primary work location is at the facility. They tend to be serviced by off-site pharmacists who come to the facility as needed. When a pharmacist cannot be available in the facility, whether it be for just a few hours each day or on a more regular basis, provisions must be in place to be able to provide medications and pharmacy services for the facility's patients [7, 11]. In Alabama, regardless of whether the facility has an on-site institutional pharmacy or contracts with a managing pharmacy, a pharmacist must be available at all times to answer pharmacy-related inquires or handle issues that might arise when a pharmacist is not physically present. There is no one required method for fulfilling this requirement, though the use of an "on-call" schedule is one way that can be utilized. However, there is still a need to provide tangible medications when a pharmacist is not on the premises to dispense them.

Alabama allows for the use of automated dispensing units (ADUs), stat medicine cabinets, and emergency medicine kits to aid in the dispensing of medications outside of the pharmacy. These dispensing systems are discussed in more detail in Chap. 13.

Key Concept
It is important to note that there must be a valid medication order from an authorized prescriber regardless of whether it is dispensed directly from the pharmacy or obtained from a dispensing cabinet, unit, or kit.

In facilities with an on-site institutional pharmacy without 24/7 pharmacist coverage, access to the pharmacy is restricted when the pharmacist is not on duty. However, in emergency situations, access to the pharmacy may be provided. This may only occur when a drug that is required to meet the immediate needs of a patient whose health would be jeopardized without the drug is not available from floor supplies or in a stat medicine cabinet. Only *one* supervisory nurse or physician in any given shift may be provided access to obtain the necessary medication(s). There must be a valid written order for any medication obtained from the pharmacy. The nurse of physician tasked with obtaining the medication must complete a form that is left in the pharmacy with the container from which the drug was removed. At minimum, this form must list:

- The patient name, date of birth, and room number.
- Drug name and strength.
- Amount removed.
- Date and time the drug was removed from the pharmacy.
- Signature of the nurse of physician removing the medication.

4.1 Repackaging, Relabeling, and Storing Medicines in Certain Residential Care Facilities

Alabama allows a pharmacy with a licensed retail pharmacy permit to repackage, relabel, and store noncontrolled prescription drugs for a patient or patients who live in a residential care facility that does not have a pharmacy on premise [12]. Some people incorrectly apply this term strictly to a traditional long-term care facility or nursing home, but there are other types of nursing facilities that provide extended care to different demographics of patients. The law specifically limits the definition of "residential care facility" to mean one that is a:

- Convalescent home.
- Nursing home.
- Extended care facility.
- Mental health or psychiatric facility.
- Rehabilitation facility.
- Developmental disability center.
- Assisted living facility.
- Specialty care–assisted living facility.

5 Other Dispensing Considerations in the Health System

5.1 Prescription Labels

The requirements for labels intended for prescription drugs in a hospital are not as extensive as they are in the community or outpatient setting. The name of the institution is not required to appear on individual unit doses nor on floor stock medications which are controlled with proof of use sheets [13]. Because directions for use change more frequently in the in-patient setting, they may be excluded from the label [13]. Instead, the directions for use most commonly appear in the facilities' medication administration record. The drug's name, strength, and direction for proper handling, safety, or use should still appear on the label.

5.2 Required Equipment in the Pharmacy

Equipment requirements for an institutional pharmacy are similar to what is required in a community pharmacy. If the facility has satellite pharmacies (smaller pharmacy areas within the same facility but away from the main pharmacy area), they must also have all required equipment. Pharmacies are required to have any technical equipment commensurate with the level and type of pharmacy practice it provides [14]. In a hospital pharmacy, this may include appropriate flow hoods to prepare sterile products such as intravenous medications or designated equipment to compound medications. It is possible that the technical equipment in a facility may differ in satellite pharmacies. For example, if a specific satellite pharmacy is not intended to prepare parenteral medications, an I.V. hood is not necessary. There are some requirements that must be present in the main pharmacy area and in any satellite pharmacy. All prescription areas must have hot and cold running water [14]. Every pharmacy must have an up-to-date drug information source. The code specifically lists "Facts and Comparisons," but allows for the use of any book or electronic media that is considered sufficient to meet the pharmacy's needs [14].

5.3 Parenteral Sterile Therapy

Parenteral sterile therapy refers to injectable medications. Some parenteral medications or sterile products can be purchased from the manufacturer in a form that is ready to be administered to the patient. However, many require some amount of preparation or dilution in the pharmacy before administration can occur. All pharmacies that engage in sterile compounding of parenteral products must register and obtain a permit with the ALBOP; this permit is renewed by the end of even-numbered years [9].

Unlike some other states, Alabama has specific requirements for who may prepare sterile products [9]. In order for a pharmacist to compound and dispense a sterile parenteral product, including cytotoxic medications, they must be certified as a sterile compounding pharmacist (sometimes referred to as a parenteral pharmacist) with ALBOP. To obtain this certification, the pharmacist must complete a (minimum) 8-h certification course that includes both didactic (classroom) and hands-on experience. The certification course must be approved by the ALBOP and include a written examination. Any pharmacist who engages in high-risk sterile compounding (e.g., certain chemotherapies) must complete an additional 4-h high-risk program approved by the ALBOP. To maintain certification, as a sterile compounding pharmacist, the pharmacist must obtain at least 2 h of ALBOP-approved continuing education (CE) hours (hands-on and didactic) in parenteral therapy in each renewal cycle.

5.4 Compounding Laws and Regulations Relevant to the Health System

Compounding for the health system patient must follow the same requirements in place for compounding the community pharmacy setting. Most institutional pharmacies, and many managing pharmacies, will engage in some degree of compounding due to the needs of their patient populations. There must be a specifically designated and adequate area or space for the compounding to occur [15]. This area must be clean, sanitary, in good state of repair, and with adequate lighting and ventilation. It must have cleanable surfaces; this includes the walls, ceilings, and floors. Potable water (water that is safe for ingestion) must be provided to the room under continuous positive pressure, and the plumbing system cannot have defects that could contaminate any compounded drug product.

Ingredients of a compounded drug should meet the federal standards of quality. Pharmacists are expected to use their professional judgment when receiving, storing, or using drug components that meet official compendia (e.g., USP) requirements or other high-quality sources [16]. Bulk drugs, chemicals, or chemicals used to compound drugs must be stored in adequately labeled containers in a clean, dry area; products that require refrigeration should be stored at the appropriate temperature.

The equipment used for compounding must be appropriate in design and capacity for the work being done [17]. It should be located in the appropriate place to facilitate its intended use of operation, cleaning, and maintenance. The surfaces of the equipment cannot contain components that are reactive, additive, or absorptive; essentially, the equipment composition should not impact or alter the purity of the compounded product. Before any equipment or utensils are used, the pharmacist must inspect it and determine it as suitable to use. It is essential to protect against contamination in compounding. Because of this, all equipment and utensils must be cleaned and sanitized before any use and stored in a way that protects from contamination. It is permissible to use automated, mechanical, electronic, limited commercial-scale manufacturing, or testing equipment as long as it is routinely inspected, calibrated, or, when necessary, checked to ensure proper performance. Potent or hazardous drugs (e.g., antibiotics, cytotoxins, and steroid hormones) require diligent and appropriate measures to prevent cross-contamination. These should include either dedicated equipment-specific or meticulous cleaning of equipment before it is sued to prepare other drugs. Proper disposal procedures must also be followed when compounding potent or hazardous drugs.

Depending on the facility, the actual compounding may be done by a pharmacy technician or a pharmacist. All compounding procedures must include a list of the components in the product, including amounts in weight or volume, and the lot number of each component [18]. If available, the procedures should list the order of component mixing, a description of the compounding process, and a designated name for the finished product. All components must be accurately weighed, measured, or subdivided as appropriate to the desired compound. It is essential that the weight and measure of the compounded product are accurate according to the written compounding procedures. To ensure this, a pharmacist must check and recheck the operations at each stage of the compounding process. Because compounding is not the same as large-scale manufacturing, there will be some degree of variability. However, any variability should be minimal. The pharmacist must determine that all finished products have a reasonable uniformity and integrity. If capsules are compounded, the pharmacist must determine that there is an acceptable degree of weight variation between the capsules.

The hospital or other health system pharmacy must keep all records related to compounding for at least 2 years.

► **Numbers of Importance** 2
Except for a few rare situations, most records that a pharmacy is required to maintain should be kept for 2 years.

5.5 Counseling Requirements

There are fewer counseling requirements in the institutional setting, but there are still some patient counseling rules. The medications that a patient is taking prior to entering a licensed healthcare facility may be discontinued, temporarily held, adjusted, and new medications may be started. It is important that the patient (or when appropriate the patient's representative or caregiver) have a good understanding of the regimen that they will be taking once they are discharged from the facility. To accomplish this, a face-to-face offer of counseling must be made by either the pharmacist of the pharmacist's designee to any patient or, where appropriate, the patient representative who is scheduled for facility discharge [19]. If the offer to counsel is accepted, the counseling must be performed orally by a pharmacist or properly supervised intern. There may be times when the pharmacist or intern attempts to counsel, but the patient or patient representative is not there or is unavailable. If this occurs, the pharmacist or intern must make known the fact that the consultation remains available and provide information on how they may be reached.

5.6 Off-Site Order Entry and Remote Work

Rules and regulations relating to off-site order entries are described in the earlier chapters of this book. An off-site order entry is permitted in institutional facilities with both (1) a maximum daily census of 75 beds and (2) lacks an on-site 24-h pharmacy 7 days of the week [20]. This allows smaller hospitals to obtain necessary medications for patients when a pharmacist is not on duty physically at the institution. There are some limitations that are worth noting. All technician functions must be verified by an onsite pharmacist before a medication is dispensed to the patient. Most off-site order entries at healthcare facilities are intentionally developed. However, the ALBOP allows for the use of off-site order entries in emergency situations so long as there are established, ALBOP-approved policies and procedures that explicitly define what constitutes an "emergency," identifies processes and security measures for off-site order entries, and includes procedures for HIPAA compliance. If the emergency plan is ever implemented, the ALBOP must be notified within 72 h of its start along with an anticipated duration. Once the emergency plan has terminated, the ALBOP should be notified.

Alabama also permits remote pharmacy work, which is defined as the practice of pharmacy when not physically located within a permitted pharmacy or facility [21]. The pharmacist must be an employee of a pharmacy or facility with a valid ALBOP permit, a facility regulated by the Alabama Department of Public Health, a facility regulated by the Alabama Department of Insurance, or a physician's office. The remote work site must be within the United States or United States territories and equipped with secure access to the facility's information system. Controls must be in place to protect confidentiality and integrity of all information. Once a pharmacist's employment ends, access to the facility's information system should be terminated. The physical act of dispensing or final product verification may not occur outside of the permitted pharmacy.

Key Concept

Many small facilities do not have the financial ability to staff a pharmacist at all times. Except in emergency situations, medications require a pharmacist review and verification before they can be dispensed. Off-site order entry and remote pharmacy work allow smaller healthcare facilities, such as rural hospitals, to obtain medication that have been ordered by an authorized prescriber even when a pharmacist is not physically present at the facility. Many facilities use medicine cabinets to dispense the medication once it has undergone the appropriate verification process.

6 Laws Related to Nursing Facilities and Pharmacy

A nursing facility is a business that provides housing, meals, and care to sick or disabled patients who require daily or more frequent medical care, nursing care, or rehabilitation services [2]. This includes places of care such as (but not limited to) long-term care facilities, skilled nursing facilities, assisted living facilities, and rehabilitation facilities. These facilities are required to provide routine and emergency drugs and biologics to residents, either directly or by obtaining them from a pharmacy through an established agreement [11].

These facilities are required to employ a licensed pharmacist or obtain the services of one [11]. It is not uncommon for nursing facilities to contract with a community pharmacy or a pharmacy company that specializes in geriatrics and nursing facilities to obtain both medications and pharmacy services. The pharmacist provides consultation on all aspects of pharmacy services in the facility. They also play an essential role in the facility's record-keeping system. The pharmacist establishes a record system that documents the receipt and disposition of controlled substances in enough detail that an accurate reconciliation can occur. The pharmacist is the one who determines whether or not the records are in appropriate order and maintained. It is also the pharmacist's responsibility to "periodically" reconcile. Unlike with other activities, there is no set frequency for how often the reconciliation of these records must occur.

Key Concept
While many consultant pharmacists help nursing facilities establish a record-keeping system for all drugs, the rules regulating nursing homes specifically require a system in place for controlled substances.

6.1 Consultant Pharmacists

Consultant pharmacists provide pharmacy services to long-term care facilities, nursing homes, homes for the aged, domiciliary, and other places that typically do not have an on-site pharmacy (although some facilities may have a pharmacy on premise). The consultant pharmacy is generally tasked with carrying out many/most of the pharmacist activity mandates for nursing facilities. Many states, including Alabama, have specific rules and regulations directed to consultant pharmacists and consultant pharmacy. The ALBOP maintains a list of all authorized consultant pharmacists in Alabama [22]. To become a consultant pharmacist, one must first become a licensed pharmacist in Alabama. Then, an initial, ALBOP-approved, certification course is required. The course must be at least 8 h long and covers specified topics (Table 12.2), and at the end, the pharmacist must pass an examination with a score of at least 75. Once this course has been successfully completed, the pharmacist completes a one-page application and sends it to the ALBOP with proof that the initial course was completed with a passing exam score. The consultant pharmacist

Table 12.2 Required topics for the initial Consultant Pharmacist certification course

Required topics
Laws and regulations (federal and state) related to services provided by consultant pharmacists
Policy and procedures
Administrative responsibilities
Professional responsibilities
The history and overview of consultant pharmacy opportunities
Drug regimen review
Ethics in consultant pharmacy
The impact of consultant pharmacy on the total healthcare system
Drug therapy/disease state monitoring

license is renewed during the normal pharmacist license renewal period during even-numbered years and must be completed by December 31. In order to renew, the consultant pharmacist must have completed at least eight *live* continuing education hours that were specifically approved by the ALBOP for consultant pharmacist continuing education credit. Multiple pharmacy organizations and both pharmacy schools within Alabama offer consultant pharmacy CE at various times throughout the year. The 8-h requirement can be obtained all in 1 year, or it can be divided across the 2-year renewal cycle.

6.2 Drug Regimen Review

A licensed pharmacist must review the drug regimen of every resident of a nursing facility at least monthly [11]. The rules for the nursing facilities only indicate that this drug regimen review must be conducted by a licensed pharmacist. However, in Alabama, it is generally intended that the review be conducted by a licensed pharmacist with a consultant pharmacist certification. If the pharmacist detects any irregularities during the review, they must report them to the attending physician and the director of nursing. In Alabama, any irregularities reported must be acted upon. This means that when a pharmacist makes a recommendation for a nursing facility patient based on this review, the recommendation must either be implemented or there must be a documented explanation as to why the recommendation was not accepted. Recommendations cannot go unacknowledged.

6.3 Storage of Medications

All medications in a nursing facility must be stored in locked compartments with appropriate temperature controls for the individual medications (e.g., drugs requiring refrigeration are stored appropriately in the refrigerator) [11]. Only authorized personnel may have access to the keys. Controlled substances, especially Schedule II drugs, must be kept separately in locked storage compartments that are permanently affixed. This measure is meant to protect the controlled medications from being removed or stolen from the facility. If a facility uses a single unit packaging drug distribution system with a minimal quantity of the controlled substance stored and a missing dose can be readily detected, the controlled substances do not have to be stored separately.

The use of emergency medication kits and stat medicine cabinets must comply with the laws, rules and regulations described earlier in this chapter.

6.4 Medication Labeling

As with any other setting, all mediation containers must be properly and plainly labeled according to all local, federal, and state requirements [11] (Table 12.3). Medications must be kept in the original container as dispensed from the pharmacy that bears the original prescription label (i.e., they cannot be transferred into other storage containers such as pill boxes). Some facilities use unit dose medications in systems such as a medication cabinet. These unit doses do not have to have all of the information required of a prescription container but should be utilized as part of a system that was collaboratively developed and approved by the pharmacist and facility administration and nursing personnel.

6.5 Destruction of Drugs

It is not unusual for nursing facilities to have regular turnover in residents (i.e., patients), and changes to a resident's medication profile are regular occurrences. There must be policies and procedures in place to facilitate the destruction of medications when necessary due to a patient's death, change in regimen, lack of use, or expiration [11]. Unless a medication can be donated to a charitable clinic (as discussed in Sect. 7), prescription drugs (including controlled substances) must be destroyed within 30 days of being discontinued or from the date of death of the resident for whom they were prescribed. Medications ordered with an "as needed" or "PRN" frequency should be destroyed if they have not been administered in the previous 90 days. If an as-needed drug has not been used in the previous 3 months, it provides the prescriber an opportunity to reevaluate the continued need for the

Table 12.3 Medication labeling requirements in Alabama nursing facilities

Prescription	Over the counter	Unit dose
Drug name Strength Patient (resident) name Ordering physician Date filled Directions for use and administration Prescription number Expiration date Number of dosage form sent Necessary auxiliary labels	Drug name Strength	Drug name Strength Control number Expiration date

medication; if the prescriber determines that the medication does need to continue to be available, it can be reobtained pursuant to a new medication order.

► **Numbers of Importance** There are important timelines on when nursing facilities should destroy medications.

- Within 30 days of a drug being discontinued from a patient's regimen.
- Within 30 days of a patient's death.
- On day 90 if a PRN medication has not been used in that time.
- On the medication's expiration date.

There are times when residents of a nursing facility require a higher level of care for an acute issue. It is difficult to determine when a person is transferred to a hospital, when or if they will return. If the patient does return to the facility, parts of their medication regimen may be different while others remain unchanged. Until that information is clear, to prevent waste of resources, facilities may retain the resident's medications until they return to the facility. When the resident returns, their previous medication orders (prior to hospital transfer) are no longer considered valid. The prescriber will provide a new set of medication orders. If a retained medication is reordered in the same way that it was used prior to hospital transfer, the medication can be administered. Any pre-hospitalization medication that is not included on the post-hospitalization orders should be considered discontinued and should be destroyed accordingly.

Controlled and noncontrolled medications can be destroyed at the nursing facility, or they may be picked up by an environmental agency that provides drug destruction services. The facility cannot return the medications to the pharmacy for destruction. Accurate records accounting for drug destruction should be completed and maintained (Table 12.4). The pharmacist should verify that the list of medications to be destroyed is accurate. In contrast, if an environmental agency is used, a registered nurse should verify the list of drugs to be destroyed and must obtain a signed copy of the destruction form as a receipt. If the destruction takes place on-site, the pharmacist and a registered nurse carry out the destruction. Both must sign a destruction form and attest the amounts listed are accurate and destroyed. On-site destruction of controlled substances requires a third witness. This third witness may be a law enforcement official or a member of management or supervisory personnel (e.g., facility administrator or charge nurse). Destruction records kept within a resident's medical record should be maintained as long as the medical record is kept. When destruction records are kept as a separate file, they must be retained for at least 2 years.

Table 12.4 Required elements of nursing facility drug destruction records [23]

Required elements
Facility name and address
Date of destruction or date drugs picked up by environmental agency
Method used in destruction [environmental agencies must indicate the proposed date and method of destruction on the record or receipt]
Prescription number
Name of pharmacy that dispensed the medication
Resident's name
Medication name and strength
Amount destroyed
Reason for destruction

7 Donating Drugs to Charitable Clinics

Alabama allows for certain facilities to transfer unused prescription medicines to charitable clinics. The law that authorizes this transfer is known as the John G. Page Jr. Act, but there are multiple rules and regulations from different regulatory authorities that govern the practice [24–27]. To qualify as a charitable clinic, it must be an established free clinic or be a community health center that is provided for under federal public health service law. Noncontrolled prescription medications that are dispensed to a patient in a (1) hospital, (2) nursing facility, 3) assisted living facility, or 4) specialty care–assisted living facility can be donated and transferred to the charitable clinic so long as they are provided free of charge and certain conditions are met (Table 12.5). In addition to these conditions, the file of the patient from whom the drugs were originally intended for at the facility must document the patient's consent (or in the case of death, the family's consent) for the drugs to be donated. Documentation of this consent must be maintained by the facility for a minimum of 2 years.

Prior to transfer, the patient's name, prescription number, and any other identifying marks must be completely removed or obliterated from the container. The only items that should remain on the label should be the (1) drug name, (2) strength, and (3) expiration date. An inventory list of all of the drugs that are being donated must accompany the drugs being transferred. At minimum, the inventory list should include for each drug the (1) drug name, (2) strength, (3) expiration date, and (4) quantity. The drugs must be physically transferred from the facility to the clinic by a person authorized in writing by the clinic's administrator to pick the drugs up for the clinic. The drugs must be picked up by the clinic within 1 week (7 days) of this inventory list being prepared or the drugs must be destroyed. The person picking up the medications must sign and date an inventory list that is to be kept at the donating facility. A representative of the clinic receiving the donated drugs must also sign and date a copy of the inventory list and maintain it at the facility for at least 2 years.

It is the responsibility of the physician or other licensed healthcare professional at the charitable clinic to determine if the drug is suitable for reuse. As with any other situation regarding prescription medications, the drugs distributed by the charitable clinic require an order or prescription from an authorized prescriber. The law

Table 12.5 Conditions for transferring prescription drugs to a charitable clinic

Conditions
Drugs are no longer needed by the original patient[a]
Drugs have been maintained according to USP and NF storage requirements
Drugs were dispensed by unit dose or an individually sealed dose[b]
Drugs are not expired[a,c]
Drugs are not controlled substances[a]

[a]Drugs transferred from a hospice care program must meet these requirements
[b]Drugs transferred from a hospice care program may be transferred if they were dispensed by unit dose or bulk packaging
[c]The expiration date of the drug must be assigned as the expiration date of the drug when dispensed by the charitable clinic

protects the facility donating the drug as well as an owner, operator, employee, or agent of the facility from both criminal and civil liabilities resulting from any acts or omissions in the transfer process unless the act or omission was the result of willful misconduct. The law also protects the pharmaceutical manufacturer from liability for any harm that may occur from the transfer. For example, if a patient receives an expired medication because the expiration date was incorrect or not communicated, the manufacturer cannot be held responsible.

References

1. *Ala. Code. § 34-23-1 (1966, Rev 2019).*
2. *Alabama Department of Public Health State Board of Health Administrative Code, Chapter 420-5-10 Nursing Facilities. § 420-5-10.-.01 Definitions (1996 and Rev. 2016).*
3. *Alabama Department of Public Health State Board of Health Administrative Code, Chapter 420-5-7 Hospitals § 420-5-7.16 Pharmaceutical Services (1982 and Rev. 2012).*
4. *Ala. Code. § 34-23-10 (1966).*
5. *Ala. Code. § 34-23-32.2 (2017).*
6. *Ala. Code. § 34-23-74 (1966, Rev 2013).*
7. *Alabama State Board of Pharmacy Administrative Code, Chapter 680-X-2 Practice of Pharmacy. § 680-X-2-.18 (1987 and Rev. 2024).*
8. *Alabama State Board of Pharmacy Administrative Code, Chapter 680-X-2 Practice of Pharmacy. § 680-X-2-.12 (1982 and Rev. 2021).*
9. *Alabama State Board of Pharmacy Administrative Code, Chapter 680-X-2 Practice of Pharmacy. § 680-X-2-.19 (1989 and Rev. 2021).*
10. *Ala. Code. § 34-23-8 (1966, Rev 2019).*
11. *Alabama Department of Public Health State Board of Health Administrative Code, Chapter 420-5-10 Nursing Facilities. § 420-5-10.16 Pharmacy Services(1996 and Rev. 2004).*
12. *Ala. Code. § 34-23-76 (2011).*
13. *Alabama State Board of Pharmacy Administrative Code, Chapter 680-X-2 Practice of Pharmacy. § 680-X-2-.13 (1982).*
14. *Alabama State Board of Pharmacy Administrative Code, Chapter 680-X-2 Practice of Pharmacy. § 680-X-2-.04 (1982 and Rev. 2020).*
15. *Ala. Code. § 34-23-152 (2003, Rev 2006).*
16. *Ala. Code. § 34-23-154 (2003).*
17. *Ala. Code. § 34-23-153 (2003).*
18. *Ala. Code. § 34-23-156.*

19. *Alabama State Board of Pharmacy Administrative Code, Chapter 680-X-2 Practice of Pharmacy. § 680-X-2-.21 (1991 and Rev. 1999).*
20. *Alabama State Board of Pharmacy Administrative Code, Chapter 680-X-2 Practice of Pharmacy. § 680-X-2-.39 (2009 and Rev. 2021).*
21. *Alabama State Board of Pharmacy Administrative Code, Chapter 680-X-2 Practice of Pharmacy. § 680-X-2-.49 (2023).*
22. *Alabama State Board of Pharmacy Administrative Code, Chapter 680-X-2 Practice of Pharmacy. § 680-X-2-.08 (1982 and Rev. 2021)).*
23. *Alabama Department of Public Health State Board of Health Administrative Code, Chapter 420-5-10 Nursing Facilities. § 420-5-10.16 Pharmacy Services (1996 and Rev. 2004).*
24. *Ala. Code. § 20-3-1 (2002).*
25. *Ala. Code. § 20-3-3 (2002).*
26. *Alabama Department of Public Health State Board of Health Administrative Code, Chapter 420-11-1 Procedures for Donation of Certain Prescription Drugs to Charitable Clinics. § 420-11-1-.02 (2002 and Rev. 2003).*
27. *Alabama Department of Public Health State Board of Health Administrative Code, Chapter 420-11-1 Tranfer Drugs to Charitable Clinics. § 420-11-1-.02 (2002 and Rev. 2003).*

13 Medication Cabinets, Kits, and Other Dispensing Systems

The line between disorder and order lies in logistics.

–Sun Tzuo

1 Key Definitions

1. Automated Dispensing Unit—an electromechanical system that performs operations or activities related to the dispensing and storage of medications [1]. The system can collect, control, and maintain required information and record.
2. Emergency Kit—a kit that contains drugs needed to effectively manage a critical care incident or need of a patient [1]. It may include controlled substances.
3. Medical Staff—licensed healthcare providers who provide medical care within a healthcare facility. Some facilities may only apply the term to physicians, while others may include other healthcare professionals.
4. Positive Identification—a user-specific password that is combined with a second identifier which may be a fingerprint, personal identification badge, retinal pattern, or other unique identifier [1].
5. Stat Medicine Cabinet—an enclosure located outside the pharmacy area that provides noncontrolled medications that are necessary to effectively manage a patient's drug regimen and which are not available from any other authorized source in sufficient time to prevent risk of harm to the patient [1].

M. N. Bulloch et al., *Pharmacy Law in Alabama*,
https://doi.org/10.1007/978-3-031-84771-4_13

2 Understanding Medicine Cabinets and Automated Systems

Automated dispensing units (ADU) or automated dispensing cabinets increase the efficiency of medication dispensing away from a centralized, on-site pharmacy [2]. This could be on a particular nursing unit within a hospital or at a facility (e.g., long-term care) that operates its own pharmacy. These machines are locked/secured medication cabinets. Their use in the hospital setting has become particularly widespread. In the past, these machines may have been placed in select areas or nursing units while most medications were dispensed from a central pharmacy. These machines facilitate first-dose availability and support more timely medication administration [3]. They can be set up to obtain one-time doses and/or routine and maintenance medications. Today, approximately 75% of hospitals use ADU as a primary method of maintenance dose distribution [4]. Less than 6% of hospitals do not have ADU on any patient care unit or area [4]. The digital link between the decentralized ADU and the electronic medical record (EMR) has been shown to reduce medication, dispensing, and storage errors and reduce workloads by decreasing the nurse time on medication administration and drug inventory activities [2, 5, 6]. Once a medication order is entered into the EMR by the prescriber, it undergoes pharmacist review and verification. Afterward, those with authorized access can obtain the medication at the appropriate frequency from the machine by logging in to the system using positive identification (refer to Chap. 12 for more information), entering the patient's/resident's information, and identifying the medication selected. ADUs come in many different brands and designs, and the law does not differentiate between them. Over 77% of hospitals use an ADU that is configured with individually secured lidded pockets [4]. This design limits access to unit dose packaging specific to the medication order. Approximately 22% of hospitals use an ADU with a matrix drawer configuration that allows access to all medications that are stocked in that drawer [4]. Most hospitals utilize barcode scanning when restocking the ADU as a method for improving patient safety [4]. Information on every transaction is recorded electronically [5].

The terminology in Alabama pharmacy law and regulation can be confusing at times because it focuses on the intended role of the dispensing system. There are specific rules relating to "stat medicine cabinets" and ADUs, which practically could be machines of the same brand and design, but with different purposes.

If a facility uses ADUs as its primary decentralized dispensing method, low stock can result in dose omissions. While there are minimum requirements for inventorying and restocking the cabinets, the need for restocking may occur more frequently depending on the medication demand. However, the pharmacist must reconcile ADU transactions at least monthly. Not only does this help maintain medication stock levels, but it also identifies situations where someone may have overridden the cabinet's security and safety measures to obtain medication. The monthly inventory helps ensure that medications are not being inappropriately removed from the cabinet, either for administration to a patient without a valid order or for diversion reasons.

Alabama law regarding ADUs or other dispensing systems outside of the pharmacy area is concise. It simply states that hospitals and nursing homes may use "vending machines or other mechanical devices" to store and dispense drugs so long as they are stocked under the supervision of a licensed pharmacist and accessed by a person in compliance with the institutional policy [7]. Beyond that, the law delegates regulation of the appropriate agencies. In Alabama, the rules regulating medicine cabinets, automated machines, and other dispensing systems are overseen by the Alabama Board of Pharmacy (ALBOP) and the Alabama Department of Public Health (ADPH).

3 Automated Dispensing Units

Both the ALBOP and the ADPH have enacted rules on the use of ADUs in Alabama (Fig. 13.1). The rules set forth by the two agencies are complementary; they either mandate the same requirements or list provisions not stipulated by the other agency. There are no contradictory rules. It is expected that pharmacists are aware of and follow all rules on ADUs, regardless of the issuing agency.

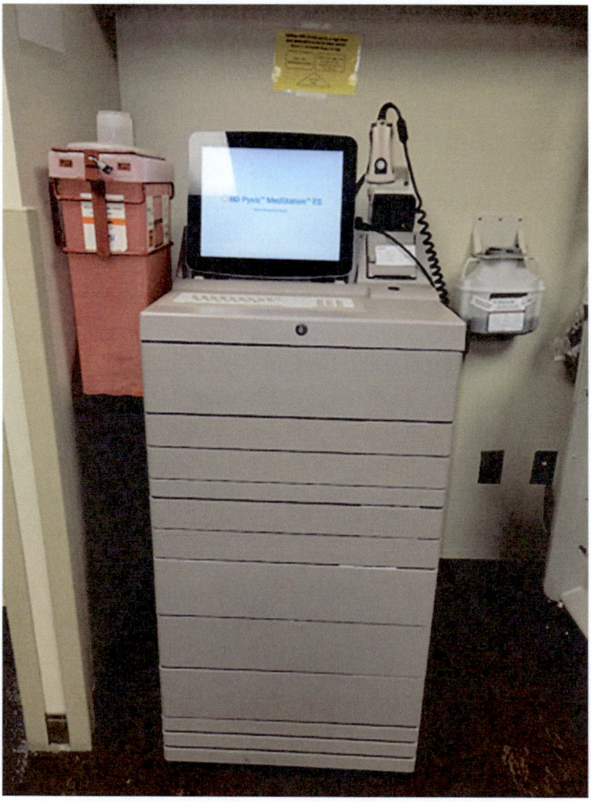

Fig. 13.1 Example of an automated dispensing unit. (Source: Marilyn Bulloch)

An ADU may be located in a licensed healthcare facility with a valid institutional pharmacy permit (indicating a pharmacy on-site) or in a facility that has a valid and current contract with a managing pharmacy to provide pharmacy services [1]. Chapter 12 includes more information on what is considered a "managing pharmacy" in Alabama. The ADU is considered an extension of the pharmacy itself [1]. Written policies and procedures that are approved by both the pharmacy and facility leadership must be maintained to govern ADU use and operation.

The managing pharmacy overseeing the machine must obtain ALBOP approval for the ADU at least 30 days before it wishes to start using it. The notice must include a copy of all ADU policies and procedures. The managing pharmacy must also notify ALBOP approval when adding or moving ADU locations at least 30 days prior to the change.

The supervising pharmacist is responsible for all ADU operations. A pharmacist (at the facility or, if applicable, the managing pharmacy) must have access to the machine and all transaction information at all times. Access to the ADU is controlled by the pharmacy and may only be granted to (1) licensed nurses, (2) licensed pharmacists, (3) registered pharmacy technicians, (4) respiratory therapists, and (4) other licensed healthcare professionals who are approved by the supervising pharmacists or medical staff. Field service personnel may be granted access to the ADU for maintenance purposes but must be under the direct observation of a licensed nurse, licensed pharmacist, or registered pharmacy technician the entire time.

The placement of an ADU does not eliminate the role of the pharmacist in the medication order process. Before a medication may be removed from the ADU, a pharmacist must review, interpret, and approve the medication order [1]. This may be completed by a pharmacist employed by the facility or the managing pharmacist. Chapter 12 describes provisions for when off-site order verification may occur. If an ordered medication is urgently needed before it can be approved by a pharmacist, the facility may allow emergency access to the medication through the ADU. However, emergency access must be authorized by the facility in its policies and procedures.

The specific medications and quantities of each kept in an ADU are determined jointly by the pharmacy, the facility's Medical Director (a lead physician administrator), and appropriate nursing leadership [1]. If medications have been delivered to the ADU by the managing pharmacy but not yet stocked into the ADU, they must be stored in compliance with the facility's policies and procedures. Restocking of an ADU is limited to a (1) licensed pharmacist, (2) registered pharmacy technician, (3) licensed nurse, or (4) other licensed healthcare professional approved by ALBOP. A pharmacist must conduct an on-site inventory of the ADU contents at least quarterly.

▶ **Numbers of Importance** Any ADU overseen by a managing pharmacy must be inventoried at least **quarterly** (e.g., every 3 months).

4 Stat Medicine Cabinets

Some institutional pharmacies do not have a licensed pharmacist working at all times, particularly during periods such as nights, weekends, and holidays where the workload and census may not support the need for a pharmacist to be scheduled to work in the pharmacy. As discussed above, many facilities use ADUs in nursing units and other patient care areas that are stocked with medications common to the patient population. In such cases, medications can be obtained from the ADU if and once reviewed and verified by a pharmacist. Other facilities may use non-electronic secure storage methods (e.g., locked drawer) that are dedicated to an individual patient. Medications on the patient's regimen are dispensed from the pharmacy when the pharmacist is on duty in sufficient amounts to administer through the next dispensing cycle. There will be times when a pharmacist is not on duty and a patient requires a new medication. If the facility has an ADU and the ADU is stocked with the necessary medication, the process is as simple as using the ADU to obtain the drug. In Alabama, there are rules that allow off-site verification of medication orders (discussed in Chap. 12) that facilitate the medication review process when a licensed pharmacist is not in-house so that the medication can be obtained from the ADU without the use of an override.

In situations where the drug is not available by ADUs, either because it is not stocked or because the facility does not use ADUs and a pharmacist is not on duty, arrangements must be made in advance by the supervising pharmacist to provide patients with necessary medications [1]. This may be accomplished using an enclosure termed by ALBOP as a stat medicine cabinet. A stat medicine cabinet may also be used to provide medications that are needed "quickly" even when a pharmacist is on duty in the facility. Each facility may have one stat medicine cabinet [1, 8]. If a facility wants to have more stat medicine cabinets, it must obtain permission from the ADPH. Facilities must have written procedures on hand for how the stat medicine cabinet will be utilized.

The medications included in the stat medicine cabinet are determined collaboratively by the supervising pharmacist and the "appropriate committee" within the facility (the name and type of committee may vary by institution) [1]. Each year, the pharmacist must review and determine the need for medications stored in the cabinet. Each cabinet must have an associated list of contents that specifies every drug (by strength) and the quantity of each stored in the cabinet [1, 8]. It is important to recognize that stat medicine cabinets may only contain *noncontrolled* substances. When a controlled substance is needed during a time when a pharmacist is not on duty, it must be obtained from an ADU, an emergency kit, or from the pharmacy itself (Chap. 12 discusses rules on pharmacy access in the absence of a pharmacist). It is also important to understand that a stat medicine cabinet is only intended to provide one-time doses or short courses of medications. It is a temporary measure and not meant to provide maintenance doses of a patient's medication regimen. As such, the stat medicine cabinet should only contain a "minimum amount of stock" of each medication, though what defines "minimum" may vary by the facility and drug [1, 8]. All medications stored in the cabinet must be packaged appropriately

Table 13.1 Required elements of policies and procedures governing the use of stat medicine cabinets in Alabama

All drugs are properly labeled
Only prepackaged drugs are available
Only amounts of drugs that are sufficient for immediate therapeutic requirements are kept in the cabinet
When the cabinet is accessed, written orders of an authorized practitioner (prescriber) and proof of use are provided
All drugs kept in the cabinet are inventoried at least every 30 days based on institutional policy
A complete audit of all cabinet activity is conducted at least once per month

based on the needs of the facility. The medications must be labeled with the medication's name, strength, and expiration date.

The supervising pharmacist and committee also determine who has access to the cabinet and write and maintain policies and procedures governing the cabinet use (Table 13.1) [1]. Access to the stat medicine cabinet is limited to authorized personnel who use a key or combination to retrieve medications. There must be some sort of record system that documents any time a medication from the cabinet is obtained and used [1, 8]. The records must include the patient name, the amount of the medication used, the prescribing physician (the rule does specify physician), the time the medication was administered, and the name of the person removing and administering the medication. The records must also include how much of each medication is placed into the cabinet each time it is stocked or restocked and the balance on hand each time a dose is removed. The policy (policies) and procedures related to the cabinet's use must include provisions for how and when used items will be replaced. At least one time per month, the pharmacist must inspect the cabinet. During this inspection, the pharmacist must reconcile cabinet use since the last inspection and replace outdated drugs. The information obtained during the inspection is included in a monthly report.

Key Concept

The ALBOP does not mandate that a stat medicine cabinet be an electronic enclosure with the ability to digitally document transactions in the same way it classifies an automated dispensing system. However, there is no rule prohibiting the use of an ADU machine as a stat medicine cabinet.

Key Concept

Controlled substances (e.g., opioids) may not be stored in a stat medicine cabinet. They may be included as appropriate in an automated dispensing system or emergency kit.

▶ **Numbers of Importance** 30
A stat medicine cabinet must be inventoried at least every 30 days.

▶ **Numbers of Importance** One per month—the minimum amount times that a complete audit of all stat medicine cabinet activity must be conducted.

5 Understanding Emergency Kits

There are times when a medication is required for patient care that has not been dispensed for a designated patient by the pharmacy. As described previously in this chapter, the use of ADU and stat medicine cabinets can be used to provide many medications when this situation occurs. However, stat medicine cabinets may not contain controlled substances, and a medication necessary to treat an acute event may not be stocked in the ADU or cabinet. Even in facilities with a pharmacy, the time to dispense the drug from the pharmacy may not allow for timely enough administration for patient's situation.

An emergency kit may be used to facilitate the prompt supply of critical medication(s) [1]. A valid medication order from an authorized prescriber is necessary to obtain and administer any of the medications within the kit.

The contents of the emergency kit, including the names and quantity of medications, are jointly determined by the supplying pharmacist and medical staff of the facility [1]. Only a pharmacist licensed in Alabama may provide medications for and seal the kit. This is an important consideration as there are mass-produced "emergency kits" sold by out-of-state companies. A copy of the kit's content is maintained by both the facility and the pharmacy supplying the kit's medications. Each kit must be labeled in a way that clearly identifies it as an "emergency" drug kit and therefore should be used only for emergencies. The kit must contain a label that lists all of the medications within the kit, including name, strength, quantity, and expiration date. The kit must contain an expiration date which is consistent with the earliest date of expiration of any medication within the kit. The kit's label must also contain the name, address(es), and telephone number(s) of the supplying pharmacist. The kit should be stored in a secured area that prevents unauthorized access and in a proper environment to preserve the medications (i.e., stored to prevent drug adulteration or deterioration). The supplying pharmacist must be notified anytime the kit is opened, and the pharmacist must restock and reseal the kit within 72 h. On the kit's expiration date, the supplying pharmacist must replace the expired medication and affix a new expiration date.

Unlike stat medicine cabinets, emergency kits are allowed to contain controlled substances. If the kit is kept in a nursing facility under the authority of the ADPH, there are additional rules regulating any controlled substances in the kit [9]. The medications must be supplied by a Drug Enforcement Administration-registered pharmacy or provider, and the maximum quantity of any controlled substance in the kit is 3 days' supply. Any kit that contains controlled substances must have security measures that include double locks, and access is limited.

▶ **Numbers of Importance** 72

The number of hours the supplying pharmacist has to stock and reseal an emergency kit that has been opened.

References

1. Alabama State Board of Pharmacy Administrative Code, Chapter 680-X-2 Practice of Pharmacy. § 680-X-2-.18 (1987 and Rev. 2024).
2. Beobide Telleria I, Ferro Uriguen A, Miró Isasi B, Martínez Arrechea S, Genua Goena MI. The impact of automation on the safety of drug dispensing in nursing homes. Farm Hosp. 2018;42(4):141–146. doi:https://doi.org/10.7399/fh.10949
3. Fung EY, Leung B, Hamilton D, Hope J. Do Automated Dispensing Machines Improve Patient Safety? Can J Hosp Pharm. 2009;62(6):516–519.
4. Pedersen CA, Schneider PJ, Ganio MC, Scheckelhoff DJ. ASHP national survey of pharmacy practice in hospital settings: Dispensing and administration-2020. Am J Health Syst Pharm. 2021;78(12):1074–1093. doi:https://doi.org/10.1093/ajhp/zxab120
5. Zheng WY, Lichtner V, Van Dort BA, Baysari MT. The impact of introducing automated dispensing cabinets, barcode medication administration, and closed-loop electronic medication management systems on work processes and safety of controlled medications in hospitals: A systematic review. Res Social Adm Pharm. 2021;17(5):832–841. doi:https://doi.org/10.1016/j.sapharm.2020.08.001
6. Alanazi MF, Shahein MI, Alsharif HM, et al. Impact of automated drug dispensing system on patient safety. Pharm Pract (Granada). 2022;20(4):2744. doi:https://doi.org/10.18549/PharmPract.2022.4.2744
7. Ala. Code. § 34-23-74 (1966, Rev 2013).
8. Alabama Department of Public Health State Board of Health Administrative Code, Chapter 420-5-10 Nursing Facilities. § 420-5-10.16 Pharmacy Services (1996 and Rev. 2004).
9. Alabama Department of Public Health State Board of Health Administrative Code, Chapter 420-5-10 Nursing Facilities. § 420-5-10.16 Pharmacy Services(1996 and Rev. 2004).

14 Compounding and Parenteral Medications

The whole is greater than the sum of its parts.

–Aristotle

1 What Is Compounding?

The Code of Alabama defines compounding as "the preparation, mixing, assembling, packaging, and labeling of a drug or device as the result of a licensed practitioner's prescription drug order or initiative based on the practitioner/patient/pharmacist relationship in the course of professional practice" [1]. During the compounding process, a new drug product is created for the purpose of meeting the needs of an individual patient [2, 3]. Instances when a patient may need a compounded drug include the following [2]:

- The patient may not be able to tolerate commercially available drugs.
- The exact preparation needed may not be commercially available.
- The patient may require a drug that is currently unavailable due to a drug shortage.
- The patient may require a drug that has been discontinued.

Compounding differs from manufacturing in that with compounding, a licensed pharmacist supervises the creation of a drug product specifically for the unique needs of a patient. This drug product is to then be dispensed directly to that patient. Whereas with manufacturing, drug products are mass produced, sold to other entities, such as pharmacies and practitioners, and then resold [2]. Compounded drugs are not approved by the United States Food and Drug Administration (FDA), whereas manufactured drugs are FDA-approved [2, 3].

M. N. Bulloch et al., *Pharmacy Law in Alabama*,
https://doi.org/10.1007/978-3-031-84771-4_14

Key Concept

Compounding is "the preparation, mixing, assembling, packaging, and labeling of a drug or device as the result of a licensed practitioner's prescription drug order or initiative based on the practitioner/patient/pharmacist relationship in the course of professional practice."

2 Pharmacist Responsibilities

In Alabama, pharmacists engaged in compounding must uphold certain responsibilities (Table 14.1) [14].

In addition, compounding pharmacists are to be knowledgeable and proficient in compounding. While no specific parameters are set regarding compounding pharmacists' continuing education requirements, pharmacists who engage in compounding are encouraged to continue learning about the topic by way of attending seminars and/or reviewing pertinent literature.

Pharmacy technicians may assist the pharmacist in compounding medications. However, the pharmacist must verify the weight or volume of all active ingredients used during the compounding process. In situations where the pharmacy receives a prescription for a compounded medication and there is not a written procedure for the compound on file, the pharmacist must direct the preparation of the compound. Rules regarding the pharmacist-to-pharmacy technician ratio apply to compounding drug products as well [4].

Key Concept

Pharmacy technicians may assist the pharmacist in compounding medications; however, the same rules regarding the pharmacist-to-pharmacy technician ratio apply.

Table 14.1 Compounding pharmacist responsibilities [14]

Verify all prescriptions
Approve or reject all components of the compounded product, drug product containers, closures, and labeling
Prepare and review all compounding records to assure that no errors have occurred in the compounding process
Assure the proper maintenance, cleanliness, and use of all equipment used in a prescription compounding practice
Assure that only personnel authorized by the supervising pharmacist shall be in the immediate vicinity of the drug compounding operation

3 Compounding Area and Equipment

Pharmacies offering compounding as a service need to ensure that their facilities abide by certain rules and regulations. The pharmacy must have a dedicated space where the compounding activities occur, and the space must be "maintained in a clean and sanitary condition." [5] Specifics regarding the space include that the walls, ceilings, and floors must be able to be cleaned (i.e., cleanable surfaces). The area needs to have proper lighting and ventilation. Potable water (drinking water or water that is safe for consumption) must be available via continuous positive pressure and free of contaminants [5].

The equipment and utensils used for compounding products should be cleaned and sanitized prior to use to prevent contamination and stored in a way to protect them from contamination. Equipment surfaces should be made of materials that are not reactive, additive, or absorptive to ensure the purity of the compounded product is not altered in any way. Regulations state that "automated, mechanical, electronic, limited commercial scale manufacturing, or testing equipment and other types of equipment may be used in the compounding of drug products." [6] If this type of equipment is used, it must be routinely inspected and calibrated, if necessary. The pharmacist is responsible for inspecting the compounding equipment immediately prior to its use. In cases where potent or hazardous drugs (i.e., antibiotics, cytotoxins, or steroid hormones) are involved in the compounding process, safety measures must be followed to prevent cross-contamination with other products. Safety measures include dedicating certain equipment for compounding these products or meticulously cleaning the equipment after use before compounding other products. Additionally, special procedures must be followed regarding the disposal of potent or hazardous drugs [6].

4 Drug Products

Pharmacists are to use their professional judgment when it comes to receiving, storing, and using drug products for compounding. Drug products should meet the official compendia requirements [7]. The United States Pharmacopeia (USP) Compounding Compendium is the standard when it comes to compounding quality measures. The United States Pharmacopeia and the National Formulary (USP-NF) provide quality standards, which include monographs, general chapters, and material reference standards for drug product ingredients. This resource is available as a yearly online subscription. While you may not be required to know all of the general chapters, it is important to understand that chapter 795 provides standards for nonsterile preparations, chapter 797 provides standards for sterile preparations, and chapter 800 provides standards for handling hazardous drugs in healthcare settings [8]. All pharmacies are required to comply with applicable USP-NF regulations [9].

The containers and closures that are used to store drug products must be free of contamination. The materials used for the containers and closures must not alter the compounded drug product in any way, including its quality, strength, or purity [10].

Key Concept

The United States Pharmacopeia (USP) Compounding Compendium is the standard when it comes to compounding quality measures. See the USP website for additional information regarding the USP Compounding Compendium, including the table of contents: https://www.usp.org/products/usp-compounding-compendium.

Chapter 795 provides standards for nonsterile preparations, chapter 797 provides standards for sterile preparations, and chapter 800 provides standards for handling hazardous drugs in healthcare settings.

5 Procedures

The ALBOP is responsible for developing written compounding procedures with the purpose of ensuring that the final compounded products are of the proper identity, strength, quality, and purity. The procedures include the following for the components used:

- Components list.
- Weight or volume.
- Lot number.
- Order of component mixing if available.
- Description of the compounding process.
- Designated name for the finished product.

The pharmacist is responsible for ensuring the procedures are followed by checking and rechecking them at each stage of the process. This is necessary to ensure that each weight and measure are accurate and in accordance with the written compounding procedures. There should be an acceptable degree of weight variation among the final compounded products. The pharmacist is responsible for ensuring that there is reasonable uniformity and integrity of all compounded products [11].

Certain procedures must be performed if a component used in the compounding process is removed from its original container and transferred to and another container. An example of this is if a pharmacist were to take a powder that is used in compounding a drug product from its original container and store it in another container. Whenever a component is transferred from its original container to another container, the following must be included on the new container [12]:

- Component name and supplier.
- Lot number and expiration date (if available).
- Strength and concentration.

It is lawful to compound drug products in anticipation of receiving a prescription. A stipulation is that only reasonable amounts may be prepared prior to receiving a prescription as opposed to preparing the product in bulk. These products that are prepared in advance must be labeled with the following information [12]:

- Complete list of ingredients or designated name of the preparation.
- Preparation date.
- Beyond use date.
- Storage under conditions dictated by composition and stability, including storage in a clean, dry place or in the refrigerator.
- Batch or lot number.

The pharmacist is responsible for inspecting the finished drug product to ensure that it has the correct labeling, which also must include all the information required for other prescriptions [12].

6 Records

Compounding records are required to comply with good compounding practices and should be retained for the same period of time in which prescription records should be retained. These records should be retained in a way so that they are readily available in case of inspection. Both the hard copy of the prescription and the computerized record should indicate that the prescription is a compounded prescription. In cases where compounding involves controlled dangerous substances or scheduled drugs, additional records are required to be kept [13].

7 Products for Over-the-Counter Sale

Pharmacies may compound drug products for sale over the counter without a prescription. In such cases, the compounded product cannot contain an ingredient that exceeds the recommended strengths and doses for drugs that are sold over the counter (OTC). The finished product must be labeled with the following information [14]:

- Product name.
- Directions for use.
- List of active ingredients.
- Necessary warnings (if applicable).

Before selling this compounded product to the patient, the pharmacist must have what the rules refer to as a "professional interaction" or "consultation" with the patient. These types of products may be compounded in advance but again only in reasonable amounts in anticipation of estimated needs. They may not be produced in bulk or sold to other pharmacies or vendors for resale purposes. These products must be stored behind the counter within the prescription department [14].

8 Products for Prescriber's Office Use

A pharmacy may compound a drug product for use in a prescriber's office. The product must be administered to the patient in the prescriber's office and must not be dispensed to the patient. The prescriber must provide the pharmacy with an order that includes the product's formula and quantity requested. The pharmacy must store a record of the compounded drug product, including the written procedure used to compound the product. The pharmacy must retain a record of the finished product's sale to the prescriber for at least 1 year. The record must include the following information: [15].

- Prescriber's name and address.
- Date of sale.
- Description and amount of the product sold.

The pharmacy can generate a prescription number for the compounded product as well as a label. The label must include the following information: [15].

- Product's name and strength.
- Quantity dispensed.
- Date on which the product was compounded.
- Beyond use date.
- Lot or batch number.
- Any additional information deemed necessary by the pharmacist.
- Pharmacy's name and address.
- Phrase "For Office Use".

> **Key Concept**
> A pharmacy may compound a drug product for use in a prescriber's office. The product must be administered to the patient in the prescriber's office and must not be dispensed to the patient.

9 Sterile Compounding

The ALBOP oversees the compounding and distribution of parenteral products in Alabama and is responsible for protecting Alabama citizens from inferior compounded drug products and inappropriate compounding procedures. Any pharmacy that is engaged in compounding sterile products must be registered and certified with the ALBOP as a parenteral sterile compounding pharmacy. Registration expires on December 31 of even-numbered years. Pharmacists who are engaged in compounding sterile products must be registered with the ALBOP. This is discussed further in Chap. 14. The supervising pharmacist is responsible for verifying that all pharmacists involved in compounding sterile products have received their parenteral certification from the ALBOP [16].

10 Prescriptions for Animals

A pharmacy may compound a drug product for an animal pursuant to receiving a prescription order from a prescriber. The compounding procedure for compounding prescriptions for animals is the same as that for compounding prescriptions for humans [17].

References

1. Ala. Code. § 34-23-150 (1975, rev. 2022) Available from: https://alison.legislature.state.al.us/code-of-alabama
2. Frequently asked questions about pharmaceutical compounding. American Pharmacists Association. Cited on 2024 July 2. Available from: https://www.pharmacist.com/Practice/Patient-Care-Services/Compounding/Compounding-FAQs
3. Compounding and the FDA: questions and answers. United States Food and Drug Administration. Cited on 2024 July 2. Available from: https://www.fda.gov/drugs/human-drug-compounding/compounding-and-fda-questions-and-answers
4. Ala. Code. § 34-23-151 (1975, rev. 2022) Available from: https://alison.legislature.state.al.us/code-of-alabama
5. Ala. Code. § 34-23-152 (1975, rev. 2022) Available from: https://alison.legislature.state.al.us/code-of-alabama
6. Ala. Code. § 34-23-153 (1975, rev. 2022) Available from: https://alison.legislature.state.al.us/code-of-alabama
7. Ala. Code. § 34-23-154 (1975, rev. 2022) Available from: https://alison.legislature.state.al.us/code-of-alabama
8. USP Compounding Compendium. United States Pharmacopeial Convention. Cited on 2024 July 12. Available from: https://www.usp.org/products/usp-compounding-compendium
9. Alabama State Board of Pharmacy Administrative Code, Chapter 680-X-2 Practice of Pharmacy. § 680-X-2-.43 (2018)
10. Ala. Code. § 34-23-155 (1975, rev. 2022) Available from: https://alison.legislature.state.al.us/code-of-alabama
11. Ala. Code. § 34-23-156 (1975, rev. 2022) Available from: https://alison.legislature.state.al.us/code-of-alabama
12. Ala. Code. § 34-23-157 (1975, rev. 2022) Available from: https://alison.legislature.state.al.us/code-of-alabama
13. Ala. Code. § 34-23-158 (1975, rev. 2022) Available from: https://alison.legislature.state.al.us/code-of-alabama
14. Ala. Code. § 34-23-159 (1975, rev. 2022) Available from: https://alison.legislature.state.al.us/code-of-alabama
15. Ala. Code. § 34-23-160 (1975, rev. 2022) Available from: https://alison.legislature.state.al.us/code-of-alabama
16. Alabama State Board of Pharmacy Administrative Code, Chapter 680-X-2 Practice of Pharmacy. § 680-X-2-.19 (1989, rev. 2021)
17. Ala. Code. § 34-23-161 (1975, rev. 2022) Available from: https://alison.legislature.state.al.us/code-of-alabama

Unique Pharmacy Settings and Practice 15

Choose a job you love, and you will never have to work a day in your life.

–Confucius

1 Consultant Pharmacy

1.1 Consultant Pharmacy Requirements

Consultant pharmacists provide pharmaceutical services to patients who reside in facilities, such as long-term care facilities, assisted living facilities, and nursing homes. Pharmacists serving in the role of consultant pharmacists in Alabama must be registered and licensed with the Alabama Board of Pharmacy (ALBOP). They must complete an online application to receive their consultant certification. Recertification occurs biennially and expires on December 31 of even-numbered years.

In addition to completing the registration, consultant pharmacists must complete an initial 8-h ALBOP-approved, consultant certification course (Table 15.1) and receive a passing score of 75 on an examination [1].

1.2 Continuing Education Requirements

Consultant pharmacists must complete eight live hours of continuing education (CE) during each pharmacist renewal cycle. These CE hours must be approved by the ALBOP. [1]

M. N. Bulloch et al., *Pharmacy Law in Alabama*,
https://doi.org/10.1007/978-3-031-84771-4_15

Table 15.1 Consultant pharmacist certification course topics [1]

State and federal consultant laws and regulations
Policies and procedures
Administrative responsibilities
Professional responsibilities
Consultant pharmacy opportunities (history and overview)
Drug regimen review
Ethics in consultant pharmacy
Impact of consultant pharmacy on the total healthcare system
Drug therapy/disease state monitoring

► **Numbers of Importance** Consultant pharmacists must complete an initial 8-h ALBOP-approved, consultant certification course and eight live CE hours every 2 years when they renew their pharmacist license.

2 Nuclear Pharmacy

2.1 Nuclear Pharmacy Requirements

Nuclear pharmacists provide radiopharmaceutical services, including the procurement, storage, preparation, labeling, quality assurance testing, distribution, record-keeping, and disposal of radiopharmaceuticals. Radiopharmaceuticals are defined as substances that "exhibit spontaneous disintegration or unstable nuclei with the emission of nuclear particles or photons and includes any such drug which is intended to be made radioactive. This definition includes nonradioactive reagent kits and nuclide generators which are intended to be used in the preparation of any such substance but does not include drugs such as carbon-containing compounds or potassium-containing salts which contain trace quantities of naturally occurring radionuclides." [2].

A licensed, certified nuclear pharmacist may only supervise one nuclear pharmacy whenever radiopharmaceutical services are being performed and ensure the pharmacy is following certain general requirements. The nuclear pharmacy area must be secure and only accessible by authorized personnel. The nuclear pharmacist must maintain accurate records for all radiopharmaceuticals, including acquisition, inventory, distribution, and disposal. Each nuclear pharmacy must have a secure area for radioactive storage and decay and comply with all federal and state rules and regulations pertaining to radiopharmaceutical procurement, storage, inventory, preparation, distribution, and disposal. In order for a radiopharmaceutical to be dispensed, there must be a prescription or medication order from a licensed medical practitioner. A nuclear pharmacist may transfer radioactive materials to an authorized user, which is someone recognized by the State Board of Health as a practitioner of the healing arts.

Once a nuclear pharmacy receives an oral order for a radiopharmaceutical, it must immediately document the following information in writing or in a data processing system: [2].

- Name of authorized user or their agent.
- Date of distribution and the time of calibration of the radiopharmaceutical.
- Name of the procedure.
- Name of the radiopharmaceutical.
- Dose or quantity of the radiopharmaceutical.
- Prescription number assigned to the order for the radiopharmaceutical.
- Any specific instructions.
- Initials of the person dispensing the radiopharmaceutical.
- Patient's name must be obtained and recorded if the order is for a therapeutic or blood-product radiopharmaceutical.

2.2 Labeling Requirements

In addition to the labeling requirements for nonradioactive pharmaceuticals, there are labeling requirements for the outer and inner shields of radiopharmaceuticals (Table 15.2) [2].

2.3 Space, Equipment, and Supplies

In addition to complying with the minimum requirements for space, equipment, and supplies for pharmacies covered in Chap. 8, nuclear pharmacies must also ensure they comply with additional requirements. In a pharmacy that compounds radiopharmaceuticals, the area where radiopharmaceuticals are stored, compounded,

Table 15.2 Radiopharmaceutical labeling requirements [2]

Immediate outer shield	Immediate inner container
Standard radiation symbol "Caution Radioactive Material" Name of the procedure Prescription number and lot number for traceability Radionucleotide and chemical form Amount of radioactivity and calibration date and time Expiration date and time Volume dispensed if liquid chemical form Number of items or weight if solid chemical form Number of ampules or vials or gaseous chemical form Molybdenum-99 content to USP limits Name of the patient or the words "physician's use only" in the absence of a patient name	Standard radiation symbol "Caution Radioactive Material" Radionuclide Chemical form Name of the procedure Prescription number of the radiopharmaceutical

Table 15.3 Required nuclear pharmacy equipment and supplies [2]

Equipment	Supplies
Fume hood	Syringes and vials required to perform practice
Shielded radiation containment drawing section	Disposable gloves and protective lab coats
Dose calibrator	Appropriate supplies to ensure aseptic technique
Well scintillation counters	Appropriate supplies to perform thin layer chromatography
Area rate meters	Lead transport shields for syringes and vials
Geiger-Mueller survey meters	Department of Transportation Type 7A-approved transport containers and other labels and supplies for shipping radioactive materials
Refrigerator	
Microscope	
Hemocytometer	
Leaded glass syringe and vial shields	
Personnel radiation detection devices	
Radioactive storage container and/or storage vault for waste materials	

distributed, and disposed of must be completely separated from the nonradioactive pharmaceuticals. Certain equipment and supplies are required in nuclear pharmacies (Table 15.3) [3].

2.4 Nuclear Pharmacist Training Requirements

Pharmacies providing nuclear pharmacy services must be registered with the ALBOP and designate a licensed, certified nuclear pharmacist as the supervising pharmacist. Recertification occurs biennially and expires on December 31 of even-numbered years. Prior to engaging in performing radiopharmaceutical services, a pharmacist must complete minimum training requirements including didactic study, training, and experience in the handling of radioactive material. The didactic training component includes completion of a course provided by an accredited college of pharmacy or other program recognized by the State of Alabama Department of Public Health (ADPH), Radiological Health Branch, and the ALBOP. The training must provide a minimum of 200 h of formal didactic training that includes the following: [2].

- Radiation physics and instrumentation.
- Radiation protection.
- Mathematics pertaining to the use and measurement of radioactivity.
- Radiation biology.
- Radiopharmaceutical chemistry.

Additionally, the pharmacist must complete at least 500 h of on-the-job training and experience handling unsealed radioactive material. This radio pharmacy internship must be completed under the supervision of a licensed nuclear pharmacist. These training and experience activities include but are not limited to the following: [2].

- Ordering, receiving, and unpackaging radioactive material safely, including performing related radiation surveys.
- Calibrating dose calibrators, scintillation detectors, and radiation monitoring equipment.
- Calculating, preparing, and verifying patient doses while maintaining radiation safety standards of shielding.
- Following appropriate internal control procedures to prevent mislabeling.
- Learning emergency procedures to handle and contain spilled materials safely, including related decontamination procedures and surveys.
- Eluting technetium-99 from generator systems, assaying the eluate for technetium-99 m, for molybdenum-99 contamination, and processing the eluate with reagent radiopharmaceuticals.
- Clinical practice concepts.

Key Concept
Pharmacies providing nuclear pharmacy services must be registered with the ALBOP and designate a licensed, certified nuclear pharmacist as the supervising pharmacist. Recertification occurs biennially and expires on December 31 of even-numbered years.

► **Numbers of Importance** A pharmacist engaged in nuclear pharmacy must complete a minimum of 200 h of formal didactic training and 500 h of on-the-job training and experience handling unsealed radioactive material.

2.5 Continuing Education Requirements

Nuclear pharmacists must complete 2 h of CE related to nuclear pharmacy prior to recertification earned in the previous calendar year during each pharmacist renewal cycle [2].

► **Numbers of Importance** Nuclear pharmacists must complete 2 h of CE related to nuclear pharmacy prior to recertification earned in the previous calendar year during each pharmacist renewal cycle.

3 Parenteral Pharmacy

3.1 Parenteral Pharmacist Requirements

Pharmacists who are engaged in compounding and dispensing sterile products must register with the ALBOP and receive their parenteral certification. As part of the parenteral certification application process, pharmacists must complete an ALBOP-approved initial training course that is a minimum of eight contact hours. The course includes a didactic and hands-on experience as well as a written examination. If pharmacists are performing high-risk sterile compounding, they need to complete an additional 4-h ALBOP-approved training in high-risk sterile compounding. The supervising pharmacist is responsible for verifying that pharmacists who are engaged in compounding and dispensing sterile products have their parenteral certification [3].

▶ **Numbers of Importance** Parenteral pharmacists must complete an ALBOP-approved initial training course that is a minimum of eight contact hours.

3.2 Continuing Education Requirements

Parenteral pharmacists must complete 2 h of parenteral CE that includes both didactic and hands-on training during each pharmacist renewal cycle. This CE requirement is for parenteral pharmacists who compound high-risk sterile products as well as those who do not compound high-risk sterile products [3]. The ALBOP's website contains a list of approved training programs for initial and renewal certification [4].

▶ **Numbers of Importance** Parenteral pharmacists must complete 2 h of parenteral CE that includes both didactic and hands-on training during each pharmacist renewal cycle.

4 Preceptors

4.1 Preceptor Qualifications

Pharmacists must express a willingness to serve as a preceptor, complete a training program, and apply to the ALBOP to receive their preceptor certification. Preceptors must be willing to cooperate with the ALBOP in the development of training requirements. Periodically, as requested by the ALBOP, preceptors provide progress updates regarding the interns and/or externs they have been supervising. It is the responsibility of preceptors to ensure that interns and externs under their supervision receive proper training that meets the ALBOP's training objectives [5].

4.2 Preceptor Training Requirements

As part of the preceptor application process, pharmacists must complete a 2-h initial ALBOP-approved preceptor training program. Pharmacists who have been approved by the ALBOP as preceptors must complete a 2-h training program during each renewal cycle or be approved by a college or school of pharmacy for providing curriculum hours. Recertification occurs biennially and expires on December 31 of even-numbered years [6]. Internships and externships may only be acquired under the supervision of a preceptor. Preceptors may supervise a maximum of three interns/externs at any given time [7].

► **Numbers of Importance** Preceptors must complete a 2-h initial ALBOP-approved preceptor training program and a 2-h training program during each pharmacist license renewal cycle or be approved by a college or school of pharmacy for providing curriculum hours.

Preceptors may supervise a maximum of three interns/externs at any given time.

References

1. Alabama State Board of Pharmacy Administrative Code, Chapter 680-X-2 Practice of Pharmacy. § 680-X-2-.08 (1982 and rev. 2021)
2. Alabama State Board of Pharmacy Administrative Code, Chapter 680-X-2 Practice of Pharmacy. § 680-X-2-.20 (1989 and rev. 2012)
3. Alabama State Board of Pharmacy Administrative Code, Chapter 680-X-2 Practice of Pharmacy. § 680-X-2-.19 (1989 and rev. 2021)
4. Pharmacist. Alabama Board of Pharmacy. Cited on 2024 July 12. Available from: https://albop.com/pharmacist/
5. Ala. Code. § 34-23-73 (1975, rev. 2022) Available from: https://alison.legislature.state.al.us/code-of-alabama
6. Alabama State Board of Pharmacy Administrative Code, Chapter 680-X-2 Practice of Pharmacy. § 680-X-2-.09 (1982 and rev. 2021)
7. Alabama State Board of Pharmacy Administrative Code, Chapter 680-X-2 Practice of Pharmacy. § 680-X-2-.16 (1984 and rev. 2022)

Requirements of Manufacturers, Wholesalers, Distributors, and Other Pharmacy Stakeholders

16

We are what we repeatedly do. Excellence, then, is not an act, but habit.

–Aristotle

1 Key Definitions

1. Drug manufacturer: A non-pharmacy facility that prepares, derives, produces, compounds, or packages drugs, chemicals, or poisons.
2. Wholesale distributor: A facility which distributes drugs for the purpose of resale to pharmacies, hospitals, practitioners, government agencies, or other entities permitted to sell drugs. The following are exempt from this definition:
   (a) A retail pharmacy selling, purchasing, or trading a drug to another pharmacy or practitioner due to temporary shortage.
   (b) Intracompany sales.
   (c) Manufacturer and distributor sales representatives distributing drug samples.
   (d) Charitable organizations distributing to nonprofit organization affiliates.
   (e) Certain purchases by hospitals or healthcare entities that are members of group purchasing organizations.
   (f) Distributing blood or blood components.
   (g) Selling, purchasing, or trading a drug; offering to sell, purchase, or trade a drug; or dispensing a drug pursuant to a prescription.
3. Private label distributor: An entity that commercially markets and distributes a drug it did not manufacture under its own brand name. It is responsible for ensuring compliance with the Food, Drug, and Cosmetic Act (FDCA) requirements and Current Good Manufacturing Practices (GMP) regulations.
4. Repackager: A facility that bottles, labels, or repackages a drug, chemical, or poison for sale or distribution that it originally purchased or acquired from a manufacturer or distributor. The definition does not apply to a physician who dispenses, administers, sells, or distributes a drug to a patient.

M. N. Bulloch et al., *Pharmacy Law in Alabama*,
https://doi.org/10.1007/978-3-031-84771-4_16

5. Third-party logistics provider (3PL): An entity that provides supply chain logistic services, including packaging, warehousing, and distribution on behalf of a manufacturer or distributor. The 3PL does not have a responsibility regarding the product's ownership, sale, or disposition.
6. Outsourcing facility: A facility at one geographic location that compounds sterile drugs. The facility must register as an outsourcing facility with the Food and Drug Administration (FDA) and abide by requirements set forth in Section 503b of the FDAC.
7. Reverse distributor: A facility that receives unwanted, unusable, or outdated drugs from pharmacies, wholesalers, 3PLs, and drug manufacturers and manages their disposal.
8. Medical oxygen: Oxygen USP is a liquid or gaseous form intended for human consumption [1].

2 Storage Facilities

Facilities that are responsible for repackaging, wholesaling, storing, and selling drugs and/or medical oxygen must be of a sufficient size and meet all federal, state, and local standards. These facilities must not be located within a residence. The facilities must protect drugs by ensuring their drug storage areas have the following proper: [1].

- Lighting.
- Ventilation.
- Temperature.
- Sanitation.
- Humidity.
- Space.
- Equipment.
- Security.

Additionally, storage facilities are to be kept clean, orderly, and free from the following: insects, rodents, birds, and vermin. All drugs must be stored at the appropriate temperature. This information may be found in the drugs' labeling or the current edition of an official compendium. If temperature storage information is unavailable, drugs should be stored at controlled room temperature as defined in an official compendium. Storage facilities' temperature and humidity must be measured and recorded. There must be a separate area for the storage of drugs that are deteriorated, outdated, misbranded, adulterated, or in secondary containers that have been opened. All drug shipments, both incoming and outgoing, must be visually inspected to ensure that no contaminated or damaged product is accepted or distributed [1].

3 Security

Permitted facilities are to be secure with only authorized personnel having access. Access to areas where drugs are stored should be limited to authorized personnel only. An alarm system must be in place to detect any access to the facility after hours. Facilities must ensure that access to the facility from the outside is limited. The rules provide an example of installing adequate lighting on the facility's outside perimeter. To prevent internal theft by facility personnel, internal security measures must be put in place [1].

4 Recordkeeping

Facilities are required to keep records regarding the receipt and/or distribution of drugs, including inventory and all transactions. Specifically, records should include the following: [1].

- Source of the drugs, including the name and address of the seller or transferor and the address of the location from which the drugs were shipped.
- Identity and quantity of the drugs received and distributed or disposed of.
- Dates of receipt and distribution or other disposition of the drug.

Facilities must retain these records for a period of at least 2 years following disposition of the drugs. During this timeframe, the records should be available for inspection and photocopying by authorized personnel. Records that are kept on-site at the facility's inspection site or kept electronically must be readily available for inspection, whereas records that are kept at a location away from the inspection site or are not kept electronically must be made available for inspection within two working days of a request. Charge back transactions, which are transactions in which a wholesale drug distributor is reimbursed for preferential pricing, are to be kept separate from other records. Any record or report that is required by the Drug Enforcement Administration (DEA) due to concerns regarding increases in purchases or pharmacies' high or unusual volumes purchased should be copied and sent to the Alabama Board of Pharmacy (ALBOP) for review [1].

Regarding recordkeeping of controlled substances, manufacturers, wholesalers, or distributors are required to obtain registration with the ALBOP annually. If these facilities sell, furnish, give away, or dispose of controlled substances or precursor agents used to manufacture controlled substances to a facility other than a manufacturer or wholesaler, they must submit copies of required DEA records and reports to the ALBOP regarding increases in purchases or high or unusual volumes of these products within 30 days [2].

▶ **Numbers of Importance** Facilities are required to keep records regarding the receipt and/or distribution of drugs, including inventory and all transactions for a period of at least 2 years following disposition of the drugs.

5 Inspections

The ALBOP as well as federal, state, and municipal law enforcement officials may enter and inspect permitted facilities from time to time. Officials are required to show appropriate identification upon arrival to the facility prior to being granted access for inspection. Inspections may involve inspecting the premises and delivery vehicles as well as auditing records and standard operating procedures. If the facility is located outside of the state of Alabama, the ALBOP may contract inspections to other states' boards of pharmacy, the National Association of Boards of Pharmacy (NABP), or other inspection agencies. For out-of-state inspections, the facility's permit holder is required to cover the costs [1].

6 Written Policies and Procedures

6.1 General

All drug manufacturers, wholesale distributors, private label distributors, repackagers, third-party logistics providers, outsourcing facilities, and reverse distributors are required to develop and follow written policies and procedures. These policies and procedures are to pertain to the receipt, security, storage, inventory, and distribution of drugs. Additionally, policies and procedures must be in place to identify, record, and report any drug loss or drug theft. The policies and procedures must detail the process for correcting any errors that occur with drug inventories. Facilities must be prepared for any disaster, emergency, or event that may disrupt normal operations and have a procedure in place to navigate any such crisis [1].

6.2 Outdated Drugs

Drug manufacturers, wholesale distributors, private label distributors, repackagers, third-party logistics providers, and outsourcing facilities must have policies and procedures to ensure that all outdated drugs are separated from other drugs. These outdated drugs must either be returned to the manufacturer or destroyed. The written documentation regarding the disposition of the outdated drugs must be retained for 2 years.

Specifically, the procedure must include the following: [1].

- A drug that is outdated, damaged, deteriorated, misbranded, or adulterated must be quarantined and physically separated from other drugs until it has been returned or destroyed.
- A drug with an immediate or sealed outer or secondary container which has been opened or used shall be identified, quarantined, and physically separated from other drugs until it has been returned or destroyed.
- If there is a concern regarding a drug's safety, identity, strength, quality, and/or purity due to the conditions in which it was returned, the drug must be returned or destroyed. The wholesale distributor and private label distributor should review the drug's conditions before or during its return as well as the drug and its container, carton, or labeling after it has been stored or shipped. An exception to this is if the drug has been examined, tested, etc. and proven to meet quality standards.

6.3 Examination of Drugs

Drug manufacturers, wholesale distributors, private label distributors, repackagers, third-party logistics providers, and outsourcing facilities must have policies and procedures regarding the examination of drugs. Once a shipment is received, the facility must visually inspect each shipping container, looking for any damage that may possibly contribute to the contamination or damage of the drug. For outgoing shipments, the facility must inspect the drugs to ensure that no damaged products are delivered [1].

6.4 Drug Recalls and Withdrawals

Drug manufacturers, wholesale distributors, private label distributors, repackagers, third-party logistics providers, and outsourcing facilities must have policies and procedures in place to handle drug recalls and withdrawals. These recalls and withdrawals can be due to the following: [1].

- Action taken by the FDA or another federal, state, or municipal law enforcement or government agency, including the ALBOP.
- Voluntary action by a drug manufacturer for the purpose of removing a drug from the market that is either detective or potentially defective.
- Action taken to promote public health and safety by replacing an existing product with an approved product or new package design.

6.5 Retail Medical Oxygen Suppliers

Retail medical oxygen suppliers are responsible for providing medical oxygen to patients. Since medical oxygen is considered a drug by the FDA and requires a prescription to be dispensed, retail medical oxygen suppliers bill patients' insurance [3]. These suppliers must develop and adhere to policies and procedures regarding medical oxygen's security, storage, inventory, and distribution. Additionally, as discussed with other drugs, they must also have a policy and procedure to identify, record, and report any medical oxygen loss or theft and correct any errors that occur with the drug's inventory. The following information is required to be included in the policies and procedures: [1].

- A procedure to make sure that personnel who deliver and supply medical oxygen are appropriately trained to deliver and supply it safely and properly.
- A designated person to make sure the supplier complies with all regulatory requirements (i.e., USP. FDA, US Department of Transportation, Occupational Safety and Health Administration, etc.) regarding the storage, packaging, labeling, shipping, dispensing, transfilling, and repacking of medical oxygen
- A procedure to provide patients for whom medical oxygen is essential to the maintenance of their lives or when the lack of it may cause them harm with information for obtaining oxygen at all times (i.e., 24 h a day, 7 days a week).
- A procedure at all locations outlining how to handle and resolve complaints and issues received.
- A procedure to ensure that all medical oxygen has a tag or label indicating its current status of use.
- A procedure to ensure that all medical oxygen cylinders that are delivered have lot numbers on them.
- A procedure to track all medical oxygen cylinders that are delivered.

The regulations state that "nothing in this section shall prohibit the non-hospital emergency distribution of medical oxygen by licensed health care providers, emergency medical technicians, first responders, fire fighters, law enforcement officers, and other emergency personnel trained in the proper use of emergency oxygen." [1] Since medical oxygen requires a prescription, medical oxygen suppliers are not to dispense it unless a patient presents a valid prescription. The prescription should be provided by a healthcare provider that is authorized to prescribe medical oxygen though their scope of practice.

As when dispensing other drugs, medical oxygen suppliers must document dispensing of medical oxygen. The following information should be recorded and retained for at least 2 years from the date when the medical oxygen was dispensed: [1].

- Patient's name and address.
- Prescriber's name and address.
- Item dispensed and quantity.
- Date of dispensing.

When supplying medical oxygen to patients, suppliers are to provide patients with instructions regarding emergency and routine contact procedures. Additionally, suppliers record in the patient record that they have provided the patient with a written plan of service. This plan details that patients and/or the patients' caregivers were provided instructions regarding how to use their medical oxygen safely and effectively. These instructions must also ensure that the patient is using the medical oxygen in compliance with their healthcare provider's prescription and intended use. It is important to note that the information described in this section applies to medical oxygen suppliers and does not pertain to licensed pharmacies or pharmacists [1].

Key Concept
Medical oxygen requires a prescription, so medical oxygen suppliers are not to dispense it unless a patient presents a valid prescription.

7 Responsibility for Operation

The facilities mentioned in this chapter with permits are to develop and retail a list of principals and people in charge (i.e., officers, directors, primary stockholders, etc.) as well as their responsibilities and qualifications. Any facility with a controlled substance permit needs to be permitted with both the ALBOP as well as the DEA and ensure that they are in compliance with all DEA regulations.

When the ALBOP receives and reviews permit applications, it considers the following factors at a minimum for the applicant as well as the principals and people in charge: [1].

- If the applicant has been convicted under federal, state, or municipal laws related to drug samples, wholesale or retail drug distribution, or distribution of controlled substances.
- Any felony convictions under federal, state, or municipal laws.
- Past experience with pharmaceutical activities.
- Any false information provided in the application regarding experience with pharmaceutical activities.
- If the applicant has ever received any federal, state, or municipal government discipline related to a license, permit, registration, etc.
- Compliance with previously granted licenses and requirements.
- Compliance with requirements to maintain and provide records to appropriate licensing authorities and/or law enforcement agencies.
- Any additional factors that the ALBOP considers relevant regarding public health and safety.

If for any reason the ALBOP determines that granting a license to an applicant would not be in the public's best interest regarding health and safety, it may deny the applicant's request for a license. If there is a transfer of the facility's ownership, the new facility owner is required to apply for a permit. Additionally, within 10 days of the change in ownership, the "Change in Ownership" form must be submitted to the ALBOP. [1]

8 Designated Representative

Drug manufacturers, wholesale distributors, private label distributors, repackagers, and third-party logistics providers are required to designate a representative who is responsible for maintaining compliance with the state of Alabama's licensing requirements. The person should be appropriately qualified by possessing the education and experience necessary to complete such responsibilities. Designated representatives must register with the ALBOP. The initial registration fee as well as the annual renewal fee is $100. The registration expires after December 31 of each year, and the applicant must pay a fee of $50 per month for each month that the renewal is late.

The ALBOP requires that the designated representative meet certain requirements (Table 16.1) [1].

If for any reason the designated representative is no longer serving in this role, whether it is due to a change in employment or a change in desire to serve in this role, the permit holder is required to submit the "Notice of Change of Designated Representative" form to the ALBOP within 10 days. If the permit holder is not able to appoint another person as the facility's designated representative at the time of the change, they must notify the ALBOP within 10 days with an action plan to identify a new designated representative. The permit holder has up to 90 days to designate a new designated representative or else they are in violation of operating a facility without a designated representative. After 90 days without a designated representative, the ALBOP may require the facility to close until there is a new designated representative in place.

Table 16.1 Designated representative requirements [1]

Be at least 21 years of age
Be a US citizen or a person who has the appropriate, legal documentation to be in the United States
Be employed by the facility on a full-time basis and be physically present at the facility at least half of the hours that the facility is open or at least 30 h per week (whichever is less)
Be actively involved in and possess knowledge regarding the facility's daily operations
Serving as the designated representative for only one physical location at any one time
Not having been previously convicted of any violation in relation to federal, state, or local drug offense laws
Not having been convicted, received adjudication, community supervision, or deferred prosecution of any felony offense or any crime related to fraud, violence, or sexual violations of the practice of pharmacy
Consent and be subject to a criminal background check (the applicant covers the cost of the background check.)

It is important to note that only drug manufacturers, wholesale distributors, private label distributors, repackagers, and third-party logistics providers are required to have a designated representative. Outsourcing facilities are required to have a supervising pharmacist at each location. The supervising pharmacist must be licensed by the ALBOP. [1]

> **Numbers of Importance** If for any reason the designated representative is no longer serving in this role, the permit holder is required to submit the "Notice of Change of Designated Representative" form to the ALBOP within 10 days.
>
> If the permit holder is not able to appoint another person as the facility's designated representative at the time of the change, they must notify the ALBOP within 10 days with an action plan to identify a new designated representative.
>
> The permit holder has up to 90 days to designate a new designated representative, or else they are in violation of operating a facility without a designated representative.
>
> After 90 days without a designated representative, the ALBOP may require the facility to close until there is a new designated representative in place.

9 Violations

Facilities with permits are required to maintain compliance with all federal, state, and municipal laws and regulations. If a facility operates in a way that endangers the health and safety of the public, then they are in violation of the rules. Any conviction of federal, state, or municipal drug laws or regulation or violation of the rules in this chapter is ground for the facility's permit to be revoked, suspended, put on probation, or be denied being issued. Additionally, the facility may be subject to a fine not to exceed $1,000 for each conviction or violation [1].

10 Permit Fees

Permits for drug manufacturers, wholesale distributors, private label distributors, repackagers, third-party logistics providers, outsourcing facilities, and reverse distributors of drugs, chemicals, or poisons for medicinal purposes are to be obtained annually. Permits for retail medical oxygen suppliers are to be obtained biannually. Permits are associated with a fee (Table 16.2) [1].

All permits regardless of whether they are annual or biannual become due on October 31 and expire on December 31. When an applicant renews a permit prior to December 31, the previous permit shall become null and void. If an applicant fails to renew a permit prior to December 31, the applicant must pay a fee of $50 per month for each month that the renewal is late in addition to the standard permit renewal fee [1].

Table 16.2 Permit fees [1]

Application	Fee ($)
Initial fee—annual permit	750
Initial fee—retail medical oxygen biannual permit	400
Renewal fee—annual permit	500
Renewal fee—retail medical oxygen biannual permit	250
Transfer of ownership of the permit	750

Key Concept

Permits for drug manufacturers, wholesale distributors, private label distributors, repackagers, third-party logistics providers, outsourcing facilities, and reverse distributors of drugs, chemicals, or poisons for medicinal purposes are to be obtained annually.

Permits for retail medical oxygen suppliers are to be obtained biannually.

All permits expire on December 31.

11 Precursor Drugs

11.1 Precursor Chemicals

Precursor chemicals are chemicals or solvents that are used to manufacture controlled substances. The DEA categorizes precursor chemicals into two lists: List I and List II [4]. Alabama rules state that all substances that are categorized as precursor chemicals and on one of these lists are considered precursor chemicals in Alabama. An exception may occur if the ALBOP objects to a precursor chemical's designation or deletion from one of the lists [5].

11.2 Licenses

Alabama rules state that "any individual, corporation, partnership, association or other entity who is a manufacturer, wholesaler, retailer or other person who sells, transfers, manufactures, purchases for resale or otherwise furnishes any listed precursor chemicals as defined or designated by any federal or state law or rule must obtain a license" from the ALBOP. [5] This biennial license expires on December 31 of even-numbered years. The initial license fee as well as the biennial renewal fee is $500. The license expires after December 31 of each year, and the applicant must pay a fee of $10 per month for each month that the renewal is late [5].

11.3 Permits

A permit must be obtained from the ALBOP "each time any individual, corporation, partnership, association or other entity having a legitimate need for using any listed precursor chemical as defined or designated by law or rule of the Alabama State Board of Pharmacy obtains such chemical(s)." [5] The applicant must submit an application and receive approval from the ALBOP. The fee for each permit is $35 [5].

References

1. Alabama State Board of Pharmacy Administrative Code, Chapter 680-X-2 Practice of Pharmacy. § 680-X-2-.23 (1990 and rev. 2024)
2. Alabama State Board of Pharmacy Administrative Code, Chapter 680-X-3-.05 Alabama Uniform Controlled Substances (1989, rev 1996)
3. Food and Drug Administration Compliance Program Guidance Manual. Food and Drug Administration. Cited on 2024 July 17. Available from: https://www.fda.gov/media/75194/download
4. List I and II Regulated Chemicals. Drug Enforcement Administration. Cited on 2024 July 17. Available from: https://www.deadiversion.usdoj.gov/schedules/orangebook/h_chemlist_listorder.pdf
5. Alabama State Board of Pharmacy Administrative Code, Chapter 680-X-2 Practice of Pharmacy. § 680-X-2-.24 (1991 and rev. 2016)

Collaborative Practice 17

If you want to go fast, go alone. If you want to go far, go together.

–African Proverb

1 Key Definitions

Several terms are introduced into the Alabama State Board of Pharmacy (ALBOP) Administrative Code regarding collaborative practice. Reviewing and understanding these definitions will make learning the rules and regulations much easier. These terms are taken directly from Chapter 680-X-2-.44 [1].

1. Agreement: Collaborative Drug Therapy Management Agreement.
2. Board of Medical Examiners: Alabama State Board of Medical Examiners (ALBME).
3. Board of Pharmacy: Alabama State Board of Pharmacy (ALBOP).
4. Collaborative Drug Therapy Management (CDTM): Practice of pharmacy whereby an individual pharmacist licensed in this state jointly and voluntarily works with an individual physician licensed in this state under a CDTM; agreement to provide a range of services to a patient of the Collaborating Physician and the Collaborating Pharmacist intended to optimize therapeutic outcomes; detect and prevent adverse medication interactions and side effects; provide education on the patient's medications used to treat the disease state so that medications are taken correctly; monitor, modify, and discontinue drug therapy as directed by the physician; provide education on managing medication side effects; communicate with third-party payors and insurers regarding prior authorization for prescription medications; and any other activity or service specified in a protocol approved by both the Board of Medical Examiners and the Board of Pharmacy, or otherwise authorized by this Rule.

M. N. Bulloch et al., *Pharmacy Law in Alabama*,
https://doi.org/10.1007/978-3-031-84771-4_17

5. Collaborating Pharmacist: A pharmacist who is licensed to practice pharmacy in Alabama, who is a party to a CDTM Agreement, and who has a direct pharmacist-patient relationship with the patient served by the Agreement.
6. Collaborating Physician: A doctor of medicine or a doctor of osteopathy licensed to practice medicine in Alabama who is a party to a CDTM Agreement, who has a direct physician-patient relationship, or otherwise authorized by this Rule, with the patient served by the Agreement, and who has prepared the patient-specific, drug or drug class-specific, disease-specific, and condition-specific plan of care based on a physical examination of the patient where required under this Rule.
7. Covering Pharmacist: A pharmacist licensed to practice pharmacy in Alabama who agrees in writing to be readily available to fulfill the duties of a Collaborating Pharmacist pursuant to a CDTM Agreement during the absence of the Collaborating Pharmacist. The Covering Pharmacist shall be an employee of the same pharmacy practice as the Collaborating Pharmacist, demonstrate the ability to provide the services listed in the Agreement, and abide by the rules and regulations of the Board of Medical Examiners and Board of Pharmacy.
8. Covering Physician: A doctor of medicine or a doctor of osteopathy licensed to practice medicine in Alabama who agrees in writing to be readily available to fulfill the duties of a Collaborating Physician pursuant to a CDTM Agreement during the absence of the Collaborating Physician. The covering physician shall be either a member of the same medical practice, practice group, or multidisciplinary medical team, or of the same or similar practice specialty as the Collaborating Physician and shall abide by the rules and regulations adopted by the Board of Medical Examiners and Board of Pharmacy.
9. Formulary: A list of legend drugs or drug classes that may be utilized under a CDTM Agreement.
10. Joint Committee: The Joint Committee on Pharmacy Collaborative Practice established for the purpose of enabling a mechanism for the exchange of information between the Board of Medical Examiners and the Board of Pharmacy on matters related to physician-pharmacist collaboration.
11. Licensed Healthcare Facility: A hospital licensed by the Alabama Department of Public Health or a Federally Qualified Health Center.
12. Patient Care Services: Services rendered by Collaborating Physicians and Collaborating Pharmacists for the benefit of the patient and which must be within the professional training and experience of the Collaborating Physician and Collaborating Pharmacist and be covered by the CDTM Agreement.
13. Protocol: A document approved by the Board of Medical Examiners and Board of Pharmacy establishing the permissible functions and activities to be performed by a Collaborating Pharmacist and signed by the parties to the CDTM Agreement.
14. Quality Assurance: Documented evaluation by the Collaborating Physician of the parties' adherence to the Agreement and patient outcomes against defined quality outcome measures, using a selected, meaningful sample of patient records, which will identify outcomes needing improvement, set performance

goals, and assess progress toward meeting established goals, with a summary of findings, conclusions, and, if indicated, recommendations for change. The physician's signature on the patient record does not constitute quality assurance monitoring.

15. Routine Scope of Practice and Services: Any patient care service provided by the Collaborating Physician and his or her practice in compliance with his or her medical education, training, experience, and the Board of Medical Examiners' laws, rules, policies and procedures, and that of the collaborating pharmacist and his or her practice in compliance with his or her pharmacy education, training, experience, and the Board of Pharmacy's laws, rules, policies, and procedures.
16. Unrestricted: An active pharmacy permit, pharmacy Drug Enforcement Administration (DEA) registration, pharmacist license, medical license, and Alabama Controlled Substances Certificate that is not revoked, suspended, or on probation at the time of application and is not subject to any conditions, restrictions, or limitations imposed by the applicable licensing board which relate directly to the delivery of healthcare services. A condition, restriction, or limitation directly relates to the delivery of healthcare services when it prevents a provider from treating certain types of patients or certain types of ailments or injuries, or otherwise limits a provider from fully engaging in the practice which would otherwise be authorized pursuant to his or her license.
17. Acute, uncomplicated illness or injury: A recent or new short-term problem with low risk of morbidity for which treatment is considered and full recovery without functional impairment is expected. For the purposes of this section, an acute, uncomplicated illness or injury includes: influenza, streptococcus, and any other condition as recommended by the Joint Committee.

2 Collaborative Drug Therapy Management

Before a pharmacist and physician can engage in CDTM, there must first be an executed agreement and written attestation that has been approved and filed by the ALBOP and the ALBME. The written attestation includes the names of the Collaborating Pharmacist, Collaborating Physician, Covering Pharmacist if applicable, and Covering Physician if applicable. It also includes the date of the agreement, the services covered by the agreement, and a formulary. The agreement and written attestation must be provided to the ALBOP and the ALBME no later than 10 days after the agreement has been signed by the parties involved. The updated agreement, including any addendums made, must be accessible at each participating practice site and be available to the ALBOP and the ALBME if requested.

Additionally, the patient, or the patient's authorized representative, must have signed a consent form agreeing to receive treatment under a CDTM agreement from the healthcare team, including a Collaborative Pharmacist. The signed consent form will become part of the patient's record [1].

► **Numbers of Importance** An agreement and written attestation must be provided to the ALBOP and the ALBME no later than 10 days after the agreement has been signed by the parties involved.

3 Eligibility Requirements

To participate in a CDTM agreement, a pharmacist and physician must hold an active, unrestricted license in the state of Alabama. The pharmacist must be licensed by the ALBOP, have no restrictions on the license, not be employed by a pharmacy that has a restricted permit, and comply with all terms and conditions for the CDTM. The physician must be licensed by the ALBME, have no restrictions on the license, and comply with all terms and conditions for the CDTM. In addition to possessing an active, unrestricted license to practice either pharmacy or medicine in Alabama, the pharmacist and physician must also have an active, unrestricted Alabama-controlled substance license. The pharmacy where the pharmacist is employed must maintain an active, unrestricted permit and DEA registration. The physician must have been in practice for at least 3 years. Alternatively, the physician could have been in practice for 1 year if they are certified by a specialty board approved by the American Board of Medical Specialties or American Osteopathic Association Bureau of Osteopathic Specialists. Lastly, both parties must pay the fees associated with a CDTM to the ALBOP and the ALBME). [1]

Key Concept
For a physician to be eligible to enter into a CDTM agreement, they must have been in practice for at least 3 years or been in practice for 1 year if they are certified by a specialty board approved by the American Board of Medical Specialties or American Osteopathic Association Bureau of Osteopathic Specialists.

4 Required Terms

4.1 Names and Titles of Collaborating Providers

The names and titles of all collaborating providers, including the Collaborating Pharmacist, Collaborating Physician, Covering Pharmacist(s), and Covering Physician(s) must be included in the agreement. The agreement needs to detail the process for changing collaborating providers. If there is a change in collaborating providers, it does not mean the agreement is automatically void unless that is explicitly stated in the agreement. Collaborating providers must sign the agreement by hand, electronically, or another method approved by the ALBOP or the ALBME. [1]

4.2 Authorized Care and Services

The authorized care and services section of the agreement must detail the nature and scope of patient care services and activities to be performed by the Collaborative Pharmacist. All patient care services and activities must be within the Collaborating Physician's routine scope of practice. Additionally, they must also be within the Collaborating Pharmacist's scope of practice authorized by the Collaborating Pharmacist's license, training, experience, and the ALBOP regulations, rules, policies, and procedures. If the Collaborating Pharmacist is providing patient care services and activities related to immunizations, opioid antagonists, and acute, uncomplicated illness or injury, there does not need to be a diagnosis made by the Collaborating Physician. For the Collaborating Pharmacist to provide all other patient care services and activities, there must be a diagnosis made and documented by the Collaborating Physician. If the Collaborating Pharmacist is engaging in modifying or discontinuing therapy, the agreement must include a protocol detailing the specific services that have been authorized for the Collaborating Pharmacist to perform as well as a formulary [1].

Key Concept
If a Collaborating Pharmacist is providing patient care services and activities related to immunizations, opioid antagonists, and acute, uncomplicated illness or injury, there does not need to be a diagnosis made by the Collaborating Physician. There must be a diagnosis made and documented by the Collaborating Physician for the Collaborating Pharmacist to provide all other patient care services and activities.

4.3 Documentation and Communication

It is the responsibility of the Collaborating Physician to document the communication in the patient's medical record. If the Collaborating Physician initiates any change to the patient's drug therapy outlined in the agreement, they have 10 days to communicate the change to the Collaborating Pharmacist. The Collaborating Physician may satisfy this requirement by sending the Collaborating Pharmacist a new prescription detailing the change in therapy via written, telephonic, or electronic means. If the Collaborating Pharmacist makes any changes to the patient's drug therapy, they also have 10 days to notify the Collaborating Physician as well as any additional physician(s) designated by the patient. The agreement includes details regarding the process for the Collaborating Pharmacist and Collaborating Physician to document in the patient's medical record, document services provided to the patient pursuant to the agreement, and communicate between one another. The Collaborating Physician is responsible for storing and keeping the records for at least 6 years from the date the patient was last contacted. If the patient is a minor, the records must be kept for at least 8 years from the date the patient was last contacted.

If the Collaborating Pharmacist is performing patient care services related to testing, screening, and treating acute, uncomplicated illness or injury, they must do the following: [1].

- Provide the patient with written instructions to follow up with a physician with whom they have an established relationship or with the Collaborating Physician.
- Provide the patient with a consent form with the drug therapy changes and patient care services detailed in the agreement to be provided to the Collaborating Physician as well as the patient's preexisting physician(s).

▶ **Numbers of Importance** If the Collaborating Physician initiates any change to the patient's drug therapy outlined in the agreement, they have 10 days to communicate the change to the Collaborating Pharmacist.

If the Collaborating Pharmacist makes any changes to the patient's drug therapy, they have 10 days to notify the Collaborating Physician as well as any additional physician(s) designated by the patient.

4.4 Override Clause

The agreement must include an override clause detailing that the Collaborating Physician may override the Collaborating Pharmacist's actions specific to services pursuant to the agreement. The override clause must include details regarding how the override will be documented as well as communicated to the Collaborating Pharmacist and the patient [1].

4.5 Expiration, Modification, and Termination

The agreement must include the date on which the agreement will be effective. Additionally, the agreement must state the term or expiration date when the agreement will expire if not renewed. All agreements must be reviewed, updated if applicable, and renewed by December 31 at least every 2 years. The agreement must include the process for modifying or terminating the agreement by either party. Agreement amendments are allowable, and they must be agreed upon by both the Collaborating Physician and the Collaborating Pharmacist. The amendment must include a description of the agreement change and the date on which the change is effective. Amendments do not automatically void the original agreement unless the amendment specifically states that it does. If the amendment involves substantive changes to the scope of patient care services or activities provided under the agreement, then it must be provided to the ALBOP and the ALBME no later than 10 days from the date when the collaborating providers sign it. The example of a substantive change provided in the rules is the addition of new therapeutic drug classes to the formulary [1].

► **Numbers of Importance** All CDTM agreements must be reviewed, updated if applicable, and renewed by December 31 at least every 2 years.

Amendments to the CDTM that involve substantive changes to the scope of patient care services or activities provided under the agreement must be provided to the ALBOP and the ALBME no later than 10 days from the date when the collaborating providers sign it.

4.6 Automatic Exclusions

The agreement must include a provision detailing when a collaborating provider will be automatically excluded from participating in the agreement. The following situations are provided in the rules as examples of these situations: [1].

- Death.
- Suspension, surrender, revocation, or retirement of a license.
- Loss or restriction of prescriptive authority.
- Suspension, surrender, or revocation of a DEA registration or Alabama Controlled Substances Certificate.
- Exclusion from any federally funded health programs.

4.7 Quality Assurance

Quality assurance is an integral component of collaborative practice as it provides the Collaborating Physician and Collaborating Pharmacist the opportunity to review the care provided to patients pursuant to the agreement on a regular basis. A certain amount of patient records referred to as a meaningful sample must be reviewed by the Collaborating Physician every quarter. The sample must include the following:

- At least 25% of the patients treated pursuant to the agreement for the first 2 years of the agreement.
- At least 10% of the patients treated pursuant to the agreement after the agreement has been in effect for 2 years.
- All patients treated pursuant to the agreement who experienced adverse outcomes.

The quality assurance review must be documented, retained by the collaborating providers, and accessible for review by the ALBOP and the ALBME. The review must be accessible for review by the ALBOP for at least 2 years and the ALBME for at least 5 years [1].

Key Concept
As part of a quality assurance review, the Collaborating Physician must review at least 25% of the patients treated pursuant to the agreement for the first 2 years of the agreement. The Collaborating Physician must review at least 10% of the patients treated pursuant to the agreement after the agreement has been in effect for 2 years. All patients treated pursuant to the agreement who experienced adverse outcomes must be reviewed.

▶ **Numbers of Importance** The quality assurance review must be documented, retained by the collaborating providers, and accessible for review by the ALBOP for at least 2 years and the ALBME for at least 5 years.

4.8 Collaborating Pharmacist Consultation

The agreement must require the Collaborating Pharmacist to communicate and consult with patients in an approved area that ensures patient confidentiality. These requirements and standards are addressed by the ALBOP in Rule 680-X-2-.27 [1].

4.9 Notice

The agreement must detail the collaborating provider(s) who is/are responsible for the costs. It also must state which party is responsible for notifying patients when an agreement expires or is terminated and when patients are to be notified if there is a change to the agreement. Patients must be promptly notified when a Collaborating Pharmacist or Collaborating Physician is no longer involved in the agreement. In the notice, the patient must be provided with the Collaborating Pharmacist's or Collaborating Physician's contact information. Additionally, patients must be provided instructions on how to obtain copies of their patient records or how to forward their records to the pharmacist or physician of their choice [1].

4.10 Testing and Screening

The rules state that agreements that include performing patient care services related to testing, screening, and treating acute, uncomplicated illness, or injury must include the following: [1].

- Patient selection criteria, which include the physician's instructions for obtaining relevant patient medical history for the purpose of identifying disqualifying health conditions, adverse reactions, and contraindications to the approved course of treatment.

- Treatment protocols, which shall include the physician's instructions for the treatment of acute, uncomplicated illness or injury based on the patient's age, symptoms, and test results, including negative results.
- Any other requirements as established by the ALBOP and the ALBME.

5 Limitations

In order for an agreement to apply to a patient, the patient must have undergone a physical examination by the Collaborating Physician within the past year and received a care plan. The care plan can be specific to the patient and/or drug, drug class, disease, or condition. The exception to this rule occurs with immunizations, uncomplicated illness or injury, and dispensing opioid antagonists. The agreement also does not apply to prescribing of controlled substance medications. Additionally, a pharmacy may not hire or employ a physician for the purpose of maintaining, establishing, or entering into a collaborative practice agreement. However, a pharmacy may employ a physician or licensed medical practitioner to conduct the quality assurance reviews required per the agreement of pharmacists who are engaged in CDTM.

There are limits to the number of providers that may collaborate. A Collaborating Physician may collaborate with a maximum of three Collaborating Pharmacists. A Collaborating Pharmacist may collaborate with a maximum of three Collaborating Physicians [1].

► **Numbers of Importance** A Collaborating Physician may collaborate with a maximum of three Collaborating Pharmacists.

A Collaborating Pharmacist may collaborate with a maximum of three Collaborating Physicians.

6 Physician Standards

Physicians who are engaged in an agreement must abide by certain standards (Table 17.1) [1].

A Covering Physician can be designated to perform the above responsibilities when the Collaborating Physician is unavailable. This Covering Physician must be pre-approved by the ALBME, and the Collaborating Physician must certify this person is still actively serving in this role annually to the ALBME. If the Covering Physician is no longer serving in this capacity, the Collaborating Physician must notify the ALBME within 10 days of the termination. In situations where the Collaborating Physician is permanently absent, the pre-approved Covering Physician may be designated the temporary Collaborating Physician for up to 60 days. During this timeframe, a new agreement designating this temporary

Table 17.1 Physician standards [1]

Provide professional medical oversight and instruction to the collaborating pharmacist
Establish and/or maintain a physician-patient relationship with each patient receiving services under the agreement, with the exception of immunizations and opioid antagonists
Be readily available to the Collaborating Pharmacist through direct telecommunication for consultation, assistance, and direction, or shall make arrangements for a substitute physician to be readily available who is pre-approved by the ALBME, who practices in a specialty substantially similar to that of the collaborating physician, and who is familiar with these rules
Collaborate with pharmacist(s) who agree to be readily available to the physician through direct telecommunication for consultation, assistance, and collaboration
Contact each patient receiving treatment by a pharmacist for an acute, uncomplicated illness or injury not later than 5 days following the first day of treatment to discuss follow-up care or refer the patient for care from a physician with whom the patient has a preexisting relationship

Collaborating Physician as the new Collaborating Physician must be drafted and submitted for approval [1].

> **Numbers of Importance** If the Covering Physician is no longer serving in this capacity, the Collaborating Physician must notify the ALBME within 10 days of the termination. When the Collaborating Physician is permanently absent, the pre-approved Covering Physician may be designated the temporary Collaborating Physician for up to 60 days.

7 Pharmacist Standards

Pharmacists who are engaged in an agreement must abide by certain standards (Table 17.2) [1].

Just as with physicians, a Covering Pharmacist can be designated to perform the above responsibilities when the Collaborating Pharmacist is unavailable. This Covering Pharmacist must be pre-approved by the ALBOP, and the Collaborating Pharmacist must certify this person is still actively serving in this role annually to the ALBOP. If the Covering Pharmacist is no longer serving in this capacity, the Collaborating Pharmacist must notify the ALBOP within 10 days of the termination. In situations where the Collaborating Pharmacist is permanently absent, the pre-approved Covering Pharmacist may be designated the temporary Collaborating Pharmacist for up to 60 days. During this timeframe, a new agreement designating this temporary Collaborating Pharmacist as the new Collaborating Pharmacist must be drafted and submitted for approval.

Additionally, if the Collaborating Pharmacist is performing patient care services related to testing, screening, and treating acute, uncomplicated illness or injury, they must do the following: [1].

Table 17.2 Pharmacist standards [1]

Establish and maintain a pharmacist-patient relationship with each patient receiving services under the agreement
Be readily available to the Collaborating Physician through direct telecommunication for consultation, assistance, and direction
Collaborate with physician(s) who agree to be readily available to the pharmacist through direct telecommunication for consultation, assistance, and collaboration

- Provide each patient with written information to advise the patient to seek follow-up care from either a physician with whom the patient has a preexisting relationship, or, if no preexisting relationship exists, to seek follow-up care from the Collaborating Physician.
- Upon request of a patient, furnish patient records to a physician designated by the patient.

▶ **Numbers of Importance** If the Covering Pharmacist is no longer serving in this capacity, the Collaborating Pharmacy must notify the ALBOP within 10 days of the termination. When the Collaborating Pharmacist is permanently absent, the pre-approved Covering Pharmacist may be designated the temporary Collaborating Pharmacist for up to 60 days.

8 Agreement Approval

An agreement must be approved by both the ALBME and the ALBOP prior to a physician, and a pharmacist may engage in CDTM. Once the agreement is signed by all participating providers, it must be submitted to the ALBME and the ALBOP within 10 days. If there is an amendment or addendum to the original agreement, it must be signed by all participating providers and submitted to the ALBME and the ALBOP within 10 days. The amendment or addendum is not considered valid and effective until the updated agreement has been approved by both the ALBME and the ALBOP.

There are fees associated with establishing collaborative practice agreements. When a physician submits an agreement to the ALBME, they must pay a $300 fee. There is an exception if the physician is engaged in CDTM at an indigent clinic. If the physician is practicing at such a site, then the fee for the agreement is $1. The Joint Committee must review and approve any application requesting the $1 agreement fee.

When a pharmacist submits an agreement to the ALBOP, they must pay a $100 fee. There is an exception if the pharmacist is engaged in CDTM at an indigent clinic. If the pharmacist is practicing at such a site, then the fee for the agreement is $1. The Joint Committee must review and approve any application requesting the $1 agreement fee.

Fees are due at the time the application is submitted and are nonrefundable [1].

9 Agreement Denial

If any of the previously mentioned components of the agreement are not followed, the ALBME or the ALBOP may deny its approval. There are eight grounds for denial outlined in the rules (Table 17.3) [1].

Before the agreement is denied, the ALBME and/or the ALBOP will conduct a hearing [1].

Table 17.3 Grounds for agreement denial [1]

1. The application or agreement that the Collaborating Physician or Collaborating Pharmacist submitted did not comply with the terms and requirements
2. The Collaborating Physician or Collaborating Pharmacist submitted false or misleading information in the application
3. The Collaborating Physician or Covering Physician has committed an offense that warrants discipline for their license to practice medicine in the state of Alabama or their controlled substance license or they are unable to practice CDTM with reasonable skill or safety to patients
4. The Collaborating Pharmacist or Covering Pharmacist has committed an offense that warrants discipline for their license to practice pharmacy in the state of Alabama or their controlled substance license or they are unable to practice CDTM with reasonable skill or safety to patients
5. The Collaborating Pharmacist or Covering Pharmacist has violated the Alabama pharmacy practice act or the law or rules of another state's Board of Pharmacy
6. One of the participating members of the agreement is under state or federal restriction, probation, discipline, or indictment related to the provision of medical services, the practice of medicine or pharmacy, or fraud
7. The Collaborating Physician or Covering Physician does not maintain an active, unrestricted license to practice medicine, an active, unrestricted DEA registration, or an active, unrestricted Alabama-controlled substance certificate
8. The Collaborating Pharmacist or Covering Pharmacist does not maintain an active, unrestricted license to practice pharmacy, an active, unrestricted Alabama-controlled substance certificate, or an active, unrestricted DEA registration for the pharmacy where the services outlined in the agreement are being provided

10 Agreement Modification, Restriction, or Termination

The ALBME and/or the ALBOP may investigate a participating member of the agreement if they believe they have violated any of the provisions of the collaborative practice agreement. If it is determined that a Collaborating Physician, Collaborating Pharmacist, Covering Physician, or Covering Pharmacist has violated any of the rules, that participating member is subject to disciplinary action. Disciplinary actions include the following: termination, modification, or restriction of the agreement, disciplinary action against the member's license, a fine, or any combination. Before any disciplinary action occurs, the ALBME and/or the ALBOP must conduct a hearing.

In situations where the ALBME and/or the ALBOP believe that there is danger to the public's health, safety, or welfare, they may invoke an emergency suspension of the agreement. The emergency suspension will become effective immediately unless otherwise stated in the order. A statement of charges and notification of a hearing will be provided. The emergency suspension may last up to 120 days [1].

11 Reporting Requirement

The ALBME may invoke disciplinary action on a physician who is engaging in CDTM if they violate any of the rules or terms of the agreement. If the ALBME believes a physician has violated the agreement and/or initiates disciplinary action, they are to report this information to the ALBOP. The ALBOP may invoke disciplinary action on a pharmacist who is engaging in CDTM if they violate any of the rules or terms of the agreement. If the ALBOP believes a pharmacist has violated the agreement and/or initiates disciplinary action, they are to report this information to the ALBME.

If one of the physicians or pharmacists voluntarily terminates their participation in the agreement, they must notify their respective board within 10 days of the termination. If the Collaborating Physician's license to practice medicine becomes inactive, revoked, suspended, restricted, or placed on probation, then the physician's participation is terminated, and they are no longer allowed to participate in the agreement. The ALBME will notify the ALBOP in cases when disciplinary action is taken regarding the physician's license or when the physician's participation in an agreement has been terminated. It is the Collaborating Physician's responsibility to notify all parties involved in the agreement, including all patients who received service through the agreement, if their license becomes inactive, revoked, suspended, restricted, or placed on probation, or if they are terminated from the agreement.

If the Collaborating Pharmacist's license to practice pharmacy becomes inactive, revoked, suspended, restricted, or placed on probation, then the pharmacist's participation is terminated, and they are no longer allowed to participate in the agreement. The ALBOP will notify the ALBME in cases when disciplinary action is taken regarding the pharmacist's license or when the pharmacist's participation in an agreement has been terminated [1].

▶ **Numbers of Importance** If one of the physicians or pharmacists voluntarily terminates their participation in the agreement, they must notify their respective board (ALBME or ALBOP) within 10 days of the termination.

12 Renewal

All CDTM agreements are to be renewed every 2 years by December 31. Prior to renewal, the Collaborating Physician and the Collaborating Pharmacist must review the agreement's terms, conditions, protocols, parties, and content to ensure it is accurate. The fee for renewing an agreement with the ALBME is $200, and the fee for renewing an agreement with the ALBOP is $50 [1].

▶ **Numbers of Importance** All CDTM agreements are to be renewed every 2 years by December 31.

13 Joint Committee

The Joint Committee's purpose is to establish a means for communication between the ALBME and the ALBOP regarding CDTM agreements. It is to serve in an advisory capacity only to the ALBME and the ALBOP. Any recommendation the Joint Committee makes is then subject to approval by both the ALBME and the ALBOP.

The following members comprise the Joint Committee:

- Two voting members of the ALBME—these members are to be appointed by the Chairman of the ALBME and will serve 2-year terms.
- ALBOP President—the term coincides with the ALBOP member's term as President.
- ALBOP Vice President—the term coincides with the ALBOP member's term as Vice President.

Joint Committee members are eligible for reappointment. If a vacancy occurs, the successor is appointed by the original appointing authority, and the member who is appointed serves the remainder of the unexpired term. The committee will appoint one of its members as the chairperson for a 1-year term. The chairperson alternates between a physician member and a pharmacist member.

The Joint Committee should not meet unless the ALBME and ALBOP have provided consent unless all four committee members are present. The ALBME Chairman and the ALBOP President may appoint a proxy if necessary to ensure that both the ALBME and the ALBOP are represented by two committee members. The Joint Committee meets at least quarterly, and the meeting schedule is subject to change based on the ALBME and ALBOP. Joint Committee members' participation in meetings is deemed an official function of their respective boards; therefore, they are eligible for compensation and reimbursement for travel expenses.

The rules state the Joint Committee has the ability to exercise the following functions and responsibilities: [1].

- Review and/or recommend changes to the current rules and regulations for physician-pharmacist collaboration.
- Discuss and/or make recommendations regarding changes to the standard protocol(s).
- Discuss and/or make recommendations regarding changes to the standard formulary(ies).
- Review and/or make recommendations regarding any expanded protocol requests.
- Review and/or make recommendations regarding any expanded formulary requests.
- Serve in an advisory role regarding issues related to applications for CDTM agreements, required education, renewal, and other matters concerning the implementation of physician-pharmacist collaborative practice.

► **Numbers of Importance** The Joint Committee is made up of four members: two voting members of the ALBME, the ALBOP President, and the ALBOP Vice President.

Key Concept
The Joint Committee chairperson serves a 1-year term and alternates between a physician member and a pharmacist member.

14 Protocols

The ALBME and the ALBOP have established standard CDTM agreement protocols and a submission checklist. In situations where a protocol does not conform to the standard protocol, it is submitted to the Joint Committee for review and approval. When determining whether to approve a nonstandard protocol, the Joint Committee takes into consideration factors, including, but not limited to, the following: [1].

- The Collaborating Physician's and Collaborating Pharmacist's education, training, experience, and specialty.
- The Collaborating Physician's and Collaborating Pharmacist's disciplinary history and any licensure restrictions.
- FDA-approved usages and recommendations.

- Is the current protocol within the standard of care for the treatment of the condition? The Joint Committee would take into consideration medications' off-label uses and whether the use is supported by evidence-based research.
- Does the protocol put patients at a level of harm that is more than necessary?
- Are the services outlined in the protocol within the Collaborating Physician's and Collaborating Pharmacist's scope of practice?

After reviewing a nonstandard protocol and considering the aforementioned factors, the Joint Committee can decide to recommend approving or denying parts of the protocol or the entire protocol.

The ALBME and the ALBOP have developed a collaborative practice agreement for a test-to-treat protocol.

Key Concept

The Collaborative Practice Agreement documents can be found on the ALBOP's website. Links to the website are provided instead of providing the documents as the information is subject to change. The ALBOP website has the most current and accurate versions available.

- Standard protocol: https://albop.com/oodoardu/2022/02/Standard-Protocol-Fillable.pdf
- Submission checklist: https://albop.com/oodoardu/2022/02/CP-Checklist.pdf
- Test-to-treat protocol application: https://albop.com/oodoardu/2024/10/Test-to-Treat-Protocol-Application-Revision-Radius.pdf

15 Formulary

The ALBME and the ALBOP have established a standard formulary of drugs and drug classes that may be utilized in a CDTM agreement. This formulary is consistent with the Joint Committee's recommendations. If a protocol includes drugs and/or drug classes that are not included on the standard formulary, it must be submitted to the Joint Committee for review. The Joint Committee will recommend approving or denying the protocol, taking into consideration the same factors when considering whether to approve a nonstandard protocol. The Joint Committee can either recommend approving or denying the addition of a drug or drug class to the protocol's formulary [1].

Key Concept

The standard formulary can be found on the ALBOP's website: https://albop.com/oodoardu/2022/02/Standard-Formulary-Fillable.pdf

16 Exclusions

These rules do not apply to a pharmacist who is licensed by the ALBOP and is employed by a licensed healthcare facility. The ALBME and the ALBOP are responsible for identifying pharmacists who meet these requirements and are therefore exempt from these rules. The ALBME and the ALBOP may request that the individual provide additional documentation and/or information before determining the individual's exemption status [1].

Reference

1. Alabama State Board of Pharmacy Administrative Code, Chapter 680-X-2 Practice of Pharmacy. § 680-X-2-.44 (2019 and rev. 2024)

Professional Conduct and the Standard of Care in Alabama Pharmacy Practice 18

If your actions inspire others to dream more, learn more, do more, and become more, you are a leader.

–John Quincy Adams

1 Alabama Code of Professional Conduct for Pharmacists and Pharmacies

The Code of Professional Conduct for Pharmacists in Alabama was first enacted in 1990 by the Alabama Board of Pharmacy (ALBOP) [1]. Since then, it has undergone three revisions, the last occurring in 2022. The rule is codified in the Alabama Administrative Code and is intended to set provisions for the safe practice of pharmacy in Alabama.

This rule sets the clear expectations that both pharmacists and pharmacies must conduct themselves in a professional manner *at all times*. This means that unprofessional actions that occur outside one's professional role, including during personal time, can fall under this authority of the rule. If violated, the ALBOP can enforce disciplinary action.

The Code of Professional Conduct outlines specific professional expectations and requirements of both pharmacists and pharmacies. Some provisions are expected of both, while others are specifically directed toward pharmacists or pharmacies. These are outlined in more detail below. A summary of the provisions is also provided (Table 18.1).

1.1 Provisions Applied to Both Pharmacists and Pharmacies

There are certain parts of pharmacy practice that are not mutually exclusive to the practitioner or the practice setting. Both have a responsibility to fulfill certain expectations and requirements in order to collectively ensure safe pharmacy practice.

M. N. Bulloch et al., *Pharmacy Law in Alabama*,
https://doi.org/10.1007/978-3-031-84771-4_18

Table 18.1 Summary of Code of Professional Conduct provisions [1]

Pharmacists and pharmacies	Pharmacist specific	Pharmacy specific
Act in a professional manner at all times Hold the health and safety of the patient as their first consideration Provide each patient the full measure of their professional abilities Strive to perfect and enlarge professional knowledge Utilize and make available professional knowledge according to best professional judgment Do not disclose personal and confidential patient information without proper patient authorization except when required by law or when disclosure is determined to be in the patient's best interest Provide patients honest, accurate, and complete information regarding professional services Do not mislead patients on the nature, cost, or value of any professional service	Observe the law Accept the ethical principles of the pharmacy profession Uphold the honor and dignity of the pharmacy profession Avoid all activity which could bring discredit to the profession Expose any activity which could bring discredit to the profession Do not agree to work under conditions that: Negatively impacts the proper exercise of professional judgment and skill Deteriorates the quality of professional services. Requires consent to unethical conduct	Do not provide an environment that: Negatively impacts the proper exercise of the pharmacist's professional judgment and skill Deteriorates the quality of professional services Requires unethical conduct Deviates from safe pharmacy practices Adversely affects public health, safety, and welfare

The most important and first consideration for all pharmacists and pharmacies is the *health* and *safety* of patients. The provision makes an important statement in naming the pharmacists "an essential health practitioner" and requires both the pharmacist and the pharmacy to provide the full measure of professional ability to all patients.

Because safety is a primary consideration, drugs or medical devices that do not meet the standards required by law (see Chap. 3) or that are not of "good quality" (e.g., adulterated) should never be *knowingly* dispensed, promoted, or distributed. Likewise, drugs or medical devices that do not provide therapeutic value to the patient should not be *knowingly* dispensed, promoted, or distributed. Violation of the provision occurs when the pharmacist or pharmacy either *knows* that they are dispensing or promoting a product that is unsafe or of no value or *condones* the action by others. In this regard, a pharmacist or pharmacy who was aware of a violation of this provision but did not act to prevent or stop it could also be held responsible.

Pharmacy is not a static profession, and the body of knowledge grows larger each day. In order to provide the best patient care, the pharmacist and pharmacy must always strive to perfect and enlarge their knowledge of pharmacy and related subjects. This knowledge should be utilized and made available according to best professional judgment.

Society places a level of trust in pharmacists and pharmacies that must be respected. Neither should engage in any activity that brings shame or discredit to the profession. This includes both illegal and unethical activities and behaviors. It is also expected that members of the profession should not be thought to condone unacceptable activities or behaviors because of the risk to the public. As such, if a pharmacist or a pharmacy becomes aware of an illegal or unethical activity or behavior, they are expected to expose it and should do so without fear or favor. This means that any action that could be viewed as retaliation or retribution toward the exposer is also a violation of the code. Likewise, reporting is considered a professional duty, and one should not expect personal or professional gain for doing so.

Confidentiality is a hallmark of legal and ethical conduct throughout medicine and pharmacy. This is outlined specifically in multiple statutes and ethical principles, including this code. The pharmacist and the pharmacy are expected to respect that professional records (those involving patients) are personal and confidential. Proper patient authorization is required before disclosing any information contained in these records. An exception to patient authorization can be made when disclosure is required by law (e.g., receiving a subpoena for individual records, inspection by an authorized federal or state agency such as the ALBOP or the Drug Enforcement Administration), or when it is considered to be in the best interest of the patient. The code does not provide guidance to this exemption, and professional judgment should be exercised to determine when such disclosures are in the best interest of a patient.

Honesty is another hallmark of pharmacy practice. Information provided to patients regarding professional services must be truthful, accurate, and complete. Neither the pharmacist nor the pharmacy should mislead patients on the nature, cost, or value of any professional service.

Although it may be permissible in other states and jurisdictions, in Alabama, the Code of Professional Conduct specifically prohibits offering a financial award or benefit (other than competitive medication pricing) to encourage or induce any person to transfer a prescription from one pharmacy to another. This means that pharmacists and pharmacies may not offer rewards such as (but not limited to) gift cards or coupons of monetary value to entice prescription transfers.

1.2 Provisions Specific to Pharmacists

The profession of pharmacy is only as honorable as its members. Pharmacists have an explicit duty to observe the law (intended broadly—not just in reference to pharmacy law), accept the profession's ethical principles, and uphold the dignity and honor of the profession.

A pharmacist is ultimately responsible for their own individual actions. No person or entity can practice pharmacy except those with a pharmacist license. Therefore, the pharmacist should not accept any working conditions that could violate their professional responsibilities. No pharmacist should agree to practice under conditions or terms which impact or interfere with the proper exercise of professional judgment or skill, nor where the quality of their professional services is subject to deterioration. Likewise, no pharmacist should work under conditions or terms that require consent to unethical conduct. The terms of this provision mean that a pharmacist cannot shift full blame to the pharmacy or employer should a negative outcome result from unsatisfactory, unsafe, or unethical working conditions or environments.

1.3 Provisions Specific to the Pharmacy

It is recognized that the pharmacy as an entity holds an authoritative role over those who work within it. As such, employees, including pharmacists and pharmacy technicians, are vulnerable to internal expectations and requirements that may not be aligned with safe patient care. To mitigate this, the Code of Professional Conduct includes a provision to the pharmacy so that the environment of the pharmacy is conducive to the safe and ethical practice of pharmacy.

While the individual pharmacist should never agree to practice under unsafe or unethical working conditions, the pharmacy itself must provide an environment that allows the pharmacist to properly and safely exercise their professional judgment and skill. Unethical conduct should be neither condoned nor required, and the environment of the pharmacy cannot be allowed to deteriorate the quality of professional services. Deviations from pharmacy practices known and recognized to be safe or the allowance of any other conditions or practice with the potential to adversely affect the public health, safety, or welfare are prohibited.

Reference

1. Alabama State Board of Pharmacy Administrative Code, Chapter 680-X-2 Practice of Pharmacy. § 680-X-2-.22 (1990 and Rev. 2022).

Ethics in Pharmacy and Medicine 19

As to diseases, make a habit of two things—to help, or at least, to do no harm.

–Hippocrates

▶ **Study Pro Tip** While the study of biomedical ethics is an essential part of pharmacy education, it is rarely tested on the MPJE. Some test takers may encounter questions regarding ethical concepts on the NAPLEX.

1 Medical Ethics

A sometimes overlooked, but essential, concept is that the primary focus of a pharmacist is the patient and not a product [1]. The underlying driver of all pharmacist actions is the identification and resolution of patients' concerns and needs [1]. The modern climate includes numerous laws and regulations, steep financial pressure, competition, and growing demand for pharmacy services [1]. In this complex environment, pharmacists often encounter quandaries arising from specific and opposing personal, professional, and societal values. The term "ethics" broadly refers to the study of the nature of morals and specific moral choices to be made [2]. Ethics is inseparable from the practice of pharmacy. It answers the question of what we *should do* and why. Certain behaviors collectively referred to are considered "norms" or standards that transcend geography, culture, religion, and other demographics [2]. Such morals include not to kill, not to lie, to obey the law, and to help those in need. In contrast, norms that bind specific groups together, including professions, are called particular morality [2]. Norms that are held by the profession of pharmacy would fall within this category. It is important to study ethics in order to

M. N. Bulloch et al., *Pharmacy Law in Alabama*,
https://doi.org/10.1007/978-3-031-84771-4_19

help prepare pharmacists to address the challenges that they will undoubtedly face in their professional careers [1].

1.1 Philosophical Theories of Ethics

1.1.1 Normative Ethics

Normative ethics sets standards for human conduct and behavior [3]. In short, they outline what one *should* do. Normative ethics evaluates whether action or behavior will be judged right or wrong. Normative ethics also outline the balance of duties we have to others. Characteristics such as integrity and respect are often learned from an early age by the people we are closest to, such as family, friends, and other social environments. There are many societal rules that are normative ethics. These include telling the truth, not stealing, and not hurting other people intentionally. There are three primary normative ethics theories: consequentialism, deontology, and virtue ethics. Each theory has a different approach to moral problem solving.

1.1.2 Utilitarianism or Consequentialism

Utilitarianism is the belief that an action is judged according to its consequences. According to utilitarianism, every action is judged good or bad according to whether or not the outcomes do more than any alternative action to increase, or minimize any decrease, in the final net balance containing more positive over negative outcomes [3]. As a moral theory, it does not allow for moral absolutes [4]. A good example of how this is applied in pharmacy is the balance of benefit for risk for any medication. How much good will a medication do for an individual patient's condition compared to the risk of an adverse effect or other undesirable consequence of medication use?

1.1.3 Deontology

Deontology asserts that an action can be judged right or wrong according to the intentions behind the action. The theory centers on rules and professional duties. An action can be considered morally correct as long as it fulfils a duty and/or does not violate a moral duty or obligation. Duties are considered the things we know are required of us regardless of what we desire to do [5]. Because morality is set by rules, there is no subjectivity or uncertainty. Unlike other ethical theories, deontology does not consider the potential consequences of an action or personal emotions driving an action [6]. An application of deontology in pharmacy could be described by the duty to disclose a medication error to a patient, despite concerns of litigation, feelings of embarrassment, or discomfort with the disclosure conversation itself. Deontology is not always practical. For example, in a mass casualty situation such as a natural disaster or major accident, deontology asserts that healthcare providers have the moral duty to provide care to every patient [6]. Yet, in emergencies, the need for triaging is often required based on available resources.

1.1.4 Virtue Ethics

Virtue ethics is the cultivation of character traits as a way to lead to more ethical actions [7]. Its roots date to Aristotle who felt that morality of a person should not be assessed based on single, isolated acts. It is the opposite of deontology. People are considered good because of intrinsic characteristics. In short, virtue ethics focuses more on how a person should *be* rather than how a person should *act* [7]. Certain feelings or emotions are neither virtue nor vice, but are correct responses to such feelings. For example, a patient with a sick child may become angry when having to wait at the pharmacy for a medication to be filled. According to virtue ethics, the ideal response to the mother's anger is patience rather than irritability. Virtue ethics also argues that a person does not stop having a positive characteristic based on one action. In the above case, the mother may normally be a very kind and polite patient, and it would be unfair to judge her character based on this one incident.

2 Principles of Biomedical Ethics

2.1 The Belmont Report

In 1974, the judges at the International Military Tribunal, tasked with the trials of those accused of war crimes during World War II, outlined the *Nuremberg Code*, which specified that consent in human experiments must be voluntary [9]. Less than two decades later in 1964, the first version of the *Declaration of Helsinki: Recommending Guiding Doctors in Clinical Research* was published [9, 10]. While the *Nuremburg Code* focused on autonomy and consent, the declaration was rooted more in what benefits or risks a patient may encounter during research [10]. Unfortunately, neither document considered participation in research by vulnerable groups such as children or adults without the capacity to make decisions [9]. It soon became apparent that a more encompassing code of biomedical ethics was needed to ensure benefit and protection for all subjects, including the vulnerable.

The Belmont Report, more formally known as the *Ethical principles and guidelines for the protection of human subjects of research*, was developed by the National Commission for the Protection of Human Subjects of Biomedical and Behavioral Research [9, 11]. The commission was created by the National Research Act of 1974 [9, 11]. The commission was charged with identifying basic ethical principles that should serve as the foundation of conduct for biomedical and behavioral research which involve human subjects and to develop guidelines to ensure that research is conducted based on these principles. The Belmont Report is named such because the location of the building where the commission initially met to outline these principles was the Smithsonian Institution's Belmont Conference Center [11]. The report itself is published in the Federal Register, which codifies it as federal regulations and gives it legal authority [9]. The Belmont Report includes three basic principles that are to serve as the justification for human actions. These include (1) autonomy or respect for persons, (2) beneficence, and (3) justice [9, 11]. While these principles were developed to apply to research, each is applicable to clinical practice. These principles are discussed in detail in Sect. 2.2.

2.2 Understanding the Principles of Biomedical Ethics in Pharmacy Practice and Research

The Belmont Report outlines three main principles of biomedical ethics, but it should not be considered an all-inclusive list of ethical principles. Two philosophers, Tom L. Beauchamp and James F. Childress, published *Principles of Biomedical Ethics* in 1979, a work which added the ethical principle of nonmaleficence and provided guidelines for use of biomedical ethical principles beyond research [9]. Interestingly, Beauchamp was a member of the commission who created the Belmont Report [9]. Additional principles have been proposed, though some can be more appropriately integrated within the definition of one of the primary principles, and others may not be specifically applicable to health care. The principles described below provide the framework for ethical behavior and decision-making within pharmacy practice.

2.2.1 Autonomy or Respect for Persons

The underlying basis for autonomy is that all persons have intrinsic and unconditional worth with the ability to make rational and moral choices and subsequently should be able to exercise self-determination [2]. This principle incorporates two considerations: (1) that individuals have autonomy which must be acknowledged and respected and (2) individuals with diminished autonomy are entitled to protection. Autonomy means that the individual is capable of making decisions based on personal goals. Respecting autonomy means respecting the individual's opinions and decisions and refraining blocking their actions unless those actions would be detrimental to others. The principle of autonomy was legally codified in a 1914 court decision where it was ruled that "Every human being of adult years and sound mind has a right to determine what shall be done with his own body" [2]. Therefore, not only is this an ethical principle but a legal one as well. In pharmacy, this means that patients have the right to make their own decisions about their health care. Respect for autonomy should be maintained even when the healthcare professional does not agree with the decision. Violating a person's autonomy can occur in different ways. It can be as simple as disregarding a patient's choice or wishes. However, autonomy can be violated in more subtle ways that the patient may not recognize. Withholding information for the individual to make a considered decision when there is no compelling reason to withhold demonstrates a lack of respect for autonomy. For example, a pharmacist may not counsel a patient on all medication-specific information out of concern that the patient would then elect not to take the medication prescribed to treat a specific condition. By only providing some, but not all, information, the patient is not afforded the right to make a fully informed decision. In research, violation of this principle occurs when informed consent is not obtained. Another, more obvious, way of violating a patient's autonomy is to act against previously stated wishes. An example of this violation is when a patient who has expressed to transition to end-of-life care is aggressively resuscitated after cardiac arrest. Another example is when a patient feels pressured or forced into taking a medication by a healthcare provider or even a family member.

2.2.1.1 Informed Consent

Informed consent is considered by some philosophers to be an independent ethical principle, and by others it is believed to best fit under the umbrella of autonomy. For the purposes of this chapter, it has been placed under autonomy but with the recognition of distinct considerations that must be respected. Informed consent is required for research and before a medical or surgical procedure. It requires honest and full disclosure of information so that the patient may make a well-informed decision based on their personal values, preferences, and goals. To provide informed consent, the patient must (1) be competent and able to understand and decide, (2) receive a full disclosure, (3) be able to comprehend the disclosure, (4) act voluntarily, and (5) consent to the proposed action [2].

Some patients lack the capacity to make informed autonomous decisions. The extent of protection required depends on the individual situation. Some patients lack the cognitive capacity to make informed choices. Adults with cognitive disabilities and children fall into this category. Others are in situations that make them vulnerable. For example, prisoners should not be subtly coerced or influenced to engage in care or research that they would not otherwise volunteer for if they were not incarcerated. In clinical practice, patients without decision-making capacity should have an appropriate surrogate who is responsible for. Incompetence is accepted when a patient is unable to understand their situation and the consequences and/or cannot comprehend a life decision of significant consequence [2]. If a presently incompetent patient was previously autonomous and expressed preferences while competent, those preferences should be respected [2]. Any patient without competence requires a surrogate decision maker. Decisions can be made according to the substituted judgment standard—what the patient (and not the decision maker) would want given the circumstances—or the best interest standards—what decision would bring the highest net benefit to the patient [2].

2.2.2 Beneficence

Beneficence is a moral obligation to assist persons in need [11]. Within this obligation are two complementary rules of beneficent actions: (1) first do no harm, and (2) maximize all possible benefits and minimize all possible harms [9, 11]. Adhering to the principle of beneficence means removing conditions that cause harm [2]. It is understood that to avoid harm, learning what is harmful must occur [11]. It is important to determine when it is appropriate to seek certain benefits even with the potential of risk, and when the benefits are outweighed by the risks [11]. Beneficence is a principle of positive and unselfish action to benefit patient and promote their benefit and welfare [2]. Beneficence is central to the patient-centered focus of pharmacy where the pharmacist's actions are centered on ensuring the most optimal outcome for the patient.

2.2.3 Nonmaleficence

Nonmaleficence is perhaps the simplest ethical principle to describe. It is the obligation to do no harm [2]. Some ethicists consider nonmaleficence to fall within the principle of beneficence, while others consider it to be a stand-alone principle. In clinical practice, it has mostly been described and applied as independent. The principle of nonmaleficence is applied each time a medication is considered for a patient when the benefits of the therapy are weighed against the potential risks and burdens that the medication may cause. It is also encountered when discontinuing therapy. In research, it refers to any risk that the research may pose to the patient, whether that risk involves any intervention being evaluated or risk from *not* providing the intervention. Though simple in definition, nonmaleficence can be challenging to avoid in pharmacy practice where almost all actions involve some degree of risk or harm.

2.2.4 Justice

Justice is the concept of treating everyone in a fair manner and providing equitable protection and opportunity [9, 11] Injustice occurs when a benefit to which a patient is entitled is denied without good reason or when a burden to obtain the benefit is imposed inappropriately [11]. There are different formulations for determining justice. These include (1) to each individual an equal share, (2) to each individual according to individual need, (3) to each individual according to individual effort, (4) to each individual according to societal contribution, and (5) to each individual according to merit [2, 11]. In research, subjects should be evaluated to determine if systematic bias is contributing to selection or exclusion of certain demographics, for example, an investigator who discusses clinical trial enrollment with their patients without insurance more often than with patients with insurance because they feel uninsured patients are more likely to participate. In clinical practice, it is difficult to balance justice with other principles. The most frequently encountered issues of justice in practice include allocation of scarce resources (medications and supplies), allocation of time for individual patients (counseling, resolving payer issues, and locating scarce resources), and care of uninsured or underinsured patients [2]. It is important to accept the requirement of fairness within the principle of justice [2]. In pharmacy, medication shortages are one, all to frequent, issue that requires the application of distributive justice across most pharmacy practice settings. When a shortage is anticipated to last a long time, professional societies or government agencies may provide guidance on how to prioritize patients, but this direction is often unavailable at the beginning of a shortage [12]. To ensure fairness, it is important that allocation of resources that are scarce be done in a way that is both transparent and appropriate for the circumstance [12]. An appeal process and mechanisms for enforcement are also important components to ensure equitable distribution [12].

2.3 Ethical Dilemmas

There will be situations that challenge these principles and, at times, two or more of the principles may conflict with one another. Ethical dilemmas are situations which, according to morals, a person should both do and not do something [8]. They invariably involve a conflict between equally desirable or undesirable alternatives. Not all ethical issues or dilemmas will involve each ethical principle. In some conflicts, it will be easier to recognize where one principle should override another. The most encountered conflict is between autonomy and beneficence. However, it is generally considered that the patient's best interests are linked to their preferences [2]. In other cases, which principle should take precedence must be weighed according to the situation. For example, a patient with insulin-dependent diabetes requires insulin injections which can cause pain. In this example, the principle of beneficence in providing the necessary medication overrides the desire to avoid pain under the principle of nonmaleficence. Other conflicts are more difficult to address. In fact, resolving an ethical issue or dilemma can be one of the most challenging parts of clinical practice because it can be difficult to identify the most appropriate solution. Consider the often-encountered scenario of a patient with a limited income and no or poor health insurance coverage who requires an expensive medication to sustain life. When less expensive alternatives or patient assistance programs are available, the conflict can be more easily resolved, but what is the best moral solution when there are no such alternatives? It is important to understand how to apply the different bioethical principles described below in order to be able to weigh them appropriately as a means to find the best possible resolution.

3 Understanding What a Profession Is

A profession is a group of people who provide a recognized service that is central to human values that cannot be provided by the average layperson [13]. The book *Ethics in Neurology* lists ten characteristics of a profession, *all* of which are applicable to pharmacy and its members [14]. (Table 19.1) In return for their societal service, professionals receive a higher degree of trust, special recognition, benefits, and more autonomy than nonprofessionals. Obtaining a degree in a particular area does not automatically make one a professional. A professional makes a lifelong commitment to the patients and society they serve.

Professionalism is the conduct, aims, or qualities that distinguish a profession [13, 15]. The term "professionalism" has been defined slightly differently by assorted pharmacy and medical organizations. In general, professionalism can be viewed as a group of internally held principles measured through behaviors [15]. The essential attitudes and behaviors that signify professionalism in pharmacy are depicted in the American College of Clinical Pharmacy's *Tenets of Professionalism for Pharmacy Students* [13]. (Table 19.2) These tenets argue that the patient is the top priority in any healthcare decision. Therefore, the patient's well-being should come first, which is in line with the patient-centered focus of pharmacy practice. A

Table 19.1 Defining characteristics of a learned profession [14]

The profession possesses a **circumscribed** and **socially valuable body of knowledge**
The **members** of the profession **determine the profession's standards of knowledge and expertise**
The profession attracts **high-quality students** who undergo an extensive **socialization process** as they are absorbed into the profession
The profession is given **authority to license practitioners** by the state with licensing and admission **boards made up largely by members of the profession**
There is an apparent **sense of community and mutuality of interests** among the members of the profession
Social policy and legislation related to the profession are **heavily influenced by members** of the profession through such mechanisms as lobbying and expert testimony
The profession has a **code of ethics** that governs practice, the tenets of which are more stringent than legal controls
A **service orientation** supersedes the proprietary interests of the professionals
A profession is a **terminal occupation** and the practitioner's singular and lifelong occupational choice
A profession is largely **free of lay control**, with its practitioners exercising a high degree of **occupational autonomy**

Table 19.2 Tenets of professionalism for pharmacy students [13]

Altruism and unselfish commitment to serve the best interests of the patient above your own
Honesty and integrity in all that you do
Respect for others
Professional presence and the establishment of trusting relationships
Professional stewardship
Dedication and commitment to excellence

professional (in this case a pharmacy student) is responsible for their own actions regardless of the setting and must recognize that the correct decision is not always an easy one. Respect for others, holding in high regard their feelings, needs, thoughts, and opinions, is an essential component of professionalism. This respect should be afforded to everyone encountered, and by doing so, it builds strong relationships with those we serve. There is an obligation to establish trusting relationships with peers, patients, and other health professionals, among others. To do that, one must maintain a professional appearance and attitude anywhere where one represents the pharmacy profession. One must communicate and present themselves in such a way as to instill confidence and trust. In the past, it was argued that this meant pharmacists should always wear a clean, pressed white coat. In modern times, this may no longer be true or practical based on the setting, but even when a white coat is not worn, a professional should still dress themselves appropriate to their environment. Pharmacy professionals should not simply perform a job, they should be actively engaged in the profession. Engagement can take many forms which may include, but is not limited to, involvement in professional organizations, advocacy efforts, mentoring, or precepting. Professionals are expected to adhere to the responsibility of lifelong learning and development. It is a certainty that information learned while in school will change over the course of time. Excellence requires continuous learning to stay up to date.

Other models of professionalism include concepts not captured by these tenets. The umbrella model of professionalism is meant to represent the holistic role of pharmacy education in the development of professionalism and places the student pharmacist as the umbrella's center shaft or handle [15]. This model emphasizes (1) empathy, (2) communication, (3) instruction and guidance from faculty, preceptors, and other pharmacists and health professionals, (4) extracurricular activities, (5) school culture and environment, (6) mentoring and modeling, and (7) professional competence and knowledge. The bicycle wheel model includes a wheel hub centered on a covenantal relationship with radiating spokes that represent pharmacist behaviors such as (1) honesty and integrity, (2) respect for others, (3) commitment to excellence, (4) care and compassion, and (5) responsibility [15]. The tire of the bicycle wheel connects the different elements while outlining methods and activities where these characteristics are displayed.

In the State of Alabama, professionalism and professional conduct are codified under Section 680-X-2.22 of the Alabama Administrative Code [16]. The requirements under this regulation are discussed in Chap. 18 of this book.

4 The Oath of a Pharmacist

Every pharmacist and pharmacy student has at one time taken the Oath of a Pharmacist. The Oath was first developed in 1983 by the American Association of Colleges of Pharmacy (AACP). [17] It was most recently revised in 2021 and adopted by AACP and the American Pharmacists Association (Fig. 19.1).

"I promise to devote myself to a lifetime of service to others through the profession of pharmacy. In fulfilling this vow:

- I will consider the welfare of humanity and relief of suffering my primary concerns.
- I will promote inclusion, embrace diversity, and advocate for justice to advance health equity.
- I will apply my knowledge, experience, and skills to the best of my ability to assure optimal outcomes for all patients.
- I will respect and protect all personal and health information entrusted to me.
- I will accept the responsibility to improve my professional knowledge, expertise, and self-awareness.
- I will hold myself and my colleagues to the highest principles of our profession's moral, ethical and legal conduct.
- I will embrace and advocate changes that improve patient care.
- I will utilize my knowledge, skills, experiences, and values to prepare the next generation of pharmacists.

I take these vows voluntarily with the full realization of the responsibility with which I am entrusted by the public."

Fig. 19.1 Oath of a Pharmacist

References

1. Kruijtbosch M, Göttgens-Jansen W, Floor-Schreudering A, van Leeuwen E, Bouvy ML. Moral dilemmas of community pharmacists: a narrative study. *Int J Clin Pharm.* 2018;40(1):74–83. https://doi.org/10.1007/s11096-017-0561-0
2. Varkey B. Principles of Clinical Ethics and Their Application to Practice. *Med Princ Pract.* 2021;30(1):17–28. https://doi.org/10.1159/000509119
3. Duignan B. Ethics – Morality, Values, Principles | Britannica. Accessed April 8, 2024. https://www.britannica.com/topic/ethics-philosophy/Normative-ethics
4. Dimmock M, Fisher A. Utilitarianism. In: *Ethics for A-Level.* 1st ed. Open Book Publishers; 2017:11–29. Accessed April 8, 2024. https://www.jstor.org/stable/j.ctt1wc7r6j.5
5. Dimmock M, Fisher A. Kantian Ethics. In: *Ethics for A-Level.* 1st ed. Open Book Publishers; 2017:31–47. Accessed April 8, 2024. https://www.jstor.org/stable/j.ctt1wc7r6j.6
6. Barrow JM, Khandhar PB. Deontology. In: *StatPearls*. StatPearls Publishing; 2024. Accessed April 8, 2024. http://www.ncbi.nlm.nih.gov/books/NBK459296/
7. Dimmock M, Fisher A. Aristotelian Virtue Ethics. In: *Ethics for A-Level.* 1st ed. Open Book Publishers; 2017:49–63. Accessed April 8, 2024. https://www.jstor.org/stable/j.ctt1wc7r6j.7
8. Braunack-Mayer AJ. What makes a problem an ethical problem? An empirical perspective on the nature of ethical problems in general practice. *J Med Ethics*. 2001;27(2):98–103. https://doi.org/10.1136/jme.27.2.98
9. Nagai H, Nakazawa E, Akabayashi A. The creation of the Belmont Report and its effect on ethical principles: a historical study. *Monash Bioeth Rev*. 2022;40(2):157–170. https://doi.org/10.1007/s40592-022-00165-5
10. 18th World Medical Assembly. Declaration of Helsinki Recommendations guiding doctors in clinical research. Published online 1964. Accessed April 18, 2024. https://www.wma.net/wp-content/uploads/2018/07/DoH-Jun1964.pdf
11. National Commission for the Protection of Human Subjects of Biomedical and Behavioral Research. The Belmont Report. Ethical principles and guidelines for the protection of human subjects of research. Published online 1979. Accessed April 8, 2024. https://www.hhs.gov/ohrp/regulations-and-policy/belmont-report/read-the-belmont-report/index.html
12. Fox ER, Wynia MK. How Should Critical Medications Be Rationed During Shortages? *AMA J Ethics*. 2024;26(4):E334–340. https://doi.org/10.1001/amajethics.2024.334
13. American College of Clinical Pharmacy, Holt S, Lau M, Wong F, Attridge R. Tenets of Professionalism for Pharmacy STudents.
14. Bernat JL. *Ethical Issues in Neurology*. 3rd ed. Lippincott Williams & Wilkins; 2008.
15. Dubbai H, Adelstein BA, Taylor S, Shulruf B. Definition of professionalism and tools for assessing professionalism in pharmacy practice: a systemic review. *J Educ Eval Health Prof.* 2019;16:22. https://doi.org/10.3352/jeehp.2019.16.22
16. Alabama State Board of Pharmacy Administrative Code, Chapter 680-X-2 Practice of Pharmacy. § 680-X-2-.22 (2011 and rev.2022). Accessed April 18, 2024. https://albop.com/oodoardu/2022/08/PHARM-680-X-2-.22-proposed-.pdf
17. American Association of Colleges of Pharmacy. Oath of a Pharmacist. Oath of a Pharmacist. Published 2021. Accessed April 8, 2024. https://www.aacp.org/resource/oath-pharmacist

Miscellaneous Laws Impacting Pharmacy Practice in Alabama

20

I would uphold the law if for no other reason but to protect myself.

–Thomas More

1 Introduction

Most pharmacy-related laws, rules, and regulations can be neatly categorized. There are some though, while equally important to pharmacy practice, that just do not easily fit into any broad category. These miscellaneous legalities should not be overlooked in pharmacy practice. Some will impact the day-to-day activities of a pharmacist more than others.

2 Practicing Pharmacy Without a License

No one can practice pharmacy in Alabama without a license issued by the Alabama Board of Pharmacy (ALBOP). [1] It is expected that a person granted a pharmacist license will uphold all federal and state laws, regulations, and rules. Anyone who practices pharmacy without a license, who permits an unlicensed person to compound or dispense prescriptions, or who *willfully* violates any pharmacy law, rule, or regulation may be subject to penalties. Some laws, rules, or regulations have specified penalties within them for violations. When they do not, the violation is considered a misdemeanor; if the person is convicted, they may be subject to a fine of up to $1000 per offense and up to 12 months in county jail.

M. N. Bulloch et al., *Pharmacy Law in Alabama*,
https://doi.org/10.1007/978-3-031-84771-4_20

3 Behind-the-Counter Medications and Products

There are some medications and products which do not require a prescription but are still kept securely behind the pharmacy counter (BTC) to control their dispensing. Not everything kept BTC is required by law or regulation; products such as over-the-counter insulin are often kept behind the pharmacy counter for patient safety and other reasons, but not particularly due to a legal mandate. One medication which is required by law to be kept and dispensed from BTC is pseudoephedrine [2]. Except when obtained by prescription, no person can obtain more than 3.6 grams of pseudoephedrine per calendar day or more than 7.5 grams within 30 days. Those purchasing pseudoephedrine must be at least 18 years of age and produce a valid, unsuspended driver's license or state-issued nondriver identification card, a valid passport, or military identification card. The purchaser must sign a record of the transaction. The information regarding the sale, including purchaser information, is submitted electronically to a monitoring database. This helps to prevent people from inappropriately obtaining more than allowable amounts from multiple pharmacies. More information on BTC products is discussed in Chap. 10.

4 Medications Related to Overdose or Substance Use Disorders

Naloxone, nalmefene, or a similarly acting drug approved by the Food and Drug Administration (FDA) for the treatment of opioid overdose may be dispensed under a standing order by the state health officer or the country health officers [3–5]. The standing order can serve as the prescription to dispense naloxone (intranasal with mucosal atomizer, nasal spray, or intramuscular with needle) or nalmefene nasal spray for an individual at risk of an opioid-related overdose or to a family member, friend, first responder, or any other individual who is in a position to assist a person at risk of an opioid-related overdose. Unlimited amounts of refills are authorized on the standing order. When a pharmacist dispenses naloxone or nalmefene under the standing order, they should provide counseling including the information covered on the standing order itself. The person receiving the medication must complete and sign the "Opioid Reversal Agent Client Form" which is included in the standing order. As of 2023, intranasal naloxone may be obtained without a prescription after the FDA reclassified it as an over-the-counter medication. Nalmefene is only approved for patients aged 12 years and older.

5 Pharmacist Reporting

5.1 Mandatory Reporting by Pharmacists

5.1.1 Communicable Diseases

Many of the healthcare rules are primarily intended to protect public health and welfare. In order to do this, the state of Alabama, like many other states, has designated several diseases that legally must be reported to the Alabama Department of Public Health (ADPH) or local affiliate. Many of these are rare or vaccine-preventable infections, but some, such as birth defects, are not communicable diseases. In most cases, pharmacists are not responsible for this reporting; that burden generally falls to the clinician or laboratory making the diagnosis. However, there is a rule in the ADPH administrative code involving pharmacists and medication dispensing. Pharmacists are required to report to the State Health Officer (or designee) whenever they dispense an *antituberculosis* (TB) medication to any patient (of any age) or an *antiretroviral* medication to an infant who is less than 18 months of age [6].

It is likely that the ADPH will have already received a report regarding the infection from the entity making the diagnosis, but the pharmacist report is a safeguard in case mandatory reporting is not submitted from the diagnosing clinician. It also helps identify cases of patients who may have been diagnosed outside of Alabama. When reporting on infant antiretroviral dispensing, the pharmacist should select "Perinatal HIV exposure." Tuberculosis should be reported as "active" or "latent." How soon the information must be reported depends on the potential danger to the general public. Latent TB and perinatal HIV exposure pose less of an immediate danger to the general public, but should be reported within 3 days of diagnosis or, in the case of the pharmacist, dispensing [7]. On the other hand, active TB is a potentially dangerous communicable infection and must be reported within 24 h. The minimum information required in these reports includes (1) patient name and (2) name and address of the prescribing physician. These reports are legally considered confidential and may only be used legally to assist with court proceedings to compel examination, treatment, commitment, or quarantine.

► **Important Concept** Pharmacists can report dispensing of antituberculosis medications or antiretrovirals to infants using one of the following:

- Online: https://epiweb.adph.state.al.us/redcap/surveys/?s=H37ENP8ADD
- Telephone: 334-206-5330
- Secure Fax: 334-206-3734

5.1.2 Child Abuse or Neglect

According to Alabama law, pharmacists are mandatory reporters when child abuse or neglect is known or suspected [8]. The pharmacist should make this report to an appropriate law enforcement official.

5.2 Prescription Drug Monitoring Program

Alabama law requires pharmacies to report dispensing of all controlled substances to the Prescription Drug Monitoring Program (PDMP). [9, 10] This includes mail order or pharmacy benefit programs which fill or dispense controlled substances to Alabama residents. In-patient (e.g., hospital) pharmacies and pharmacies servicing long-term care facilities are not included in this mandate as long as the controlled substance is administered to a patient within the facility's premises. Failure of either the licensed pharmacy *or* the pharmacist to comply with this law can result in disciplinary action. The PDMP is responsible for monitoring pharmacies for reporting compliance and notifying the ALBOP if noncompliance is detected [10].

5.3 Adverse Drug Reactions

No medication or vaccine is without risk. One main purpose of preclinical trials is to identify potential adverse events (AEs) that could occur with the use of a therapeutic. However, the contained sample size in even the best designed study may not be able to fully illustrate a medication's safety profile. There are times when the extent of an AE, or even the actual AE itself, is not known until the medication is being used in a broad patient population. Manufacturers are required to report all post-marketing AEs to the Food and Drug Administration (FDA). [11] Healthcare providers are *not* required to report AEs but may voluntarily submit reports electronically to the FDA's Adverse Event Reporting System (FAERS).

In contrast, federal law mandates healthcare providers, including pharmacists, to report AEs that occur with immunizations. The Vaccine Adverse Event Reporting System (VAERS) was implemented to be a national early warning system to detect safety issues with vaccines used in the United States. [12] Anyone can use the system to report an adverse event. However, the National Childhood Vaccine Injury Act of 1986 *requires* that *all* healthcare providers report to VAERS certain vaccine-specific effects [12, 13]. These AEs can be found on the VAERS website (https://vaers.hhs.gov/reportevent.html) in a table that lists the vaccine along with the AE and interval from vaccination that is relevant. For example, if a patient experiences vasovagal syncope within 1 h of receiving a pneumococcal vaccine, the incident must be reported to VAERS. Vasovagal syncope occurring beyond 1 h does not have to be reported. It is important to recognize that the list of mandatory reported AEs does not include every potential AE, and not all vaccines have *specific* AEs which must be reported. However, if the AE that occurred would prevent the patient from receiving any additional doses of the vaccine (e.g., it becomes a contraindication), it must be reported—regardless of what the vaccine is or what AE occurred. Though not required, healthcare providers are encouraged to report any AE, even if it is not among those required to report, or any vaccine administration errors.

5.4 Privacy Violations

Pharmacies take strong measures to ensure compliance with patient privacy, but there are occasions where a breach of protected health information (PHI) compromises the security or privacy of PHI. The federal HIPPA Breach Notification Rule requires all HIPAA-covered entities, such as pharmacies, and their business associates, to make a notification anytime PHI is breached [14]. Notifications must be made within 60 days of when the breach was discovered. The notification can be made by postal mail or email (only if the person has agreed to receive electronic communications—though most people do; if contact information is outdated for ten or more impacted persons, the entity has to post the notice on their website for at least 90 days or provide the notice in major print or broadcast media in the local area (e.g., a local newspaper or local television station). Additionally, the entity has to provide a toll-free telephone number—which must remain active for at least 90 days—where people can call to determine if their PHI has been involved in the breach. Other notification requirements exist for large breaches and breaches involving specific scenarios that are beyond the scope of this chapter. Finally, breaches must be submitted electronically to the Secretary of Health and Human Services. Instructions and forms for this can be found at https://www.hhs.gov/hipaa/for-professionals/breach-notification/breach-reporting/index.html

6 Immunization Training

The pharmacy has become one of the most popular places for patients to receive immunizations. In Alabama, vaccines may be administered by licensed pharmacists, registered interns, externs, or technicians, under special provisions [15]. In order to administer vaccines, the person must have a current certificate in basic cardiopulmonary resuscitation (CPR). Interns, externs, and technicians may only administer vaccines under the direct supervision of a licensed pharmacist.

The allowance of technicians to administer vaccines is relatively new to Alabama and arose from the COVID-19 pandemic. Technicians wishing to vaccinate must complete a minimum 2 h of Accreditation Council for Pharmacy Education-approved practical training program that must include hands-on injection training, the recognition and treatment of emergency reactions to vaccines, and pass a successful examination to assure sufficient knowledge. The technician should submit to the ALBOP documentation that they have completed the course and have other requirements (e.g., CPR certification) within 10 days of course completion. The technician will receive a certificate of immunization authority which must be displayed in a conspicuous place in the pharmacy.

While interns, externs, and technicians may perform the immunization, it is the pharmacist who is ultimately responsible for ensuring the safety and compliance of immunization practices. Only FDA-authorized or FDA-licensed vaccines may be administered, with the exception of an emergency vaccine being ordered and administered according to the Advisory Committee on Immunization Practices (ACIP) recommendations. Children may receive vaccines at a pharmacy, but the vaccine must be ordered and administered according to the ACIP's vaccination schedule. Vaccines must be stored appropriately to ensure their stability and efficacy. Because most vaccines involve needles, the pharmacist must ensure compliance with blood-borne pathogen safety requirements, including the appropriate use of FDA-cleared sharps disposal containers and medical waste disposal.

Reactions to vaccines do occur. The pharmacist is responsible for reporting any adverse event to the Vaccine Adverse Event Reporting System. This includes any reaction that may occur from a vaccine they themselves administered or which were administered by an intern, extern, or technician under their direct supervision. The pharmacy must have either an epinephrine kit or epinephrine autoinjector available should a reaction requiring its use occur.

In order to maintain their immunization authority, pharmacists must complete a minimum of two ALBOP-approved hours of immunization-related continuing education during each renewal cycle.

7 Off-Site Vaccine Order Entry Processing

Off-site vaccine order entry processing occurs when a licensed pharmacist (or registered intern or technician under the direct supervision of a pharmacist) remotely accesses their own pharmacy's electronic database from outside the pharmacy in order to process vaccines [16]. This may be necessary when pharmacy personnel are providing immunizations at a site away from the walls of the pharmacy, such as at a mobile clinic. It must be completed in real time at the remote site using technology that is afterward returned to the pharmacy for secure storage. All related records (hard copy or electronic) are maintained at the pharmacy for a minimum of 2 years from the date of entry.

Off-site vaccine order entry processing is limited to:

- Interpreting/clarifying vaccine orders.
- Data entry of vaccine order information.
- Drug regimen review.
- Providing clinical vaccine information.

8 Third-Party Prescription Program

The "Third-Party Prescription Program" is any system of providing reimbursement of pharmaceutical services under a contractual agreement or arrangement of a provider of such services (third-party program (TPP)) and another party who is not the consumer of those services [17]. An example of this is a contract between a pharmacy and an insurance plan to reimburse the pharmacy for prescription medications that the pharmacy dispenses to patients covered by that insurance plan. Alabama law has several provisions that outline the arrangements between TPPs and pharmacies. No TPP may establish business in Alabama until it has provided written notice of the plan's provisions to all pharmacies in the state, and each pharmacy has had at least 30 days from receiving the notice to enroll in the program if they choose [18]. However, they specifically exclude the Alabama Medicaid Program and the Public Education Employees' Health Insurance Plan (PEEHIP). [19]

Any agreement or contract between a TPP and a pharmacy must include a statement that describes the method and amount of reimbursement to the pharmacy for services provided to plan beneficiaries, frequency of payments from the TPP to the pharmacy, and the method for adjudication of complaints or settlements of disputes between the two parties [20]. The TPP may not withhold payments to the pharmacy beyond the timeframe specified in the contract or agreement [21]. Like any other type of business, the pharmacy is providing a service and should be paid according to the terms of the contract. Individual claims that are incomplete or illegible may be returned to the pharmacy and resubmitted once appropriate corrections have been made. A TPP and a pharmacy may not enter into a contract or agreement which includes reimbursement rates or procedures to obtain reimbursement for services rendered to patients covered by the plan that are less than the "usual and customary rates" paid by other patients not covered by the plan for similar services [22].

The TPP must notify all pharmacies enrolled in the program at least 30 days before the cancellation of benefit coverage of any group enrolled in the program [23]. The program is to notify patients enrolled in the program of the cancellation and must make "reasonable" efforts to obtain the plan identification cards of those whose benefits are being cancelled. In reality, this rarely occurs. The TPP must notify the pharmacy that the program has been canceled/discontinued and that the TPP has been unsuccessful in attempting to regain possession of the card. If for some reason a patient is able to use the plan identification card after the cancellation (e.g., have medications filled and the plan billed for them), the person is liable for all money paid for the services. If the TPP did not notify the pharmacy of the cancellation and that they could not regain the card, the TPP must pay the pharmacy for the services rendered. With the use of electronic submission of insurance claims, this situation is uncommon since the pharmacy should receive an electronic rejection of the claim if the patient is no longer covered.

9 The Pharmacy Audit Integrity Act

The Alabama Pharmacy Audit Integrity Act (PAIA) was enacted to establish minimum and uniform standards and criteria for the audit of records by or on behalf of certain entities [24]. The law applies to any audit of pharmacy records conducted by a managed care company, nonprofit hospital, medical service organization, health benefit plan, third-party payor, pharmacy benefit manager (PBM), health program administered by a department of the state of Alabama (excluding the Alabama Medicaid Agency), or any entity that represents these companies, groups, or departments [25]. It is mean to apply to routine audits conducted to ensure pharmacies are complying with requirements and agreements set forth for the payment of pharmacy services and medications. The PAIA only applies to routine audits and is not applicable to audits or investigations involving alleged fraud, willful misrepresentation, or waste abuse [26].

Some auditing entities conduct the audits themselves, and others contract with a third-party company to conduct the audit. The auditing entity cannot compensate any employee or contractor who is conducting the audit based on the amount to be recouped by the pharmacy [27]. This helps maintain the ethical integrity of the audit. The PAIA outlines a specific audit procedure that must be followed (Table 20.1), which includes a provision that the contract with the pharmacy must identify and describe in detail the audit procedures [28]. Although the act lists several different auditing entities, the procedures themselves often generically state "PBM." Pharmacy Benefit Managers (PBMs) may provide auditing guidelines in their provider manual, but if they do not, they must include a documented checklist of all items to be audited and the manual when they notify a pharmacy of the audit. Pharmacies must be audited under the same standards and parameters as other similarly situated pharmacies audited by the entity. Audits must be conducted under rules appliable at the time of the prescription. If the audit includes a prescription dispensed in 2023, the auditor may not use rules updated in 2024; it must use the 2023 rules.

Key Concept
Although not a law or an official rule or regulation, ALBOP has an official policy that third-party auditors are not to be allowed within the actual pharmacy area to conduct an on-site audit.

▶ **Numbers of Importance** During an audit, a PBM may only review a maximum of 150 prescriptions.

The PAIA limits the amount of time covered in an audit to 2 years from the date the claim was submitted or adjudicated [28]. No audit may be conducted more than 6 months after the date that a health plan terminates its contract with a PBM.

When the audit identifies negative findings or the appearance of overpayment, the entity moves to recoup the money from the pharmacy. This means that the pharmacy has to return money that it was paid. Pharmacies have extensive records; in some areas, the auditors use a process called extrapolation where they only review a small number of claims submitted. If any of the claims reviewed are out of compliance, they extrapolate the discrepancies over the total number of claims submitted. For example, if the auditors review 200 claims out of 100,000 total claims and identify errors in 30 of them, they seek recoupment of 15% of payments submitted for all 100,000 claims. There may not be any errors at all in the unreviewed claims, but the auditor assumes there are. The PAIA specifically *prohibits* the auditing entity from using extrapolation to calculate penalties or amounts to be charged back or recouped unless it is required by federal requirements or federal plans [27]. In fact, in Alabama, no more than 150 unique prescriptions may be reviewed during an

Table 20.1 Audit procedures required by the Pharmacy Audit Integrity Act [28]

An entity conducting an on-site audit must give the pharmacy written notice at least 2 weeks before conducting the initial on-site audit for each audit cycle
The audit may not be initiated or scheduled in the first five calendar days of any month
The auditing entity must have a provider manual that lists auditing guidelines which include the name, date, and edition/volume
For on-site audits, the pharmacy must be provided with a list of material that is copied or removed during the audit. The PBM may document this material on either a checklist or an auditing acknowledgment form
The pharmacy must produce items requested either during the course of the audit or within 30 days of the on-site audit
The auditor(s) conducting an on-site audit may not interfere with the delivery of pharmacist services and must use every effort to minimize inconvenience and disruptions to pharmacy operations during the audit
Any audit involving clinical or professional judgment must be conducted by or in consultation with a licensed pharmacist
Clerical or recordkeeping errors (e.g., typographical errors) may not be considered fraud. However, these errors may be subject to recoupment if the error resulted in overpayment to the pharmacy
A pharmacy has the right to submit amended claims through an online submission to correct clerical or recordkeeping errors in lieu of recoupment of a claim when no financial harm to the patient or plan has occurred as long as the prescription was dispensed according to state law and plan limits
A PBM must provide proof of intent to commit fraud or that the clerical or recordkeeping error resulted in actual financial harm to themselves, a health insurance plan managed by the PBM, or a consumer in order to recoup funds
No one is subject to criminal penalties for errors unless there is proof of intent to commit fraud, waste, or abuse
Any amount of money to be charged back or recouped due to overpayment cannot exceed the amount that the pharmacy was overpaid
The cost of the drugs dispensed cannot be included in the calculation of overpayment as long as it was dispensed according to a prescriber's order and within plan limits
The dispensing fee cannot be included in the calculation of the overpayment unless the prescription is considered a misfill (a prescription that was not actually dispensed, the prescriber denied the authorization request, a prescription where an additional dispensing fee was charged, or the prescription dispensed was a medication error)
The auditing entity cannot require any documentation that is not required by state or federal law. Information is considered valid if it is documented on the prescription, computerized treatment notes, pharmacy system, or any other acceptable medical records
Unless allowed by state or federal law, auditors only have access to previous audit reports on a specific pharmacy conducted by the same auditor for the same PBM, health plan, or insurer. Audit reports or other information gained from an audit on a pharmacy cannot be used to conduct an audit for a different PBM or insurance plan
Audit results are disclosed to the health benefit plan according to contract terms
A pharmacy may use records of a hospital, physician, or other authorized practitioner of the healing arts for drugs or medical supplies, written or transmitted by any means of communications to validate the pharmacy record with respect to orders or refills of a prescription or narcotic medication
If a PBM or its representative conducts an audit, the sample size is limited to a maximum of 150 prescriptions. A refill does not constitute a separate prescription
Reasonable costs associated with the audit are the responsibility of the auditing entity if the sample of claims reviewed exceeds 100 unique prescription hard copies
A pharmacy must be given at least 30 days from the receipt of the preliminary audit report to produce documentation to address any discrepancy found, with reasonable extension granted upon request
Audit documents must be signed by the auditors assigned to the audit
The audit report must contain clear contact information of the representative of the auditing organization

audit [28]. When an audit identifies overpayment or underpayment, a projection based on the number of patients served with a similar diagnosis or on the number of similar orders or refills for similar drugs can be used, but the amount recouped is based on the actual overpayment or underpayment of actual claims.

The preliminary audit report must be delivered to the pharmacy within 90 days of the audit conclusion, though reasonable extensions may be granted upon request [28]. The pharmacy has 30 days to provide documentation to address any identified discrepancies. The final audit report must be delivered to the pharmacy within 180 days of the receipt of the preliminary audit report or the final appeal. The entity conducting the audit must establish a written appeals process under which a pharmacy can appeal an unfavorable preliminary audit report [29]. If the entity finds that the unfavorable audit report (or any portion of it) is unsubstantiated, the entity must dismiss the report or the applicable portion of it. If, after the appeal, issues raised in the appeal are not resolved to the satisfaction of one of the parties, the party may request mediation unless the contract outlines other terms of resolution. A certified mediator is selected by a list of mediators maintained by the Alabama Supreme Court. The cost of the mediation is paid by a joint agreement of both parties or according to the decision of the mediator. Recoupment of disputed funds or repayment of funds to the entity by the pharmacy occurs after the final internal disposition of the audit, including the appeals process if applicable.

If the identified discrepancy for an individual audit exceeds $25,000, future payments in excess of that amount to the pharmacy may be withheld pending finalization of the audit [28]. However, interest cannot accrue during the audit period.

Key Concept
Auditors cannot use extrapolation to calculate penalties or amounts to be recouped.

▶ **Study Prep Tip** The PAIA is an important law for pharmacists to understand, but the intricate details of the law are less likely to appear on the MPJE than other laws which are more broadly applicable to pharmacy practice. Although it is possible that a question of any sort could appear on the MPJE, content will most likely focus on responsibilities that a pharmacist should be aware of. Test takers may find it useful to focus on the act's requirements of pharmacies and pharmacists.

10 Right to Select a Pharmacy or Pharmacist

Alabama patients have the legal right to select the pharmacy or pharmacist of their choice [30]. Health insurance policies and employee benefit plans may not prevent or interfere with this selection. If both Pharmacy Z and Pharmacy G accept payment from the insurance plan, the insurance company or plan cannot force the patient to use Pharmacy Z instead of Pharmacy G.

These plans cannot deny any pharmacy or pharmacist the right to participate as a contracting provider. This may be confusing because not all pharmacies and pharmacists accept certain health insurance plans for payment. The law does not require the plans to pay the pharmacies a particular amount nor to prevent the insurance company from charging patients less for using a preferred pharmacy over a nonpreferred pharmacy. If a pharmacy does not accept a particular insurance plan or policy, the patient can choose to either pay out-of-pocket for the medication or to use a pharmacy that does accept their plan.

11 Insurance Coverage for Drugs to Treat Life-Threatening Illnesses

Alabama has a specific law dedicated to ensuring that medical insurance companies do not exclude coverage of prescription medications *solely* because they are not approved by the FDA for a particular indication [31]. If the medication is recognized as a viable treatment for an indication in the medical literature, by the Commissioner of Insurance, by the United States Pharmacopeia Drug Information, the American Medical Association Drug Evaluations, or the American Hospital Formulary Service Drug Information, the indication is considered valid. This law does not apply to investigational drugs or medications where the FDA has determined its use to be contraindicated for the indication.

12 Drug Disposal and Donation

An ultimate user is a person who lawfully obtained a prescription medication for themselves, a member of their household, or an animal in the household [32]. There may be times when people feel the need to return prescription medications to the pharmacy. For example, a patient who has been receiving a controlled substance while on hospice care may pass away with the leftover medication; the family may not want the medication around where it could be stolen or used for illicit purposes.

Pharmacies are allowed to receive, collect, and dispose of prescription medications, including controlled substances. The pharmacy must notify the ALBOP that it wishes to do so. The pharmacy must submit to the ALBOP the necessary authorization to be a collector of controlled substances by the Drug Enforcement Administration (DEA) within 10 days of receiving the authorization from the DEA. The pharmacy must also notify ALBOP when it stops providing these services.

13 Medications in Medical Offices

13.1 Dispensing of Prescription Drugs by Alabama Department of Public Health Registered Nurses

Registered nurses (RNs) who are employed by either the ADPH or a country health department are allowed to dispense prescription drugs for diseases and programs approved by the ALBOP. [33] These specifically include (1) tuberculosis, (2) sexually transmitted diseases, (3) family planning (e.g., contraceptives), (4) hypertension, (5) meningitis, and (6) pertussis. In a unique exception to standard clinician—diagnosis—prescribing rules and expectations, these RNs may dispense appropriate prescription drugs to the sexual partners of patients infected with *Chlamydia trachomatis*, *Neisseria gonorrhoeae*, or *Trichomonas vaginalis* without ever testing the person for the infection, examining them, or even having a clinician-patient relationship, as long as the patient is age 12 years or older. The ADPH administrative code rationalizes this rule by stating that these partners are "unlikely to seek treatment or evaluation." The medications themselves are dispensed to the infected patients to deliver to their sex partners.

14 Sale of Pure Alcohol

The early twentieth century was a time when many laws relating to alcohol were passed in Alabama, including those referencing its medicinal use. Though these laws practically may not seem culturally applicable in the modern practice of pharmacy, they are still valid laws within the state (Table 20.2). The laws were written at a time when terminology and the structure of pharmacy were different than that existing today. In fact, many predate many major state and federal pharmacy laws overall and provide some of the earliest legal references to pharmacists and prescriptions.

It is important to note that these laws apply to pure alcohol or grain alcohol—and do not apply to FDA-approved medications which may contain a small amount of alcohol within them. Several of the laws use the phrase "retail druggist," which today would refer to any community pharmacist whether they worked for an independent pharmacy or a corporate chain pharmacy. Most of the laws refer to physicians, which would exclude physician extenders such as Nurse Practitioners or Physician Assistants from any allowable practices. When used medically, the law is clear that it must be determined that the alcohol is being used for medicinal purposes and not as a drink or beverage [34]. At the time many of these laws were written, temperance laws and Prohibition legally banned alcohol as a beverage, and lawmakers wanted to make sure that the medical community was not utilizing the prescribing process as a way to get around that ban. In fact, before a physician can legally prescribe alcohol for medicinal purposes, they must file an affidavit with the probate judge in the county of their medical practice, affirming that they will only prescribe it for valid medicinal reasons [35].

Table 20.2 Alabama laws related to the medicinal use of alcohol [36–43]

A licensed or registered pharmacist may sell pure alcohol for medicinal purposes only upon receipt of a valid prescription from an authorized Alabama physician who has examined the patient prior to issuing the prescription
A maximum of one-half pint alcohol may be sold and delivered on any one prescription
A licensed or registered pharmacist may sell up to 5 gallons of grain alcohol to chemists and bacteriologists actually engaged in scientific work. The purchaser must sign a written or printed statement with their name, address, occupation, and purpose for the alcohol and certify that the alcohol is purchased only for that purpose
A licensed or registered pharmacist may sell up to 5 gallons of alcohol to be used in the arts, for scientific purposes, or mechanical purposes. The purchaser must sign a written or printed statement with their name, address, occupation, and purpose for the alcohol and certify that the alcohol is purchased only for that purpose
A licensed or registered pharmacist may compound prescriptions or medicines using medicinal alcohol without being required to pay a special tax required of liquor dealers
A licensed or registered pharmacist may sell up to 1 gallon at a time of grain or pure alcohol to Alabama-licensed and practicing physicians for use in compounding or dispensing remedies in their medical practice
Prescriptions for medicinal alcohol must state (1) the disease or ailment for which the alcohol is being used for, (2) method of use or administration, (3) quantity of dose(s), (4) interval of time between doses or time of doses, (5) a statement by the physician that the alcohol is medically necessary, (6) physician name and address, (7) patient name and address, (8) date of prescription issued/written, and (9) a statement of the number of alcohol prescriptions written for that patient in the past 12 months or a statement that there have been no alcohol prescriptions for that patient
Any prescription for medicinal alcohol must be filled/dispensed on the day the prescription was issued or the following day
A signed copy of any prescription for medicinal alcohol must be filed by the prescribing physician with the office of the county probate judge
All prescriptions for medicinal alcohol are examined by a grand jury (retrospectively)
The pharmacist dispensing the medicinal alcohol prescription must provide a copy of the prescription to the alcoholic beverage control board by the end of the month in which the prescription was dispensed
Refills for prescriptions for medicinal alcohol are not permitted
In towns with a population > 2000, a prescription for medicinal alcohol may not be filled at any pharmacy where a physician is an owner or has a financial interest
Prescribing or dispensing of whiskey, rum, gin, or brandy for medicinal purposes is not permissible

From a practical perspective, some of the laws outline practices that are no longer commonly utilized. For example, the law enacted in 1915 allows pharmacists to sell grain alcohol to bacteriologists for research [36]. Today, the scientist would obtain such a product from a larger, nonpharmacy source, most likely more suited to providing research chemicals. Still, because the laws have not been repealed, it is helpful to be aware of them and their opportunities and limitations.

15 Tax Exemption

Medications prescribed and dispensed for human consumption are exempt from Alabama sales tax [44]. Depending on the city and/or county, it is possible that local sales tax may be charged. However, medications prescribed by physicians to patients aged 65 years and older and filled by licensed pharmacists are exempt by state law from county or municipal sales tax too [45].

16 Abortion of a Viable Unborn Child

Abortion overall is prohibited in Alabama, except under specific circumstances that are determined by a physician [46]. In general, the legal precepts involving abortion in Alabama are outside the scope of pharmacy law. However, the state does have certain restrictions centered on potentially abortifacient medications for which a pharmacist should be familiar with. Because the medications used in medication abortion have other indications (including some that are entirely unrelated to family planning), the medications themselves are still available for dispensing. The ALBOP policy (which is not of the same weight as a regulation) states that a pharmacist may fill medications to treat ectopic pregnancies, miscarriages, or other non-abortifacient treatments [47]. The policy indicates that the prescription should contain a "proper and well-documented diagnosis from the physician" that specifies what the medication is being used for. If a medication is used to induce an abortion in compliance with the specific circumstances authorized by state law, it must be dispensed and administered by a physician [48].

17 Federal Reference Books

Federal organizations such as the United Stated Food and Drug Administration and the Centers for Disease Control have published a variety of reference books known by their color (Table 20.3) [49–54]. While it is not crucial to know every detail regarding each book, it is important to know the general material covered within each book.

Table 20.3 Federal reference books [49–54]

Book	General material covered
Red	Drug pricing
Orange	List of approved drug products with therapeutic equivalence evaluations
Yellow	International travel vaccines
Green	Animal drug products
Purple	Biological products
Pink	Vaccine-preventable diseases

References

1. *Ala. Code. § 34-23-13 (1966).*
2. *Ala. Code. § 20-2-190 (1991, Rev 2017).*
3. *Ala. Code. § 20-2-280 (2015).*
4. *Ala. Code. § 20-2-283 (2016).*
5. Harris S. Standing order of the state health officer opioid reversal agent distribution for overdose prevention. Published online September 21, 2023. Accessed June 27, 2024. https://www.alabamapublichealth.gov/pharmacy/assets/standingorder.pdf
6. *Alabama Department of Public Health State Board of Health Administrative Code, Chapter 420-4-1 Reporting § 420-4-1-.04 (1982 and Rev 2024).*
7. Alabama Department of Public Health. Reportable Diseases/Conditions in Alabama. Published online April 14, 2024. Accessed June 26, 2024. https://www.alabamapublichealth.gov/blog/assets/nd-reportable-diseases.pdf
8. *Ala. Code. § 26-14-3 (1965, Rev. 2017).*
9. *Ala. Code. § 20-2-213 (2004, Rev 2016).*
10. *Alabama Department of Public Health Administrative Code, Chapter 420-7-2-.12 Reporting to Database by Dispensers § 420-7-2-.12 (2014).*
11. 21 CFR 314.80 – Postmarketing reporting of adverse drug experiences. Accessed July 19, 2024. https://www.ecfr.gov/current/title-21/part-314/section-314.80
12. VAERS – Report an Adverse Event. Accessed July 19, 2024. https://vaers.hhs.gov/reportevent.html
13. Rep. Waxman HA [D C 24. H.R.5546 – 99th Congress (1985-1986): National Childhood Vaccine Injury Act of 1986. Published October 18, 1986. Accessed July 19, 2024. https://www.congress.gov/bill/99th-congress/house-bill/5546
14. Office for Civil Rights. Breach Notification Rule. Published September 14, 2009. Accessed July 17, 2024. https://www.hhs.gov/hipaa/for-professionals/breach-notification/index.html
15. *Alabama State Board of Pharmacy Administrative Code, Chapter 680-X-2 Practice of Pharmacy. § 680-X-2-.46 (2021).*
16. *Alabama State Board of Pharmacy Administrative Code, Chapter 680-X-2 Practice of Pharmacy. § 680-X-2-.47 (2021).*
17. *Ala. Code. § 34-23-111 (1981).*
18. *Ala. Code. § 34-23-117 (1981).*
19. *Ala. Code. § 34-23-116 (1981).*
20. *Ala. Code. § 34-23-112 (1981).*
21. *Ala. Code. § 34-23-114 (1981).*
22. *Ala. Code. § 34-23-115 (1981).*
23. *Ala. Code. § 34-23-113 (1981).*
24. *Ala. Code. § 34-23-182 (2012).*
25. *Ala. Code. § 34-23-183 (2012).*
26. *Ala. Code. § 34-23-187 (2012).*
27. *Ala. Code. § 34-23-186 (2012).*
28. *Ala. Code. § 34-23-184 (2012).*
29. *Ala. Code. § 34-23-185 (2012).*
30. *Ala. Code. § 27-45-3 (1988).*
31. *Ala. Code. § 27-1-10.1 (1994).*
32. *Alabama State Board of Pharmacy Administrative Code, Chapter 680-X-2 Practice of Pharmacy. § 680-X-2-.42 (2013).*
33. *Alabama Department of Public Health Administrative Code, Chapter 420-4-1 Notifiable Diseases. § 420-4-1-.12 (1975 and Rev 2024).*
34. *Ala. Code. § 28-4-155 (1919).*
35. *Ala. Code. § 28-4-156 (1919).*
36. *Ala. Code. § 28-4-151 (1915).*

37. *Ala. Code. § 28-4-152 (1915).*
38. *Ala. Code. § 28-4-153 (1915).*
39. *Ala. Code. § 28-4-154 (1919).*
40. *Ala. Code. § 28-4-157 (1919).*
41. *Ala. Code. § 28-4-159 (1919).*
42. *Ala. Code. § 28-4-160 (1915).*
43. *Ala. Code. § 28-4-162 (1919).*
44. *Ala. Code. § 40-23-4.1 (1981).*
45. *Ala. Code. § 40-23-4 (2024).*
46. *Ala. Code. § 26-23H-4 (2019).*
47. Alabama Board of Pharmacy. Dispensing of medications for non-abortifacient treatments. Published online February 15, 2023. Accessed July 22, 2024. https://albop.com/oodoardu/2023/02/POLICY-23-001.pdf
48. *Ala. Code. § 26-23E-7 (2013).*
49. Micromedex. Micromedex source information. Last reviewed May 31, 2024. Accessed July 30, 2024. https://www.nlm.nih.gov/research/umls/rxnorm/sourcereleasedocs/mmx.html
50. United States Food and Drug Administration. Approved drug products with therapeutical equivalence evaluations | Orange Book. Last reviewed July 12, 2024. Accessed July 30, 2024. https://www.fda.gov/drugs/drug-approvals-and-databases/approved-drug-products-therapeutic-equivalence-evaluations-orange-book
51. Centers for Disease Control and Prevention. CDC Yellow Book. Last reviewed August 14, 2023. Accessed July 30, 2024. https://wwwnc.cdc.gov/travel/page/yellowbook-home
52. United States Food and Drug Administration. Approved animal drug products (Green Book). Last reviewed February 1, 2024. Accessed July 30, 2024. https://www.fda.gov/animal-veterinary/products/approved-animal-drug-products-green-book
53. United States Food and Drug Administration. Purple Book: lists of licensed biological products with reference product exclusivity and biosimilarity or interchangeability evaluations. Last reviewed August 3, 2020. Accessed July 30, 2024. https://www.fda.gov/drugs/therapeutic-biologics-applications-bla/purple-book-lists-licensed-biological-products-reference-product-exclusivity-and-biosimilarity-or
54. Centers for Disease Control and Prevention. Epidemiology and prevention of vaccine-preventable diseases table of contents. Last reviewed May 17, 2023. Accessed July 30, 2024. https://www.cdc.gov/pinkbook/hcp/table-of-contents/index.html

Notes

M. N. Bulloch et al., *Pharmacy Law in Alabama*,
https://doi.org/10.1007/978-3-031-84771-4

Index

M. N. Bulloch et al., *Pharmacy Law in Alabama*,
https://doi.org/10.1007/978-3-031-84771-4

MIX
Papier aus verantwortungsvollen Quellen
Paper from responsible sources
FSC® C105338

If you have any concerns about our products,
you can contact us on
ProductSafety@springernature.com

In case Publisher is established outside the EU,
the EU authorized representative is:
Springer Nature Customer Service Center GmbH
Europaplatz 3, 69115 Heidelberg, Germany

Printed by Libri Plureos GmbH
in Hamburg, Germany